ANNUAL EDITIONS

Human Development 10/11

Thirty-Ninth Edition

EDITOR

Karen L. Freiberg

University of Maryland, Baltimore County

Dr. Karen Freiberg has an interdisciplinary educational and employment background in nursing, education, and developmental psychology. She received her BS from the State University of New York at Plattsburgh, her MS from Cornell University, and her PhD from Syracuse University. Dr. Freiberg has worked as a school nurse, a pediatric nurse, a public health nurse for the Navajo Indians, an associate project director for a child development clinic, a researcher in several areas of child development, and a university professor. She is the author of an award-winning textbook, *Human Development: A Life-Span Approach,* which is now in its fourth edition. Dr. Freiberg is currently on the faculty at the University of Maryland, Baltimore County.

Mc Graw Hill

Connect
Learn
Succeed™

The McGraw·Hill Companies

Connect
Learn
Succeed™

ANNUAL EDITIONS: HUMAN DEVELOPMENT 10/11, THIRTY-NINTH EDITION

Published by McGraw-Hill, a business unit of The McGraw-Hill Companies, Inc., 1221 Avenue of
the Americas, New York, NY 10020. Copyright © 2011 by The McGraw-Hill Companies, Inc.
All rights reserved. Previous edition(s) 2008, 2009, 2010. No part of this publication may be reproduced
or distributed in any form or by any means, or stored in a database or retrieval system, without the
prior written consent of The McGraw-Hill Companies, Inc., including, but not limited to, in any
network or other electronic storage or transmission, or broadcast for distance learning.

Some ancillaries, including electronic and print components, may not be available to customers
outside the United States.

Annual Editions® is a registered trademark of The McGraw-Hill Companies, Inc.

Annual Editions is published by the **Contemporary Learning Series** group within the
McGraw-Hill Higher Education division.

1 2 3 4 5 6 7 8 9 0 WDQ/WDQ 1 0 9 8 7 6 5 4 3 2 1 0

ISBN 978–0–07–805062–6
MHID 0–07–805062–6
ISSN 0278–4661

Managing Editor: *Larry Loeppke*
Developmental Editor: *Dave Welsh*
Editorial Coordinator: Mary Foust
Editorial Assistant: *Cindy Hedley*
Production Service Assistant: *Rita Hingtgen*
Permissions Coordinator: *DeAnna Dausener*
Senior Marketing Manager: *Julie Keck*
Senior Marketing Communications Specialist: *Mary Klein*
Marketing Coordinator: *Alice Link*
Director Specialized Production: *Faye Schilling*
Senior Project Manager: *Joyce Watters*
Design Specialist: *Margarite Reynolds*
Production Supervisor: *Sue Culbertson*
Cover Graphics: *Kristine Jubeck*

Compositor: Laserwords Private Limited
Cover Image: © SuperStock Inc. (inset); Ryan McVay/Getty Images (background)

Library in Congress Cataloging-in-Publication Data
Main entry under title: Annual Editions: Human Development, 2010/2011.
  1. Human Development—Periodicals. I. Freiberg, Karen L., *comp*. II. Title: Human Development.
658'.05

Editors/Academic Advisory Board

Members of the Academic Advisory Board are instrumental in the final selection of articles for each edition of ANNUAL EDITIONS. Their review of articles for content, level, and appropriateness provides critical direction to the editors and staff. We think that you will find their careful consideration well reflected in this volume.

ANNUAL EDITIONS: Human Development 10/11
39th Edition

EDITOR

Karen L. Freiberg
University of Maryland, Baltimore County

Preface

In publishing ANNUAL EDITIONS we recognize the enormous role played by the magazines, newspapers, and journals of the public press in providing current, first-rate educational information in a broad spectrum of interest areas. Many of these articles are appropriate for students, researchers, and professionals seeking accurate, current material to help bridge the gap between principles and theories and the real world. These articles, however, become more useful for study when those of lasting value are carefully collected, organized, indexed, and reproduced in a low-cost format, which provides easy and permanent access when the material is needed. That is the role played by ANNUAL EDITIONS.

The "Information Age" has created a few Internet addicts and many other technology users who spend several hours each day using electronic media (Google, MySpace, Facebook, Twitter, video games, iPods, cell phones, etc.). Several articles in this new anthology address this information boom and discuss how we are adapting to electronic stimulation in our daily lives.

The Internet has made genealogy one of our most popular new hobbies. People want to trace their ancestry, geographic origins, and possible genetic health risks. The first unit of *Annual Editions: Human Development, 39th edition* presents information to make the science of genetics easier to understand.

As humans develop through the circle of life, it is customary to track changes from infancy through old age. The arrangement of articles in this collection is chronological by age. However, many subjects are treated in abridged form in many units because they are not age specific. Some examples are intelligence, emotional responsivity, socialization, culture, spirituality, education, gender, and nutrition. A Topic Guide is included in this publication to help readers find current, appropriate educational information in the many areas of development which transcend age boundaries.

At conception a new human being is created, but each unique individual carries genetic materials from biological relatives alive and dead, and may pass them on to future generations.

Development through infancy proceeds from sensory and motor responses to verbal communication, thinking, conceptualizing, and learning from others.

Childhood brings rapid physical growth, improved cognition, and social learning.

Adolescence is when the individual begins to test out sexual maturity. Values and identity are questioned. Separation from parents begins. Under the influence of sex hormones, the brain undergoes multiple changes. Emotions may fluctuate rapidly.

Early adulthood usually establishes the individual as an independent person. Employment, further education, and the beginning of one's own family are all aspects of setting up a distinct life, with both its own characteristics and the characteristics and customs of previous generations.

During middle adulthood persons have new situations to face, new transitions to cope with. Children grow up and leave home. Signs of aging become apparent. Relationships change, roles shift. New abilities may be found and opportunities created.

Finally, during late adulthood, people assess what they've accomplished. Some are pleased. Some feel they could have done more or lived differently. In the best of instances, individuals accept who they are and are comfortable with themselves.

As you explore this anthology, you will discover that many articles ask questions that have no answers. As a student, I felt frustrated by such writing. I wanted answers, right answers, right away. However, over time I learned that maturity includes accepting relativity and acknowledging extenuatory circumstances. Life frequently has no right or wrong answers, but rather various alternatives with multiple consequences. Instead of right versus wrong, a more helpful consideration is "What will bring about the greater good for the greater number?" Controversies, whether about terrorism, stem cells, or vaccinations, can promote healthy discussions. Different viewpoints should be weighed against societal standards. Different philosophies should be celebrated for what they offer in creating intellectual abilities in human beings to adapt to changing circumstances.

The Greek sophists were philosophers who specialized in argumentation, rhetoric (using language persuasively), and dialectics (finding synthesis or common ground between contradictory ideas). This was sophistication. However, from their skilled thinking came the derogatory term "sophism," suggesting that some argumentation was deceptive rather than wise. The term sophomore, which now means second-year student, comes from this variation of sophism, combining "sophos" (wise) with "moros" (dull or foolish). "Sophomoric" translates to exhibiting immaturity and lack of judgment, while "sophisticated" translates to having acquired knowledge. Educators strive to have their students move from knowing all the answers (sophomoric) to asking intelligent questions (sophisticated).

This anthology is dedicated to seekers of knowledge and searchers for what is true, right, or lasting. To this end, those articles have been selected that provide you with information that will stimulate discussion and give your thoughts direction, but not those that tell you what to think. May you be "seeking" learners all through your own years of human development. May each suggestive answer you discover open your mind to more erudite (instructive) learning, questioning, and sophistication.

Karen Freiberg

Karen L. Freiberg, PhD
Editor

Contents

UNIT 1
Genetic and Prenatal Influences on Development

Part A. Genetic Influences

Part B. Prenatal Influences

The concepts in bold italics are developed in the article. For further expansion, please refer to the Topic Guide.

UNIT 2
Development during Infancy and Early Childhood

The concepts in bold italics are developed in the article. For further expansion, please refer to the Topic Guide.

UNIT 3
Development during Childhood: Cognition and Schooling

The concepts in bold italics are developed in the article. For further expansion, please refer to the Topic Guide.

UNIT 4
Development during Childhood: Family and Culture

The concepts in bold italics are developed in the article. For further expansion, please refer to the Topic Guide.

UNIT 5
Development during Adolescence and Young Adulthood

The concepts in bold italics are developed in the article. For further expansion, please refer to the Topic Guide.

UNIT 6
Development during Middle and Late Adulthood

The concepts in bold italics are developed in the article. For further expansion, please refer to the Topic Guide.

Part B. Late Adulthood

The concepts in bold italics are developed in the article. For further expansion, please refer to the Topic Guide.

Correlation Guide

The *Annual Editions* series provides students with convenient, inexpensive access to current, carefully selected articles from the public press. **Annual Editions: Human Development 10/11** is an easy-to-use reader that presents articles on important topics such as *genetics and prenatal development, school-age development, family and culture's roles in development, later-life development,* and many more. For more information on *Annual Editions* and other *McGraw-Hill Contemporary Learning Series* titles, visit www.mhhe.com/cls.

This convenient guide matches the units in **Annual Editions: Human Development 10/11** with the corresponding chapters in two of our best-selling McGraw-Hill Human Development textbooks by Santrock.

Annual Editions: Human Development 10/11	A Topical Approach to Life-Span Development, 5/e by Santrock	Life-Span Development, 12/e by Santrock
Unit 1: Genetic and Prenatal Influences on Development	**Chapter 2:** Biological Beginnings	**Chapter 2:** Biological Beginnings
Unit 2: Development during Infancy and Early Childhood	**Chapter 2:** Biological Beginnings **Chapter 4:** Health **Chapter 5:** Motor, Sensory, and Perceptual Development **Chapter 7:** Information Processing **Chapter 8:** Intelligence **Chapter 9:** Language Development **Chapter 10:** Emotional Development **Chapter 12:** Gender and Sexuality **Chapter 15:** Peers and the Sociocultural World	**Chapter 4:** Physical Development in Infancy **Chapter 5:** Cognitive Development in Infancy **Chapter 6:** Socioemotional Development in Infancy **Chapter 7:** Physical and Cognitive Development in Early Childhood **Chapter 8:** Socioemotional Development in Early Childhood
Unit 3: Development during Childhood: Cognition and Schooling	**Chapter 3:** Physical Development and Biological Aging **Chapter 6:** Cognitive Developmental Approaches **Chapter 7:** Information Processing **Chapter 8:** Intelligence **Chapter 16:** Schools, Achievement, and Work	**Chapter 5:** Cognitive Development in Infancy **Chapter 7:** Physical and Cognitive Development in Early Childhood **Chapter 9:** Physical and Cognitive Development in Middle and Late Childhood
Unit 4: Development during Childhood: Family and Culture	**Chapter 2:** Biological Beginnings **Chapter 3:** Physical Development and Biological Aging **Chapter 4:** Health **Chapter 9:** Language Development **Chapter 10:** Emotional Development **Chapter 12:** Gender and Sexuality **Chapter 16:** Schools, Achievement, and Work	**Chapter 6:** Socioemotional Development in Infancy **Chapter 8:** Socioemotional Development in Early Childhood **Chapter 10:** Socioemotional Development in Middle and Late Childhood
Unit 5: Development during Adolescence and Young Adulthood	**Chapter 3:** Physical Development and Biological Aging **Chapter 4:** Health **Chapter 7:** Information Processing **Chapter 8:** Intelligence **Chapter 9:** Language Development **Chapter 10:** Emotional Development **Chapter 12:** Gender and Sexuality **Chapter 14:** Families, Lifestyles, and Parenting **Chapter 15:** Peers and the Sociocultural World	**Chapter 11:** Physical and Cognitive Development in Adolescence **Chapter 12:** Socioemotional Development in Adolescence **Chapter 13:** Physical and Cognitive Development in Early Adulthood **Chapter 14:** Socioemotional Development in Early Adulthood
Unit 6: Development during Middle and Late Adulthood	**Chapter 3:** Physical Development and Biological Aging **Chapter 4:** Health **Chapter 7:** Information Processing **Chapter 8:** Intelligence **Chapter 9:** Language Development **Chapter 10:** Emotional Development **Chapter 12:** Gender and Sexuality **Chapter 15:** Peers and the Sociocultural World **Chapter 17:** Death, Dying, and Grieving	**Chapter 15:** Physical and Cognitive Development in Middle Adulthood **Chapter 16:** Socioemotional Development in Middle Adulthood **Chapter 17:** Physical Development in Late Adulthood **Chapter 18:** Cognitive Development in Late Adulthood **Chapter 19:** Socioemotional Development in Late Adulthood **Chapter 20:** Death, Dying, and Grieving

Topic Guide

This topic guide suggests how the selections in this book relate to the subjects covered in your course. You may want to use the topics listed on these pages to search the Web more easily.

On the following pages a number of websites have been gathered specifically for this book. They are arranged to reflect the units of this Annual Editions reader. You can link to these sites by going to *http://www.mhhe.com/cls*.

All the articles that relate to each topic are listed below the bold-faced term.

Adolescence
5. Truth and Consequences at Pregnancy High
16. In Defense of Distraction
17. Informing the ADHD Debate
24. Girls Gone Bad?
25. Disrespecting Childhood
28. A Peaceful Adolescence
29. Young, Gay, and Murdered
30. Interview with Dr. Craig Anderson: Video Game Violence
31. Jail Time Is Learning Time

Adulthood
17. Informing the ADHD Debate
28. A Peaceful Adolescence
32. Finding a Job in the 21st Century
33. Hold Me Tight
35. 50 Reasons to Love Being 50+
36. *Are You Ready for* Act II?
37. Tearing: Breakthrough in Human Emotional Signaling

Aggression
21. The Angry Smile
25. Disrespecting Childhood
26. Don't Blame the Caveman
30. Interview with Dr. Craig Anderson: Video Game Violence
31. Jail Time Is Learning Time

Aging
35. 50 Reasons to Love Being 50+
36. *Are You Ready for* Act II?
38. Healthy Aging in Later Life
40. Lost and Found
41. Life after Death
42. Navigating Practical Dilemmas in Terminal Care

Anxiety
33. Hold Me Tight

Attachment
9. Long-Term Studies of Preschool: Lasting Benefits Far Outweigh Costs
11. Easing the Separation Process for Infants, Toddlers, and Families
29. Young, Gay, and Murdered
33. Hold Me Tight

Brain development
7. Reading Your Baby's Mind
11. Easing the Separation Process for Infants, Toddlers, and Families
14. Get Smart
16. In Defense of Distraction
17. Informing the ADHD Debate
30. Interview with Dr. Craig Anderson: Video Game Violence
34. Emotions and the Brain: Laughter
35. 50 Reasons to Love Being 50+

Career
31. Jail Time Is Learning Time
32. Finding a Job in the 21st Century
36. *Are You Ready for* Act II?

Children
9. Long-Term Studies of Preschool: Lasting Benefits Far Outweigh Costs
11. Easing the Separation Process for Infants, Toddlers, and Families
12. Accountability Comes to Preschool: Can We Make It Work for Young Children?
13. "Early Sprouts": Establishing Healthy Food Choices for Young Children
15. An Educator's Journey toward Multiple Intelligences
17. Informing the ADHD Debate
18. Ten Big Effects of the No Child Left behind Act on Public Schools
20. A "Perfect" Case Study: Perfectionism in Academically Talented Fourth Graders
21. The Angry Smile
22. Where Personality Goes Awry
23. The Blank Slate
24. Girls Gone Bad?
25. Disrespecting Childhood
27. The End of White America?
34. Emotions and the Brain: Laughter

Cognition
4. The Mystery of Fetal Life: Secrets of the Womb
7. Reading Your Baby's Mind
14. Get Smart
15. An Educator's Journey toward Multiple Intelligences
16. In Defense of Distraction
17. Informing the ADHD Debate
31. Jail Time Is Learning Time
38. Healthy Aging in Later Life

Creativity
19. Single-Sex Classrooms Are Succeeding
32. Finding a Job in the 21st Century
33. Hold Me Tight
35. 50 Reasons to Love Being 50+
38. Healthy Aging in Later Life

Culture
5. Truth and Consequences at Pregnancy High
11. Easing the Separation Process for Infants, Toddlers, and Families
16. In Defense of Distraction
21. The Angry Smile
23. The Blank Slate
24. Girls Gone Bad?
25. Disrespecting Childhood
26. Don't Blame the Caveman
27. The End of White America?
28. A Peaceful Adolescence
29. Young, Gay, and Murdered

Internet References

The following Internet sites have been selected to support the articles found in this reader. These sites were available at the time of publication. However, because websites often change their structure and content, the information listed may no longer be available. We invite you to visit http://www.mhhe.com/cls for easy access to these sites.

Annual Editions: Human Development 10/11

General Sources

Association for Moral Education
http://www.amenetwork.org/

This association is dedicated to fostering communication, cooperation, training, curriculum development, and research that links moral theory to educational practices.

Behavior Analysis Resources
http://www.coedu.usf.edu/behavior/bares.htm

Dedicated to promoting the experimental, theoretical, and applied analysis of behavior, this site encompasses contemporary scientific and social issues, theoretical advances, and the dissemination of professional and public information.

Healthfinder
http://www.healthfinder.gov

Healthfinder is a consumer health site that contains the latest health news, prevention and care choices, and information about every phase of human development.

UNIT 1: Genetic and Prenatal Influences on Development

American Academy of Pediatrics (AAP)
http://www.aap.org

AAP provides data on optimal physical, mental, and social health for all children. The site links to professional educational sources and current research.

Basic Neural Processes
http://psych.hanover.edu/Krantz/neurotut.html

An extensive tutorial on brain structures is provided here.

Center for Evolutionary Psychology
http://www.psych.ucsb.edu/research/cep/

A link to an evolutionary psychology primer is available on this site. Extensive background information is included.

Conception
http://www.thefertilitydiet.com

The *Fertility Diet* guides couples toward diet and lifestyle choices that can make a real difference in fertility.

Genetics Education Center
http://www.kumc.edu/gec/

The University of Kansas Medical Center provides information on human genetics and the human genome project at this site. Included are a number of links to research areas.

Harvard Heart Letter
http://www.health.harvard.edu/newsweek

The Harvard Heart Letter provides monthly advise on the latest developments in heart health, new treatments, prevention, and research breakthroughs.

International HapMap Project
http://www.hapmap.org

Scientists from six countries work together to catalog human genetic variations that affect health and disease.

MedlinePlus Health Information/Prenatal Care
http://www.nlm.nih.gov/medlineplus/prenatalcare.html

On this site of the National Library of Medicine and the National Institutes of Health, you'll find prenatal-related sections such as General Information, Diagnosis/Symptoms, Nutrition, Organizations, and more.

UNIT 2: Development during Infancy and Early Childhood

Autism
http://www.autism-society.org

ASA, the nation's leading grassroots autism organization, exists to improve the lives of all affected by autism. It has many excellent resources for those needing more information about autism.

BabyCenter
http://www.babycenter.com

This well-organized site offers quick access to practical information on a variety of baby-related topics that span the period from preconception to toddlerhood.

Center for Childhood Obesity Research (CCOR)
http://www.hhdev.psu.edu/ccor/index.html

CCOR reports on obesity in toddlers and school-age children.

Children's Nutrition Research Center (CNRC)
http://www.kidsnutrition.org

CNRC is dedicated to defining the nutrient needs of healthy children, from conception through adolescence, and of pregnant and nursing mothers.

Early Childhood Care and Development
http://www.ecdgroup.com

Child development theory, programming and parenting data, and research can be found on this site of the Consultative Group. It is dedicated to the improvement of conditions of young children at risk.

Zero to Three: National Center for Infants, Toddlers, and Families
http://www.zerotothree.org

Zero to Three is dedicated solely to infants, toddlers, and their families. Organized by recognized experts in the field, it provides technical assistance to communities, states, and the federal government.

Internet References

UNIT 3: Development during Childhood: Cognition and Schooling

Children Now
http://www.childrennow.org

Children Now focuses on improving conditions for children who are poor or at risk. Articles include information on education, the influence of media, health, and security.

Council for Exceptional Children
http://www.cec.sped.org

This is the home page of the Council for Exceptional Children, which is dedicated to improving education for exceptional children and the gifted child.

Educational Resources Information Center (ERIC)
http://www.eric.ed.gov/

Sponsored by the U.S. Department of Education, this site will lead to numerous documents related to elementary and early childhood education.

Federation of Behavioral, Psychological, and Cognitive Science
http://www.thefederationonline.org

The federation's mission is fulfilled through legislative and regulatory advocacy, education, and information dissemination to the scientific community. Hotlink to the National Institutes of Health's Project on the Decade of the Brain.

The National Association for the Education of Young Children (NAEYC)
http://www.naeyc.org

NAEYC is the nation's largest organization of early childhood professionals. It is devoted to improving the quality of early childhood education programs for children from birth through the age of eight.

Project Zero
http://pzweb.harvard.edu

Following 30 years of research on the development of learning processes in children and adults, Project Zero is now helping to create communities of reflective, independent learners; to enhance deep understanding within disciplines; and to promote critical and creative thinking.

Teaching Technologies
http://www.inspiringteachers.com/bttindex.html

This is an excellent website for aspiring as well as experienced teachers.

UNIT 4: Development during Childhood: Family and Culture

Harborview Injury Prevention and Research Center
http://depts.washington.edu/hiprc/

Systematic reviews of childhood injury prevention and interventions on such diverse subjects as adolescent suicide, child abuse, accidental injuries, and youth violence are offered on this site.

Families and Work Institute
http://www.familiesandwork.org/index.html

The Families and Work Institute conducts policy research on issues related to the changing workforce, and it operates a national clearinghouse on work and family life.

iVillage Pregnancy and Parenting
http://parenting.ivillage.com

This resource focuses on issues concerning single parents and their children. The articles range from parenting children from infancy through adolescence.

Parentsplace.com: Single Parenting
http://www.parentsplace.com

This site provides links to resources valuable to parents, with topics ranging from pregnancy to teens.

Passive Aggressive Diaries
http://www.PassiveAggressiveDiaries.com

Passive Aggressive Diaries is a website blog that invites people to share their stories of passive aggressive behavior.

UNIT 5: Development during Adolescence and Young Adulthood

Alcohol & Drug Addiction Resource Center
http://www.addict-help.com/

An online source for questions regarding alcohol and drug addiction.

ADOL: Adolescent Directory On-Line
http://site.educ.indiana.edu/aboutus/AdolescenceDirectoryonLine ADOL/tabid/4785/Default.aspx

The ADOL site contains a wide array of web documents that address adolescent development. Specific content ranges from mental health issues to counselor resources.

AMA—Adolescent Health On-Line
http://www.ama-assn.org/ama/pub/category/1947.html

This AMA adolescent health initiative describes clinical preventive services that primary care physicians and other health professionals can provide to young people.

American Academy of Child and Adolescent Psychiatry
http://www.aacap.org/

Up-to-date data on a host of topics that include facts for families, public health, and clinical practice may be found here.

Depression
http://www.depression-primarycare.org

This site provides depression-related information for clinicians, organizations, and patients.

UNIT 6: Development during Middle and Late Adulthood

Alzheimer's Disease Research Center
http://alzheimer.wustl.edu/

ADRC facilitates advanced research on clinical, genetic, neuropathological, neuroanatomical, biomedical, neuropsychological, and psychosocial aspects of Alzheimer's disease and related brain disorders.

Internet References

American Association of Retired Persons

http://www.aarp.org

Founded in 1958, AARP is a nonprofit, nonpartisan membership organization that helps people 50 and over improve the quality of their lives. AARP has 40 million members and has offices in all 50 states, the District of Columbia, Puerto Rico and the U.S. Virgin Islands.

Lifestyle Factors Affecting Late Adulthood

http://www.school-for-champions.com/health/lifestyle_elderly.htm

The way a person lives his or her life in the later years can affect the quality of life. Find here information to improve a senior's lifestyle plus a few relevant links.

National Aging Information and Referral Support Center

http://www.nausa.org/informationandreferral/index-ir.php

This service by the States United for Action in Aging is a central source of data on demographic, health, economic, and social status of older Americans.

Department of Health and Human Services—Aging

http://www.hhs.gov/aging/index.html

This is a complete site, with links and topics on aging.

UNIT 1

Genetic and Prenatal Influences on Development

Unit Selections

1. **The Identity Dance,** Gunjan Sinha
2. **Seeking Genetic Fate,** Patrick Barry
3. **Fat, Carbs and the Science of Conception,** Jorge E. Chavarro, Walter C. Willett, and Patrick J. Skerrett
4. **The Mystery of Fetal Life: Secrets of the Womb,** John Pekkanen
5. **Truth and Consequences at Pregnancy High,** Alex Morris

Key Points to Consider

- Will genetic technology result in more attempts to alter genes than environmental factors in the 21st century?

- Will life experiences still conspire to switch new DNA sequences on and off?

- Would you spend hundreds of dollars to discover your genetic roots and your risk factors for known diseases?

- How can diet affect conception?

- What are the ethical concerns about "selling" ova to help infertile couples have their own children?

- How prevalent is surrogate motherhood today? How do gestational carriers feel about surrogacy?

- Should tax dollars support the 15% of unmarried teenage girls who become pregnant each year?

Student Website

www.mhhe.com/cls

Internet References

American Academy of Pediatrics (AAP)
http://www.aap.org
Basic Neural Processes
http://psych.hanover.edu/Krantz/neurotut.html
Center for Evolutionary Psychology
http://www.psych.ucsb.edu/research/cep/
Conception
http://www.thefertilitydiet.com
Genetics Education Center
http://www.kumc.edu/gec/
Harvard Heart Letter
http://www.health.harvard.edu/newsweek
International Hap Map Project
http://www.hapmap.org
MedlinePlus Health Information/Prenatal Care
http://www.nlm.nih.gov/medlineplus/prenatalcare.html

Genetic scientists have made quantum leaps in this decade, finding ways to treat abnormal human conditions by manipulating cells, genes, and the immune system. The total human genome was mapped in 2003. This knowledge of the human complement of twenty-three pairs of chromosomes with their associated genes in the nucleus of every cell has the potential for allowing cures for previously incurable diseases. The use of stem cells (undifferentiated embryonic cells) in animal research has documented the possibility of morphing stem cells into any kind of human cells. Stem cells will turn into desired tissue cells when the gene sequences of cytosine, adenine, thymine, and guanine (CATG) of the desired tissues are expressed. Scientists are using their knowledge of the human genome and embryonic stem cells to alter behaviors as well as to cure diseases. Cloning (complete reproduction) of a human already exists when one egg fertilized by one sperm separates into identical twins. Monozygotic twin research suggests that one's genetic CATG sequencing does not determine human behaviors, diseases, and traits without environmental input. Nature versus nurture is better phrased nature plus nurture. Genes appear to have mechanisms by which environmental factors can turn them on or leave them dormant.

Genetic precursors of human development and the use of stem cells, morphing, and cloning will be hot topics of the next several years as more genetic manipulation becomes feasible. As DNA sequences associated with particular human traits (genetic markers) are uncovered, pressure will appear to alter these traits. Will the focus be on altering the CATG sequencing, or altering the environmental factors that will "operate" on the genes?

Human embryology (the study of the first through seventh weeks after conception) and human fetology (the study of the eighth week of pregnancy through birth) have given verification to the idea that behavior precedes birth. The genetic hardwiring of CATG directs much of this behavior. However, the developing embryo/fetus reacts to the internal and external environments provided by the mother as well. Substances diffuse through the placental barrier from the mother's body. The embryo reacts to toxins (viruses, antigens) that pass through the umbilical cord. The fetus reacts to an enormous number of other stimuli, such as the sounds from the mother's body (digestive rumblings, heartbeat) and the mother's movements, moods, and medicines. How the embryo/fetus reacts (weakly to strongly, positively to negatively) depends, in large part, on his or her genetic preprogramming. Genes and environment are so inextricably intertwined that the effect of each cannot be studied separately. Prenatal development always has strong environmental influences and vice versa.

The two articles in the genetic influences section of this unit describe how decoding of the human genome will affect our future views about human development. The information in them is central to many ongoing discussions of human development. The potentialities for altering structures and behaviors, by altering the CATG messages of DNA on chromosomes within cells

or by cloning humans, are massive. We all need to understand what is happening. We need to make knowledgeable and well-thought-out choices for our futures.

The first article, "The Identity Dance," addresses the interplay of genes and environment. It presents research on identical twins suggesting that life factors conspire to switch genetic sequences of CATG on, or off, to create personality traits, diseases, and other human behaviors. What will we, the human race, choose to do with the technology in our hands: alter gene sequences or alter environment? The author poses several questions about human twins which should stimulate lively debates.

The second article, "Seeking Genetic Fate," discusses the possibility of having one's own DNA mapped in order to understand more about one's ancestry, geographical origins, and health risks. While humans share about 99.5% of their genes in common, the last 0.5% is of interest in that it produces human variations. Scientists have developed ways to look at single nucleotide polymorphisms, or SNPs, which can reveal much of these genetic variations. While personal genomics is possible, the technology is still evolving. There is no way at present to be absolutely sure the predictive power of SNPs is accurate. Many genetic diseases, for example, are triggered by environmental factors. Having the tag SNP does not always result in becoming diseased.

The third article, "Fat, Carbs and the Science of Conception," discusses how important good fats (unsaturated) and good carbs (complex) are to fertility. The famous longitudinal Nurses' Health Study at Harvard University has data to document the findings that trans fats and fast (easily digested) carbs in the diet are detrimental to conception.

The fourth article, "The Mystery of Fetal Life: Secrets in the Womb," answers questions regarding fetal psychological development. Human behaviors such as intelligence and personality may be profoundly influenced by the environment of the mother's uterus. Nurture occurs before and after birth. John Pekkanen addresses issues such as over-the-counter drugs, caffeine, infections, pets, and environmental pollutants. He reviews what is known about fetal memory, including the much misunderstood "Mozart effect."

The final topic selected for inclusion in this unit of this anthology deals with the large numbers of very young mothers who know very little about prenatal influences on development when they become pregnant. For many years adolescent childbearing was on the decline in the United States. Today it is on the increase. About 15% of women between 15 and 19 in the United States become pregnant each year. Many of them are poor, uneducated, and unmarried. The risks of having a premature, low birth-weight, or small-for-gestational-age infant increases with teen pregnancy and lack of prenatal care or knowledge of prenatal health considerations. Many babies born small and early are at risk for mental and physical disabilities. Alex Morris in "Truth and Consequences at Pregnancy High" questions the value of providing free or low cost education to these pregnant teens. Prenatal influences are profound. Spending money on prenatal care can ultimately save taxpayers billions of dollars to educate children born with disabilities.

The Identity Dance

The battle between genes and the environment is over. As the dust settles, scientists piece together how DNA and life experience conspire to create personality.

GUNJAN SINHA

Sandra and Marisa Peña, 32-year-old identical twins, seem to be exactly the same. They have the same thick dark hair, the same high cheekbones, the same habit of delicately rubbing the tip of the nose in conversation. They had the same type of thyroid cyst at the same age (18) in the same place (right side). When San Diego is mentioned, they both say, simultaneously and with the same intonation, "Oh, I love San Diego!" They live together, work one floor away from each other at MTV, wear the same clothes, hang out with the same friends. They even have the same dreams.

The sisters are as alike as two people can be. At the same time, they are opposites. Sandra is outgoing and confident; Marisa is reserved. They have the same pretty face, but those cheekbones make shy Marisa look mysterious and brooding, while Sandra looks wholesome and sweet. Sandra tends to speak for her sister: "Marisa's always been more quiet, more subdued, an introvert"; Marisa nods her assent. They see themselves as a duo—but more like complementary photo negatives rather than duplicates of each other. "I think we balance each other out," says Sandra. "Definitely," Marisa chimes in. Sandra begins, "In every family photo, I'm smiling, she's—" " 'I'm not," Marisa says with a laugh.

When their father passed away ten years ago from pancreatic cancer and their mother died soon after, the deeper differences between the two became obvious. Their family had been very loving and protective, and the sisters were traumatized by the sudden loss. But as Marisa sank into a depression, Sandra picked up and changed her life. She left San Antonio for Germany to live with her boyfriend. Marisa stayed put, catatonic with sadness. It was the first time the two had ever been apart.

Then, after a few months in Germany, Sandra headed to New York City—the buzzing metropolis in which she had dreamed of living since she was a teenager. Marisa soon followed Sandra, but when she arrived in New York, "She just couldn't let go of [her sadness]," says Sandra. "I didn't know what to do with her."

In recent years, we've, come to believe that genes influence character and personality more than anything else does. It's not just about height and hair color—DNA seems to have its clutches on our very souls. But spend a few hours with identical twins, who have exactly the same set of genes, and you'll find that this simplistic belief crumbles before your eyes. If DNA dictates all, how can two people with identical genes—who are living, breathing clones of each other—be so different?

To answer such questions, scientists have begun to think more broadly about how genes and life experience combine to shape us. The rigid idea that genes determine identity has been replaced with a more flexible and complex view in which DNA and life experience conspire to mold our personalities. We now know that certain genes make people susceptible to traits like aggression and depression. But susceptibility is not inevitability. Gene expression is like putty: Genes are turned on and off, dialed up or down both by other genes and by the ups and downs of everyday life. A seminal study last year found that the ideal breeding ground for depression is a combination of specific genes *and* stressful triggers—simply having the gene will not send most people into despair. Such research promises to end the binary debate about nature vs. nurture—and usher in a revolution in understanding who we are.

We've come to believe genes influence character more than anything else—DNA seems to have its clutches on our souls.

"While scientists have been trying to tease apart environmental from genetic influences on diseases like cancer, this is the first study to show this effect [for a mental disorder]," says Thomas Insel, director of the National Institute of Mental Health. "This is really the science of the moment."

About ten years ago, technological advances made it possible to quickly identify human genes. That breakthrough launched a revolution in human biology—and in psychiatry. Not only were scientists rapidly discovering genes linked to illnesses such as cancer and birth defects like dwarfism, they also found genes associated with such traits as sexual preference and aggression as well as mental illnesses such as schizophrenia.

Genetic discoveries transformed the intellectual zeitgeist as well, marking a decisive shift from the idea that environment alone shapes human personality. Nurture-heavy theories about behavior dominated in the 1960s and 1970s, a reaction in part to the legacy of Nazi eugenics. By the 1990s, the genome was exalted as "the human blueprint," the ultimate dictator of our attributes. Behavioral geneticists offered refreshingly simple explanations for human identity—and for social problems. Bad parenting, poor neighborhoods or amoral television didn't cause bad behavior; genes did. No wonder all those welfare programs weren't working.

"People really believed that there must be something exclusively genetically wrong with people who are not successful. They were exhausted with these broken-hearted liberals saying that it's all social," says Andreas Heinz, professor of psychiatry at Humboldt and Freie University in Berlin, who has been studying the influence of genes and environment on behavior for years. The idea that violent behavior in particular might be genetically "set" was so accepted that in 1992, the director of the agency overseeing the National Institute of Mental Health compared urban African-American youth with "hyperaggressive" and "hypersexual" monkeys in a jungle.

Behavioral genetics had a simple argument: Bad parenting, poor neighborhoods or TV didn't cause bad behavior. Genes did.

Genetic explanations for behavior gained ground in part through great leaps in our understanding of mood disorders. In the early 1990s, research at the federal labs of Stephen Suomi and Dee Higley found that monkeys with low levels of serotonin—now known to be a major player in human anxiety and depression—were prone to alcoholism, anxiety and aggression. Around the same time, Klaus-Peter Lesch at the University of Würtzburg in Germany identified the serotonin transporter gene, which produces a protein that ferries serotonin between brain cells. Prozac and other drugs work by boosting levels of serotonin in the brain, so this gene seemed like an obvious target in the search for the genetic roots of depression.

Lesch, who was working on the connection between this gene and psychiatric disorders, later found that people who had at least one copy of the short version of this gene were much more likely to have an anxiety disorder. Short and long versions of genes function much like synonymous words: Different lengths, or "spellings," generate subtle but critical differences in biology.

Genetics couldn't explain why some people bounce back from terrible trauma that shatters others, or why some people are ruthlessly ambitious and others laid-back.

Despite these groundbreaking insights, it quickly became clear that complex human behaviors couldn't be reduced to pure genetics. Apart from a few exceptions, scientists couldn't find a gene that directly caused depression or schizophrenia or any other major mental of mood disorder. The new research also failed to answer a lot of common-sense questions: If identical twins are genetically indistinguishable, how could just one end up schizophrenic or homosexual? And it couldn't address subtler questions about character and behavior. Why do some people bounce back from terrible trauma that shatters others? Why are some people ruthlessly ambitious and others laid-back?

Thanks to misfit monkeys like George, a rhesus macaque living in a lab in Maryland, researchers have clues to the missing element. In most ways, George is a typical male monkey. He's covered in sandy fur and has a rubbery, almost maniacal grin. But a couple of things set George apart. After he was born, Higley and Suomi's team separated George from his mother, raising him instead in a nursery with other macaque infants his own age. George has another strike against him: a short version of the serotonin transporter gene (monkeys, like people, can have either a short form or a long form of the gene).

But the most notable thing about George is that he is an alcoholic. Each day, George and his simian chums have happy hour, with alcohol freely available in their cage for one hour. Unlike his buddies, George drinks like the resident barroom lush—he sways and wobbles and can't walk a straight line.

And his problems go beyond the bottle. He's reluctant to explore new objects, and he is shy around strangers. He always seems to be on edge and tends to get aggressive and impulsive quickly. In short, he's a completely different animal from his cousin Jim, who also has the short version of the transporter gene but was raised by his biological mom. Jim's "normal" upbringing seems to have protected him from the gene: This monkey is laid-back and prefers sugar water to booze.

After studying 36 family-raised monkeys and 79 nursery-raised animals, the team found that the long version of the gene seems to help the animals shrug off stress. The short form of the gene, by contrast, doesn't directly *cause* alcoholism: Monkeys with the short gene and a normal family upbringing have few personality problems. But the short version of the gene definitely puts the animals at a disadvantage when life gets tough. Raised without the care and support of their mothers, their predisposition toward anxiety and alcoholism comes to the fore.

"Maternal nurturing and discipline seem to buffer the effect of the serotonin gene," says Suomi. "If they don't have good mothers, then the [troubled] behavior comes out loud and clear."

The implications of this research are tantalizing, since people also carry long and short versions of the transporter gene. These variants, unlike those that have been identified as making people susceptible to diseases like breast cancer or Alzheimer's, are very common: Among Caucasians, about one-fifth of the population has two copies of the short gene (everyone gets one copy from Mom and the other from Dad), and another third have two copies of the long gene. The rest have one of each. (The gene has not yet been studied in other populations.) The evidence indicated that this gene was related to resilience and depression in humans. Why, then, had researchers thus far failed to find a convincing correlation between the gene and the risk of depression?

Terrie Moffitt and Avshalom Caspi, a husband-and-wife team of psychologists at King's College in London, had the insight that environmental influences might be the missing part of the puzzle. Moffitt and Caspi turned to a long-term study of almost 900 New Zealanders, identified these subjects' transporter genes and interviewed the subjects about traumatic experiences in early adulthood—like a major breakup, death in the family or serious injury—to see if the difficulties brought out an underlying genetic tendency toward depression.

The results were striking: 43 percent of subjects who had the short genes and who had experienced four or more tumultuous events became clinically depressed. By contrast, only 17 percent of the long-gene people who had endured four or more stressful events wound up depressed—no more than the rate of depression in the general population. People with the short gene who experienced no stressful events fared pretty well too—they also became depressed at the average rate. Clearly, it was the combination of hard knocks and short genes that more than doubled the risk of depression.

Caspi and Moffitt's study, published last summer, was one of the first to examine the combined effects of genetic predisposition and experience on a specific trait. Psychiatrists were delighted. "It's just a wonderful story," says Insel. "It changed the way we think about genes and psychiatric disorders."

Moffitt and Caspi have found a similar relationship between another gene and antisocial behavior. Abused and neglected children with a gene responsible for low levels of monoamine oxidase in the brain were nine times more likely to engage in violent of other antisocial behavior as adults than were people with the same gene who were not mistreated. Finnish scientists have since found similar effects on genes for novelty seeking—a trait associated with attention deficit hyperactivity disorder. Children who had the genes and who were also raised by strict, emotionally distant parents were much more likely to engage in risky behavior and make impulsive decisions as adults than children with the same genes who were raised in more tolerant and accepting environments.

While scientists don't exactly know how genes are influenced by environment at the molecular level, there are clues that genes have the equivalent of molecular "switches" and can be programmed—turned on or off, up or down—very early. Both Lesch and Suomi have shown that the level of biochemicals such as the serotonin transporter molecule can be "set" as early as in the womb, at least in mice and monkeys.

Mothers of multiples will tell you their babies were distinct the moment they were born.

The prenatal environment also has a major influence on differences between identical twins. Mothers of multiples will tell you that their babies were distinct the moment they were born, and research backs them up. Twins experience different environments even in the womb, as they compete with each other for nutrients. One can beat out the other, which is why they often have different birth weights: Marisa Pena is a bit taller and heavier than her sister.

Prenatal experiences are just the first in a lifetime of differentiating factors. Only about 50 percent of the characteristics twins have in common are due to genes alone. Researchers now believe that an illness suffered by only one twin, or different amounts of attention from peers or parents, can set the stage for personality differences. This makes it easier to understand why the Pena sisters reacted as they did: By the time their parents died, "these twins had had a lifetime of experiences which might have made them react differently," says Moffitt. "In addition, some pairs of identical twins individuate themselves in early childhood. They seem to take on the roles of 'the shy one' and 'the outgoing one' and then live up to those roles." in other words, they customize their environment, and the world treats them accordingly.

The new science of nature *and* nurture isn't as straightforward as the DNA-is-destiny mantra, but it is more accurate. "People have a really hard time understanding the probabilistic nature of how genes impact traits like depression," says Kenneth Kendler, director of the Virginia Institute for Psychiatric and Behavioral Genetics at Virginia Commonwealth University, who heads a major twin registry. "They think that if something is heritable, then it can't be modified by the environment." The knowledge that the traits we inherit are also contingent on what the world does to us promises more insight into why people act and feel differently—even when they look exactly the same.

GUNJAN SINHA is an award-winning science writer based in Frankfurt, Germany.

Additional reporting by Jeff Grossman.

From *Psychology Today,* March/April 2004, pp. 52, 57–58, 60–61, 63, 95. Copyright © 2004 by Sussex Publishers, LLC. Reprinted by permission.

Seeking Genetic Fate

Personal genomics companies offer forecasts of disease risk, but the science behind the packaging is still evolving.

PATRICK BARRY

"Resistant!!!" shouts the title of Lindsay Richman's post. Apparently, she was elated to learn that her DNA reduces her susceptibility to norovirus infections, the principal cause of the common stomach flu.

So she posted a comment on a discussion board on the website for 23andMe, a company based in Mountain View, Calif., that specializes in the fledgling industry of personal genomics. To get a glimpse of her own DNA, Richman had sent the company $400 and a vial of her spit. From her point of view, what happened next was a mystery—a black box. But a few weeks later, out popped her results on a password-protected website, complete with social networking tools for sharing and discussing her genetic inheritance with other customers.

In the string of online responses to Richman's post, others who share her genetic good fortune compared notes on the last time they'd had any symptoms of stomach flu. Richman, a 26-year-old real estate agent in New York City, hasn't had stomach flu since she was 8, she wrote.

In other discussions, people compared their genetic profiles and brainstormed on how lifestyle choices and environmental exposures might influence their risks for various conditions, such as Parkinson's disease and prostate cancer.

Now that prices charged by personal genomics companies such as 23andMe, Navigenics, deCODE genetics and DNA Direct have dropped, ranging from a few hundred to a few thousand dollars, many people curious about their genetic inheritance, and how it relates to their health, have easier access to DNA testing.

Serving to "crowdsource" the search for new links among genes, behavior and disease, these companies' customers represent a small army of amateur genome sleuths who could prove to be a new force in pushing genomic research forward. But the genetic report cards these amateurs are reading may not be as definitive as they assume. Despite progress in linking genetic differences with disease risk and other traits, the predictive power of these links has fallen short of expectations.

In April, the *New England Journal of Medicine* published a review and a set of essays grappling with this shortfall in DNA's predictive power and searching for the best way to take research forward. An essay by Peter Kraft and David Hunter, epidemiologists at the Harvard School of Public Health in Boston, was revealingly titled, "Genetic risk prediction—are we there yet?"

Their answer, in a nutshell: No. Which leads to the crucial question of what, exactly, customers of personal genomics companies are looking at when logging on to the digital oracle to peek at their genetic fates.

The leap from a tube of saliva to a ledger of traits, health risks and ancestral history involves a lot of science—some credible, some flimsy. As more and more people become consumers of genetic information services, these people may want to first open that black box and take a good look inside.

The Black Box

It's certainly not the most dignified way to join the genomics era.

Inside the small, brightly colored DNA-sample kit that arrives in the mail lies a clear plastic tube capped by a blue plastic funnel—the easier to spit into. Users are instructed to fill the tube to a little line, which the directions say can take five minutes or more. Five minutes of repetitive spitting.

In that saliva float cheek cells that have sloughed off from the soft tissue lining the mouth. Snapping the tube's lid shut releases a preservative that keeps the cells intact during their voyage to the lab.

"The reason we collect so much spit is to get a lot of your DNA," explains Brian Naughton, a founding scientist at 23andMe. The machines that read the sequence of DNA chemical "letters" of the genetic code are quite accurate and robust against noise. Repeat the scan with DNA from the same person, and the two results will be more than 99.9 percent identical, according to the company.

"It's clearly reproducible," says George M. Church, a geneticist at Harvard Medical School in Boston. Testing a person again with another company's service using a different model of DNA reading machine will also produce nearly identical results. Church says.

Spit and Learn

The technology that personal genomics companies use does not read the sequence of genetic code letter by letter. Instead, the machines look for single-letter variations at specific locations. From a person's vial of spit, DNA is extracted from cells. The gene chip takes it from there.

DNA on a Chip

Resembling a computer chip, a gene chip has millions of microscopic spots. Each contains anchored, single DNA strands with specific sequences of genetic code with common single-letter variations.

Get Together

When spread over the gene chip, DNA from a person's spit sample joins with strands already attached to the chip that have the complementary genetic sequence. A fluorescent molecule marks joined strands.

Revealing Spots

Thanks to the fluorescent tags, glowing dots signal where a sample DNA strand has the matching genetic sequence to the known sequence of a pre-attached strand. A computer analyzes the results, producing a list of single-letter variations.

These machines use gene chips to read up to a million letters of genetic code at once. Since the first gene chips that could skim the entire genome debuted in 2005, the cost to scan a person's DNA has dropped dramatically.

Despite what some customers might assume, most personal genomics companies do *not* produce a complete sequence of a customer's genome. An entire human genome contains about 6 billion letters of genetic code distributed among a person's 23 pairs of chromosomes (the inspiration for the name 23andMe). These machines don't read every DNA letter. Instead, they read individual letters at 500,000 to a million different spots in the genome, capturing just 8 to 16 *thousandths* of one percent of the full genome.

But that genome sliver is carefully selected to represent much of the genetic variation among people. "It's really coverage of that genetic variation that you're going for," Naughton explains.

Nearly all of a person's genetic code is identical to that of every other person—roughly 99.5 percent of it matches up letter for letter. At certain spots along the length of a person's chromosomes, though, the genetic code can differ from other people's by a single letter. In the sequence of the familiar A's, T's, C's and G's, the four information-carrying nucleotides in DNA, some people might have a T at a certain

location while others have a C. These small variations are called single nucleotide polymorphisms, or SNPs (pronounced "snips").

The human genome contains about 10 million known SNPs. That estimate is the latest from the International HapMap Project, an ongoing scientific collaboration that's mapping these genetic variations. But SNPs near each other on a chromosome tend to get inherited together, making it possible to group neighboring SNPs into units of inheritance called haplotypes. A few tag SNPs are enough to identify each group, so it takes only about 500,000 tag SNPs to reveal a person's haplotypes. That's why most gene chips test for at least 500,000 SNPs, and why checking this tiny sliver of the genome—these tag SNPs—can reveal much of the genetic variation that makes a person unique.

Tag SNPs usually aren't part of any known gene. But the surrounding DNA inherited along with a SNP can contain one or more genes important for various diseases. The SNP is often a proxy.

This much of the black box is fairly reliable: the raw data on at least hundreds of thousands of a person's SNPs. Some personal genomics companies make this mountain of raw data directly available to their customers.

But that's the easy part. The other, more problematic half of the black box is interpretation. What exactly does having one SNP variant or another mean for a person's risk for heart disease, diabetes, colon cancer?

In short, there's no single answer for how reliable these interpretations are. Some SNPs have clear, strong and well-understood links with specific traits or diseases. Many others have only small effects, and the biological mechanisms for the links are often unknown.

Reviewing the available scientific evidence for each disease or trait is the biggest challenge for these companies, says Michele Cargill, director of human genetics for Navigenics. "You really have to read each [study] very, very carefully. It takes a lot of time and it's all done manually."

For example, the resistance to norovirus infection that Richman enjoys is linked to a SNP called rs601338, which is located on each of the two chromosome 19s she inherited from her parents. At this location, a person can have either an A or a G for this SNR Chromosomes with an A lack a functioning copy of a gene called *FUT2*. This gene produces a certain molecule on the outer surfaces of the cells that line the intestines. As it turns out, noroviruses must bind to this molecule in order to enter and infect the cells. People like Richman, who inherited the ASNP from both of her parents, do not have a working copy of the *FUT2* gene, so their intestinal cells lack the molecule that noroviruses need to cause an infection.

In this case, the link is strong. A single SNP can indicate whether a person has a working copy of a certain gene, and the biological mechanisms tying this gene to the virus's ability to enter the person's cells are well understood. In nearly all studies, people who lacked a functional copy of the *FUT2* gene didn't get sick, even when deliberately exposed to this

Chances Are

Writer Patrick Barry sent his own vial of spit to 23andMe and in return had access to an online summary, featured in this Web screenshot, of his risk for type 2 diabetes. Also, the company's chart of Marker Effects illustrates how risk can change from one variation on a genome to another. The genetic answer to the risk for this disease is not straightforward.

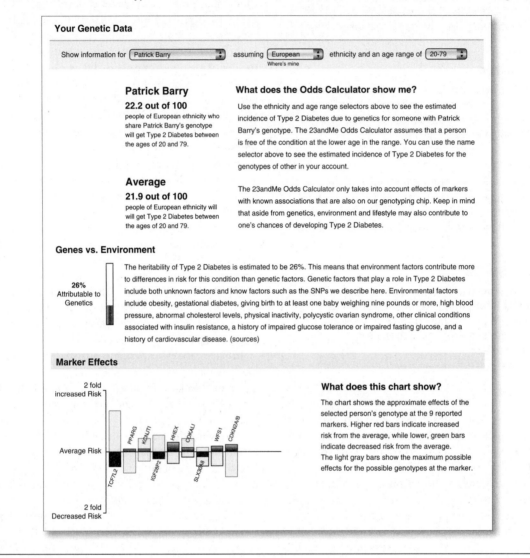

type of virus. It's as close as one ever gets in biology to a slam dunk.

About 1,300 genes have known, strong links to medical conditions, Church notes. Some disorders, such as sickle-cell anemia, are truly genetic diseases that a person has from birth. Others such as Parkinson's disease, macular degeneration, Alzheimer's disease and breast cancer arise later in life and can be influenced by environment and lifestyle, even though some genes are known to significantly change the odds that a person will get the disease.

But the relatively clear-cut cases are the exception, not the rule. For many traits and diseases, finding reasonably strong and reliable links with SNPs has proven more difficult than many scientists had expected.

Beware Weak Links

To search for these links, researchers use gene chips similar to those used by personal genomics companies. With these gene chips, scientists scan the DNA of two groups of people: a few hundred or thousand people with the disease in question and a few hundred or thousand without it. If the two groups are well matched in terms of other important traits such as age, ethnicity, smoking habits and so on, a SNP that appears more frequently among people with the disease than among the control group may be associated with the disease.

At first, these studies tended to "discover" a lot of illusory links—false connections that crop up by pure chance in the mountains of data produced by these studies (*SN: 6/21/08, p. 20*).

Haplotype in a Haystack

Personal genomics companies read only a tiny portion of a person's genome. But it's a telling portion, with efforts focused on identifying SNPs and haplotypes. SNPs are spots in the DNA where one person has a different chemical letter than another. Certain congregations of SNPs are flags for haplotypes, which are patterns of

genetic variation found in different populations. The illustration maps tag SNPs: (a) shows differences among four people in the same genetic sequence in part of one chromosome; (b) shows three SNPs highlighted in four haplotypes. The tag SNPs (c) can identify the haplotypes of the individuals.

a SNPs

	SNP ▼		SNP ▼		SNP ▼
Person 1	A A C A C G C C A	. . .	. T T C G G G G T C	. . .	. A G T C G A C C G	. . . .
Person 2	A A C A C G C C A	. . .	. T T C G A G G T C	. . .	. A G T C A A C C G	. . . .
Person 3	A A C A T G C C A	. . .	. T T C G G G G T G	. . .	. A G T C A A C C G	. . . .
Person 4	A A C A G G C C A	. . .	. T T C G G G G T G	. . .	. A G T C G A C C G	. . . .

b Haplotypes

▼▼▼

Haplotype 1	C T C A A A G T A C G G T T C A G G C A
Haplotype 2	T T G A T T G C G C A A C A G T A A T A
Haplotype 3	C C C G A T C T G T G A T A C T G G T G
Haplotype 4	T C G A T T C C G C G G T T G A G A C A

▼   ▼   ▼

c Tag SNPs   A/G   T/C   C/G

In the last few years, scientists have learned to correct for these statistical sins, but even with most false positives weeded out, these studies often point to large numbers of potentially suspect SNPs. For example, dozens of well-established SNPs contribute to the risk for Type 2 Diabetes, the form of the disease that emerges in late adulthood and is hastened by a diet high in sugar.

Unfortunately, most of these SNPs alter risk by only a tiny amount—a 2 percent change in risk for this one, a 5 percent change for that one, a 10 percent change for a third. Even a 10 percent change would mean that the odds of developing diabetes sometime in that person's lifetime would increase from the typical 22 percent to 24 percent. Not exactly a crystal ball–caliber revelation.

"People will tell you that if they know that they have a slightly higher risk for diabetes, then they could change their diet," Kraft says. "But you don't really need an expensive genome test to tell you that."

Even more problematic, though, is the fact that new links continue to trickle in. When the risks from individual SNPs are added, a person's overall risk of the disease could be slightly positive. But a newly discovered SNP could tilt the balance in the other direction.

"Our best guess about your risk today might turn out to be very different five years from now," Kraft says. "Your risk as a

function of time is a random walk. It bounces up and down as we learn more."

These problems also plague other common illnesses such as heart disease, as well as complex traits such as height and intelligence. In each of these cases, large numbers of SNPs are involved because the underlying biology is complicated. Heart disease, for example, is an umbrella term for various cardiovascular problems that could depend on genes for heart muscle proteins, blood vessel strength and elasticity, cholesterol metabolism, blood clotting and others. And each of these functions often arises from webs of interactions among dozens or hundreds of genes. These interactions produce the feedback loops that fine-tune a cell's behavior and make it robust, and these interactions add to genetic complexity (SN: 12/6/08, p. 22).

"It's very early days in terms of what we've learned about common, complex diseases," Kraft says.

Some in the genome research community say that studies with ever larger numbers of subjects are needed to find SNPs that have even weaker links but that many people have. The hope is that the cumulative effects will point to significant predictions. Others suggest that studies have already found all the important, common SNPs that there are to find, and that new studies should instead search for SNPs that are held by a small minority of people but that exert a stronger influence on disease.

Seeking Genetic Roots

DNA holds clues not only to an individual's medical future, but also to their family's past. Genetic profiles offered by many companies can show customers their ancestral histories.

After all, DNA is the ultimate genealogical record. A mutation that arose in the DNA of a person who lived 10,000 years ago could have been passed down to his or her children and grandchildren, becoming a kind of hidden family heirloom. Because the odds of that same single-letter mutation occurring again independently are negligibly small, somebody alive today who has that particular SNP almost certainly descended from that person who lived 10,000 years ago.

Of course, a DNA test can't pinpoint who that ancestor was. But by mapping where in the world a particular SNP is common among indigenous people, scientists can make a fairly good estimate of where its primogenitor lived.

DNA in small organelles called mitocnondria is inherited only from a person's mother. So a mitochondrial DNA SNP must have come from the mother, and her mother, and her mother, and so on for perhaps hundreds of generations. And DNA in the Y sex chromosome can come only from a boy's father and each previous father. Retracing the lineage of a mutation on other chromosomes is messy, since other chromosomes are shuffled at each generation. But mitochondrial DNA and Y chromosomes each offer a straight line of descent.

Modern tests look at more than 2,000 SNPs on both the mitochondrial DNA and—if the customer is male—the Y chromosome. The science behind these results is fairly robust, and estimates of geographical ancestry will only improve as scientists gather more DNA samples from people around the world.

—Patrick Barry

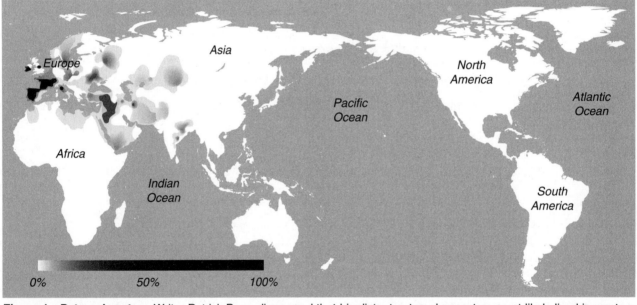

Figure 1   Paternal roots: Writer Patrick Barry discovered that his distant paternal ancestors most likely lived in western Europe. The map's color spectrum shows the probabilities that his father's family line, as identified by haplotype groups, originated in certain geographic regions.

Selling, Knowing Risk

Until more progress is made, some scientists say, selling risk information about complex diseases is premature.

"The justification is just not there for claiming that these [SNPs] have any clinical utility at this stage" for complex diseases, says Allan Balmain, a cancer geneticist at the University of California, San Francisco. He says that, in his opinion, personal genomics companies are "just exploiting the naïveté in the general population."

These companies plan to use their growing databases of DNA samples—and their legions of curious customers—for novel research. Other research scientists are cautiously optimistic.

Customers who have sent their DNA samples to these companies are not a random sample of the population, a fact that could bias the results. And information about family history, health habits and environmental exposures are gathered through unmonitored online surveys, rather than by professional clinicians. With careful study design and quality control for the data, though, these obstacles could be surmountable. "Their data set is not in itself bad," Balmain says. "Some of these things may turn out to be very useful."

Eventually, though, these companies may need to move beyond SNPs, as many researchers have begun to do. Much of the genetic variation among people comes in forms other than changes to single letters of code. Some people have long

Sometimes Even the Best Minds Need a Little R&R

So, pull the shades, turn off the PDA, and enjoy a guilty pleasure . . . *SCI FI* Magazine. We take you unblushingly into the world of the future . . . the world of what may be . . . and we have FUN with it. After all, who doesn't love those effects from the *Transformers* movies, or the gossip about a possible new *Star Trek* TV series, or those *Stargate Universe* secrets? Don't you deserve a little "me" time to pour over the paparazzi spread to see what kind of trouble the Hollywood sci fi set is getting into? Or even the review on the latest sci fi online game?

Yes, we know it's bubble-gum, it's popular media, it's psycho-babble. But its just so darn cool! . . . Next time someone scoffs that sci fi is useless, mind numbing drivel, you might want to remind them how many of those miraculous gadgets from the original *Star Trek* are now in everyday use.

Go ahead. Order a subscription for yourself today. It can be just our little secret.

chunks of DNA within their genomes that other people lack. Along with these insertions and deletions, the number of copies of some genes varies from person to person. While these kinds of structural differences are far less numerous than SNPs, each of them can involve hundreds or thousands of letters of genetic code, so together they account for about four times more genetic variation than SNPs do *(SN: 4/25/09, p. 16).*

Modified gene chips can detect some small insertions and deletions, but the best way to tally these changes is with the more thorough, and more expensive, approach of DNA sequencing.

Current state-of-the-art technologies can sequence an entire human genome for about $5,000, compared with millions of dollars just four years ago. "I think nobody anticipated just how fast the cost of sequencing would change," Church says. "I think we're already at the tipping point. It's already getting feasible to sequence large portions of genomes, maybe all the coding regions, for studies and for individuals."

Unfortunately, Naughton says, 23andMe doesn't store frozen saliva samples for most customers, only for those participating in research projects. So if Richman someday wants to upgrade to a full genome sequence to learn even more about her genetic inheritance, she'll have to go through all that spitting again.

Explore More

International HapMap Project: www.hapmap.org

PATRICK BARRY is a science writer based in San Francisco.

From *Science News,* July 4, 2009, vol. 176, no. 1, pp. 16–21. Copyright © by Society for Science & the Public. Reprinted by permission.

Fat, Carbs and the Science of Conception

In a groundbreaking new book, Harvard researchers look at the role of diet, exercise and weight control in fertility. Guarantee: you will be surprised.

JORGE E. CHAVARRO, MD, WALTER C. WILLETT, MD, AND PATRICK J. SKERRETT

Every new life starts with two seemingly simple events. First, an active sperm burrows into a perfectly mature egg. Then the resulting fertilized egg nestles into the specially prepared lining of the uterus and begins to grow. The key phrase in that description is "seemingly simple." Dozens of steps influenced by a cascade of carefully timed hormones are needed to make and mature eggs and sperm. Their union is both a mad dash and a complex dance, choreographed by hormones, physiology and environmental cues.

A constellation of other factors can come into play. Many couples delay having a baby until they are financially ready or have established themselves in their professions. Waiting, though, decreases the odds of conceiving and increases the chances of having a miscarriage. Fewer than 10 percent of women in their early 20s have issues with infertility, compared with nearly 30 percent of those in their early 40s. Sexually transmitted diseases such as chlamydia and gonorrhea, which are on the upswing, can cause or contribute to infertility. The linked epidemics of obesity and diabetes sweeping the country have reproductive repercussions. Environmental contaminants known as endocrine disruptors, such as some pesticides and emissions from burning plastics, appear to affect fertility in women and men. Stress and anxiety, both in general and about fertility, can also interfere with getting pregnant. Add all these to the complexity of conception and it's no wonder that infertility is a common problem, besetting an estimated 6 million American couples.

It's almost become a cliché that diet, exercise and lifestyle choices affect how long you'll live, the health of your heart, the odds you'll develop cancer and a host of other health-related issues. Is fertility on this list? The answer to that question has long been a qualified "maybe," based on old wives' tales, conventional wisdom—and almost no science. Farmers, ranchers and animal scientists know more about how nutrition affects fertility in cows, pigs and other commercially important animals than fertility experts know about how it affects reproduction in humans. There are small hints scattered across medical journals, but few systematic studies of this crucial connection in people.

We set out to change this critical information gap with the help of more than 18,000 women taking part in the Nurses' Health Study, a long-term research project looking at the effects of diet and other factors on the development of chronic conditions such as heart disease, cancer and other diseases. Each of these women said she was trying to have a baby. Over eight years of follow-up, most of them did. About one in six women, though, had some trouble getting pregnant, including hundreds who experienced ovulatory infertility—a problem related to the maturation or release of a mature egg each month. When we compared their diets, exercise habits and other lifestyle choices with those of women who readily got pregnant, several key differences emerged. We have translated these differences into fertility-boosting strategies.

At least for now, these recommendations are aimed at preventing and reversing ovulatory infertility, which accounts for one quarter or more of all cases of infertility. They won't work for infertility due to physical impediments like blocked fallopian tubes. They may work for other types of infertility, but we don't yet have enough data to explore connections between nutrition and infertility due to other causes. And since the Nurses' Health Study doesn't include information on the participants' partners, we weren't able to explore how nutrition affects male infertility. From what we have gleaned from the limited research in this area, some of our strategies might improve fertility in men, too. The plan described in The Fertility Diet doesn't guarantee a pregnancy any more than do in vitro fertilization or other forms of assisted reproduction. But it's virtually free, available to everyone, has no side effects, sets the stage for a healthy pregnancy, and forms the foundation of a healthy eating strategy for motherhood and beyond. That's a winning combination no matter how you look at it.

Slow Carbs, Not No Carbs

Once upon a time, and not that long ago, carbohydrates were the go-to gang for taste, comfort, convenience and energy. Bread, pasta, rice, potatoes—these were the highly recommended, base-of-the-food-pyramid foods that supplied us with half or more of our calories. Then in rumbled the Atkins and South Beach diets. In a scene out of George Orwell's "1984," good became bad almost overnight as the two weight-loss juggernauts turned carbohydrates into dietary demons, vilifying them as the source of big bellies and jiggling thighs. Following the no-carb gospel, millions of Americans spurned carbohydrates in hopes of shedding pounds. Then, like all diet fads great and small, the no-carb craze lost its luster and faded from prominence.

It had a silver lining, though, and not just for those selling low-carb advice and products. All the attention made scientists and the rest of us more aware of carbohydrates and their role in a healthy diet. It spurred several solid head-to-head comparisons of low-carb and low-fat diets that have given us a better understanding of how carbohydrates affect weight and weight loss. The new work supports the growing realization that carbohydrate choices have a major impact—for better and for worse—on the risk for heart disease, stroke, type 2 diabetes and digestive health.

New research from the Nurses' Health Study shows that carbohydrate choices also influence fertility. Eating lots of easily digested carbohydrates (fast carbs), such as white bread, potatoes and sugared sodas, increases the odds that you'll find yourself struggling with ovulatory infertility. Choosing slowly digested carbohydrates that are rich in fiber can improve fertility. This lines up nicely with work showing that a diet rich in these slow carbs and fiber before pregnancy helps prevent gestational diabetes, a common and worrisome problem for pregnant women and their babies. What do carbohydrates have to do with ovulation and pregnancy?

More than any other nutrient, carbohydrates determine your blood-sugar and insulin levels. When these rise too high, as they do in millions of individuals with insulin resistance, they disrupt the finely tuned balance of hormones needed for reproduction. The ensuing hormonal changes throw ovulation off-kilter.

Knowing that diet can strongly influence blood sugar and insulin, we wondered if carbohydrate choices could influence fertility in average, relatively healthy women. The answer from the Nurses' Health Study was yes. We started by grouping the study participants from low daily carbohydrate intake to high. One of the first things we noticed was a connection between high carbohydrate intake and healthy lifestyles.

Women in the high-carb group, who got nearly 60 percent of their calories from carbs, ate less fat and animal protein, drank less alcohol and coffee, and consumed more plant protein and fiber than those in the low-carb group, who got 42 percent of calories from carbohydrates. Women in the top group also weighed less, weren't as likely to smoke and were more physically active. This is a good sign that carbohydrates can be just fine for health, especially if you choose good ones.

The *total* amount of carbohydrate in the diet wasn't connected with ovulatory infertility. Women in the low-carb and high-carb groups were equally likely to have had fertility problems. That wasn't a complete surprise. As we described earlier, different carbohydrate sources can have different effects on blood sugar, insulin and long-term health.

Evaluating total carbohydrate intake can hide some important differences. So we looked at something called the glycemic load. This relatively new measure conveys information about both the amount of carbohydrate in the diet and how quickly it is turned to blood sugar. The more fast carbs in the diet, the higher the glycemic load. (For more on glycemic load, go to health.harvard .edu/ newsweek.) Women in the highest glycemic-load category

were 92 percent more likely to have had ovulatory infertility than women in the lowest category, after accounting for age, smoking, how much animal and vegetable protein they ate, and other factors that can also influence fertility. In other words, eating a lot of easily digested carbohydrates increases the odds of ovulatory infertility, while eating more slow carbs decreases the odds.

Because the participants of the Nurses' Health Study complete reports every few years detailing their average daily diets, we were able to see if certain foods contributed to ovulatory infertility more than others. In general, cold breakfast cereals, white rice and potatoes were linked with a higher risk of ovulatory infertility. Slow carbs, such as brown rice, pasta and dark bread, were linked with greater success getting pregnant.

Computer models of the nurses' diets were also revealing. We electronically replaced different nutrients with carbohydrates. Most of these substitutions didn't make a difference. One, though, did. Adding more carbohydrates at the expense of naturally occurring fats predicted a decrease in fertility. This could very well mean that natural fats, especially unsaturated fats, improve ovulation when they replace easily digested carbohydrates.

In a nutshell, results from the Nurses' Health Study indicate that the *amount* of carbohydrates in the diet doesn't affect fertility, but the *quality* of those carbohydrates does. Eating a lot of rapidly digested carbohydrates that continually boost your blood-sugar and insulin levels higher can lower your chances of getting pregnant. This is especially true if you are eating carbohydrates in place of healthful unsaturated fats. On the other hand, eating whole grains, beans, vegetables and whole fruits—all of which are good sources of slowly digested carbohydrates—can improve ovulation and your chances of getting pregnant.

Eating whole grains, beans, vegetables and whole fruits—all sources of 'slow carbs'— can improve ovulation and chances of pregnancy.

Balancing Fats

In 2003, the government of Denmark made a bold decision that is helping protect its citizens from heart disease: it essentially banned trans fats in fast food, baked goods and other commercially prepared foods. That move may have an unexpected effect—more little Danes. Exciting findings from the Nurses' Health Study indicate that trans fats are a powerful deterrent to ovulation and conception. Eating less of this artificial fat can improve fertility, and simultaneously adding in healthful unsaturated fats whenever possible can boost it even further.

Women, their midwives and doctors, and fertility researchers have known for ages that body fat and energy stores affect reproduction. Women who don't have enough stored energy to sustain a pregnancy often have trouble ovulating or stop menstruating altogether. Women who have too much stored energy often have difficulty conceiving for other reasons, many of which affect ovulation. These include insensitivity to the hormone insulin, an excess of male sex hormones and overproduction of leptin, a hormone that helps the body keep tabs on body fat.

A related issue is whether *dietary* fats influence ovulation and reproduction. We were shocked to discover that this was largely uncharted territory. Until now, only a few studies have explored this connection. They focused mainly on the relationship between fat intake and characteristics of the menstrual cycle, such as cycle length and the duration of different phases of the cycle. In general, these studies suggest that more fat in the diet, and in some cases more saturated fat, improves the menstrual cycle. Most of these studies were very small and didn't account for total calories, physical activity or other factors that also influence reproduction. None of them examined the effect of dietary fat on fertility.

The dearth of research in this area has been a gaping hole in nutrition research. If there is a link between fats in the diet and reproduction, then simple changes in food choices could offer delicious, easy and inexpensive ways to improve fertility. The Nurses' Health Study research team looked for connections between dietary fats and fertility from a number of different angles. Among the 18,555 women in the study, the total amount of fat in the diet wasn't connected with ovulatory infertility once weight, exercise, smoking and other factors that can influence reproduction had been accounted for. The same was true for cholesterol, saturated fat and monounsaturated fat—none were linked with fertility or infertility. A high intake of polyunsaturated fat appeared to provide some protection against ovulatory infertility in women who also had high intakes of iron, but the effect wasn't strong enough to be sure exactly what role this healthy fat plays in fertility and infertility.

Trans fats were a different story. Across the board, the more trans fat in the diet, the greater the likelihood of developing ovulatory infertility. We saw an effect even at daily trans fat intakes of about four grams a day. That's less than the amount the average American gets each day.

Eating more trans fat usually means eating less of another type of fat or carbohydrates. Computer models of the nurses' diet patterns indicated that eating a modest amount of trans fat (2 percent of calories) in place of other, more healthful nutrients like polyunsaturated fat, monounsaturated fat or carbohydrate would dramatically increase the risk of infertility. To put this into perspective, for someone who eats 2,000 calories a day, 2 percent of calories translates into about four grams of trans fat. That's the amount in two tablespoons of stick margarine, one medium order of fast-food french fries or one doughnut.

Fats aren't merely inert carriers of calories or building blocks for hormones or cellular machinery. They sometimes have powerful biological effects, such as turning genes on or off, revving up or calming inflammation and influencing cell function. Unsaturated fats do things to improve fertility—increase insulin sensitivity and cool inflammation—that are the opposite of what trans fats do. That is probably why the largest decline in fertility among the nurses was seen when trans fats were eaten instead of monounsaturated fats.

The Protein Factor

At the center of most dinner plates sits, to put it bluntly, a hunk of protein. Beef, chicken and pork are Americans' favorites, trailed by fish. Beans lag far, far behind. That's too bad. Beans are an excellent source of protein and other needed nutrients, like fiber and many minerals. And by promoting the lowly bean from side dish to center stage and becoming more inventive with protein-rich nuts, you might find yourself eating for two. Findings from the Nurses' Health Study indicate that getting more protein from plants and less from animals is another big step toward walking away from ovulatory infertility.

Scattered hints in the medical literature that protein in the diet may influence blood sugar, sensitivity to insulin and the production of insulin-like growth factor-1—all of which play important roles in ovulation—prompted us to look at protein's impact on ovulatory infertility in the Nurses' Health Study.

We grouped the participants by their average daily protein intake. The lowest-protein group took in an average of 77 grams a day; the highest, an average of 115 grams. After factoring in smoking, fat intake, weight and other things that can affect fertility, we found that women in the highest-protein group were 41 percent more likely to have reported problems with ovulatory infertility than women in the lowest-protein group.

When we looked at animal protein intake separately from plant protein, an interesting distinction appeared. Ovulatory infertility was 39 percent more likely in women with the highest intake of animal protein than in those with the lowest. The reverse was true for women with the highest intake of plant protein, who were substantially less likely to have had ovulatory infertility than women with the lowest plant protein intake.

That's the big picture. Computer models helped refine these relationships and put them in perspective. When total calories were kept constant, adding one serving a day of red meat, chicken or turkey predicted nearly a one-third increase in the risk of ovulatory infertility. And while adding one serving a day of fish or eggs didn't influence ovulatory infertility, adding one serving a day of beans, peas, tofu or soybeans, peanuts or other nuts predicted modest protection against ovulatory infertility.

Eating more of one thing means eating less of another, if you want to keep your weight stable. We modeled the effect that juggling the proportions of protein and carbohydrate would have on fertility. Adding animal protein instead of carbohydrate was related to a greater risk of ovulatory infertility. Swapping 25 grams of animal protein for 25 grams of carbohydrates upped the risk by nearly 20 percent. Adding plant protein instead of carbohydrates was related to a lower risk of ovulatory infertility. Swapping 25 grams of plant protein for 25 grams of carbohydrates shrank the risk by 43 percent. Adding plant protein instead of animal protein was even more effective. Replacing 25 grams of animal protein with 25 grams of plant protein was related to a 50 percent lower risk of ovulatory infertility.

These results point the way to another strategy for overcoming ovulatory infertility—eating more protein from plants and less from animals. They also add to the small but growing body of evidence that plant protein is somehow different from animal protein.

Milk and Ice Cream

Consider the classic sundae: a scoop of creamy vanilla ice cream crisscrossed by rivulets of chocolate sauce, sprinkled with walnuts and topped with a spritz of whipped cream. If you are having trouble getting pregnant, and ovulatory infertility is suspected, think of it as temporary health food. OK, maybe that's going a bit too far. But a fascinating finding from the Nurses' Health Study is that a daily serving or two of whole milk and foods made from whole milk—full-fat yogurt, cottage cheese, and, yes, even ice cream—seem to offer some protection against ovulatory infertility, while skim and low-fat milk do the opposite.

The results fly in the face of current standard nutrition advice. But they make sense when you consider what skim and low-fat milk do, and don't, contain. Removing fat from milk radically changes its balance of sex hormones in a way that could tip the scales against ovulation and conception. Proteins added to make skim and low-fat milk look and taste "creamier" push it even farther away.

It would be an overstatement to say that there is a handful of research into possible links between consumption of dairy products and fertility. The vanishingly small body of work in this area is interesting, to say the least, given our fondness for milk, ice cream and other dairy foods. The average American woman has about two servings of dairy products a day, short of the three servings a day the government's dietary guidelines would like her to have.

The depth and detail of the Nurses' Health Study database allowed us to see which foods had the biggest effects. The most potent fertility food from the dairy case was, by far, whole milk, followed by ice cream. Sherbet and frozen yogurt, followed by low-fat yogurt, topped the list as the biggest contributors to ovulatory infertility. The more low-fat dairy products in a woman's diet, the more likely she was to have had trouble getting pregnant. The more full-fat dairy products in a woman's diet, the less likely she was to have had problems getting pregnant.

Our advice on milk and dairy products might be criticized as breaking the rules. The "rules," though, aren't based on solid science and may even conflict with the evidence. And for solving the problem of ovulatory infertility, the rules may need tweaking. Think about switching to full-fat milk or dairy products as a temporary nutrition therapy designed to improve your chances of becoming pregnant. If your efforts pay off, or if you stop trying to have a baby, then you may want to rethink dairy—especially whole milk and other full-fat dairy foods—altogether. Over the long haul, eating a lot of these isn't great for your heart, your blood vessels or the rest of your body.

Before you sit down to a nightly carton of Häagen-Dazs ("*The Fertility Diet* said I needed ice cream, honey"), keep in mind that it doesn't take much in the way of full-fat dairy foods to measurably affect fertility. Among the women in the Nurses' Health Study, having just one serving a day of a full-fat dairy food, particularly milk, decreased the chances of having ovulatory infertility. The impact of ice cream was seen at two half-cup servings a week. If you eat ice cream at that rate, a pint should last about two weeks.

Equally important, you'll need to do some dietary readjusting to keep your calorie count and your waistline from expanding. Whole milk has nearly double the calories of skim milk. If you have been following the U.S. government's poorly-thought-out recommendation and are drinking three glasses of milk a day, trading skim milk for whole means an extra 189 calories a day. That could translate into a weight gain of 15 to 20 pounds over a year if you don't cut back somewhere else. Those extra pounds can edge aside any fertility benefits you might get from dairy foods. There's also the saturated fat to consider, an extra 13 grams in three glasses of whole milk compared with skim, which would put you close to the healthy daily limit.

Aim for one to two servings of dairy products a day, both of them full fat. This can be as easy as having your breakfast cereal with whole milk and a slice of cheese at lunch or a cup of whole-milk yogurt for lunch and a half-cup of ice cream for dessert. Easy targets for cutting back on calories and saturated fat are red and processed meats, along with foods made with fully or partially hydrogenated vegetable oils.

Once you become pregnant, or if you decide to stop trying, going back to low-fat dairy products makes sense as a way to keep a lid on your intake of saturated fat and calories. You could also try some of the nondairy strategies for getting calcium and protecting your bones. If you don't like milk or other dairy products, or they don't agree with your digestive system, don't force yourself to have them. There are many other things you can do to fight ovulatory infertility. This one is like dessert—enjoyable but optional.

The Role of Body Weight

Weighing too much or too little can interrupt normal menstrual cycles, throw off ovulation or stop it altogether. Excess weight lowers the odds that in vitro fertilization or other assisted reproductive technologies will succeed. It increases the chances of miscarriage, puts a mother at risk during pregnancy of developing high blood pressure (pre-eclampsia) or diabetes, and elevates her chances of needing a Cesarean section. The dangers of being overweight or underweight extend to a woman's baby as well.

Weight is one bit of information that the participants of the Nurses' Health Study report every other year. By linking this information with their accounts of pregnancy, birth, miscarriage and difficulty getting pregnant, we were able to see a strong connection between weight and fertility. Women with the lowest and highest Body Mass Indexes (BMI) were more likely to have had trouble with ovulatory infertility than women in the middle. Infertility was least common among women with BMIs of 20 to 24, with an ideal around 21.

Keep in mind that this is a statistical model of probabilities that links weight and fertility. It doesn't mean you'll get pregnant only if you have a BMI between 20 and 24. Women with higher and lower BMIs than this get pregnant all the time without delay or any medical help. But it supports the idea that weighing too much or too little for your frame can get in the way of having a baby.

We call the range of BMIs from 20 to 24 the fertility zone. It isn't magic—nothing is for fertility—but having a weight in that range seems to be best for getting pregnant. If you aren't in or near the zone, don't despair. Working to move your BMI in that direction by gaining or losing some weight is almost as good. Relatively small changes are often enough to have the desired effects of healthy ovulation and improved fertility. If you are too lean, gaining five or 10 pounds can sometimes be enough to restart ovulation and menstrual periods. If you are overweight, losing 5 percent to 10 percent of your current weight is often enough to improve ovulation.

Being at a healthy weight or aiming toward one is great for ovulatory function and your chances of getting pregnant. The "side effects" aren't so bad, either. Working to achieve a healthy weight can improve your sensitivity to insulin, your cholesterol, your blood pressure and your kidney function. It can give you more energy and make you look and feel better.

While dietary and lifestyle contributions to fertility and infertility in men have received short shrift, weight is one area in which there has been some research. A few small studies indicate that overweight men aren't as fertile as their healthy-weight counterparts. Excess weight can lower testosterone levels, throw off the ratio of testosterone to estrogen (men make some estrogen, just as women make some testosterone) and hinder the production of sperm cells that are good swimmers. A study published in 2006 of more than 2,000 American farmers and their wives showed that as BMI went up, fertility declined. In men, the connection between increasing weight and decreasing fertility can't yet be classified as rock solid. But it is good enough to warrant action, mainly because from a health perspective there aren't any downsides to losing weight if you are overweight. We can't define a fertility zone for weight in men, nor can anyone else. In lieu of that, we can say to men who are carrying too many pounds that shedding some could be good for fertility and will be good for overall health.

The Importance of Exercise

Baby, we were born to run. That isn't just the tagline of Bruce Springsteen's anthem to young love and leavin' town. It's also a perfect motto for getting pregnant and for living a long, healthy life. Inactivity deprives muscles of the constant push and pull they need to stay healthy. It also saps their ability to respond to insulin and to efficiently absorb blood sugar. When that leads to too much blood sugar and insulin in the bloodstream, it endangers ovulation, conception and pregnancy. Physical activity and exercise are recommended and even prescribed for almost everyone—except women who are having trouble getting pregnant. Forty-year-old findings that too much exercise can turn off menstruation and ovulation make some women shy away from exercise and nudge some doctors to recommend avoiding exercise altogether, at least temporarily. That's clearly the right approach for women who exercise hard for many hours a week and who are extremely lean. But taking it easy isn't likely to help women who aren't active or those whose weights are normal or above where they should be. In other words, the vast majority of women.

Some exciting results from the Nurses' Health Study and a handful of small studies show that exercise can be a boon for fertility. These important findings are establishing a vital link between activity and getting pregnant. Much as we would like to offer a single prescription for conception-boosting exercise, however, we can't. Some women need more exercise than others, for their weight or moods, and others are active just because they enjoy it. Some who need to be active aren't, while a small number of others may be too active.

Instead of focusing on an absolute number, try aiming for the fertility zone. This is a range of exercise that offers the biggest window of opportunity for fertility. Being in the fertility zone means you aren't overdoing or underdoing exercise. For most women, this means getting at least 30 minutes of exercise every day. But if you are carrying more pounds than is considered healthy for your frame (i.e., a BMI above 25), you may need to exercise for an hour or more. If you are quite lean (i.e., your BMI is 19 or below), aim for the middle of the exercise window for a few months. Keep in mind that the fertility zone is an ideal, not an absolute. Hospital delivery rooms are full of women who rarely, or never, exercise. Not everyone is so lucky. If you are having trouble getting pregnant, then maybe the zone is the right place for you.

Whether you classify yourself as a couch potato or an exercise aficionado, your fertility zone should include four types of activity: aerobic exercise, strength training, stretching and the activities of daily living. This quartet works together to control weight, guard against high blood sugar and insulin, and keep your muscles limber and strong. They are also natural stress relievers, something almost everyone coping with or worrying about infertility can use.

Exercise has gotten a bad rap when it comes to fertility. While the pioneering studies of Dr. Rose Frisch and her colleagues convincingly show that too much exercise coupled with too little stored energy can throw off or turn off ovulation in elite athletes, their work says nothing about the impact of usual exercise in normal-weight or overweight women. Common sense says that it can't be a big deterrent to conception. If it were, many of us wouldn't be here. Our ancestors worked hard to hunt, forage, clear fields and travel from place to place. Early *Homo sapiens* burned twice as many calories each day as the average American does today and were fertile despite it—or because of it.

Results from the Nurses' Health Study support this evolutionary perspective and show that exercise, particularly vigorous exercise, actually improves fertility. Exercising for at least 30 minutes on most days of the week is a great place to start. It doesn't really matter how you exercise, as long as you find something other than your true love that moves you and gets your heart beating faster.

JORGE E. CHAVARRO and WALTER C. WILLETT are in the Department of Nutrition at the Harvard School of Public Health. PATRICK J. SKERRETT is editor of the Harvard Heart Letter. For more information, go to health.harvard.edu/newsweek or thefertilitydiet.com.

Acknowledgements—Adapted from THE FERTILITY DIET by Forge E. Chavarro, M.D., Sc. D., Walter C. Willett, M.D., Dr. P.H., and Patrick F. Skerrett. Adapted by permission from The McGraw Hill Companies, Inc. Copyright © 2008 by the President and Fellows of Harvard College.

The Mystery of Fetal Life: Secrets of the Womb

JOHN PEKKANEN

In the dim light of an ultrasound room, a wand slides over the abdomen of a young woman. As it emits sound waves, it allows us to see into her womb. The video screen brightens with a grainy image of a 20-week-old fetus. It floats in its amniotic sac, like an astronaut free of gravity.

The fetal face stares upward, then turns toward us, as if to mug for the camera. The sound waves strike different tissues with different densities, and their echoes form different images. These images are computer-enhanced, so although the fetus weighs only 14 ounces and is no longer than my hand, we can see its elfin features.

Close up, we peek into the fetal brain. In the seconds we observe, a quarter million new brain cells are born. This happens constantly. By the end of the nine months, the baby's brain will hold 100 billion brain cells.

The sound waves focus on the chest, rendering images of a vibrating four-chambered heart no bigger than the tip of my little finger. The monitor tells us it is moving at 163 beats a minute. It sounds like a frightened bird fluttering in its cage.

We watch the rib cage move. Although the fetus lives in an airless environment, it "breathes" intermittently inside the womb by swallowing amniotic fluid. Some researchers speculate that the fetus is exercising its chest and diaphragm as its way of preparing for life outside the womb.

The clarity of ultrasound pictures is now so good that subtle abnormalities can be detected. The shape of the skull, brain, and spinal cord, along with the heart and other vital organs, can be seen in breathtaking detail.

In this ultrasound exam, there are no hints to suggest that anything is abnormal. The husband squeezes his wife's hand. They both smile.

The fetus we have just watched is at the midpoint of its 40-week gestation. At conception 20 weeks earlier, it began as a single cell that carried in its nucleus the genetic code for the human it will become.

After dividing and redividing for a week, it grew to 32 cells. Like the initial cell, these offspring cells carry 40,000 or so genes, located on 23 pairs of chromosomes inherited from the mother and father. Smaller than the head of a pin, this clump of cells began a slow journey down the fallopian tube and attached itself to the spongy wall of the uterus.

Once settled, some embryonic cells began to form a placenta to supply the embryo with food, water, and nutrients from the mother's bloodstream. The placenta also filtered out harmful substances in the mother's bloodstream. The embryo and mother exchange chemical information to ensure that they work together toward their common goal.

Instructed by their genes, the cells continued to divide but didn't always produce exact replicas. In a process still not well understood, the cells began to differentiate to seek out their own destinies. Some helped build internal organs, others bones, muscles, and brain.

At 19 days postconception, the earliest brain tissues began to form. They developed at the top end of the neural tube, a sheath of cells that ran nearly the entire length of the embryo.

The human brain requires virtually the entire pregnancy to emerge fully, longer than the other organ systems. Even in the earliest stage of development, the fetus knows to protect its brain. The brain gets the most highly oxygenated blood, and should there be any shortage, the fetus will send the available blood to the brain.

Extending downward from the brain, the neural tube began to form the spinal cord. At four weeks, a rudimentary heart started to beat, and four limbs began sprouting. By eight weeks, the two-inch-long embryo took human form and was more properly called a fetus. At 10 to 12 weeks, it began moving its arms and legs, opened its jaws, swallowed, and yawned. Mostly it slept.

"We are never more clever than we are as a fetus," says Dr. Peter Nathanielsz, a fetal researcher, obstetrician, and professor of reproductive medicine at Cornell University. "We pass far more biological milestones before we are born than we'll ever pass after we're born."

Not long ago, the process of fetal development was shrouded in mystery. But through the power of scanning techniques, biotechnology, and fetal and animal studies, much of the mystery of fetal life has been unveiled.

We now know that as the fetus matures it experiences a broad range of sensory stimulation. It hears, sees, tastes, smells, feels, and has rapid eye movement (REM) sleep, the sleep stage we associate with dreaming. From observation of its sleep and wake cycles, the fetus appears to know night from day. It learns and remembers, and it may cry. It seems to do everything in utero that it will do after it is born. In the words of one researcher, "Fetal life is us."

Studies now show that it's the fetus, not the mother, who sends the hormonal signals that determine when a baby will be born. And we've found out that its health in the womb depends in part on its mother's health when she was in the womb.

Finally, we've discovered that the prenatal environment is not as benign, or as neutral, as once thought. It is sensitive to the mother's health, emotions, and behavior.

The fetus is strongly affected by the mother's eating habits. If the mother exercises more than usual, the fetus may become temporarily short of oxygen. If she takes a hot bath, the fetus feels the heat. If she smokes, so does the fetus. One study has found that pregnant women exposed to more sunlight had more outgoing children.

We now know that our genes do not encode a complete design for us, that our "genetic destiny" is not hard-wired at the time of conception. Instead, our development involves an interplay between genes and the environment, including that of the uterus. Because genes take "cues" from their environment, an expectant mother's physical and psychological health influences her unborn child's genetic well-being.

Factors such as low prenatal oxygen levels, stress, infections, and poor maternal nutrition may determine whether certain genes are switched on or off. Some researchers believe that our time in the womb is the single most important period of our life.

"Because of genetics, we once thought that we would unfold in the womb like a blueprint, but now we know it's not that simple," says Janet DiPietro, an associate professor of maternal and child health at the Johns Hopkins School of Public Health and one of a handful of fetal-behavior specialists. "The mother and the uterine environment she creates have a major impact on many aspects of fetal development, and a number of things laid down during that time remain with you throughout your life."

The impact of the womb on our intelligence, personality, and emotional and physical health is beginning to be understood. There's also an emerging understanding of something called fetal programming, which says that the effects of our life in the womb may be not felt until decades after we're born, and in ways that are more powerful than previously imagined.

Says Dr. Nathanielsz, whose book *Life in the Womb* details the emerging science of fetal development: "It's an area of great scientific importance that until recently remained largely unknown."

I'm pregnant. Is it okay to have a glass of wine? Can I take my Prozac? What about a Diet Coke?

Years ago, before she knew she was pregnant, a friend of mine had a glass of wine with dinner. When she discovered she was pregnant, she worried all through her pregnancy and beyond.

She feels some guilt to this day, even though the son she bore turned out very well.

Many mothers have experienced the same tangled emotions. "There's no evidence that a glass of wine a day during pregnancy has a negative impact on the developing fetus," says Dr. John Larsen, professor and chair of obstetrics and gynecology at George Washington University. Larsen says that at one time doctors gave alcohol by IV to pregnant women who were experiencing preterm labor; it relaxed the muscles and quelled contractions.

Larsen now sometimes recommends a little wine to women who experience mild contractions after a puncture from an amniocentesis needle, and some studies suggest that moderate alcohol intake in pregnancy may prevent preterm delivery in some women.

Even though most experts agree with Larsen, the alcohol message that most women hear calls for total abstinence. Experts worry that declaring moderate alcohol intake to be safe in pregnancy may encourage some pregnant women to drink immoderately. They say that pregnant women who have an occasional drink should not think they've placed their baby at risk.

What is safe? Some studies show children born to mothers who consumed three drinks a day in pregnancy averaged seven points lower on IQ tests than unexposed children. There is evidence that six drinks a day during pregnancy puts babies at risk of fetal alcohol syndrome (FAS), a constellation of serious birth defects that includes mental retardation. The higher the alcohol intake, the higher the FAS risk.

Are there drugs and drug combinations that women should avoid or take with caution during pregnancy? Accutane (isotretinoin), a prescription drug for acne and psoriasis, is known to cause birth defects. So too are some anticonvulsant drugs, including Epitol, Tegretol, and Valproate. Tetracycline, a widely prescribed antibiotic, can cause bone-growth delays and permanent teeth problems for a baby if a mother takes it during pregnancy.

Most over-the-counter drugs are considered safe in pregnancy, but some of them carry risks. Heavy doses of aspirin and other nonsteroidal anti-inflammatory drugs such as ibuprofen can delay the start of labor. They are also linked to a life-threatening disorder of newborns called persistent pulmonary hypertension (PPHN), which diverts airflow away from the baby's lungs, causing oxygen depletion. The March issue of the journal *Pediatrics* published a study linking these nonprescription painkillers to PPHN, which results in the death of 15 percent of the infants who have it.

OTC Drugs

In 1998, researchers at the University of Nebraska Medical Center reported dextromethorphan, a cough suppressant found in 40 or more OTC drugs including Nyquil, Tylenol Cold, Dayquil, Robitussin Maximum Strength, and Dimetapp DM, caused congenital malformations in chick embryos. The research was published in *Pediatric Research* and supported by the National Institutes of Health.

Although no connection between dextromethorphan and human birth defects has been shown, the Nebraska researchers noted that similar genes regulate early development in virtually all species. For this reason, the researchers predicted that dextromethorphan, which acts on the brain to suppress coughing, would have the same harmful effect on a human fetus.

Many women worry about antidepressants. Some need them during pregnancy or took them before they knew they were pregnant. A study published in the *New England Journal of Medicine* found no association between fetal exposure to antidepressants and brain damage. The study compared the IQ, temperament, activity level, and distractibility of more than 125 children whose mothers took antidepressants in pregnancy with 84 children whose mothers took no drugs known to harm the fetus.

The two groups of children, between 16 months and eight years old when tested, were comparable in every way. The antidepressants taken by the mothers included both tricyclates such as Elavil and Tofranil and selective serotonin reuptake inhibitors such as Prozac.

Not all mood-altering drugs may be safe. There is some evidence that minor tranquilizers taken for anxiety may cause developmental problems if taken in the first trimester, but there is no hard proof of this. Evidence of fetal damage caused by illegal drugs such as cocaine is widely accepted, as is the case against cigarette smoking. A 1998 survey found that 13 percent of all mothers who gave birth smoked. Evidence is striking that cigarette smoking in pregnancy lowers birth weight and increases the risks of premature birth, attention deficit hyperactive disorder, and diminished IQ.

A long-running study based on information from the National Collaborative Perinatal Project found that years after they were born, children were more apt to become addicted to certain drugs if their mother took them during delivery.

"We found drug-dependent individuals were five times more likely to have exposure to high doses of painkillers and anesthesia during their delivery than their nonaddicted siblings," says Stephen Buka of the Harvard School of Public Health. Buka suspects this is caused by a modification in the infant's brain receptors as the drugs pass from mother to child during an especially sensitive time.

Caffeine

Coffee consumption has worried mothers because there have been hints that caffeine may be harmful to the fetus. Like most things in life, moderation is the key. There's no evidence that 300 milligrams of caffeine a day (about three cups of coffee, or four or five cups of most regular teas, or five to six cola drinks) harms a developing baby. Higher caffeine consumption has been weakly linked to miscarriage and difficulty in conceiving.

Expectant mothers concerned about weight gain should be careful of how much of the artificial sweetener aspartame they consume. Marketed under brand names such as NutraSweet and Equal, it's found in diet soft drinks and foods.

The concern is this: In the body, aspartame converts into phenylalanine, a naturally occurring amino acid we ingest when we eat protein. At high levels, phenylalanine can be toxic to brain cells.

When we consume phenylalanine in protein, we also consume a number of other amino acids that neutralize any ill effects. When we consume it in aspartame, we get none of the neutralizing amino acids to dampen phenylalanine's impact. And as it crosses the placenta, phenylalanine's concentrations are magnified in the fetal brain.

If a fetal brain is exposed to high levels of phenylalanine because its mother consumes a lot of aspartame, will it be harmed? One study found average IQ declines of ten points in children born to mothers with a fivefold increase of phenylalanine blood levels in pregnancy. That's a lot of aspartame, and it doesn't mean an expectant mother who drinks moderate amounts of diet soda need worry.

Researchers say consuming up to three servings of aspartame a day—in either diet soda or low-calorie foods—appears to be safe for the fetus. However, a pregnant woman of average weight who eats ten or more servings a day may put her unborn baby at risk. In testimony before Congress, Dr. William Pardridge, a neuroscience researcher at UCLA, said it's likely that the effect of high phenylalanine levels in the fetal brain "will be very subtle" and many not manifest until years later.

One wild card concerns the 10 to 20 million Americans who unknowingly carry a gene linked to a genetic disease called phenylketonuria (PKU), which can lead to severe mental retardation. Most carriers don't know it, because PKU is a recessive genetic disorder, and both mother and father must carry the defective gene to pass PKU on to their child. A carrier feels no ill effects. According to researchers, a pregnant woman who unknowingly carries the PKU gene might place her unborn child at risk if she consumes even relatively moderate amounts of aspartame. There is no hard evidence that this will happen, but it remains a serious concern. PKU can be detected in the fetus by amniocentesis; a restrictive diet can prevent the worst effects of PKU on the child.

How does a mother's getting an infection affect her unborn baby? And should she be careful of cats?

Many experts think pregnant women should be more concerned about infections and household pets than a glass of wine or can of diet drink. There's overwhelming evidence of the potential harm of infections during pregnancy. We've known for a long time that rubella (German measles), a viral infection, can cause devastating birth defects.

More worrisome are recent studies showing that exposure to one of the most common of winter's ills—influenza—may put an unborn child at risk of cognitive and emotional problems. If flu strikes in the second trimester, it may increase the unborn baby's risk of developing schizophrenia later in life. While the flu may be a trigger, it's likely that a genetic susceptibility is also needed for schizophrenia to develop.

Some evidence exists that maternal flu may also lead to dyslexia, and suspicions persist that a first-trimester flu may cause fetal neural-tube defects resulting in spina bifida. The common cold, sometimes confused with the flu, has not been linked to any adverse outcomes for the baby.

"Infections are probably the most important thing for a pregnant woman to protect herself against," says Lise Eliot, a developmental neurobiologist at the Chicago Medical School. "She should always practice good hygiene, like washing her hands frequently, avoiding crowds, and never drinking from someone else's cup." She adds that the flu vaccine has been approved for use during pregnancy.

Some researchers recommend that pregnant women avoid close contact with cats. Toxoplasmosis, a parasitic infection, can travel from a cat to a woman to her unborn child.

Most humans become infected through cat litter boxes. An infected woman might experience only mild symptoms, if any, so the illness usually goes undetected. If she is diagnosed with the infection, antiparasitic drugs are helpful, but they don't completely eliminate the disease. The infection is relatively rare, and the odds of passing it from mother to child are only one in five during the first two trimesters, when the fetal harm is most serious. The bad news is that a fetus infected by toxoplasmosis can suffer severe brain damage, including mental retardation and epilepsy. Some researchers also suspect it may be a latent trigger for serious mental illness as the child grows older.

Cerebral Palsy

An expectant mother may not realize she has potentially harmful infections. The prime suspects are infections in the reproductive tract. Researchers suspect most cerebral-palsy cases are not caused by delivery problems, as has been widely assumed. There's strong evidence that some cases of cerebral-palsy may be linked to placental infections that occur during uterine life. Other cerebral-palsy cases may be triggered by oxygen deprivation in early development, but very few appear to be caused by oxygen deprivation during delivery. It's now estimated that only 10 percent of cerebral-palsy cases are related to delivery problems.

Maternal urinary-tract infections have been linked to lower IQs in children. Another infection, cytomegalovirus (CMV), has been linked to congenital deafness. Sexually transmitted diseases such as chlamydia are suspected to be a trigger for preterm birth. Despite the serious threat posed to developing babies, infections during pregnancy remain poorly understood.

"We just don't know right now when or how the uterine infections that really make a difference to the fetus are transmitted in pregnancy," says Dr. Karin Nelson, a child neurologist and acting chief of the neuro-epidemiology branch of the National Institute of Neurologic Disorders and Stroke at NIH. "Nor do we know all the potential problems they may cause."

Because of this, researchers offer little in the way of recommendations other than clean living and careful sex. They recommend that any woman contemplating pregnancy get in her best physical condition, because a number of studies have found that a woman's general health before she becomes pregnant is vital to fetal health. They also recommend a thorough gynecological exam because it may detect a treatable infection that could harm the fetus.

Rachel Carson was right about pesticides. So if you're pregnant, how careful should you be about what you eat?

In her book *Silent Spring,* author Rachel Carson noted that when pregnant mammals were exposed to synthetic pesticides, including DDT and methoxychlor, the pesticides caused developmental abnormalities in offspring. Carson, a scientist, noted that some pesticides mimicked the female hormone estrogen and caused the male offspring to be feminized.

About the time of Carson's 1962 book, another story was emerging about diethylstilbestrol (DES), a man-made female hormone administered in the 1940s and '50s to prevent miscarriages. In the 1960s it became clear that many young daughters of DES mothers were turning up reproductive malformations and vaginal cancers. Sons born to DES mothers suffered reproductive problems, including undescended testicles and abnormal sperm counts.

Endocrine Disrupters

Over the years, suspicion grew from both animal and human studies that something in the environment was disrupting fetal development. In the 1990s it was given a name—endocrine disruption. The theory was that DES and the pesticides cited by Carson caused defects in offspring because they disrupted the normal endocrine process. They did this by mimicking hormones inside the human body.

It's now clear that DDT and DES are the tip of the iceberg. Today more than 90,000 synthetic chemicals are used, most made after World War II. New chemicals are produced every week. They are used in everything from pesticides to plastics.

How many of these man-made chemicals might act as endocrine disrupters? More than 50 have been identified, and hundreds more are suspects.

To understand the threat from endocrine disrupters, it helps to understand what human hormones do. Secreted by endocrine glands, these tiny molecules circulate through the bloodstream to the organs. They include estrogen, adrenalin, thyroid, melatonin, and testosterone. Each is designed to fit only into a specific receptor on a cell, like a key that fits only one lock. When a hormone connects with the cell receptor, it enters the cell's nucleus. Once there, the hormone acts as a signaling agent to direct the cell's DNA to produce specific proteins.

During fetal life, the right type and concentration of hormones must be available at the right time for normal fetal development to occur. Produced by both mother and fetus, hormones are involved in cell division and differentiation, the development of the brain and reproductive organs, and virtually everything else needed to produce a baby.

"We know from animal experiments and wildlife observations that periods in development are very sensitive to alterations in the hormone levels," says Robert Kavlock, director of reproductive toxicology for the Environmental Protection Agency.

The damage is done when chemical mimickers get into cells at the wrong time, or at the wrong strength, or both. When this happens, something in the fetus will not develop as it should.

After years of witnessing the harmful impact on wildlife, we now know that humans are not immune to endocrine disrupters. More troubling, because of the pervasiveness of these chemicals, is that we can't escape them. We get them in the food we eat, the water we drink, the products we buy.

One of the most dramatic examples came to light in the 1970s when researchers wanted to find out why so many babies born in the Great Lakes region suffered serious neurological defects. They found the answer in polychlorinated biphenyls (PCBs), organic chemicals once used in electrical insulation and adhesives. Heavy PCB contamination of Great Lakes fish eaten by the mothers turned out to be the cause.

It is not clear how PCBs cause fetal brain damage, but it's believed to happen when they disrupt thyroid hormones. Severe thyroid deficiency in pregnancy is known to cause mental retardation. Another study found reduced penis size in boys born to mothers exposed to high levels of PCBs.

The U.S. manufacture of PCBs ended in 1977. PCB levels found in the mothers and the fish they ate suggested at the time that only very high exposure caused a problem for developing babies. Now we know this isn't true.

Because PCBs don't break down, they've remained a toxin that continues to enter our bodies through the food we eat. They have leached into soil and water and are found in shellfish and freshwater fish and to a smaller degree in ocean fish. Bottom-feeding freshwater fish, such as catfish and carp, have the highest PCB concentrations.

PCBs store in fat tissue and are found in dairy products and meats. Fatty meats, especially processed meats like cold cuts, sausages, and hot dogs, are usually heaviest in PCBs. They get into these products because farm animals graze on PCB-contaminated land. However, eating fish from PCB-contaminated water remains the primary way we get these chemicals into our systems. In pregnant women, PCBs easily cross the placenta and circulate in the fetus.

PCBs are ubiquitous. They've been detected in the Antarctic snow. If you had detection equipment sensitive enough, you'd find them in the milk at the supermarket.

What concerns experts are findings from studies in the Netherlands and upstate New York that found even low maternal PCB exposures pose risk to a fetus.

The Dutch study followed 418 children from birth into early childhood. In the final month of pregnancy, researchers measured the maternal PCB blood levels, and at birth they measured PCB levels in the umbilical cord. None of the mothers was a heavy fish eater or had any history of high PCB exposure, and none of their PCB levels was considered high by safety standards.

At 3½ years of age, the children's cognitive abilities were assessed with tests. After adjusting for other variables, the researchers found that maternal and cord blood PCB levels correlated with the children's cognitive abilities. As the PCB blood levels went up, the children suffered more attention problems and their cognitive abilities went down. It should be noted that the brain damage in these Dutch children was not devastating. They were not retarded or autistic. But on a relative scale, they had suffered measurable harm.

The Dutch researchers concluded that the in utero PCB exposure, and not any postnatal exposure, caused the children's brain damage. The study also revealed that these children had depressed immune function.

"All we can say now," says Deborah Rice, a toxicologist at the EPA's National Center for Environmental Assessment in Washington, "is we have strong evidence that PCB levels commonly found among women living in industrialized society can cause subtle neurological damage in their offspring." But one of the difficulties, according to Rice, is that we really don't yet know what an unsafe maternal PCB level might be.

"I think the bottom line is that women should be aware of PCBs and aware of what they're putting in their mouth," adds Rice.

The Dutch study is a warning not only about the potential impact of low levels of PCBs but about the potential harm from low levels of other endocrine disrupters.

More news arrived in March when the results from the federal government's on-going Fourth National Health and Nutrition Examination Survey (NHANES) became public. The survey of 38,000 people revealed that most of us have at least trace levels of pesticides, heavy metals, and plastics in our body tissues. In all, NHANES tested for 27 elements.

The survey found widespread exposure to phthalates, synthetic chemicals used as softeners in plastics and other products. Phthalates are one of the most heavily produced chemicals and have been linked in animal studies to endocrine disruption and birth defects. The likely sources of human exposure are foods and personal-care products such as shampoos, lotions, soaps, and perfumes; phthalates are absorbed through the skin.

Dr. Ted Schettler, a member of the Greater Boston Physicians for Social Responsibility, suspects endocrine disrupters may be linked to increases in the three hormone-driven cancers—breast, prostate, and testicular. The rate of testicular cancer among young men has nearly doubled in recent years, and the rates of learning disabilities and infertility also have increased.

"We can't blame all that is happening on toxic chemicals," says Schettler, who coauthored *In Harm's Way,* a report on how chemical contaminants affect human health. "But we need to ask ourselves if we're seeing patterns that suggest these chemicals are having a major impact on fetal development and human populations. We also need to ask what level of evidence we're going to need before we take public-health measures. That's a political question."

The EPA's Kavlock says, "We don't know the safe or unsafe levels for many of these chemicals." Nor do we know how many of the thousands of man-made chemicals in the environment will turn out to be endocrine disrupters or cause human harm. The EPA received a mandate from Congress in 1996 to find the answers, but it will be a long wait.

"If we devoted all the toxicology testing capacity in the entire world to look for endocrine-disrupting chemicals, we couldn't do all the chemicals. There's just not enough capacity," Kavlock says. "So we are focusing on 500 to 1,000 chemicals that are the major suspects. It will take many years and a lot of money just to understand how they interact with hormonal-system and fetal development."

What is all this bad stuff we can get from eating fish or from microwaving food in plastics? Do vitamins help?

Methylmercury is a heavy metal that can cause fetal brain damage. NHANES revealed that 10 percent of American women of child-bearing age—a representative sample of all American women—had methylmercury blood and hair levels close to "potentially hazardous levels." The EPA and some non-government experts consider these existing methylmercury levels already above what is safe.

Dr. Jill Stein, an adolescent-medicine specialist and instructor at Harvard Medical School, has studied methylmercury's toxicity. She says the acceptable levels of methylmercury in the NHANES report were too high and that many more women are in the danger zone. "The NHANES data tells me that more than 10 percent of American women today are carrying around enough mercury to put their future children at risk for learning and behavior problems," she says.

Like PCBs and other toxic chemicals, mercury is hard to avoid because it is abundant in our environment. It comes from natural and man-made sources, chiefly coal-fired power plants and municipal waste treatment. Each year an estimated 160 tons of mercury is released into the nation's environment. In water, mercury combines with natural bacteria to form methylmercury, a toxic form of the metal. It is easily absorbed by fish. When a pregnant woman consumes the contaminated fish, methylmercury crosses the placenta and the fetal blood-brain barrier.

The world became aware of methylmercury's potential for harm more than 40 years ago in the fishing village of Minamata in Japan. People there were exposed to high levels of the heavy metal from industrial dumping of mercury compounds into Minamata Bay. The villagers, who ate a diet heavy in fish caught in the bay, experienced devastating effects. The hardest hit were the unborn. Women gave birth to babies with cerebral-palsy-like symptoms. Many were retarded.

Mercury

Fish are the major source of mercury for humans. The Food and Drug Administration recommends that pregnant women not eat swordfish, king mackerel, shark, and tilefish. These fish are singled out because large oceangoing fish contain more methylmercury. Smaller ocean fish, especially cod, haddock, and pollock, generally have low methylmercury levels. A whitefish found off the coast of Alaska, pollock is commonly found in fish sticks and fast-food fish. Salmon have low methylmercury

levels, but they are a fatty fish and apt to carry higher levels of PCBs.

Like the Dutch PCB studies, recent studies of maternal methylmercury exposure have turned up trouble. They've shown that the so-called "safe" maternal levels of the metal can cause brain damage during fetal development.

One study was carried out in the 1990s by a Danish research team that studied 917 children in the Faroe Islands, where seafood is a big part of the diet. Children were grouped into categories depending on their level of maternal methylmercury exposure; they were assessed up to age seven by neurological tests. None of the children's methylmercury exposure levels was considered high, yet many of the children had evidence of brain damage, including memory, attention, and learning problems.

"Subtle effects on brain function therefore seem to be detectable at prenatal methylmercury exposure levels currently considered safe," the study concluded. In a follow-up report published in a 1999 issue of the *Journal of the American Medical Association,* the authors said the blood concentrations of methylmercury found in the umbilical cord corresponded with the severity of the neurological damage suffered by the children.

In a study of 237 children, New Zealand researchers found similar neurological harm, including IQ impairment and attention problems, in children whose mothers' exposure to methylmercury came from fish they ate during pregnancy.

"The children in these studies were not bathed in methylmercury," notes Rita Schoeny, a toxicologist in the EPA's Office of Water. "Can people in the U.S. be exposed to the same levels of mercury in the course of their dietary practice? We think so."

Jill Stein and other experts worry that the more scientific studies we do, the more we'll realize that in fetal development there may be no such thing as a "safe" maternal level for methylmercury, PCBs, and scores of other synthetic chemicals.

"We keep learning from studies that these chemicals are harmful to fetal development at lower and lower doses," Stein says. "It's what we call the declining threshold of harm."

What about canned tuna? It has been assumed to contain low methylmercury levels because most of it comes from smaller fish. The FDA offers no advisories about it. But according to EPA researchers, a recent State of Florida survey of more than 100 samples of canned tuna found high levels of methylmercury. The more-expensive canned tuna, such as albacore and solid white tuna, usually carried higher methylmercury levels, according to the survey. This apparently is because more expensive canned tuna comes from larger tuna. In some of the canned tuna, the methylmercury levels were high enough to prevent their export to several countries, including Canada.

Some of the methylmercury levels were "worrisomely high," according to Kathryn Mahaffey, a toxicologist and director of the division of exposure assessment at the EPA. They were high enough to cause concern for pregnant women.

"A big problem is the tremendous variability out there in the tuna supply," adds Stein. "You have no idea when you're eating a can of tuna how much methylmercury you're getting."

"Even if you ate just a small serving of some of these canned tunas each day," says Mahaffey, "you'd be substantially above a level we would consider safe."

Mahaffey and Stein agree that an expectant mother who ate even a few servings a week with methylmercury levels found in some of the canned tuna would put her developing baby at risk of brain and other neurological damage.

Now that we know a developing fetus is sensitive to even low levels of toxic chemicals, women can exercise some basic precautions to help protect their developing babies.

Don't microwave food that is wrapped in plastic or is still in plastic containers. "There are endocrine-disrupting chemicals in these plastics," Schettler says, "that leach right into the food when it's microwaved. This has been well documented and measured." Studies suggest that even at very low levels these chemicals can have an adverse effect on the fetus's hormonal system.

The EPA's Kavlock considers the fruits and vegetables you buy at the supermarket to be safe in pregnancy, but Schettler says you should try to eat organic foods to avoid even trace amounts of pesticides. Wash fruits and vegetables before eating them. Avoid pesticides or insecticide use around the house during pregnancy as well as the use of chemical solvents for painting or remodeling.

Herbicides and pesticides have leached into reservoirs that supply home drinking water, and filtration plants can't remove them all. Some are known to be endocrine disrupters. Home water filters can reduce contaminants; the best ones use active charcoal as a filtering agent.

Experts agree that a pregnant woman, or a woman who may get pregnant, can eat fish but should be careful about the kind she eats and how much of it. EPA's Rice cautions any woman who is pregnant or thinking of becoming pregnant to avoid eating any sport fish caught in a lake or river.

Vegetable Fats

Rice adds that the PCB risk with fish can be reduced. "Trim the fish of fat and skin, and broil or grill it," see says. "That way you cook off fat and minimize your PCB exposure." There is not much you can do to reduce the methylmercury levels in fish because it binds to protein.

"Fat is important for a baby's neurological development before and after birth, so pregnant women should consider vegetable fats like olive oil and flaxseed oil as a source," Rice adds. She says low fat dairy and meat products carry fewer PCBs than higher-fat ones.

The EPA has issued a PCB advisory for the Potomac River in the District, Virginia, and Maryland, citing in particular catfish and carp. You can go to www.epa.gov/ost/fish/epafish.pdf for EPA advisories on PCB and methylmercury environmental contamination. From there you can connect to state websites for advisories on local waters and specific fish.

Women can help prevent neurological and other birth defects by taking vitamin supplements before pregnancy. A daily dose of 400 micrograms of folic acid can reduce the risk of such problems as spina bifida by more than 70 percent as well as prevent brain defects and cleft lip and palate. Indirect evidence from a study published last year in the *New England Journal of Medicine* suggests that folic acid may also help prevent congenital heart defects.

To be effective, folic acid should be taken before pregnancy to prevent developmental defects. Folic acid comes in multivitamins and prenatal vitamins and is found naturally in legumes, whole-wheat bread, citrus fruits, fortified breakfast cereal, and leafy green vegetables. Despite the proven value of folic acid, a recent March of Dimes survey found that only 32 percent of American women of childbearing age—including pregnant women—took folic-acid supplements.

What can a fetus learn in the womb? And does playing Mozart make a baby lots smarter?

Developmental psychologist Anthony DeCasper wanted to answer two questions: What does a fetus know, and when does it know it?

DeCasper's aim was to find out if a fetus could learn in utero and remember what it learned after it was born. He enlisted the help of 33 healthy expectant mothers and asked each to tape-record herself reading passages from Dr. Seuss's *The Cat in the Hat* or from another children's book, *The King, the Mice, and the Cheese*. The mothers were randomly assigned to play one of these readings, each of which lasted two or three minutes, to their unborn children three times a day during the final three weeks of their pregnancies.

DeCasper, a professor of developmental psychology at the University of North Carolina at Greensboro, could do the experiment because it was known that fetuses could hear by the third trimester and probably earlier. DeCasper had shown earlier that at birth, babies preferred their mother's voice to all other voices. Studies in the early 1990s found that fetuses could be soothed by lullabies and sometimes moved in rhythm to their mother's voice. Fetuses hear their mother's voice from the outside, just as they can hear any other voice, but they hear the mother's voice clearer and stronger through bone conduction as it resonates inside her.

A little more than two days after birth, each of the newborns in DeCasper's study was given a specially devised nipple. The device worked by utilizing the baby's sucking reflex. When the baby sucked on the nipple, it would hear its mother's voice. But if it paused for too long a time between sucks, it would hear another woman's voice. This gave the baby control over whose voice it would hear by controlling the length of its pause between sucks.

DeCasper also placed small earphones over the infant's ears through which it could hear its mother's voice read from the books.

"Now two days or so after it was born, the baby gets to choose between two stories read by its own mother," DeCasper said. "One was the story she'd recited three times a day for the last three weeks of pregnancy, and the other is one the baby's never heard before, except for the one day his mother recorded it. So the big question was: Would the babies prefer the story they'd heard in the womb, or wouldn't they? The answer was a clear yes—the babies preferred to hear the familiar story."

DeCasper did a second experiment by having women who were not the baby's mothers recite the same two stories. The babies again showed a strong preference for the story they'd heard in the womb.

"These studies not only tell us something about the fidelity with which the fetal ear can hear," DeCasper says, "but they also show that during those two or three weeks in the womb, fetal learning and memory are occurring."

British researchers observed expectant mothers who watched a TV soap opera. The researchers placed monitors on the mother's abdomens to listen in on fetal movements when the program aired. By the 37th week of pregnancy, the babies responded to the show's theme music by increasing their movements, an indication they remembered it.

Soon after the babies were born, the researchers replayed the theme music to them. This time, instead of moving more, the babies appeared to calm down and pay attention to the music. The researchers considered this a response to familiar music.

Fetal Memory

"The fact that we find evidence of fetal memory doesn't mean fetuses carry conscious memories, like we remember what we ate for breakfast," explains Lise Eliot, author of *What's Going On in There?*, a book on early brain development. "But we now know there is a tremendous continuity from prenatal to postnatal life, and the prenatal experience begins to shape a child's interaction with the world it will confront after birth. Babies go through the same activity patterns and behavioral states before and after birth. Well before it is born, the baby is primed to gravitate to its mother and its mother's voice."

Some researchers speculate a baby's ability to remember in the womb may be a way of easing its transition from prenatal life to postnatal life. A baby already accustomed to and comforted by its mother's voice may be reassured as it enters a new world of bright lights, needle pricks, curious faces, and loud noises.

The question arises: Can the uterine environment affect a baby's intelligence? Twins studies have shown that genes exert an all-powerful influence on IQ. The role of environment in IQ has traditionally meant the nurturance and stimulation the baby receives after birth.

Bernie Devlin, a biostatistician and assistant professor of psychiatry at the University of Pittsburgh, did an analysis of 212 twins studies on intelligence. In a paper published in *Nature*, he concluded that the accepted figure of 60 to 80 percent for IQ heritability is too high. It should be closer to 50 percent, he says, which leaves more room for environmental factors. Devlin says the one environmental factor that's been missing in understanding human intelligence is time in the womb.

"I'm surprised that the impact of fetal life on a child's intelligence had not been accounted for in these IQ studies," Devlin says. "I know it's very complicated, but it's surprising that people who study the heritability of intelligence really haven't considered this factor."

What is the impact of life in the womb on intelligence? Devlin thinks it's equal to if not greater than the impact of a child's upbringing. In other words, it's possible a mother may have more influence over her child's intelligence before birth than after.

As the brain develops in utero, we know it undergoes changes that affect its ultimate capacity. Nutritional and hormonal influences from the mother have a big impact. And twins studies show that the heavier twin at birth most often has the higher IQ.

A number of studies from the United States and Latin America also found that a range of vitamins, as well as sufficient protein in the mother's prenatal diet, had an impact on the child's intelligence.

Links between specific vitamins and intelligence have been borne out in two studies. An animal study conducted at the University of North Carolina and published in the March issue of *Developmental Brain Research* found that rats with a choline deficiency during pregnancy gave birth to offspring with severe brain impairments. Choline, a B-complex vitamin involved in nerve transmission, is found in eggs, meat, peanuts, and dietary supplements.

The August 1999 issue of the *New England Journal of Medicine* reported that expectant mothers with low thyroid function gave birth to children with markedly diminished IQs as well as motor and attention deficits. The study said one cause of hypothyroidism—present in 2 to 3 percent of American women—is a lack of iodine in the American diet. Women whose hypothyroidism was detected and treated before pregnancy had children with normal test scores. Hypothyroidism can be detected with a blood test, but expectant mothers who receive little or late prenatal care often go undiagnosed or are diagnosed too late to help their child.

Although most American women get the nutrition they need through diet and prenatal vitamins, not all do. According to a National Center for Health Statistics survey, more than one in four expectant mothers in the U.S. received inadequate prenatal care.

Devlin's *Nature* article took a parting shot at the conclusions reached in the 1994 book *The Bell Curve*, in which Richard J. Herrnstein and Charles Murray argued that different social classes are a result of genetically determined, and therefore unalterable, IQ levels. The lower the IQ, the argument goes, the lower the social class.

Not only does the data show IQ to be far less heritable than that book alleges, Devlin says, but he suspects improvements in the health status of mostly poor expectant mothers would see measurable increases in the IQs of their offspring.

Devlin's argument is supported by Randy Thornhill, a biologist at the University of New Mexico. Thornhill's research suggests that IQ differences are due in part to what he calls "heritable vulnerabilities to environmental sources of developmental stress." In other words, vulnerable genes interact with environmental insults in utero resulting in gene mutations that affect fetal development. Thornhill says environmental insults may include viruses, maternal drug abuse, or poor nutrition.

"The developmental instability that results," Thornhill says, "is most readily seen in the body's asymmetry when one side of the body differs from the other. For example, on average an individual's index fingers will differ in length by about two millimeters. Some people have much more asymmetries than others."

But the asymmetries we see on the outside also occur in the nervous system. When this happens, neurons are harmed and memory and intelligence are impaired. Thornhill says the more physical asymmetries you have, the more neurological impairment you have. He calculates that these factors can account for as much as 50 percent of the differences we find in IQ.

Thornhill adds that a fetus that carries these genetic vulnerabilities, but develops in an ideal uterine environment, will not experience any serious problems because the worrisome mutations will not occur.

"The practical implications for this are tremendous," Thornhill says. "If we can understand what environmental factors most disrupt fetal development of the nervous system, then we'll be in a position to remove them and have many more intelligent people born."

Studies on fetal IQ development suggest that the current emphasis on nurturance and stimulation for young children be rethought. The philosophy behind initiatives such as Zero to Three and Early Head Start makes sense. The programs are based on evidence that the first three years are very important for brain development and that early stimulation can effect positive changes in a child's life. But Devlin and Thornhill's research suggests a stronger public-health emphasis on a baby's prenatal life if we are to equalize the opportunities for children.

Does that mean unborn babies need to hear more Mozart? Companies are offering kits so expectant mothers can play music or different sounds to their developing babies—the prenatal "Mozart effect." One kit promises this stimulation will lead to "longer new-born attention span, better sleep patterns,

accelerated development, expanded cognitive powers, enhanced social awareness and extraordinary language abilities." Will acceptance to Harvard come next?

"The number of bogus and dangerous devices available to expectant parents to make their babies smarter constantly shocks me," says DiPietro. "All these claims are made without a shred of evidence to support them."

Adds DeCasper: "I think it is dangerous to stimulate the baby in the womb. If you play Mozart and it remembers Mozart, is it going to be a smarter baby? I haven't got a clue. Could it hurt the baby? Yes, I think it could. If you started this stimulation too early and played it too loud, there is evidence from animal studies that you can destroy the ear's ability to hear sounds in a particular range. That's an established fact. Would I take a risk with my fetus? No!"

DeCasper and other researches emphasize that no devices or tricks can enhance the brainpower of a developing baby. Their advice to the expectant mother: Take the best possible care of yourself.

"The womb is a quiet, protective place for a reason," DiPietro concludes. "Nature didn't design megaphones to be placed on the abdomen. The fetus gets all the stimulation it needs for its brain to develop."

Mr. John Pekkanen is a contributing editor to *The Washingtonian*. From "Secrets of the Womb," by John Pekkanen, *The Washingtonian*, August 2001, pages 44–51, 126–135.

Truth and Consequences at Pregnancy High

The education of a teenage mother.

Alex Morris

Before the sun has risen over the Bronx River, an alarm chimes in 17-year-old Grace Padilla's bedroom. Sliding from the lower bunk, she pads to the bathroom, flips on the light, brushes her teeth, then gathers up her hair into a short ponytail, which she wraps with a long row of black extensions and knots into a tight bun. She's quick and efficient, with none of the preening one might expect of a high-school junior. At 6:30 A.M., she goes back into the bedroom to wake her 2-year-old daughter.

Along with her grandparents, her mother, her sister, and her child, Grace lives in a small two-bedroom apartment on the second floor of a nondescript brick building in Hunts Point, where nearly half the residents live below the poverty line and roughly 15 percent of girls ages 15 to 19 become pregnant each year. It's the highest teen-pregnancy rate in the city, more than twice the national average.

"Lilah, wake up," Grace whispers, leaning in close. Lilah bats her mother away with a tiny hand and nestles up closer to Grace's own mother, Mayra, who had moments before returned home from her night shift as a cashier at a local food-distribution center and slipped, exhausted, into Grace's place in the bed.

"Come on, let's go get dressed," Grace pleads, pulling her daughter from under the covers as Lilah begins crying, flailing her arms and legs.

"Come *on*," Grace begs. She fights to keep her mounting frustration in check and then counts down the seconds before she'll make Lilah go stand against the wall, her usual form of punishment. "Five . . . four . . . three . . . two . . . one."

The threat is enough. Lilah's body goes slack, her screaming dissipates to a whimper. Grace is able to wrestle her into the clothes she'd laid out beforehand. But the child's screams have woken Grace's grandparents, who are now in the galley kitchen, arguing in Spanish. Her grandfather has Alzheimer's. He accidentally makes decaffeinated coffee, which infuriates his wife.

At 7:20, Grace smoothes a tiny hat over Lilah's curls, bundles her into a coat, then jostles schoolbooks into a bag. In the empty lot across the street, a rooster starts to crow.

When Grace arrives at Jane Addams High School for Academics and Careers, she joins the daily parade of mothers—pushing strollers, grasping the chubby fists of toddlers, perching bundled babies on cocked hips—making their way to basement room B17, the headquarters of the school's Living for the Young Family Through Education (LYFE) center. Run by the Department of Education, the

LYFE program operates in 38 schools in the five boroughs, teaching parenting skills and providing on-site day care to teen parents who are full-time students in New York City's public schools. Jane Addams hosts one of the most active branches in the city, with sixteen mothers currently in the program.

While the students sign in on a clipboard, social worker Ana C. Martínez flits among them with her checklist of concerns. Is this baby eating enough? (Yes.) Does that one still have a cough? (No.) When will the heat be turned back on in one young mother's apartment? (Uncertain.) If it isn't soon, has she considered going to a shelter? (She has.)

"How's the baby?" Martínez asks Grace.

"She's fine," Grace answers.

Satisfied, Martínez turns her attention to Lilah. "Can I get a hug?"

"No," the child replies coyly, pretending to hide behind her mother's legs.

"Pretty please?"

Lilah finally concedes, jumping into the woman's arms.

Martínez laughs. "We have to play that game every morning, don't we?"

The girls cluster around a table laid out with bagels and jam, which Martínez serves every morning, both to entice her charges to be at school on time and also to make sure they get enough to eat ("Some don't at home," she clucks). She admits that the LYFE program, which serves 500 families and costs taxpayers about $13 million a year, has its naysayers, people who think that it makes life too easy for the mothers and diverts money from students who've made more-responsible choices. "But the reality is, teens are having kids, and we've got to work with them," she says. "They're entitled to an education."

Grace greets Jasmine Reyes—a soft-spoken senior whose 2-year-old daughter, Jayleen, is Lilah's best friend in day care—before going over to peer at Nelsy Valerio's infant. When Iruma Moré enters the room with her 8-month-old daughter, Dymia, Grace beelines for the baby, unwrapping her from a pile of blankets.

"Dymia, Dymia, *Dy-mi-a,*" she chants, bouncing the child on her lap. "She's so little," Grace marvels wistfully.

Iruma giggles. "I try to feed her all the time," she says, as she drops into a chair next to a locker crammed full of diapers. Though all four of Iruma's older sisters were teen mothers, she didn't know her school had day care until her sophomore year. "I started seeing the mothers coming in with their babies and stuff, and I always used to wonder where they take them," she says. One day, she looked through a doorway and it was like peering into a magic cupboard—a roomful of babies with soft skin and fine hair. Iruma thought she might like to have one of her own. By her junior year, she was pregnant. "I wasn't using nothing, no protection, so I mean, I knew it was gonna come sooner or later."

The nursery is a clown's paradise, brightly painted and well outfitted with funds donated by makeup artist Bobbi Brown. (In addition to the traditional high-school curriculum, Jane Addams teaches a number of vocations, including cosmetology, which Grace is studying.) Grace and Iruma each commandeer a crib and begin to strip down their daughters to their underwear, so that a caretaker can check the children for marks. Then the mothers fill out a form about when their child last ate, the child's mood, how the baby has been sleeping. Just before the bell rings for second period, they leave the nursery and head upstairs to school. For the next seven hours, they'll get to be kids again themselves.

Grace got pregnant in January 2006, less than a month after her 14th birthday and soon after she lost her virginity to a 15-year-old boy from the neighborhood named Nikko Vega. He was the only person she'd slept with, or even wanted to. After he broke up with a girlfriend ("A ho," Grace sniffs), she began cutting her eighth-grade classes to meet him at his apartment. Even then, she had full curves and a round and inviting face. She was normally sweet, but if pressed, she could fire off a string of expletives so fast the words blurred together. Nikko liked that about her. One day, the two of them found themselves playing more than Nintendo, and they just let it happen.

"It was heat-of-the-moment stuff," Grace says of having sex for the first time. Getting pregnant wasn't even on her mind. But it was on Nikko's: "A couple of hours after, I was thinking, like, *Damn.*" He eventually asked Grace if she should go on birth control, but they knew that would make her mom suspicious. They decided to take their chances, though it bothered Nikko to be so reckless. "A lot of people I knew had kids young, and I didn't want to be one of them," he admits. He had hoped to go to college on a football scholarship, had even made a pact with his friends to put off fatherhood. "Like, ever since we were younger, we all spoke about, 'No kids.' All of us."

Grace got pregnant at 14. She told Nikko that she wanted to keep the baby and that she was happy, "in a sad sort of way."

"It didn't work," Grace says archly. "Everybody he grew up with has a kid now."

Grace didn't know she was pregnant for months. She didn't get morning sickness, headaches, or cramps. She still did step dancing, played football after school, rode roller coasters when her mom took her to a theme park, fit into her regular clothes. She hadn't been having her period long enough for its absence to be a major cause for concern. When she went to a neighborhood clinic to get tested, just in case, and the results came back positive, she was shocked. "I didn't really know what to do," she says. "I didn't know what to ask. I was just like, 'What?'"

When she told Nikko, he walked away without saying a word, but a couple of hours later, he returned, driven back by the hangdog devotion he has for Grace and by fear of her disapproval. She told him that she wanted to keep the baby and that she was happy about the decision,

"in a sad sort of way." She loved babies, but she wasn't sure what she was getting into. To the extent that he could be there for her, an extent that even he understood to be meager, Nikko said he was onboard.

It took Grace a month to work up the nerve to tell her mother. When Mayra came home from work one day, Grace, her older sister, Samantha, and her cousin were sitting in front of the building waiting for her "like there was a funeral." In the elevator ride up to the apartment, Mayra looked from one girl to the next. "Which one of you is pregnant?" she asked. She thought Samantha would answer, but when she didn't, the realization set in that it was her younger daughter who was in trouble.

"How could you?" Mayra screamed, standing in their living room, shaking with anger. "How could you? You see our situation, you see what I have on my plate. How could you be so selfish?"

Grace ran to her bedroom, sobbing. Mayra stayed in the living room, sobbing. Mayra's own mother walked in the door and demanded to know what was going on.

"Your granddaughter," Mayra wailed, "your *14-year-old* granddaughter decided you needed to see a great-grandkid."

"Oh my God," the old woman said. "*¡Ay, Dios mío! ¡Ay, Dios mío, ayúdenos!*"

For a month, Mayra cried every day. Having gotten married at 16 and had Samantha at 17, she was loath to become a grandmother at 36. She had asked Grace repeatedly if she had started having sex, and the girl had always denied it. Between her parents and her own children, the apartment was already overcrowded, and money stretched thin. She threatened to send Grace to live with her father, who had left the family a decade ago. For years, they hadn't been able to track him down. Now he had a new family in Philadelphia, and Grace had been in cautious contact. But when they called to tell him about the pregnancy, he made it clear that she wasn't welcome. Grace hasn't spoken to him since.

Mayra was surprised to find herself seriously considering abortion as an option. The South Bronx has a high birthrate in part because in this largely Hispanic and Catholic community, the idea of terminating a pregnancy meets with such intense disapproval. Her mother told her that she would not be able to live under the same roof if they went through with it, but Mayra didn't see how Grace could manage to raise a child, nor did she want to put her daughter through the difficulty of labor only to give the baby away. Grace guessed that she was about four months along and agreed to visit an abortion clinic. The sonogram showed that the baby was due in ten weeks.

"Ten weeks?" Mayra asked. "This is a 14-year-old who's been to theme parks, eaten junk food the whole time, had no prenatal care. Ten weeks? I don't know what this baby's gonna be like."

The nurse nodded sympathetically, but there was nothing to be done. "There's nowhere in this country where they'll do that abortion at seven months."

Mayra set about preparing for the baby. She arranged for Grace to be enrolled in Jane Addams, the closest school that had a LYFE program. She put a call out to friends and family for a crib, a stroller, secondhand baby clothes. She started making doctors appointments, pleading her daughter's way into clinics that didn't have openings until after the baby was due. Grace looked so young when she brought her in, no one could believe she was the one who was pregnant.

Grace's water broke in the hallway of Jane Addams the second week of her freshman year, a full month before her due date. Thinking she had wet her pants, she called her mother from a bathroom stall.

"Um, I want to go home," she said when Mayra picked up.

"Why? What happened?"

"My pants are all wet."

"What do you mean your pants are all wet? Did a car splash you or something?"

"No. Like, they're all wet. Like, I went into the bathroom, and they're all wet."

"Oh my God," Mayra cut in. "Your water broke. Oh my God! You're gonna have this baby in that school!"

When Grace arrived at Albert Einstein hospital, she was having contractions. Her mother stepped outside to calm her nerves with a cigarette, and Grace took the moment alone to ask her doctor if it was possible that she might die in childbirth. He reassured her that the chances were infinitesimally slim. "He sugarcoated it," she says. "He was a nice guy."

By the time Nikko arrived the following afternoon, Grace was in the throes of "the worst pain I ever felt in my life," she says, gasping just at the thought. She refused to allow him in the room. "I was in so much pain I really just wanted to kill him. I said, 'I advise security, doctors, nurses, everybody on this floor, if that man reaches this room, it's gonna be chaos, because this is all his fault.' "

On Sunday, September 17, 2006, at 2:55 A.M., Delilah Joli Vega was born, alert and healthy.

At the McDonald's on Prospect Avenue, teenagers crowd the counter, munching fries and competing for attention, the boys with their hooded sweatshirts pulled down low over their eyes, the girls in tight jeans and baby tees, nameplate jewelry shimmering, hair ruthlessly slicked back into high ponytails. As Iruma orders a pile of cheeseburgers and two Happy Meals, Grace and Jasmine drag high chairs up to the table and settle in with Nikko. The conversation is no different from that at any other table in the place, except for the constant interruption. There's drama going down on Grace's block— "Dumbass Samantha was talking about, 'Oh, if Sasha did punch A. J. in the face, it wasn't' cause A. J. hit her, it was over Killah . . .'"—but she can't focus on the story with Lilah sending golden arcs of boxed apple juice into the air.

"Lilah, you're spilling the juice," Grace points out. "You're. Spilling. The. Juice."

Jayleen, Jasmine's daughter, looks over at Lilah, then squeezes her own juice box with vigor.

"You must want to get smacked," Grace tells her, raising her eyebrows before turning to the girl's mother. "I been telling you about that, Jasmine."

"Later, later," Jasmine pleads, not in the mood for a parenting lesson. But the fact is the mothers often act as a check on one another, imparting what parenting wisdom they have, holding one another to a certain standard. Grace, particularly, prides herself on her parenting skills. She's observant. She's strict. Her mother, Mayra, taught her how to take care of Lilah but refused to do the tasks for her. Grace was the one who changed Lilah's diapers, fed her, got up in the middle of the night when she cried. "She's not Baby Alive, is she?" Mayra would ask. "There's no off-button on her."

Having teenage parents does mean that Lilah is prone to mimic teenage behavior. "Her attitude is serious," says Grace. "She'll be like, 'Mind your business.' Mind *my* business? You better be talking to the milkman! I love her, but sometimes I just want to bop her on her head." But the good manners Lilah displays in front of company—if not always at home—testify to Grace's efforts.

Even now, as Lilah eyes the chicken nuggets that Iruma has been tearing into bite-size chunks for Dymia, she doesn't reach out and take one. "Hee dat icken, Mommy?" she asks politely.

"I see that chicken," Grace answers. "But you asked for a burger, so now you're gonna eat a burger."

"She didn't ask for a burger. You said she wanted a burger," Jasmine points out. "You're mad mean."

Grace shrugs off the comment, as a girl from their school pauses on her way past their table.

"Hey! What's up, baby?" she coos at Dymia before turning to Iruma. "She's getting so big. Oh my God!"

Iruma pushes her glasses up on her nose and smiles contentedly. "Yeah, she getting big."

"Oh my God, you're so cute!" The girl stares at Dymia, shaking her head in amazement.

In the South Bronx, the stigma of having a child at a young age is remarkably absent, not just because teen parenthood has long been pervasive but also because the family structure is such that children often grow up raising younger siblings, nieces, and nephews. Adding a child of their own into the mix doesn't seem like it will change much in terms of daily routine, but it does feel like a rite of passage, a one-way ticket to adulthood. Motherhood cements a girl's fertility, her femininity. Louder than any clingy top or painted lip, it broadcasts that now she's a woman. And for some girls, that's appealing. When *The Tyra Banks Show* did an online survey of 10,000 girls across the country, one-fifth of them said they wanted to become teen moms. The latest Centers for Disease Control report shows a 3 percent increase in teen pregnancy in 2006 after more than a decade of decline. At Jane Addams, round bellies orbit the hallways like planets. The school doesn't keep track of pregnancies, but according to the attendance officer, one week this spring, seven girls out of a student body of about 1,500 were out of school to give birth.

The mothers watch as the girl from school continues on her way, joining a booth where a group of teenagers have piled in together, plopping on each other's laps, laughing loudly at each other's jokes. None of them have children. They seem not to have a single care. The chasm between being a parent and being a kid was difficult to intuit until it was crossed. Now Grace knows it well. When Nikko once teased her about all the fun she would have without him if she went to college, she leveled a cold stare at him and asked, "How am I gonna have fun in college with a child?"

Iruma fishes her cell phone out of a bag and presses a few buttons. Hip-hop starts to blare from the little speakers, setting a more festive mood. The moms relax. Jayleen and Lilah bounce in time to the music.

"Jayleen, you want to dance for everybody?" Jasmine asks. "You want to get on the table and dance?"

Jayleen tries to climb out of her high chair, and Jasmine lifts her up onto the bench, where she plants her feet and shakes her little bottom back and forth.

"Oh, she gotta donk, she gotta donk," Jasmine chants, as Jayleen's dance grows increasingly outrageous. The moms laugh.

Sometimes it's hard not to act their age. "You need to be adult and mature, but you're still young," says Grace. "Adults have fun all the time. They still joke, they still laugh. They can't take your kid away just because of that."

When grace gets home from school one afternoon, her grandparents have two eyes of the gas stove burning to drive away the apartment's chill. She steers Lilah away from the flame and to the refrigerator, where she allows her to choose a snack. Lilah points at a pitcher of red liquid, and Grace fixes her a bottle, waiting for Nikko to get home from the GED program he started the week before. When he does, he waves a sheet of loose-leaf paper in front of her. It's his first assignment, a short essay on why he should be a candidate for the program.

"I need to finish school for my 2-year-old daughter," he starts off in an even hand. "I need to finish school for her because she follows everything that I do, and I feel that it is time for me to step up to the plate." At the bottom of the page, his teacher has written "good ideas, good motivation" and given him a B-plus. Grace seems pleased. "Oh snap, babe. Now what are you gonna do to get an A-minus?"

She's only half-joking. Even if it is sometimes misplaced, Grace has a highly evolved sense of propriety. She expects to be treated a certain way, expects Nikko to embrace his responsibilities as a father. Her loyalties now are to Lilah, and her world is delineated: There are the players and hustlers and birds, people best avoided; then there are the "cousins" and *títís* and "brothers," people she may not be related to by blood but who do well by her and her daughter. She's not quite sure yet where Nikko falls. "He be all right," she says.

It took a long time for Mayra to accept Nikko as a de facto member of the family. It wasn't just his role in the pregnancy—she understood that Grace was equally at fault—it was his own neglectful upbringing that gave her pause. She refused to have his name listed on Lilah's birth certificate until her own mother interjected. "You're gonna leave her birth certificate just blank under father, like she doesn't know who her child's father is?" the older woman asked, horrified.

Since Lilah was born, Nikko has spent a smattering of nights in jail, mostly for getting in neighborhood fights or, as he says, "being in the wrong place at the wrong time." Because his mother did not force him to go to school, he has not a single high-school credit. When Mayra took him to family court for child support (a requirement of the LYFE program), Mayra told the judge that she didn't expect any money from Nikko, that she would prefer he get an education rather than a job now, so that he could support his child later; but the judge still awarded them $25 a month—less than the cost of a box of diapers—which Nikko's mother agreed to pay until her son turned 18. Grace and Mayra have still not seen a cent.

In the end, though, it was hard to keep blaming Nikko, a child, for what Mayra saw as his mother's failings. When he didn't have a winter coat, she bought him one. When he was hungry, she fed him. When his mother kicked him out after a fight with her boyfriend, Mayra temporarily let him stay with them. Over time, he grew on her. "I basically showed her a lot of respect," says Nikko. "A lot of butt kissing," corrects Grace. Mayra realizes that, in his capacity, he is a good father: He's present. Though other girls are still dating the fathers of their children, Nikko is the only boy who visits the LYFE center. A certificate stating that he completed LYFE's fatherhood-training program hangs in a frame over Grace's bed. "The only reason I don't press it is because this baby knows who her daddy is," says Mayra. "And she loves her daddy."

Still, both Mayra and Grace find their patience sputtering. In the three years since Grace got pregnant, Nikko hadn't held a single job or completed a single class. Mayra sees the writing on the wall. She knows that the statistics are not in Nikko and Grace's favor: Only 40 percent of teenagers who have children get their high-school diplomas, and 64 percent of children born to unmarried high-school dropouts live in poverty. "Life isn't about you anymore," Mayra is quick to inform him. "You brought someone else into this world that you have to care for. If you're gonna be that type of person that's gonna just not

do nothing—and because of that, statistics is gonna land you back in jail—you may as well say bye to them now while Lilah's small and can get over you fast. Because this baby's not visiting nobody in jail." At the beginning of this year, to make good on her word, she gave him one month to prove to her that he was in school or had landed a job. Right at the deadline, he signed up for his GED.

Sometimes Grace feels that she's leaving Nikko behind. She talks of going to college, studying business, opening her own beauty salon, getting her child out of Hunts Point, away from the "hustlers and divas." She expects that there will come a day when she alone is responsible for providing for Lilah. "You can hope, we can all hope that Nikko's gonna do something to better himself and want to be there and provide for his family," Mayra tells her. "But the fact remains, if he doesn't, he wouldn't be the first boy. You wouldn't be the first single mother."

One evening early this spring, the young family has the Padilla apartment to themselves. Mayra sleeps soundly behind the closed door of the bedroom, resting up for her night shift at eleven. Grace's grandparents are at church, her sister out with friends. At times like these, Grace likes to pretend the apartment belongs to her and Nikko, that she doesn't live with her mother and he doesn't crash at a friend's place, that they've managed to make a life for themselves and Lilah on their own.

Nikko prepares a bowl of popcorn, while Grace flips through channels on the TV, stopping at a music video she knows Lilah likes. The little girl follows along with the dance in the best rendition a 2-year-old could possibly muster, stroking her hips as they wiggle furiously and then flapping her wrists like a drag queen. When she looks behind her to make sure her parents are watching, Nikko and Grace laugh at her presumption. As parents, they share an easy rapport. She teases and prods him gently; he defers to her with a good-natured grin.

Later, there's homework to be done. Grace has a field trip tomorrow, so her load is light, but Nikko struggles to write an essay on the three branches of government. Once he finishes his GED, he's hoping to enroll in junior college. Grace pulls out her U.S. history folder, shows him a few photocopied papers, then goes into the kitchen to heat up frozen chicken patties.

After they eat, she gives Lilah a bath, crouching by the bathtub and allowing her daughter to splash around as long as she likes. "You a monkey," she says, laughing as Lilah dunks her head under the water and then shakes out her curls. "When she was a baby, the funnest part was the bath because her faces were just priceless." While Nikko heats up a bottle of chocolate milk, Grace towels Lilah off, rubs her down with lotion as the child tries to squirm out of her grasp—"She likes running around naked"—and dresses her in a diaper and footed fleece pajamas. Nikko puts his homework aside to give Lilah her bottle, stretching her out across his lap and rocking her gently. He waits until she's asleep to kiss Grace good-bye.

"Love you, babe," he says.

"Love you too."

UNIT 2

Development during Infancy and Early Childhood

Unit Selections

Key Points to Consider

- If mothers' milk is the best milk for babies, why are fewer mothers choosing to breastfeed?

- How much do babies understand at birth? What emotions do they feel? Are there social and emotional "milestones" to help caregivers trace progress?

- Have you heard that vaccines cause autism? Have you looked at the science behind these claims?

- Are there inexpensive and easy ways to boost a baby's brain power? Can any caregiver incorporate them into daily activities?

- At what age can toddlers understand other people's feelings?

- Shy children: are they socially competent or lonely? What does it mean when a child clings to a parent at separation time?

- Should preschools focus on pre-reading and pre-math skills? If so, how much? What else should good preschools provide for their charges?

- Can young children be helped to prefer healthy foods over empty-calorie foods?

Student Website

www.mhhe.com/cls

Internet References

Autism
http://www.autism-society.org

BabyCenter
http://www.babycenter.com

Center for Childhood Obesity Research (CCOR)
http://www.hhdev.psu.edu/ccor/index.html

Children's Nutrition Research Center (CNRC)
http://www.kidsnutrition.org

Early Childhood Care and Development
http://www.ecdgroup.com

Zero to Three: National Center for Infants, Toddlers, and Families
http://www.zerotothree.org

Development during infancy and early childhood is more rapid than in any other life stage, excluding the prenatal period. Newborns are quite well developed in some areas, and incredibly deficient in others. Babies' cerebral hemispheres already have their full complement of neurons (worker cells). The neuroglia (supportive cells) are almost completely developed and will reach their final numbers by age one. In contrast, babies' legs and feet are tiny, weak, and barely functional. Look at newborns from another perspective, however, and their brains seem somewhat less superior. The neurons and neuroglia present at birth must be protected. We may discover ways to make more cerebral neurons in the future, but such knowledge now is in its infancy and does not go very far. By contrast, the cells of the baby's legs and feet (skin, fat, muscles, bones, blood vessels) are able to replace themselves by mitosis indefinitely. Their numbers will continue to grow through early adulthood; then their quantity and quality can be regenerated through advanced old age.

The developing brain in infancy is a truly fascinating organ. At birth it is poorly organized. The lower (primitive) brain parts (brain stem, pons, medulla, cerebellum) are developed enough to allow the infant to live. The lower brain directs vital organ systems (heart, lungs, kidneys, etc.). The higher (advanced) brain parts (cerebral hemispheres) have allocated neurons, but the nerve cells and cell processes (axons, dendrites) are small, underdeveloped, and unorganized. During infancy, these higher (cerebral) nerve cells (that allow the baby to think, reason, and remember) grow at astronomical rates. They migrate to permanent locations in the hemispheres, develop myelin sheathing (insulation), and conduct messages. Many twentieth-century researchers, including Jean Piaget, the father of cognitive psychology, believed that all brain activities in the newborn were reflexive, based on instincts for survival. They were wrong. New research has documented that fetuses can learn, and newborns can think as well as learn.

The role played by electrical and chemical activity of neurons in actively shaping the physical structure of the brain is particularly awe-inspiring. The neurons are produced prenatally. After birth, the flood of sensory inputs from the environment (sights, sounds, smells, tastes, touch, balance, and kinesthetic sensations) drives the neurons to form circuits and become wired to each other. Trillions of connections are established in a baby's brain. During childhood, the connections that are seldom or never used are eliminated or pruned. The first three years are critical for establishing these connections. Environments that provide both good nutrition and lots of sensory stimulation actually produce richer, more connected brains.

The first selection on infancy asks and partially answers the question, "Why are fewer mothers in the United States choosing to breastfeed today, when the nutritional benefits of human milk far outweigh formula milk?" Data clearly demonstrate that human milk for human infants is associated with fewer gastrointestinal disturbances and protection against many infections, including all diseases for which the mother has developed antibodies. The rates of otitis media (ear infections) are much lower in breastfed babies, as is the incidence of SIDS. Breast milk is associated with long-term reduced risk for diabetes, asthma,

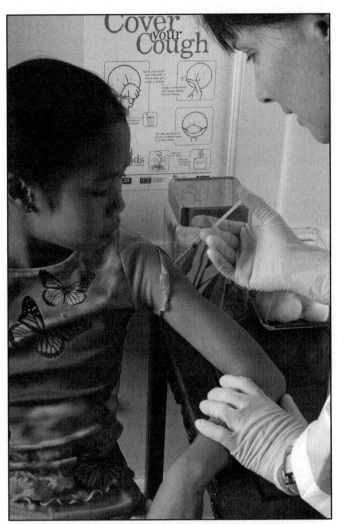

© The McGraw-Hill Companies, Inc./Jill Braaten, photographer

leukemia, and obesity. The partial answer in this article is that the formula industry blocks the public from realizing all these benefits in order to sell more formula.

The second selection on infancy, "Reading Your Baby's Mind," addresses a concern of many parents: "How much does this baby understand?" With electroencephalography and laser eye tracking, scientists are providing surprising answers. In short, a lot! They feel empathy when others are stressed, as well as fear and contentment from birth onwards. This article explains how infant minds develop, the role of the environment, and gives milestones of progress in the first 18 months of life.

The third infancy article, "Vaccination Nation," by Chris Mooney, explains how the fear of vaccinations developed in America. "Vaccines do not cause autism." This is the opening sentence. Ample research by unbiased scientists, working pro bono, are reviewed. However, once a claim is made and people become frightened, it is hard to contain their fears. Thimerosal, once blamed for causing brain damage, has been removed from vaccines since 2001! The sad result of the unsupported assertions about poisons in vaccines is that fewer children are getting inoculations. Polio, measles, mumps, diphtheria, tetanus, pertussis, and rubella, largely unknown diseases, can become epidemic again and cause unprecedented loss of life. The question remains, "How can people be persuaded that vaccines are safe and that they can prevent devastating diseases?"

The first early childhood article addresses "Long-Term Studies of Preschool: Lasting Benefits Far Outweigh Costs." Many industrialized nations subsidize high-quality early childhood education. The United States does not. Long-term studies of three excellent preschool programs in the United States have documented long-lasting benefits. While national preschool funding would be an expensive investment, the authors argue that it would be worth the costs.

"How to Help Your Toddler Begin Developing Empathy," explains that toddlers can understand that other people have feelings, separate from those the young child is experiencing. The ability to comprehend this is the foundation for developing empathy with others. Rebecca Pariakian and Claire Lerner explain how to encourage youngsters to think about others. This takes time, and a lot of patience. Moving from "I, me, and mine" to "you and yours" is a complex skill that continues to develop over one's lifetime.

The second selection for early childhood deals with attachment and bonding between young children and their primary caregivers. Attachment is a good thing! Theories of attachment are reviewed by the author, Nancy Balaban. Separation from the beloved caregiver, once strong attachment bonds have developed, can be stressful. This article gives many suggestions for easing the process.

Deborah Stipek, in the third early childhood article, "Accountability Comes to Preschool: Can We Make It Work for Young Children?," gives sketches of what a good preschool can do, and what will happen if the nonacademic aspects of preschools are dropped in favor of a narrow set of reading and math skills. Young children, advises Stipek, need preschool programs that emphasize social skills, emotional well-being, and health habits, as well as an enthusiasm for learning. Preschools should not evolve into the kindergartens or first grades of yesteryear.

The last selected writing for this collection of articles about infancy and early childhood addresses the importance of a healthy diet. High nutritional value foods are necessary for the rapid growth in this stage of life. Healthy development is promoted by eating lean proteins, whole grains, calcium-rich foods and beverages, and plenty of vegetables and fruits. Empty calorie snacks, excess sugar and salt, and artificially flavored beverages dull the appetite for more nutritious choices. The authors of "'Early Sprouts': Establishing Healthy Food Choices for Young Children" have many exciting suggestions for helping young children really like the foods that are best for them.

HHS Toned Down Breast-Feeding Ads

Formula Industry Urged Softer Campaign

Marc Kaufman and Christopher Lee

In an attempt to raise the nation's historically low rate of breast-feeding, federal health officials commissioned an attention-grabbing advertising campaign a few years ago to convince mothers that their babies faced real health risks if they did not breast-feed. It featured striking photos of insulin syringes and asthma inhalers topped with rubber nipples.

Plans to run these blunt ads infuriated the politically powerful infant formula industry, which hired a former chairman of the Republican National Committee and a former top regulatory official to lobby the Health and Human Services Department. Not long afterward, department political appointees toned down the campaign.

The ads ran instead with more friendly images of dandelions and cherry-topped ice cream scoops, to dramatize how breast-feeding could help avert respiratory problems and obesity. In a February 2004 letter (pdf), the lobbyists told then-HHS Secretary Tommy G. Thompson they were "grateful" for his staff's intervention to stop health officials from "scaring expectant mothers into breast-feeding," and asked for help in scaling back more of the ads.

The formula industry's intervention—which did not block the ads but helped change their content—is being scrutinized by Congress in the wake of last month's testimony by former surgeon general Richard H. Carmona that the Bush administration repeatedly allowed political considerations to interfere with his efforts to promote public health.

Rep. Henry A. Waxman's Committee on Oversight and Government Reform is investigating allegations from former officials that Carmona was blocked from participating in the breast-feeding advocacy effort and that those designing the ad campaign were overruled by superiors at the formula industry's insistence.

"This is a credible allegation of political interference that might have had serious public health consequences," said Waxman, a California Democrat.

The milder campaign HHS eventually used had no discernible impact on the nation's breast-feeding rate, which lags behind the rate in many European countries.

Some senior HHS officials involved in the deliberations over the ad campaign defended the outcome, saying the final ads raised the profile of breast-feeding while following the scientific evidence available then—which they say did not fully support the claims of the original ad campaign.

But other current and former HHS officials say the muting of the ads was not the only episode in which HHS missed a chance to try to raise the breast-feeding rate. In April, according to officials and documents, the department chose not to promote a comprehensive analysis by its own Agency for Healthcare Research and Quality (AHRQ) of multiple studies on breast-feeding, which generally found it was associated with fewer ear and gastrointestinal infections, as well as lower rates of diabetes, leukemia, obesity, asthma and sudden infant death syndrome.

The report did not assert a direct cause and effect, because doing so would require studies in which some women are told not to breast-feed their infants—a request considered unethical, given the obvious health benefits of the practice.

A top HHS official said that at the time, Suzanne Haynes, an epidemiologist and senior science adviser for the department's Office on Women's Health, argued strongly in favor of promoting the new conclusions in the media and among medical professionals. But her office, which commissioned the report, was specifically instructed by political appointees not to disseminate a news release.

Wanda K. Jones, director of the women's health office, said agency media officials have "all been hammering me" about getting Haynes to stop trying to draw attention to the AHRQ report. HHS press officer Rebecca Ayer emphatically told Haynes and others in mid-July that there should be "no media outreach to anyone" on that topic, current and former officials said.

Both HHS and AHRQ ultimately sent out a few e-mail notices, but the report was generally ignored. Requests to speak with Haynes were turned down by other HHS officials.

Regarding the changes made to the earlier HHS ad campaign, Kevin Keane, then HHS assistant secretary for public affairs and now a spokesman for the American Beverage Association, said formula companies lobbied hard, as did breast-feeding advocates.

"We took heat from the formula industry, who didn't want to see a campaign like this. And we took some heat from the advocates who didn't think it was strong enough," Keane said. "At the end of the day, we had a ground-breaking campaign that goes further than any other administration ever went."

But the campaign HHS used did not simply drop the disputed statistics in the draft ads. The initial idea was to startle women with images starkly warning that babies could become ill. Instead, the final ads cited how breast-feeding benefits babies—an approach that the ad company hired by HHS had advised would be ineffective. The department also pulled back on several related promotional efforts.

After the 2003–05 period in which the HHS ads were aired, the proportion of mothers who breast-fed in the hospital after their babies were born dropped, from 70 percent in 2002 to 63.6 percent in 2006, according to statistics collected in Abbott Nutrition's Ross Mothers Survey, an industry-backed effort that has been measuring breast-feeding rates for more than 30 years. In 2002, 33.2 percent of women were doing any breast-feeding at six months; by 2006, that rate had declined to 30 percent.

The World Health Organization recommends that, if at all possible, women breast-feed their infants exclusively for at least six months.

The breast-feeding ad campaign originated in a formal "Blueprint for Action on Breastfeeding" released in 2000 by David Satcher, who had been appointed surgeon general by President Bill Clinton. The Office on Women's Health convinced the nonprofit Ad Council to donate $30 million in media time, and it hired an ad agency to work alongside scientists from the National Institutes of Health, the Centers for Disease Control and Prevention, and elsewhere.

Officials met with dozens of focus groups before concluding that the best way to influence mothers was to delineate in graphic terms the risks of not breast-feeding, an approach in keeping with edgy Ad Council campaigns on smoking, seat belts and drunken driving. For example, an ad portraying a nipple-tipped insulin bottle said, "Babies who aren't breastfed are 40% more likely to suffer Type 1 diabetes."

Gina Ciagne, the office's public affairs specialist for the campaign, said, "We were ready to go with our risk-based campaign—making breast-feeding a real public health issue—when the formula companies learned about it and came in to complain. Before long, we were told we had to water things down, get rid of the hard-hitting ads and generally make sure we didn't somehow offend."

Ciagne and others involved in the campaign said the pushback coincided with a high-level lobbying campaign by formula makers, which are mostly divisions of large pharmaceutical companies that are among the most generous campaign donors in the nation.

The campaign the industry mounted was a Washington classic—a full-court press to reach top political appointees at HHS, using influential former government officials, now working for the industry, to act as go-betweens.

Two of the those involved were Clayton Yeutter, an agriculture secretary under President George H.W. Bush and a former chairman of the Republican National Committee, and Joseph A. Levitt, who four months earlier directed the Food and Drug Administration's Center for Food Safety and Applied Nutrition food safety center, which regulates infant formula. A spokesman for the International Formula Council said both were paid by a formula manufacturer to arrange meetings at HHS.

In a Feb. 17, 2004, letter to Thompson (pdf), Yeutter began "Dear Tommy" and explained that the council wished to meet with him because the draft ad campaign was inappropriately "implying that mothers who use infant formula are placing their babies at risk," and could give rise to class-action lawsuits.

Yeutter acknowledged that the ad agency "may well be correct" in asserting that a softer approach would garner less attention, but he said many women cannot breast-feed or choose not to for legitimate reasons, which may give them "guilty feelings." He asked, "Does the U.S. government really want to engage in an ad campaign that will magnify that guilt?"

He also praised Keane, the HHS public affairs official, for making "helpful changes" and removing "egregious statements," but asked that more be done. Two months later, Yeutter wrote Thompson to thank him for meeting with a group that included Levitt and an official of the council. The group members supported breast-feeding, he said, but they wanted HHS to use "positive visual images."

The formula companies also approached Carden Johnston, then president of the American Academy of Pediatrics. Afterward, Johnston wrote a letter to Thompson advising him that "we have some concerns about this negative approach and how it will be received by the general public."

The letter made a strong impression at HHS, former and current officials said. But it angered many of the medical group's members and the head of its section on breast-feeding, Lawrence M. Gartner, a Chicago physician. Gartner told Thompson in a letter that the 800 members of the breast-feeding section did not share Johnston's concerns and had not known of his letter.

"This campaign needed to be much stronger than it was," Gartner said, adding that in his view, the original ads were backed by solid scientific evidence.

According to former and current HHS officials, Cristina V. Beato, then an acting assistant secretary at HHS, played a key role—in addition to that of Keane—in toning down the ads. They said she stressed to associates that it was essential to "be fair" to the formula companies.

Beato was then serving in an acting capacity because lawmakers refused to vote on her confirmation because of complaints that she had padded her official resume. In a 2004 interview with the ABC newsmagazine "20/20," which described some of the industry's efforts to change the breast-feeding ad campaign, Beato confirmed that she "met with the industry, because they kept calling my office, every two weeks." She said in a telephone interview that their complaints played no role in her decisions.

"I brought together our top public health people to examine the health claims, and they examined the science and concluded what should be in and what should be out," Beato said.

Duane Alexander, head of the government's National Institute of Child Health and Human Development, was among the officials contacted by the industry who later supported eliminating some of the ads.

Staff researcher Madonna Lebling contributed to this report.

Reading Your Baby's Mind

New research on infants finally begins to answer the question: what's going on in there?

PAT WINGERT AND MARTHA BRANT

Little Victoria Bateman is blond and blue-eyed and as cute a baby as there ever was. At 6 months, she is also trusting and unsuspecting, which is a good thing, because otherwise she'd never go along with what's about to happen. It's a blistering June afternoon in Lubbock, Texas, and inside the Human Sciences lab at Texas Tech University, Victoria's mother is settling her daughter into a high chair, where she is the latest subject in an ongoing experiment aimed at understanding the way babies think. Sybil Hart, an associate professor of human development and leader of the study, trains video cameras on mother and daughter. Everything is set. Hart hands Cheryl Bateman a children's book, "Elmo Pops In," and instructs her to engross herself in its pages. "Just have a conversation with me about the book," Hart tells her. "The most important thing is, do not look at [Victoria.]" As the two women chat, Victoria looks around the room, impassive and a little bored.

After a few minutes, Hart leaves the room and returns cradling a lifelike baby doll. Dramatically, Hart places it in Cheryl Bateman's arms, and tells her to cuddle the doll while continuing to ignore Victoria. "That's OK, little baby," Bateman coos, hugging and rocking the doll. Victoria is not bored anymore. At first, she cracks her best smile, showcasing a lone stubby tooth. When that doesn't work, she begins kicking. But her mom pays her no mind. That's when Victoria loses it. Soon she's beet red and crying so hard it looks like she might spit up. Hart rushes in. "OK, we're done," she says, and takes back the doll. Cheryl Bateman goes to comfort her daughter. "I've never seen her react like that to anything," she says. Over the last 10 months, Hart has repeated the scenario hundreds of times. It's the same in nearly every case: tiny babies, overwhelmed with jealousy. Even Hart was stunned to find that infants could experience an emotion, which, until recently, was thought to be way beyond their grasp.

And that's just for starters. The helpless, seemingly clueless infant staring up at you from his crib, limbs flailing, drool oozing, has a lot more going on inside his head than you ever imagined. A wealth of new research is leading pediatricians and child psychologists to rethink their long-held beliefs about the emotional and intellectual abilities of even very young babies.

In 1890, psychologist William James famously described an infant's view of the world as "one great blooming, buzzing confusion." It was a notion that held for nearly a century: infants were simple-minded creatures who merely mimicked those around them and grasped only the most basic emotions—happy, sad, angry. Science is now giving us a much different picture of what goes on inside their hearts and heads. Long before they form their first words or attempt the feat of sitting up, they are already mastering complex emotions—jealousy, empathy, frustration—that were once thought to be learned much later in toddlerhood.

They are also far more sophisticated intellectually than we once believed. Babies as young as 4 months have advanced powers of deduction and an ability to decipher intricate patterns. They have a strikingly nuanced visual palette, which enables them to notice small differences, especially in faces, that adults and older children lose the ability to see. Until a baby is 3 months old, he can recognize a scrambled photograph of his mother just as quickly as a photo in which everything is in the right place. And big brothers and sisters beware: your sib has a long memory—and she can hold a grudge.

Babies yet to utter an INTELLIGENT SYLLABLE are now known to feel a range of COMPLEX EMOTIONS like envy and empathy.

The new research is sure to enthrall new parents—See, Junior *is* a genius!—but it's more than just an academic exercise. Armed with the new information, pediatricians are starting to change the way they evaluate their youngest patients. In addition to tracking physical development, they are now focusing much more deeply on emotional advancement. The research shows how powerful emotional well-being is to a child's future health. A baby who fails to meet certain key "emotional milestones" may have trouble learning to speak, read and, later, do well in school. By reading emotional responses, doctors have begun to discover ways to tell if a baby as young as 3 months is showing early signs of possible psychological disorders, including depression, anxiety, learning disabilities and perhaps autism. "Instead of just asking if they're crawling or sitting, we're asking more questions about how they share their world with their caregivers," says Dr. Chet Johnson, chairman of the American Academy of Pediatrics' early-childhood committee. "Do they point to things? When they see a new person, how do they react? How children do on social and emotional and language skills are better predictors of success in adulthood than motor skills are." The goal: in the not-too-distant future, researchers hope doctors will routinely identify at-risk kids years earlier than they do now—giving parents crucial extra time to turn things around.

One of the earliest emotions that even tiny babies display is, admirably enough, empathy. In fact, concern for others may be hard-wired into babies' brains. Plop a newborn down next to another crying infant, and chances are, both babies will soon be wailing away. "People have always known that babies cry when they hear other babies cry," says Martin Hoffman, a psychology professor at New York University who did the first studies on infant empathy in the 1970s. "The question was, why are they crying?" Does it mean that the baby is truly concerned for his fellow human, or just annoyed by the racket? A recent study conducted in Italy, which built on Hoffman's own work, has largely settled the question. Researchers played infants tapes of other babies crying. As predicted, that was enough to start the tears flowing. But when researchers played babies recordings of their own cries, they rarely began crying themselves. The verdict: "There is some rudimentary empathy in place, right from birth," Hoffman says. The intensity of the emotion tends to fade over time. Babies older than 6 months no longer cry but grimace at the discomfort of others. By 13 to 15 months, babies tend to take matters into their own hands. They'll try to comfort a crying playmate. "What I find most charming is when, even if the two mothers are present, they'll bring their own mother over to help," Hoffman says.

Part of that empathy may come from another early-baby skill that's now better understood, the ability to discern emotions from the facial expressions of the people around them. "Most textbooks still say that babies younger than 6 months don't recognize emotions," says Diane Montague, assistant professor of psychology at LaSalle University in Philadelphia. To put that belief to the test, Montague came up with a twist on every infant's favorite game, peekaboo, and recruited dozens of 4-month-olds to play along. She began by peeking around a cloth with a big smile on her face. Predictably, the babies were delighted, and stared at her intently—the time-tested way to tell if a baby is interested. On the fourth peek, though, Montague emerged with a sad look on her face. This time, the response was much different. "They not only looked away," she says, but wouldn't look back even when she began smiling again. Refusing to make eye contact is a classic baby sign of distress. An angry face got their attention once again, but their faces showed no pleasure. "They seemed primed to be alert, even vigilant," Montague says. "I realize that's speculative in regard

to infants . . . I think it shows that babies younger than 6 months find meaning in expressions."

This might be a good place to pause for a word about the challenges and perils of baby research. Since the subjects can't speak for themselves, figuring out what's going on inside their heads is often a matter of reading their faces and body language. If this seems speculative, it's not. Over decades of trial and error, researchers have fine-tuned their observation skills and zeroed in on numerous consistent baby responses to various stimuli: how long they stare at an object, what they reach out for and what makes them recoil in fear or disgust can often tell experienced researchers everything they need to know. More recently, scientists have added EEGs and laser eye tracking, which allow more precise readings. Coming soon: advanced MRI scans that will allow a deeper view inside the brain.

When infants near their first birthdays, they become increasingly sophisticated social learners. They begin to infer what others are thinking by following the gaze of those around them. "By understanding others' gaze, babies come to understand others' minds," says Andrew Meltzoff, a professor of psychology at the University of Washington who has studied the "gaze following" of thousands of babies. "You can tell a lot about people, what they're interested in and what they intend to do next, by watching their eyes. It appears that even babies know that . . . This is how they learn to become expert members of our culture."

Meltzoff and colleague Rechele Brooks have found that this skill first appears at 10 to 11 months, and is not only an important marker of a baby's emotional and social growth, but can predict later language development. In their study, babies who weren't proficient at gaze-following by their first birthday had much less advanced-language skills at 2. Meltzoff says this helps explain why language occurs more slowly in blind children, as well as children of depressed mothers, who tend not to interact as much with their babies.

In fact, at just a few months, infants begin to develop superpowers when it comes to observation. Infants can easily tell the difference between human faces. But at the University of Minnesota, neuroscientist Charles Nelson (now of Harvard) wanted to test how discerning infants really are. He showed a group of 6-month-old babies a photo of a chimpanzee, and gave them time to stare at it until they lost interest. They were then shown another chimp. The babies perked up and stared at the new photo. The infants easily recognized each chimp as an individual—they were fascinated by each new face. Now unless you spend a good chunk of your day hanging around the local zoo, chances are you couldn't tell the difference between a roomful of chimps at a glance. As it turned out, neither could babies just a few months older. By 9 months, those kids had lost the ability to tell chimps apart; but at the same time, they had increased their powers of observation when it came to human faces.

Nelson has now taken his experiment a step further, to see how early babies can detect subtle differences in facial expressions, a key building block of social development. He designed a new study that is attempting to get deep inside babies' heads by measuring brain-wave activity. Nelson sent out letters to the parents of nearly every newborn in the area, inviting them to participate. Earlier this summer it was Dagny Winberg's turn. The 7-month-old was all smiles as her mother, Armaiti, carried her into the lab, where she was fitted with a snug cap wired with 64 sponge sensors. Nelson's assistant, grad student Meg Moulson, began flashing photographs on a screen of a woman. In each photo, the woman had a slightly different expression—many different shades of happiness and fear. Dagny was given time to look at each photo until she became bored and looked away. The whole time, a computer was closely tracking her brain activity, measuring her mind's minutest responses to the different photos. Eventually, after she'd run through 60 photos, Dagny had had enough of the game and began whimpering and fidgeting. That ended the session. The point of the experiment is to see if baby brain scans look like those of adults. "We want to see if babies categorize emotions in the ways that adults do," Moulson says. "An adult can see a slight smile and categorize it as happy. We want to know if babies can do the same." They don't have the answer yet, but Nelson believes that infants who display early signs of emotional disorders, such as autism, may be helped if they can develop these critical powers of observation and emotional engagement.

Halfway across the country, researchers are working to dispel another baby cliché: out of sight, out of mind. It was long believed that babies under 9 months didn't grasp the idea of "object permanence"—the ability to know, for instance, that when Mom leaves the room, she isn't gone forever. New research by psychologist Su-hua Wang at the University of California, Santa Cruz, is showing that babies understand the concept as early as 10 weeks. Working with 2- and 3-month-olds, she performs a little puppet show. Each baby sees a duck on a stage. Wang covers the duck, moves it across the stage and lifts the cover. Sometimes the duck is there. Other times, the duck disappears beneath a trapdoor. When they see the duck has gone missing, the babies stare intently at the empty stage, searching for it. "At 2½ months," she says, "they already have the idea that the object continues to exist."

A strong, well-developed ability to connect with the world—and with parents in particular—is especially important when babies begin making their first efforts at learning to speak. Baby talk is much more than mimickry. Michael Goldstein, a psychologist at Cornell University, gathered two groups of 8-month-olds and decked them out in overalls rigged up with wireless microphones and transmitters. One group of mothers was told to react immediately when their babies cooed or babbled, giving them big smiles and loving pats. The other group of parents was also told to smile at their kids, but randomly, unconnected to the babies' sounds. It came as no surprise that the babies who received immediate feedback babbled more and advanced quicker than those who didn't. But what interested Goldstein was the way in which the parents, without realizing it, raised the "babble bar" with their kids. "The kinds of simple sounds that get parents' attention at 4 months don't get the same reaction at 8 months," he says. "That motivates babies to experiment with different sound combinations until they find new ones that get noticed."

A decade ago Patricia Kuhl, a professor of speech and hearing at the University of Washington and a leading authority on early language, proved that tiny babies have a unique ability to learn a foreign language. As a result of her well-publicized findings, parents ran out to buy foreign-language tapes, hoping their little Einsteins would pick up Russian or French before they left their cribs. It didn't work, and Kuhl's new research shows why. Kuhl put American 9-month-olds in a room with Mandarin-speaking adults, who showed them toys while talking to them. After 12 sessions, the babies had learned to detect subtle Mandarin phonetic sounds that couldn't be heard by a separate group of babies who were exposed only to English. Kuhl then repeated the experiment, but this time played the identical Mandarin lessons to babies on video- and audiotape. That group of babies failed to learn any Mandarin. Kuhl says that without the emotional connection, the babies considered the tape recording just another background noise, like a vacuum cleaner. "We were genuinely surprised by the outcome," she says. "We all assumed that when infants stare at a television, and look engaged, that they are learning from it." Kuhl says there's plenty of work to be done to explain why that isn't true. "But at first blush one thinks that people—at least babies—need people to learn."

So there you have it. That kid over there with one sock missing and smashed peas all over his face is actually a formidable presence, in possession of keen powers of observation, acute emotional sensitivity and an impressive arsenal of deductive powers. "For the last 15 years, we've been focused on babies' abilities—what they know and when they knew it," says the University of Washington's Meltzoff. "But now we want to know what all this predicts about later development. What does all this mean for the child?"

Some of these questions are now finding answers. Take shyness, for instance. It's long been known that 15 to 20 percent of children are shy and anxious by nature. But doctors didn't know why some seemed simply to grow out of it, while for others it became a debilitating condition. Recent studies conducted by Nathan Fox of the University of Maryland show that shyness is initially driven by biology. He proved it by wiring dozens of 9-month-olds to EEG machines and conducting a simple experiment. When greeted by a stranger, "behaviorally inhibited" infants tensed up, and showed more activity in the parts of the brain associated with anxiety and fear. Babies with outgoing personalities reached out to the stranger. Their EEG scans showed heightened activity in the parts of the brain that govern positive emotions like pleasure.

Just because your baby is MORE PERCEPTIVE than you thought doesn't mean she'll be DAMAGED if she cries for a minute.

But Fox, who has followed some of these children for 15 years, says that parenting style has a big impact on which kind of adult a child will turn out to be. Children of overprotective parents, or those whose parents didn't encourage them to overcome shyness and childhood anxiety, often remain shy and anxious as adults. But kids born to confident and sensitive parents who gently help them to take emotional risks and coax them out of their shells can often overcome early awkwardness. That's an important finding, since behaviorally inhibited kids are also at higher risk for other problems.

Stanley Greenspan, clinical professor of psychiatry and pediatrics at George Washington University Medical School, is one of the leaders in developing diagnostic tools to help doctors identify babies who may be at risk for language and learning problems, autism and a whole range of other problems. He recently completed a checklist of social and emotional "milestones" that babies should reach by specific ages. "I'd like to see doctors screen babies for these milestones and tell parents exactly what to do if their babies are not mastering them. One of our biggest problems now is that parents may sense intuitively that something is not right," but by the time they are able to get their child evaluated, "that family has missed a critical time to, maybe, get that baby back on track."

So what should parents do with all this new information? First thing: relax. Just because your baby is more perceptive than you might have thought doesn't mean she's going to be damaged for life if she cries in her crib for a minute while you answer the phone. Or that he'll wind up quitting school and stealing cars if he witnesses an occasional argument between his parents. Children crave—and thrive on—interaction, one-on-one time and lots of eye contact. That doesn't mean filling the baby's room with "educational" toys and posters. A child's social, emotional, and academic life begins with the earliest conversations between parent and child: the first time the baby locks eyes with you; the quiet smile you give your infant and the smile she gives you back. Your child is speaking to you all the time. It's just a matter of knowing how to listen.

With T. Trent Gegax, Margaret Nelson, Karen Breslau, Nadine Joseph and Ben Whitford

Vaccination Nation

The decadelong controversy surrounding the safety of vaccines is over—or is it? A fierce debate continues over what really puts our children at risk.

CHRIS MOONEY

Vaccines do not cause autism. That was the ruling in each of three critical test cases handed down on February 12 by the U.S. Court of Federal Claims in Washington, D.C. After a decade of speculation, argument, and analysis—often filled with vitriol on both sides—the court specifically denied any link between the combination of the MMR vaccine and vaccines with thimerosal (a mercury-based preservative) and the spectrum of disorders associated with autism. But these rulings, though seemingly definitive, have done little to quell the angry debate, which has severe implications for American public health.

The idea that there is something wrong with our vaccines—that they have poisoned a generation of kids, driving an "epidemic" of autism—continues to be everywhere: on cable news, in celebrity magazines, on blogs, and in health news stories. It has had a particularly strong life on the Internet, including the heavily trafficked *Huffington Post,* and in pop culture, where it is supported by actors including Charlie Sheen and Jim Carrey, former *Playboy* playmate Jenny McCarthy, and numerous others. Despite repeated rejection by the scientific community, it has spawned a movement, led to thousands of legal claims, and even triggered occasional harassment and threats against scientists whose research appears to discredit it.

You can see where the emotion and sentiment come from. Autism can be a terrible condition, devastating to families. It can leave parents not only aggrieved but desperate to find any cure, any salvation. Medical services and behavioral therapy for severely autistic children can cost more than $100,000 a year, and these children often exhibit extremely difficult behavior. Moreover, the incidence of autism is apparently rising rapidly. Today one in every 150 children has been diagnosed on the autism spectrum; 20 years ago that statistic was one in 10,000. "Put yourself in the shoes of these parents," says journalist David Kirby, whose best-selling 2005 book, *Evidence of Harm,* dramatized the vaccine-autism movement. "They have perfectly normal kids who are walking and happy and everything—and then they regress." The irony is that vaccine skepticism—not the vaccines themselves—is now looking like the true public-health threat.

The decadelong vaccine-autism saga began in 1998, when British gastroenterologist Andrew Wakefield and his colleagues published evidence in *The Lancet* suggesting they had tracked down a shocking cause of autism. Examining the digestive tracts of 12 children with behavioral disorders, nine of them autistic, the researchers found intestinal inflammation, which they pinned on the MMR (measles, mumps, and rubella) vaccine. Wakefield had a specific theory of how the MMR shot could trigger autism: The upset intestines, he conjectured, let toxins loose in the bloodstream, which then traveled to the brain. The vaccine was, in this view, effectively a poison. In a dramatic press conference, Wakefield announced the findings and sparked an instant media frenzy. For the British public, a retreat from the use of the MMR vaccine—and a rise in the incidence of measles—began.

In the United States, meanwhile, fears would soon arise concerning another means by which vaccines might induce autism. Many vaccines at the time contained thimerosal, a preservative introduced in the 1930s to make vaccines safer by preventing bacterial contamination. But thimerosal is 50 percent mercury by weight, and mercury is known to be a potent neurotoxin, at least in large doses. In 1999 new federal safety guidelines for mercury in fish stirred concerns about vaccines as well.

The U.S. government responded by ordering that thimerosal be removed from all vaccines administered to children under age 6, or reduced to trace amounts. (Some inactivated influenza vaccines were exempted.) The step was described as a "precautionary" measure. There was no proof of harm, government researchers said, just reason to worry that there might be. Meanwhile, scientists launched numerous studies to determine whether thimerosal had actually caused an autism epidemic, while some parents and their lawyers started pointing fingers and developing legal cases.

Within weeks of this year's federal court decisions—which examined and vindicated both the MMR vaccine and thimerosal environmental lawyer Robert F. Kennedy Jr. wrote a column in *The Huffington Post* in which he continued to press his case that the government has peddled unsafe vaccines to an unsuspecting public. It is a cause he has championed since 2005, when he published "Deadly Immunity" in *Rolling Stone* and *Salon* magazines. The article was a no-holds-barred denunciation of the U.S. public-health establishment, purporting to tell the story of how "government health agencies colluded with Big Pharma to hide the risks of thimerosal from the public . . . a chilling case study of institutional arrogance, power, and greed." Half a decade after the original thimerosal concerns were first raised, Kennedy claimed to have found the smoking gun: the transcript of a "secret" 2000 meeting of government, pharmaceutical, and independent researchers with expertise in vaccines. Kennedy's conclusion: The generational catastrophe was real; our kids had been poisoned. If true, it would be perhaps the greatest biomedical catastrophe in modern history.

But for Kennedy to be right, a growing consensus in the medical establishment had to be wrong. Indeed, Kennedy blasted a leading organ of science that had just vindicated both the MMR vaccine and thimerosal, the Institute of Medicine (IOM). "The CDC [Centers for Disease Control and Prevention] paid the Institute of Medicine to conduct a new study to whitewash the risks of thimerosal," Kennedy wrote, "ordering researchers to 'rule out' the chemical's link to autism." In reality, the IOM—a branch of the National Academy of Sciences (NAS), the government's top independent scientific adviser—carefully creates firewalls between the funding it receives to conduct scientific assessments and the results it ultimately produces. "Funders don't control the composition of the committee, and they don't meet with the committee," says Harvard public-health researcher Marie McCormick, who chaired the IOM vaccine-safety committee in question. "And on no NAS or IOM committee are the members paid; they all work pro bono. There's no reason for them not to look at the data."

The same year Kennedy's article came out, journalist David Kirby published *Evidence of Harm—Mercury in Vaccines and the Autism Epidemic: A Medical Controversy.* He followed a group of parents from the Coalition for SafeMinds, an autism activist organization. They had grown convinced that vaccines and other environmental factors had caused their children's conditions. Kirby's chronicle of the parents' efforts to publicize the dangers of vaccines became a best seller and greatly advanced SafeMinds' cause.

"It's not hard to scare people," says pediatrician and leading vaccine advocate Paul Offit. "But it's extremely difficult to unscare them."

Yet even as vaccine hysteria reached a fever pitch in the wake of Kennedy's and Kirby's writings, the scientific evidence was leaning strongly in the other direction. In discounting the dangers of both the MMR vaccine and thimerosal, the IOM had multiple large epidemiological studies to rely on. For MMR, the IOM examined 16 studies. All but two, which were dismissed because of "serious methodological flaws," showed no evidence of a link. For thimerosal, the IOM looked at five studies, examining populations in Sweden, Denmark, the United Kingdom, and the United States (studies that vaccine critics contend were flawed). Since then, further research has strengthened and vindicated the committee's original conclusion. It is a conclusion that has been "independently reached by scientific and professional committees around the world," as a recent science journal commentary noted. Either the scientific community has found a clear, reassuring answer to the questions raised about thimerosal in vaccines, or there is a global scientific conspiracy to bury the truth.

Whether the public is hearing the scientific community's answer is another matter. "It's not hard to scare people," says pediatrician and leading vaccine advocate Paul Offit, who himself coinvented a vaccine. "But it's extremely difficult to unscare them."

A backlash against vaccine skeptics is beginning to mount. Standing up to fellow celebrities, actress Amanda Peet, who recently vaccinated her baby daughter, has become a spokeswoman for the provaccine group Every Child by Two. Offit's book *Autism's False Prophets* has further galvanized vaccine defenders—not only by debunking the science of those who claim vaccines are dangerous but also by contending that the parents of autistic children and the children themselves are indeed victims, not of vaccines but of medical misinformation.

The provaccine case starts with some undeniable facts: Vaccines are, as the IOM puts it, "one of the greatest achievements of public health." The CDC estimates that thanks to vaccines, we have reduced morbidity by 99 percent or more for smallpox, diphtheria, measles, polio, and rubella. Averaged over the course of the 20th century, these five diseases killed nearly 650,000 people annually. They now kill fewer than 100. That is not to say vaccines are perfectly safe; in rare cases they can cause serious, well-known adverse side effects. But what researchers consider unequivocally unsafe is to avoid them. As scientists at the Johns Hopkins Bloomberg School of Public Health recently found while investigating whooping cough outbreaks in and around Michigan, "geographic pockets of vaccine exemptors pose a risk to the whole community."

When it comes to autism, vaccine defenders make two central claims. First, the condition is likely to be mostly genetic rather than environmentally caused; and second, there are reasons to doubt whether there is really a rising autism epidemic at all.

It is misleading to think of autism as a single disorder. Rather, it is a spectrum of disorders showing great variability in symptoms and expression but fundamentally characterized by failed social development, inability to communicate, and obsessive repetitive behavior. Autism generally appears in children at early ages, sometimes suddenly, and its genetic component has long been recognized. Studies have shown that if one identical twin has autism, there is at least a 60 percent chance that the other also does. "From my point of view, it's a condition associated with genetic defects and developmental biology problems," says Peter Hotez, a George Washington University microbiologist and father of an autistic child. Hotez, who is also president of the Sabin Vaccine Institute, says, "I don't think it's possible to explain on the basis of any vaccine toxin that is acquired after the baby is born." Still, scientists cannot fully rule out environmental triggers—including various types of toxicity—that might interact with a given individual's preexisting genetic inclination. Autism is a complex disorder with multiple forms of expression and potentially multiple types of causation that are incompletely understood.

As for whether autism is rising, a number of experts say it is hard to know. Is the increase real, or is it largely the result of more attention to the condition, an expansion of the autism spectrum to embrace many different heterogeneous disorders, a new focus on children classified as autistic in federal special education programs during the 1990s, and other factors? It could be some combination of all these things.

But if environmental triggers of autism cannot be ruled out, the idea that those triggers can be found in the MMR vaccine or in thimerosal has crumbled under the weight of scientific refutation. Epidemiological studies have cast grave doubt on Andrew Wakefield's MMR hypothesis—and so have subsequent scandals. Nearly all of Wakefield's coauthors have since retracted the autism implications of their work; *The Lancet* has also backed away from the study. A series of investigative stories published in *The Times* of London unearthed Wakefield's undisclosed ties to vaccine litigation in the U.K. and, more recently, suggested he fabricated his data (which Wakefield denies).

As for thimerosal, government precautions notwithstanding, it was never clear how threatening it might be. The federal mercury standards that first heightened concern were developed for methylmercury, not ethylmercury, the form contained in thimerosal. Ethylmercury has less risk of accumulating to a toxic dose because it does not last as long in the body. And, according to the IOM's 2004 report, there had never been any evidence of a major incident of mercury poisoning leading to autism.

The strongest argument against the idea that thimerosal poisoned a generation of children does not emerge from the body of published studies alone. There is the added detail that although thimerosal is no longer present in any recommended childhood vaccines save the inactivated influenza vaccine—and hasn't been, beyond trace amounts, since 2001—no one is hailing the end of autism. "If you thought thimerosal was related to autism, then the incidence of autism should have gone down," Harvard's McCormick explains. "And it hasn't."

Children who would have been classified as mentally retarded or learning disabled were now being classified on the autism spectrum.

In 2005 David Kirby stated that if autism rates didn't begin to decline by 2007, "that would deal a severe blow to the autismthimerosal hypothesis." But as McCormick notes, despite the absence of thimerosal in vaccines, reports of autism cases have not fallen. In a 2008 study published in *Archives of General Psychiatry,* two researchers studying a California Department of Developmental Services database found that the prevalence of autism had actually continued increasing among the young. Kirby concedes that these findings about the California database represent a "pretty serious blow to the thimerosalcauses-autism hypothesis," though he does not think they thoroughly bury it. In an interview, he outlined many problems with relying on the California database, suggesting potential confounding factors such as the state's high level of immigration. "Look, I understand the desire to try to end this and not scare parents away from vaccination," Kirby says. "But I also feel that sometimes that desire to prove or disprove blinds people on both sides."

Kirby says—and even some vaccine defenders agree—that some small subgroup of children might have a particular vulnerability to vaccines and yet be missed by epidemiological studies. But the two sides disagree as to the possible size of that group. "If one or two or three children every year are getting autism from vaccines, you would never pick that up," Offit says. Kirby, in contrast, feels that while the idea of thimerosal as the "one and only cause of autism has gone out the window," he still believes there is an "epidemic" with many environmental triggers and with thimerosal as a possible contributing factor.

Meanwhile, in the face of powerful evidence against two of its strongest initial hypotheses—concerning MMR and thimerosal—the vaccine skeptic movement is morphing before our eyes. Advocates have begun moving the goalposts, now claiming, for instance, that the childhood vaccination schedule hits kids with too many vaccines at once, overwhelming their immune systems. Jenny McCarthy wants to "green our vaccines," pointing to many other alleged toxins that they contain. "I think it's definitely a response to the science, which has consistently shown no correlation," says David Gorski, a cancer surgeon funded by the National Institutes of Health who in his spare time blogs at Respectful Insolence, a top medical blog known for its provaccine stance. A hardening of antivaccine attitudes, mixed with the despair experienced by families living under the strain of autism, has heightened the debate—sometimes leading to blowback against scientific researchers.

Paul Shattuck did not set out to enrage vaccine skeptics and the parents of autistic children. Currently an assistant professor at the George Warren Brown School of Social Work at Washington University in St. Louis, he has dedicated the last decade of his professional life to helping people with autism in their families. "Some of my dearest friends have kids with autism," he says.

But in 2006 Shattuck came under fire after he published an article in the journal *Pediatrics* questioning the existence of an autism epidemic. No one doubts that since the early 1990s the number of children diagnosed with autism has dramatically increased, a trend reflected in U.S. special education programs, where children enrolled as autistic grew from 22,445 in 1994–1995 to 140,254 in 2003–2004. Yet Shattuck's study found reasons to doubt that these numbers were proof of an epidemic. Instead, he suggested that "diagnostic substitution"—in which children who previously would have been classified as mentally retarded or learning disabled were now being classified on the autism spectrum—played a significant role in the apparent increase.

Shattuck did not reject the idea that rising autism levels might be in part due to environmental causes; he merely showed the increase was largely an artifact of changing diagnostic practices, which themselves had been enabled by rising levels of attention to autism and its listing as a diagnostic category in special education. Yet simply by questioning autism epidemic claims in a prominent journal, he became a target. "People were obviously Googling me and tracking me down," he recalls. Shattuck emphasizes that most e-mails and calls merely delivered "heartfelt pleas from people with very sick kids who've been led to believe a particular theory of etiology." The bulk weren't menacing, but a few certainly were.

Others attacked Shattuck's research on the Web and insinuated that he had fabricated his data or committed scientific misconduct. "It was dismaying to feel like people were calling me a traitor to autistic kids and families," he says.

"If there has been a more harmful urban legend circulating in our society than the vaccine-autism link," University of Pennsylvania bioethicist Arthur Caplan wrote in *The Philadelphia Inquirer,* "it's hard to know what it might be." One type of harm, as Shattuck's story shows, is to individual scientists and the scientific process. There is a real risk that necessary research is being held back as scientists fear working in such a contested field. Shattuck's experience is not unique. Offit cannot go on a book tour to promote *Autism's False Prophets* because of the risk involved in making public appearances. He has received too many threats.

Yet another cost comes in the rush toward unproven, and potentially dangerous, alternative therapies to treat autism. It is easy to sympathize with parents of autistic children who desperately want to find a cure, but this has led to various pseudoremedies whose efficacy and safety have been challenged by science. These include facilitated communication, secretin infusion, chelation therapy (which involves pumping chemicals into the blood to bind with heavy metals such as mercury), and hormonal suppression. It is estimated that more than half of all children with autism are now using "complementary and alternative" treatments.

Disease, however, is the greatest danger associated with holding back vaccines amid the ongoing investigation of dubious claims. Both the vaccinated and the unvaccinated populations are placed at greater risk. Given enough vaccine exemptions and localized outbreaks, it is possible that largely vanquished diseases could become endemic again. (That is precisely what happened with measles in 2008 in the U.K., following the retreat from the MMR vaccine in the wake of the 1998 scare.) The public-health costs of such a development would be enormous—and they would not impact everyone equally. "If vaccine rates start to drop, who's going to get affected?" Peter Hotez asks. "It's going to be people who live in poor, crowded conditions. So it's going to affect the poorest people in our country."

Paradoxically, the great success of vaccines is a crucial reason why antivaccination sentiment has thrived, some scientists say. Most of the diseases that vaccines protect against have largely been licked. As a consequence, few people personally remember the devastation they can cause. So with less apparently on the line, it is easier to indulge in the seeming luxury of vaccine skepticism and avoidance. Even before the recent spike in attention to thimerosal, members of the public were alarmingly skeptical of vaccines. In a 1999 survey, 25 percent felt their children's immune systems could be harmed by too many vaccinations, and 23 percent shared the sentiment that children receive more vaccinations than are healthy. There is every reason to think that those numbers—gathered before the vaccine-autism controversy reached anything like its current intensity—have risen since.

In the United States, population pockets with low vaccination rates (such as in Boulder, Colorado, and Ashland, Oregon) have existed for some time, and the great fear among many governmental medical authorities is that high-profile claims about vaccine dangers will widen the phenomenon, with potentially disastrous consequences. Already, medical and religious vaccination exemptions are climbing: In New York State they totaled 4,037 in 2006, nearly twice as many as in 1999. In New Jersey they came to 1,923 in 2006 versus only 727 in 1990. It is not just exemptors: The far larger concern, according to McCormick and others, is those parents referred to as "vaccine hesitaters." They have heard all the noise about vaccines and will probably get their children shots because they feel they have to, but their skepticism is growing.

Offit points to still another threat: litigation. The wave of autism-related claims filed with the U.S. government's Vaccine Injury Compensation Program is unprecedented. Since 2001 autism claims have outnumbered nonautism cases almost four to one. Following the science, the court has now dismissed many of them, but there is the possibility that civil litigation will follow. "I still think it's going to be another 10 years before this really washes out in litigation," Offit says. If the legal atmosphere becomes too difficult for vaccine manufacturers, they could stop producing them or be forced out of business.

Ultimately, that is why the vaccineautism saga is so troubling— and why it is so important to explore how science and so many citizens fell out of touch.

"It wouldn't have been possible without the Internet," says journalist Arthur Allen, who has covered the vaccine-autism story since 2002, when he wrote a high-profile *New York Times Magazine* article that took the thimerosal risk seriously. Over time Allen changed his mind, coming to reject the idea that vaccines are to blame. Still, he recognizes why it persists. "If people believe something happened to them, there are so many people on the Web you can find who believe the same thing." The Internet has become a haven for a number of autism support groups that continually reinforce the vaccine-autism argument. This has led to the radicalization of some elements who have denounced scientists as "vaccine barbarians," "pharmaceutical and medical killers," and so on. And after all we have heard about environmental and chemical risks—some accurate, some not—people are now easily persuaded about all manner of toxin dangers.

But if the Internet has made it easier for pockets of antiscience feeling to grow and flourish, scientific authorities also deserve some of the blame. "I don't think they woke up that this was a serious problem until maybe 2008," David Gorski says about the growing antivaccine sentiment. George Washington University's Hotez notes that "the office of the surgeon general, the secretary of Health and Human Services, and the head of the CDC have not been very vocal on this issue." True, the CDC, the Food and Drug Administration, and other governmental organizations feature accurate and up-to-date information about vaccine risks on their websites. But that is very different from launching a concerted communications campaign to ensure that the public retains faith in vaccination.

Some outspoken scientists may have actually increased the polarization on this issue. For example, calling those against vaccines "scientifically illiterate"—or, as CDC vaccine expert Stephen Cochi reportedly put it to one journalist, "junk scientists and charlatans"— may just lead to a further circling of the wagons.

The most promising approach to the vaccine-autism issue comes from the government itself. Consider the work of Roger Bernier, a CDC scientist who turned to emphasizing the public-engagement aspects of the vaccine problem after hearing one parent declare any new government research on the topic "dead on arrival." The central problem Bernier has confronted: how to deal with a situation in which so many parents are unswervingly convinced that their children have been harmed, in which they could be harming their children even more by using untested therapies, and in which dangerous misinformation abounds.

"There's no end to the kind of noise people can make about vaccines," he observes. "And so if you're in the vaccine community, what's the best approach to this? I don't think it is ignoring people." Instead, Bernier has headed up a series of award-winning projects that bring together average citizens with scientists and policymakers to reach joint recommendations on vaccines, holding public dialogues across the country to break down boundaries between the experts and everybody else, literally putting multiple perspectives around a table. His example suggests that while science's first and greatest triumph in this area was to develop vaccinations to control or eradicate many diseases, the challenge now—not yet achieved, and in some ways even more difficult—is to preserve public support for vaccine programs long after these scourges have largely vanished from our everyday lives.

"The problem is not only research," Bernier says. "The problem is trust."

CHRIS MOONEY will continue to report on the vaccineautism controversy on his blog. The Intersection, at blogs.discovermagazine.com/intersection.

From *Discover*, June, 2009, pp. 59–60, 62, 64, 65 and 75. Copyright © 2009 by Discover Syndication. Reprinted by permission via PARS International.

Long-Term Studies of Preschool: Lasting Benefits Far Outweigh Costs

Mr. Bracey and Mr. Stellar summarize the findings of three studies that provide strong evidence of long-term positive outcomes for high-quality preschool programs. All that remains now, they argue, is for the U.S. to make a commitment to universal, free preschool.

GERALD W. BRACEY AND ARTHUR STELLAR

The November 2001 issue of the *Kappan* contained a special section offering a cross-national perspective on early childhood education and day care. Day-care programs in England, Italy, and Sweden were described and contrasted with day care in the U.S. The other countries, especially Sweden, have coherent, comprehensive programs based on a set of assumptions about the positive outcomes of early education. In the U.S., by contrast, there is a "nonsystem." Sharon Lynn Kagan and Linda Hallmark wrote that, in the U.S., "not only has early childhood never been a national priority, but decades of episodic, on-again, off-again efforts have yielded a set of uncoordinated programs and insufficient investment in the infrastructure. Often, the most important components of high-quality education and care—financing, curriculum development, and teacher education—are neglected."[1]

According to Kagan and Hallmark, the U.S. has historically resisted major government intrusions into the early years of education because such intervention would signal a failure on the part of the family. This resistance has produced a vicious circle: parents resist government intervention in the education of young children on ideological grounds; the government, for its part, doesn't produce high-quality day care; parental resistance to government day care solidifies because of the low quality of the care. Today, the ideology that seeks to keep government out of family matters is still very much alive. David Salisbury of the Cato Institute put it this way: "The key to producing intelligent, healthy children does not lie in putting more of them in taxpayer-funded preschools. . . . Instead of forcing mothers into the workplace through heavy taxation, the government should reduce the tax burden on families and, thereby, allow child care to remain in the capable hands of parents."[2]

This view of day care is most unfortunate, as evidence is now strong that high-quality day care produces long-term

positive outcomes. Three studies of specific programs provide the evidence.

The "granddaddy" of these three studies is known as the High/Scope Perry Preschool Project.[3] In the mid-1960s, African American children whose parents had applied to a preschool program in Ypsilanti, Michigan, were randomly assigned to receive the program or not. Those who tested the children, interviewed the parents, or were the children's teachers once they reached school age did not know to which group the children had been assigned. Random assignment eliminates any systematic bias between the groups, although it cannot *guarantee* that they will be the same. By keeping the information on group assignment confidential, the experimenters sought to minimize any kind of Pygmalion effects stemming from expectations about the children who had been in preschool and those who had not. Few preschool programs existed at the time, and children in the control group remained at home.

Parents of the preschool children had completed an average of 9.4 years of school. Only 20% of the parents had high school diplomas, compared to 33% of all African American adults at the time of the study. The children attended preschool for a half day for eight months. The first group of children, entering in 1962, received one year of the preschool program; later groups received two. The program also included weekly, 90-minute home visits by members of the project staff.

The vision of childhood underlying the High/Scope Program was shaped by Piaget and other theorists who viewed children as active learners. Teachers asked questions that allowed children to generate conversations with them. Those who developed the program isolated 10 categories of preschool experience that they deemed important for developing children: creative representation, language and literacy, social relations and personal initiative, movement, music, classification, seriation (creating series and patterns), number, space, and time. Children participated in individual, small-and large-group activities. The curriculum and instruction flowed from both constructivist and cognitive/developmental approaches.[4]

Teachers rarely assessed the children's specific knowledge. This approach stood in marked contrast to another preschool curriculum, Direct Instruction (DI). DI attempts to impart specific bits of knowledge through rapid-fire drill and highly programmed scripts.

A study of the Perry preschoolers and controls at age 40 is in progress. Other studies took place when the subjects reached ages 19 and 27. At age 19, the preschoolers had higher graduation rates and were less likely to have been in special education. The graduation rate effect, though, was limited to females. The preschoolers also had higher scores on the Adult Performance Level Survey, a test from the American College Testing Program that simulates real-life problem situations.

By the time the two groups turned 27, 71% of the preschool group had earned high school diplomas or GEDs, compared to 54% of the control group. The preschoolers also earned more, were more likely to own their own homes, and had longer and more stable marriages. Members of the control group were arrested twice as often, and five times as many members of the control group (35%) had been arrested five or more times.

The second study is called the Abecedarian Project and has been run out of the University of North Carolina, Chapel Hill, since 1972.[5] The study identified children at birth and provided them full-day care, 50 weeks a year, from birth until they entered school. Adults would talk to the children, show them toys or pictures, and offer them opportunities to react to sights and sounds in the environment. As the children grew, these adult/child interactions became more concept and skill oriented. For older preschoolers, they also became more group oriented. Some children continued in the program until age 8, while another group of children began to receive an enrichment program after they started school.

Although the children were randomly assigned, it is important to note that children in the "control" group were not without assistance. To reduce the chances that any differences might come from nutritional deficiencies affecting brain growth, the researchers supplied an enriched baby formula. Social work and crisis intervention services were also available to families in the control group. If the researchers' assessments indicated that the children were lagging developmentally, the families were referred to a relevant social agency. As a consequence of these policies and services, four of the children in the control group were moved to the head of the waiting list for what the researchers called "scarce slots in other quality community child centers."

In the decade following the start of the Perry Project, early childhood education became more prevalent, especially in university areas like Chapel Hill. Thus some of the families in the control group sent their children to other preschool programs. It seems likely, therefore, that some children in the control group received benefits similar to those provided to the children in the experimental group. These benefits would tend to reduce the differences seen between experimental and control groups.

A 1988 follow-up study of the subjects at age 21 found that young adults who had taken part in the Abecedarian Project completed more years of schooling than the controls (12.2 versus 11.6). As with the Perry Project, this difference was most evident among the females in the study. More members of the experimental group were still in school (42% versus 20%), and more had enrolled in four-year colleges (35.9% versus 13.7%). Forty-seven percent of the experimental group worked at skilled jobs, such as electrician, compared to just 27% of the control group. The subjects who had attended the Abecedarian preschool were less likely to smoke or to use marijuana, but they were no less likely to use alcohol or to indulge in binge drinking.

The researchers administered reading and math tests at ages 8, 12, 15, and 21. Subjects who had been in the program for eight years showed much better reading skills than those in the control group. The "effect sizes" obtained for reading ranged from 1.04 at age 8 to .79 at age 21. Effect sizes for math ranged from .64 at age 8 to .42 at age 21. Judgment must be used in interpreting effect sizes, but all researchers would consider these to be large, with the possible exception of the .42 for math at age 21, which might be considered "medium."

For subjects who had terminated the program when they entered school, the reading effect sizes ran from .75 at age 8 to .28 at age 21. The impact of math for the same group actually grew over time, from .27 at age 8 to .73 at age 21. In general, it appears that participants who continued with the Abecedarian program into the elementary grades were affected more than those who stopped at the end of preschool.

Subjects who received the school-only program showed smaller effect sizes. For reading, the effect size was .28 at age 8 and dwindled to just .11 at age 21. Once again, math showed increased impact over time, from .11 at age 8 to .26 at age 21.

The third major long-term study of preschool outcomes is known as the Chicago Child-Parent Center Program (CPC).[6] It was a much larger study than the Perry or Abecedarian project, but the children were not randomly assigned to experimental and control groups. The CPC was also much more diffuse than the other projects, taking place in some 20 centers, and initially teachers had more latitude over what kinds of materials were incorporated. Later, all centers adopted a program developed through the Chicago Board of Education that emphasized three major areas: body image and gross motor skills, perceptual/motor and arithmetic skills, and language.

As with the other projects, extensive parent involvement was emphasized. Project staff members visited the homes of participants, and parents often accompanied children on field trips. In a 2000 follow-up study, subjects at age 21 who had taken part in the project had lower crime rates, higher high school completion rates, and fewer retentions in grade.

Quality Concerns

There is now some evidence to suggest that even diffuse programs that are broad in scope, such as Head Start, produce increases in high school graduation rates and in college attendance.[7] It seems clear, though, that high-quality programs are more effective. As laid out by Steven Barnett of Rutgers University, to be high quality, programs should have the following characteristics:

- low child/teacher ratios,
- highly qualified and well-paid teachers,
- intellectually rich and broad curricula,
- parents engaged as active partners with the program, and
- starting dates at or before the child reaches age 3.[8]

According to Kagan and Hallmark, many programs in the U.S. do not meet these criteria. Samuel Meisels of the Erikson Institute posits that the proposed "national reporting system" for Head Start will not bring such qualities to Head Start, either.[9] Indeed, Meisels worries that the system might reduce the quality of Head Start and psychologically damage children.

Costs and Benefits

The three preschool programs discussed here cost money, substantially more money than Head Start and even more than most preschools provided by private companies. The question arises as to whether the benefits from the programs are worth these costs. Cost-benefit analyses on all three conclude that they are.

A recent analysis of the Abecedarian Project by Leonard Masse and Steven Barnett of Rutgers University concluded that the benefit/cost ratio for the program was 4 to 1.[10] That is, society received four dollars in return for every dollar invested. This is not as high as analyses suggested for the Perry and Chicago projects. These yielded benefit/cost ratios on the order of 7 to 1. As we noted, though, a number of children in the Abecedarian project control groups attended some other preschools, and this could have reduced the differences between the groups.

Masse and Barnett estimated that children who took part in the program would earn $143,000 more over their lifetimes than those who did not. Their mothers would earn $133,000 more. The latter figure might surprise readers at first, but Masse and Barnett cite other studies finding that given stable, continuous child care, mothers are able to effectively reallocate their time to allow them to establish better, longer-term, and more productive relationships with employers.

Masse and Barnett also infer that the children of the children who participated in high-quality preschool programs will earn more as a consequence. Although it is difficult to quantify such projected earnings increases, they estimate a lifetime increase of $48,000 for the children of the participants. Although clearly conjectural, the logic is straightforward: the children who participated will experience outcomes, such as higher educational attainment, that are associated with higher earnings for future generations.

The cost-benefit analysts warn that these programs can be expensive. They estimated the cost of the Perry Project at $9,200 per child, per year, while the Abecedarian cost figure comes in at $13,900 (both estimates in constant 2002 dollars). This compares to $7,000 for Head Start. They worry that governments might experience "sticker shock" if they try to replicate these projects on a large-scale basis, but they caution that "costs alone offer little guidance. The costs of a program must

be compared against the benefits that the program generates. Benefit/cost ratios that are greater than one indicate that a program is worthy of consideration regardless of the absolute level of program costs."[11]

The programs described in this article all involved children living in poverty. Little if any research exists on long-term benefits for middle-class children. Masse and Barnett argue that, if we limit the programs to children under age 5 and assume that 20% of those children live in poverty, the annual cost for high-quality preschool for those 20% would be $53 billion per year.

Governments, however, appear to be looking at absolute costs. The Education Commission of the States reports that eight states have cut back on funds available for preschool in 2002–03. Moreover, today, in early 2003, state government budgets are in their worst shape since World War II. Still, sentiment for universal preschool is growing. After reviewing the evidence on the impact of early childhood education, the Committee for Economic Development led off a monograph as follows:

> The Committee for Economic Development (CED) calls on the federal and state governments to undertake a new national compact to make early education available to all children age 3 and over. To ensure that all children have the opportunity to enter school ready to learn, the nation needs to reform its current, haphazard, piecemeal, and underfunded approach to early learning by linking programs and providers to coherent state-based systems. The goal should be universal access to free, high-quality prekindergarten classes, offered by a variety of providers for all children whose parents want them to participate.[12]

Such a program makes much more sense to us than a program that tests all children in reading, math, and science in grades 3 through 8. Alas, Chris Dreibelbis of the CED reports that, while the CED monograph has been well received in both the education and business communities, there is little movement that might make its proposal a reality.[13]

Notes

1. Sharon L. Kagan and Linda G. Hallmark, "Early Care and Education Policies in Sweden: Implications for the United States," *Phi Delta Kappan*, November 2001, p. 241.

2. David Salisbury, "Preschool Is Overhyped," *USA Today*, 18 September 2002.

3. John R. Berrueta-Clement et al., *Changed Lives: The Effects of the Perry Preschool Program on Youths Through Age 19* (Ypsilanti, Mich.: High/ Scope Press, 1984); and Lawrence J. Schweinhart, Helen V. Barnes, and David P. Weikart, *Significant Benefits: The High/Scope Perry Preschool Study Through Age 27* (Ypsilanti, Mich.: High/Scope Press, 1993).

4. Mary Hohmann and David P. Weikart, *Educating Young Children: Active Learning Practices for Preschool and Child Care Programs* (Ypsilanti, Mich.: High/Scope Press, 1995).

5. Frances A. Campbell et al., "Early Childhood Education: Young Adult Outcomes for the Abecedarian Project," *Applied Developmental Science*, vol. 6, 2002, pp. 42–57; and

Frances A. Campbell, "The Development of Cognitive and Academic Abilities: Growth Curves from an Early Childhood Experiment," *Developmental Psychology*, vol. 37, 2001, pp. 231–42.

6. Arthur J. Reynolds et al., "Age 21 Benefit-Cost Analysis of the Chicago Child-Parent Center Program," paper presented to the Society for Prevention Research, Madison, Wis., 21 May–2 June 2001; and idem, "Long-Term Effects of an Early Childhood Intervention on Educational Achievement and Juvenile Arrest," *Journal of the American Medical Association*, 9 May 2001.

7. Eliana Garces, Duncan Thomas, and Janet Currie, "Longer Term Effects of Head Start," Working Paper No. 8054, National Bureau of Economic Research, December 2000, available at www.nber.org/papers/w8054; and Janet Currie and Duncan Thomas, "School Quality and the Longer-Term Effects of Head Start," *Journal of Human Resources*, Fall 2000, pp. 755–74.

8. W. Steven Barnett, "Early Childhood Education," in Alex Molnar, ed., *School Reform Proposals: The Research Evidence* (Greenwich, Conn.: Information Age Publishing, 2002),

available at www.asu.edu/educ/epsl. Click on Education Policy Research Unit, then, under "archives," click on "research and writing."

9. Samuel J. Meisels, "Can Head Start Pass the Test?," *Education Week*, 19 March 2003, p. 44.

10. Leonard N. Masse and W. Steven Barnett, *Benefit Cost Analysis of the Abecedarian Early Childhood Intervention Project* (New Brunswick, N.J.: National Institute for Early Childhood Research, Rutgers University, 2002).

11. Ibid., p. 14.

12. *Preschool for All: Investing in a Productive and Just Society* (New York: Committee for Economic Development, 2002), p. 1.

13. Personal communication, 3 February 2003.

GERALD W. BRACEY is an associate for the High/Scope Educational Research Foundation, Ypsilanti, Mich., and an associate professor at George Mason University, Fairfax, Va. He lives in the Washington, D.C., area. **ARTHUR STELLAR** is president and CEO, High/Scope Educational Research Foundation, Ypsilanti, Mich.

From *Phi Delta Kappan*, June 2003, pp. 780–783. Copyright © 2003 by Phi Delta Kappan. Reprinted by permission of Phi Delta Kappan and Gerald W. Bracey and Arthur Stellar.

How to Help Your Toddler Begin Developing Empathy

REBECCA PARIAKIAN AND CLAIRE LERNER

Empathy is the ability to imagine how someone else is feeling in a particular situation and respond with care. This is a very complex skill to develop. Being able to empathize with another person means that a child:

- Understands that he is a separate individual, his own person;
- Understands that others can have different thoughts and feelings than he has;
- Recognizes the common feelings that most people experience—happiness, surprise, anger, disappointment, sadness, etc.;
- Is able to look at a particular situation (such as watching a peer saying good-bye to a parent at child care) and imagine how he—and therefore his friend—might feel in this moment; and
- Can imagine what response might be appropriate or comforting in that particular situation—such as offering his friend a favorite toy or teddy bear to comfort her.

Understanding and showing empathy is the result of many social-emotional skills that are developing in the first years of life. Some especially important milestones include:

- Establishing a secure, strong, loving relationship with you. Feeling accepted and understood by you helps your child learn how to accept and understand others as he grows.
- Beginning to use social referencing, at about 6 months old. This is when a baby will look to a parent or other loved one to gauge his or her reaction to a person or situation. For example, a 7-month-old looks carefully at her father as he greets a visitor to their home to see if this new person is good and safe. The parent's response to the visitor influences how the baby responds. (This is why parents are encouraged to be upbeat and reassuring—not anxiously hover—when saying good-bye to children at child care. It sends the message that "this is a good place" and "you will be okay.") Social referencing, or being sensitive to a parent's reaction in new situations, helps the babies understand the world and the people around them.

- Developing a theory of mind. This is when a toddler (between 18 and 24 months old) first realizes that, just as he has his own thoughts, feelings and goals, others have their own thoughts and ideas, which may be different from his.
- Recognizing one's self in a mirror. This occurs between 18 and 24 months and signals that a child has a firm understanding of himself as a separate person.

What Can You Do: Nurturing Empathy in Your Toddler

Empathize with your child. *Are you feeling scared of that dog? He is a nice dog but he is barking really loud. That can be scary. I will hold you until he walks by.*

Talk about others' feelings. *Kayla is feeling sad because you took her toy car. Please give Kayla back her car and then you choose another one to play with.*

Suggest how children can show empathy. *Let's get Jason some ice for his boo-boo.*

Read stories about feelings. Some suggestions include:

- *I Am Happy: A Touch and Feel Book of Feelings* by Steve Light
- *My Many Colored Days* by Dr. Seuss
- *How Are You Peeling* by Saxton Freymann and Joost Elffers
- *Feelings* by Aliki
- *The Feelings Book* by Todd Parr
- *Baby Happy Baby Sad* by Leslie Patricelli
- *Baby Faces* by DK Publishing
- *When I Am/Cuando Estoy* by Gladys Rosa-Mendoza

Be a role model. When you have strong, respectful relationships and interact with others in a kind and caring way, your child learns from your example.

Use "I" messages. This type of communication models the importance of self-awareness: I don't like it when you hit me. It hurts.

Validate your child's difficult emotions. Sometimes when our child is sad, angry, or disappointed, we rush to try and fix it right away, to make the feelings go away because we want to protect him from any pain. However, these feelings are part of life and ones that children need to learn to cope with. In fact, labeling and validating difficult feelings actually helps children learn to handle them: *You are really mad that I turned off the TV. I understand. You love watching your animal show. It's okay to feel mad. When you are done being mad you can choose to help me make a yummy lunch or play in the kitchen while mommy makes our sandwiches.* This type of approach also helps children learn to empathize with others who are experiencing difficult feelings.

Use pretend play. Talk with older toddlers about feelings and empathy as you play. For example, you might have your child's stuffed hippo say that he does not want to take turns with his friend, the stuffed pony. Then ask your child: *How do you think pony feels? What should we tell this silly hippo?*

Think through the use of "I'm sorry." We often insist that our toddlers say "I'm sorry" as a way for them to take responsibility for their actions. But many toddlers don't fully understand what these words mean. While it may feel "right" for them to say "I'm sorry", it doesn't necessarily help toddlers learn empathy. A more meaningful approach can be to help children focus on the other person's feelings: *Chandra, look at Sierra—she's very sad. She's crying. She's rubbing her arm where you pushed her. Let's see if she is okay.* This helps children make the connection between the action (shoving) and the reaction (a friend who is sad and crying).

Be patient. Developing empathy takes time. Your child probably won't be a perfectly empathetic being by age three. (There are some teenagers and even adults who haven't mastered this skill completely either!) In fact, a big and very normal part of being a toddler is focusing on *me, mine,* and *I.* Remember, empathy is a complex skill and will continue to develop across your child's life.

Easing the Separation Process for Infants, Toddlers, and Families

Nancy Balaban

Seven-month-old Max sits on his mother's lap while she talks with Alice, Max's primary caregiver. She says good-bye, kisses Max, and hands him to Alice. Max bursts into tears. "Mommy will be back after your nap," Alice tells him.

They sit on the floor to look at Max's family pictures. "Oh, look, here's Mommy and Sandy, your dog. Woof-woof!" As Max begins to calm, Alice cuddles him and reads him his favorite book.

It's a common sight, one we see every day in child care centers and family child care homes. Families and children say goodbye in the morning and then say hello at the end of the day—a repeated demonstration that separation and attachment are two sides of the same coin; a daily declaration of love.

The Power of Attachment

Attachment and separation are the stuff of which life is made. Feelings about saying goodbye aren't restricted to child care situations. Separating from someone we love and care about is a lifelong experience that affects every one of us many times during the course of our lives. How many separation experiences has each of us had!

We begin life with a separation from our nine-month inner home. We leave home to go to school or camp or college. We graduate and leave again. We move to a new home, take a new job, go on a vacation trip. Some get married, some get divorced, and usually we all suffer the ultimate separation, the death of a loved one. The task of adjustment to these separations challenges us at every stage of life, from infancy on. Characteristic of all these experiences is leaving the familiar and heading into the unknown. Where would we be without the strength of our attachments?

The bonds between family and child promote resilience, self-regulation, and a positive sense of self. Because firm ties to another help us develop autonomy and the belief that we are lovable, it is critical to encourage and value strong attachments not only between children and parents, but also between teachers and the infants and toddlers they care for (Honig 2002a). If attachment is misunderstood as dependence, it may be wrongly discouraged.

Infants' and toddlers' trusting attachments to their teachers are critical in helping them cope with the stress of separation.

I saw an example of this recently. A director admonished a teacher for holding a two-year-old on her lap several times during the morning because "you are spoiling and babying the child."

Attachment Fosters Children's Development

We know a lot about attachment. According to Eliot (2000), babies are programmed to grow attached to their parents or primary caregivers due to development in their brain's frontal lobe. The attachment relationship "seems to be responsible for modulating stress. Attachment and brain development are a two-way street" (p. 311). Quality child care, in Eliot's view, is key in protecting babies' brains and emotional development.

In quality child care infants' and toddlers' trusting attachments to their teachers are critical in helping them cope with the stress of separation. Since stress can cause elevated levels of the hormone cortisol, a potential hazard to the brain, and since attachment seems to offer protection, we have another powerful reason to nurture and treasure our attachments with others.

Thanks to the seminal work of Ainsworth and Wittig (1969); Bowlby (1969); Mahler, Pine, and Bergman (1975), and a more recent explication by Honig (2002b), we understand that the young child's slow developmental journey leads to the creation of a person who is both attached to the parent yet separate—a paradox: bound yet free, close yet apart. This human dilemma has been defined as a "developmental necessity" (Resch 1977).

According to the theory of Margaret Mahler (Mahler, Pine, & Bergman 1975), children and their parents travel together through a series of developmental phases that enable the children, at around age three, to become certain that "I'm me and no one else." This process becomes partially observable, for example, around seven to nine months, when a baby may become fussy about going to anyone other than a parent. This can be hard on visiting grandparents, other relatives, or care-givers, and embarrassing to parents. However, this is really a baby's way of saying to the adult, "I love you, and I don't want to be messing around with anyone else." Baby and parent hopefully withstand this mild storm and then head together into toddlerhood, where the emotional weather gets a bit more turbulent.

It's exciting when a just-walking child, lured by enchant-ing sights and sounds, wanders off without a backward glance. But somewhere around 18 to 24 months, according to Mahler's theory, this runabout toddler becomes aware of her own vulner-ability: "Hey, wait a minute. I'm too little to be away from you too long; I can't take care of myself. I need you!" So parents, who have figured out how to give the toddler some rein with-out the bit, suddenly find this young wanderer clinging to their legs or climbing into their lap for what Mahler calls "emotional refueling."

It's at this point that parents as well as teachers must cope with toddlers' being pulled in two directions at once. One moment they strike out on their own ("I do it myself!"); then moments later they plop down in a lap, seeking security and safety. By negotiating this tempestuous time, parents and tod-dlers not only become separate from one another, but as long as the parent is a reliable, loving, secure base, the two also become more securely joined.

In some groups children develop attachments to several caregivers.

The Internal Parent

By the time most babies become toddlers, they are beginning to be able to hold in their minds an internal image of their attach-ment person or persons. My colleague Virginia Casper (pers. comm. 2005) calls this a "love memory." Imagine a grand-mother at an airport bidding her grandson goodbye. She can draw on the love memory of her grandson to alleviate the pain of parting, and he can do the same by thinking about her. Toddlers also try to rely on love memories for comfort, especially at the moment of separation. However, at a time of great stress, a still fragile love memory may not be available. As this dear memory image recedes, the toddler could feel as though the person has disappeared.

Here is an example. I was standing next to a two-year-old and his father, waiting for an elevator. When the elevator door opened, the father stepped in, assuming the child was following. But the door shut, leaving the child with me, a stranger. Scream-ing, the toddler threw himself on the floor. To him, his father had been swallowed alive. My assurance that "he's coming right back" did no good. Finally the elevator returned, miraculously spitting out his worried father and reuniting him with the terri-fied child. This example sheds light on the fragility of that inner image and why infants and toddlers need time and sensitivity to cope with the stress of separation.

Adults' experiences from their own childhood may influence their feelings about separation.

Variations in Attachment

While Mahler's theory of developmental phases is one among others, in your work you may see some aspects of the behaviors she describes. Although attachment to a secure base and the reac-tion to strangers are universal (Eliot 2000), there are variations on the theme. In some groups children develop attachments to several caregivers. For example, perhaps you have seen a toddler arrive at her familiar early care setting with an aunt and a cousin, as well as a grandparent in tow, and then bid goodbye to them all. While this may lessen the stress of separating within the familiar community group, it may make it difficult for the child to go to a stranger (Gonzalez-Mena 2005). At the other extreme, there are families who do not risk forming attachments with their babies due to living conditions of dire poverty and widespread infant mortality (Rogoff 2003; Gonzalez-Mena 2005).

Other factors come into play in the drama of attachment and separation. Consider temperament, which may influence the manner in which infants and toddlers react to separation (Kristal 2005). How adaptable is an infant to new situations? How eas-ily soothed when upset? How intense is a toddler in expressing emotions? These temperamental factors put a stamp on the way a child faces the world. Adults as well come with assorted tem-peraments that affect how they separate from their children. A parent might be wary in saying goodbye, while the child might be easygoing.

How teachers regard a child's temperament is another con-sideration. Teachers may be influenced by their own cultural socialization goals. A recent study found that in China teachers view shy, sensitive children as socially and academically com-petent, while in North America teachers are likely to view shy, sensitive children as lonely and depressed (Carlson, Feng, & Harwood 2004).

In early care programs we need to remember that adults' experiences from their own childhood may influence their feel-ings about separation. A parent was very tense bringing her son to the classroom, because her own long-ago early childhood experience involved a punitive teacher. She wrote,

> The pain of separation is not only from your child but from your own childhood. . . . The past lives on . . . the dangers that lurked in [my world] are simply nowhere to be found in [my son's]. I know that I can never get my childhood back, and still, when I enter his classroom, with its smell of milk and warm bodies, the adult veneer begins to crack. (Franks 1989)

Family circumstances—a new baby, a parent away from home for a period of time, a move to a new home, the death of a pet, marital stress or violence—also affect how children react to separation. Even a change in the family constellation can affect

Five Tips for Creating a Curriculum of Trust

1. Use a primary caregiving system in which each early care teacher forms a miniature family group of three or four children, focusing on routines like feeding, changing, napping, and playing (Baker & Manfredi/Petitt 2004). Although the caregiver-child relationship is close, it is not exclusive. The best system relies on the cooperation and mutual helpfulness of the caregiving team. If a teacher is comforting a baby and another child from her primary group requires attention, the teacher needs to know that another staff member will pitch in to help.

   The primary caregiver provides a secure base for the child and the family. The relationship eases a child's anxiety and reassures the family not only during the transition from home to center care, but throughout the whole of the child's stay. Primary caregiving has been described as being "best for everyone involved" (Bernhardt 2000, 74).

2. Institute a gradual easing into the program for the family and child together. A slow entry process gives the child time to adjust, the parent time to know the early care teacher, and the teacher time to know the child and family. Many programs invite a family member and the child to stay only a short time on the child's first day and then increase the time each day for two or three days, until the adult says, "Goodbye, I'll be back later," and the teacher supports the separation.

   Programs must explain the purpose of the plan for gradual adjustment to families before they enter. An easing-in process isn't simple when a parent must go to work, but trying to facilitate it is worth the effort. The payback is a happy child and a trusting parent.

3. Be there to support the everyday goodbyes. Hugging, kissing, crying, waving at the window or door, saying "I love you"—all allow feelings to come out in the open. Emphasizing that Mom or Dad or Grandma will be back is very important, because young children are not always sure that is so. Since separation is a central concern in early childhood, teacher support may be required throughout the year. When teachers form a secure base with children, children are able to explore and learn.

   Research shows that the quality of early relationships with teachers is an important predictor of children's future social relations with peers and their later school satisfaction and achievement (Howes & Ritchie 2002). Teachers and caregivers are important people.

4. Anticipate and be prepared for regressions or shifts in behavior during a child's first weeks in the program. For example, a toddler who is toilet trained may lose control during the separation period. An easygoing baby may cling like Velcro to the parent. One child may increase thumb sucking, another may bite or hit occasionally, while others may resist going to sleep, refuse to eat, have frequent tantrums, or begin waking at night at home. Knowing that these behaviors may occur enables teachers to be accepting when a child hits. Saying "He doesn't like it when you hit, so let's find another toy for you" establishes the child's trust in a teacher who is there to help.

5. Offer children tangible reminders of their parents, such as photographs or a favorite toy or blanket. Provide books about hello and goodbye, play peekaboo games (Szamreta 2003), use important words from a child's home language, and ensure consistent classroom routines.

a child (Kristal 2005), as happened for a 23-month-old who had been secure in early care for over a year:

> Amanda's father brought her to the center accompanied by her grandparents, freshly arrived from China. They were there to help her mother, who was about to give birth. Amanda was engrossed at the water table but became frantic as the three family members began to leave without saying goodbye. Her father held her for a long time while she sobbed. The abrupt departure, the new family arrangement, plus the impending birth affected Amanda's usual ability to separate.

Children with Special Needs

Although children with special needs or disabilities are as attached to their parents as most children, they may experience a delay in the expression of their separation reactions (Foley 1986), and their cues may be subtle or difficult to read. A study of separation reactions in children with mild retardation, ages three to five years, with developmental ages one-and-a-half to two-and-a-half, revealed that the children did not give strong clues to their feelings (Kessler, Ablon, & Smith 1969). Their regressive behavior was often attributed to the retardation itself, and their aimless running around to hyperactivity rather than separation reactions. The teachers encouraged the children's responses to separation by talking about where their mothers were, what the mothers were doing, and when they were coming back. When the teachers also helped parents recognize that their children's behavior reflected feelings of anxiety about separation, the mothers began to understand the depth of their children's attachment.

Children with special needs may be put on a school bus without due consideration for their feelings about separating from their families and connecting to new teachers. In a program for two-year-olds with cerebral palsy, the teachers seldom saw the families because the children arrived by bus. One boy spent a lot of time crying, refusing the teacher's attention. Sensing that he missed his family, the teacher asked his mother to ride the bus with him and come into the classroom. Her short visits and time on the bus gave her son the security he needed to sustain the separation. The staff were able to help him by reflecting his feelings, saying, "I know you miss your mom, but you'll see her soon when the bus takes you home after school."

In another early intervention program, teachers encouraged families to use a predictable daily ritual for saying goodbye—for example, a kiss, a hug, and a high-five, always in the same order. Teachers and families sent a "communication book" back and forth daily, between center and home, in which each wrote facts important for the other to know.

The Effects of Culture

Cultural preferences may influence how some separations take place. In a small study of mothers' preferences in toddler attachment behaviors, Anglo mothers disliked clinginess and preferred their children playing at a distance. Puerto Rican mothers, on the other hand, preferred their toddlers to sit close by and display respectfulness (Harwood & Miller 1991). As teachers, we need to understand the importance of cultural beliefs and what separation means to families of diverse cultures.

Another study that included a small group of young Korean American children revealed that the children were taught by their families that it is a virtue to hide their feelings and to show deference to teachers (Chu 1978). Their teachers were not Korean American, so we must wonder what the teachers thought. Did they think the children didn't miss their families because they didn't cry? Or did the teachers think that the children's self-control was a sign of precocious maturity? Did the teachers know that Korean culture values undemonstrative behavior?

The challenge for early care teachers is to understand that a family's point of view about raising their child is valid for that family as long as it does no harm. There is abundant information to help teachers understand the variety of familial and cultural beliefs that exist (see "Resources on Different Cultural Approaches to Childrearing"). However, we can learn from families themselves, if we listen well and do not rush to judge practices that are different from our own. It is more respectful to say "Please tell me how you [bathe/feed/give guidance to/toilet train] your child" than to share our ideas of the "correct" way. We need to listen and learn, even if what we hear makes us uncomfortable (such as "I put her on the potty starting at three months"). While an accepting attitude takes considerable practice and requires the support of others, it can forge strong teacher-family relationships.

A Curriculum of Trust

By developing a curriculum of trust, teachers can help infants and toddlers, when away from their families in early care, to achieve well-being and comfort as well as the ability to learn (see "Five Tips for Creating a Curriculum of Trust"). Recognition that separation reactions in young children can be expected and are valid provides an unparalleled contribution to children's development. It is you—early care teachers—who can show children and families that participation in a quality early care and education program is a unique opportunity for children's growth. When teachers and caregivers ease the separation process by building trust, they help children build competence, confidence, and self-assurance.

Resources on Different Cultural Approaches to Childrearing

Carlson, V. J., & R.L. Harwood. Dec 1999/ Jan 2000. Understanding and negotiating cultural differences concerning early developmental competence: The six raisin solution. *Zero to Three.* Adapted version online: www.zerotothree.org/vol20-3.html#six-solution.

Gonzalez-Mena, J. 2005. Attachment and separation. In *Diversity in early care and education,* 4th ed., 79–91. New York: McGraw-Hill.

Gonzalez-Mena, J. 2005. A framework for understanding differences. In *Diversity in early care and education,* 4th ed., 61–77. New York: McGraw-Hill.

Gonzalez-Mena, J., & N. Bhavnagri. 2000. Diversity and infant/toddler caregiving. *Young Children* 55 (5): 31–35.

Harkness, S., & C.M. Super, eds. 1996. Parental theories in the management of young children's sleep in Japan, Italy, and the United States. In *Parents' cultural belief systems: Their origins, expressions, and consequences,* 364–84. New York: Guilford.

References

Ainsworth, M.D.S., & B.A. Wittig. 1969. Attachment and exploratory behavior of one-year-olds in a strange situation. In *Determinants of infant behavior,* ed. B.M. Foss, 111–36. London: Methuen.

Baker, A.C., & L.A. Manfredi/Petitt. 2004. *Relationships, the heart of quality care: Creating community among adults in early care settings.* Washington, DC: NAEYC.

Balaban, N. 2006. *Everyday goodbyes: Starting school and early care—A guide to the separation process.* New York: Teachers College Press.

Bernhardt, J.L. 2000. A primary caregiving system for infants and toddlers: Best for everyone involved. *Young Children* 55 (2): 74–80.

Bowlby, J. 1969. *Attachment and loss. Volume I: Attachment.* New York: Basic Books.

Carlson, V.J., X. Feng, & R.L. Harwood. 2004. The "ideal baby": A look at the intersection of temperament and culture. *Zero to Three* 24 (4): 22–28. Cited in Balaban 2006, 64.

Chu, H. 1978. The Korean learner in an American school. In *Teaching for cross-cultural understanding.* Arlington, VA: Arlington Public Schools. Cited in Farver, Kim, & Lee 1995, 1097.

Eliot, L. 2000. *What's going on in there? How the brain and mind develop in the first five years.* New York: Bantam.

Farver, J.A.M., Y.K. Kim, & Y. Lee. 1995. Cultural differences in Korean- and Anglo-American preschoolers' social interaction and play behaviors. *Child Development* 66: 1088–99.

Foley, G. 1986. Emotional development of children with handicaps. In *The feeling child: Affective development reconsidered,* ed. N. Curry, 57–73. New York: Haworth Press. Cited in Balaban 2006, 66.

Franks, L. 1989. Hers: The little red chair. *New York Times,* March 12, Late City Final Edition, Sec. 6.

Gonzalez-Mena, J. 2005. *Diversity in early care and education: Honoring differences.* Rev. ed. New York: McGraw-Hill.

Harwood, R., & J.G. Miller. 1991. Perceptions of attachment behavior: A comparison of Anglo and Puerto Rican mothers. *Merrill-Palmer Quarterly* 37 (4): 583–99.

Honig, A.S. 2002a. Attachment to early childhood caregivers. In *Secure relationships: Nurturing infant/toddler attachment in early care settings,* 21–38. Washington, DC: NAEYC.

Honig, A.S. 2002b. *Secure relationships: Nurturing infant/toddler attachment in early care settings.* Washington, DC: NAEYC.

Howes, C., & S. Ritchie. 2002. *A matter of trust: Connecting teachers and learners in the early childhood classroom.* New York: Teachers College Press.

Kessler, J.W., G. Ablon, & E. Smith. 1969. Separation reactions in young, mildly retarded children. *Children* 16: 2–7.

Kristal, J. 2005. *The temperament perspective: Working with children's behavioral styles.* Baltimore, MD: Brookes.

Mahler, M.S., F. Pine, & A. Bergman. 1975. *The psychological birth of the human infant: Symbiosis and individuation.* New York: Basic Books.

Resch, R. 1977. On separating as a developmental phenomenon: A natural study. *Psychoanalytic Contemporary Science* 5: 197–269.

Rogoff, B. 2003. *The cultural nature of human development.* New York: Oxford University Press.

Szamreta, J.M. 2003. Peekaboo power to ease separation and build secure relationships. *Young Children* 58 (1): 88–94.

NANCY BALABAN, EdD, is on the faculty of the Infant and Parent Development and Early Intervention program in the Bank Street Graduate School of Education, New York City. She is the author of many articles and a recent book about separation, *Everyday Goodbyes: Starting School and Early Care—A Guide to the Separation Process.*

Accountability Comes to Preschool

Can We Make It Work for Young Children?

Early childhood educators are justifiably concerned that demands for academic standards in preschool will result in developmentally inappropriate instruction that focuses on a narrow set of isolated skills. But Ms. Stipek believes that teaching preschoolers basic skills can give them a good foundation for their school careers, and she shows that it is possible to do this in ways that are both effective and enjoyable.

DEBORAH STIPEK

Pressures to raise academic achievement and to close the achievement gap have taken a firm hold on elementary and secondary schools. Now, preschools are beginning to feel the heat. Testing for No Child Left Behind isn't required until third grade. But as elementary schools ratchet up demands on children in the early grades and as kindergarten becomes more academic, children entering school without basic literacy and math skills are at an increasingly significant disadvantage.

Accountability is also beginning to enter the preschool arena. Both the House and Senate versions of the Head Start reauthorization bill require the development of educational performance standards based on recommendations of a National Academy of Sciences panel. Head Start programs would then be held accountable for making progress toward meeting these goals, and their funding would be withdrawn after some period of time if they failed. States and districts are likely to follow with initiatives designed to ensure that children in publicly funded early childhood education programs are being prepared academically to succeed in school.

There are good reasons for the increased attention to academic skills in preschool, especially in programs serving economically disadvantaged children. Children from low-income families enter kindergarten on average a year to a year and a half behind their middle-class peers in terms of school readiness. And the relatively poor cognitive skills of low-income children at school entry predict poor achievement in the long term. Meredith Phillips, James Crouse, and John Ralph estimated in a meta-analysis that about half of the total black/white gap in math and reading achievement at the end of high school is explained by the gap between blacks and whites at school entry.[1] Preschool education can give children from economically disadvantaged homes a better chance of succeeding in school by contributing to their cognitive skills. Moreover, all young children are capable of learning far more than is typically believed, and they enjoy the process.

Until recently, kindergarten was a time for children to *prepare* for school. Today, it *is* school.

This new focus on academic preparation will undoubtedly have significant implications for the nature of preschool programs, and it could have negative consequences. Until recently, kindergarten was a time for children to *prepare* for school. Today, it *is* school—in most places as focused on academic skill as first grade used to be. Will the same thing happen to preschool? We need to think hard about how we will balance the pressure to prepare young children academically with their social/emotional needs. How will we increase young children's academic skills without undermining their enthusiasm for learning or reducing the attention we give to the many other domains of development that are important for their success?

The early childhood education community has resisted a focus on academic skills primarily because experts are worried that it will come in the form of whole-group instruction, rigid pacing, and repetitive, decontextualized tasks—the kind of "drill and kill" that is becoming commonplace in the early elementary grades and that is well known to suffocate young children's natural enthusiasm for learning. My own recent observations in preschools suggest that these concerns are well founded.

I am seeing children in preschool classrooms counting by rote to 10 or 20 in a chorus. When I interview the children, many have no idea what an 8 or a 10 is. They can't tell me, for example, how many cookies they would have if they started with 7 and I gave them one more, or whether 8 is more or less than 9. I am seeing children recite the alphabet, call out letters shown on flashcards, and identify letter/ sound connections on worksheets (e.g., by drawing a line from a *b* to a picture of a ball). Some can read the word *mop* but have no idea that they are referring to a tool for cleaning floors, and they are not able to retell in their own words a simple story that had been read to them.[2] I am seeing young children recite by rote the days of the week and the months of the year while the teacher points to the words written on the board—without any understanding of what a week or a month is and without even a clear understanding that the written words the teacher points to are connected to the words they are saying. In these classrooms every child in the class gets the same task or is involved in the same activity, despite huge variability in their current skill levels. Some children are bored because they already know what is being taught; others are clueless.

Alternatives to Drill and Kill

The good news is that young children can be taught basic skills in ways that engage rather than undermine their motivation to learn. Motivating instruction must be child-centered—adapted to the varying skills and interests of children.

Good teachers embed instruction in activities that make sense to young children. They teach vocabulary, for example, by systematically using and reinforcing the meaning of new words in the context of everyday activities. When children are blowing bubbles, the teacher might introduce different descriptive terms (e.g., "shimmer") or names of shapes (e.g., "oval" versus "round"). Teachers promote oral language by reading stories, encouraging story making, joining in role play, asking children to explain how things work, giving children opportunities to share experiences, helping them to expand what they say, and introducing and reinforcing more complex sentence structures. Comprehension and analytic skills can be developed by reading to children and asking them to predict what will happen next and to identify patterns and draw conclusions. Print awareness is promoted by creating a book area, having materials and other things in the classroom labeled, and pointing out features of books being read to children. Phonics can be taught through songs, rhyming games, and language play. Early writing skills can be encouraged and developed in the context of pretend play (e.g., running a restaurant or post office) and by having children dictate stories or feelings to an adult and gradually begin to write some of the words themselves.

> **Good teachers are busy asking questions, focusing children's attention, helping them document and interpret what they see, and providing scaffolds and suggestions.**

Young children develop basic number concepts best by actively manipulating objects, not by rote counting.[3] Mathematics, like literacy, can be learned in the context of playful activities. A pretend restaurant can provide many opportunities for learning math. Children can match one straw for each glass for each person, count out amounts to pay for menu items (five poker chips for a plastic pizza,

four chips for a glass of apple juice, and so on), tally the number of people who visit the restaurant, or split the pizza between two customers. Questions about relative quantities (less and more, bigger and smaller) can be embedded in restaurant activities and conversations. (Who has *fewer* crackers or *more* juice left in her glass?) Children can categorize and sort objects (e.g., put all the large plates on this shelf and the tall glasses on the shelf below). Measurement of weight and even a basic notion of fractions can be learned by cooking for the restaurant (a half cup of milk, a quarter cup of sugar); volume can be learned by pouring water from measuring cups into larger containers.

Effective teaching of young children cannot be delivered through a one-size-fits-all or scripted instructional program, in part because teachers need to be responsive to children's individual skills and interests. Good teachers know well what each child knows and understands, and they use that knowledge to plan appropriate and varied learning opportunities. For example, whereas one child may dictate a few sentences to the teacher for his journal each day, another might actually write some of the words herself. While some children are asked to count beans by ones, others are asked to count them by twos or by fives.

Teaching in the kinds of playful contexts mentioned above can be direct and explicit. Young children are not left to their own devices—to explore aimlessly or to invent while the teacher observes. To the contrary, effective and motivating teaching requires a great deal of active teacher involvement. Teachers need to have clear learning goals, plan activities carefully to achieve those goals, assess children's learning regularly, and make modifications when activities are not helping children learn.

Good teachers are busy asking questions, focusing children's attention, helping them document and interpret what they see, and providing scaffolds and suggestions. Which object do you think will float, the small metal ball or the block of wood? Why do you think the wood floated and the ball didn't, even though the wood block is bigger? On the paper, let's put an "F" for float after the pictures of the objects that float and an "S" after the pictures of the objects that sink. Then we can look at our summary of findings to figure out how the floating objects and the sinking objects are different from each other. Teachers need to assess children's understanding and skill levels both informally—as they listen to children's replies and comments during classroom activities—and more formally—interacting with each child individually for a few minutes every few weeks. And teachers need to use what they learn from their assessments to plan instructional interventions that will move *each child* from where he or she is to the next step.

Effective teachers also maintain children's enthusiasm for learning by being vigilant and seizing opportunities to use children's interests to teach. I once observed a brilliant teacher turn a child's comment about new shoes (which most teachers would have found distracting) into a multidisciplinary lesson. She asked the students to take off one shoe and use it to measure the length of their leg, from their waist to their ankle. Some had to learn how to find their waist and ankle to accomplish the task (physiology and vocabulary). They also had to count each time they turned the shoe and keep track of where they ended up (math). The teacher then led a conversation about who had the longest and the shortest leg (comparisons). Then they measured arms and talked about whether arms were shorter or longer than legs and by how much (introduction to subtraction and idea of averages). The conversation finally turned to other objects that could be used as measuring instruments.

This teacher didn't always rely on spontaneous teaching opportunities. She had a very well-planned instructional program. But she also took good advantage of children's interests and seized opportunities to build academic lessons out of them.

Beyond Academic Skills

Ironically, to achieve high academic standards, we need to be more, not less, concerned about the nonacademic aspects of children's development. Children's social skills and dispositions toward learning, as well as their emotional and physical well-being, directly affect their academic learning.

Fortunately, efforts to promote development on important nonacademic dimensions need not reduce the amount of time children spend learning academic skills. As I describe below, efforts to support positive social, emotional, and physical development can be embedded in the academic instructional program and the social climate of the classroom.

Social skills. Children who have good social skills—who are empathic, attentive to others' needs, helpful, respectful, and able to engage in sustained social interactions—achieve academically at a higher level than children who lack social skills or are aggressive.[4] The higher achievement results in part because children who are socially adept develop positive relationships with teachers and peers. They are motivated to work hard to please their teachers, and they feel more comfortable and secure in the classroom. Aggressive and disruptive children develop conflictual relationships with teachers and peers and spend more time being disciplined (and thus less time engaged in academic tasks).

Social skills can be taught in the context of classroom routines and activities designed to teach academic skills. Lessons about appropriate social behavior can be provided as stories that are read to children and discussed. Opportunities to develop skills in collaboration can be built into tasks and activities designed to teach literacy and math skills. Teachers can encourage children to develop social problem-solving skills when interpersonal conflicts arise by helping them solve the problem themselves—"Is there another way you could have let Sam know that you wanted to play with the airplane?"—rather than solving the problem for them—"Sam, give the airplane to Jim. It's his turn."

A program called "Cool Tools," designed to promote social and academic skills, begins with preschoolers at the UCLA laboratory elementary school—the Corinne A. Seeds University Elementary School. Children create an alphabet that decorates the walls of their classroom: "S" is for "share," "K" is for "kindness," "H" is for "help," "C" is for "cooperation." Teachers also take advantage of events in the world and in the community. Following the tsunamis in Southeast Asia, the children made lists of what survivors might need. They donated the coins they had collected for their study of money in mathematics to a fund for survivors, and they made muffins and granola and sold them to parents and friends to raise additional funds. Thus literacy and math instruction, and a little geography, were embedded in activities designed to promote feelings of responsibility and generosity.

Dispositions toward learning. Children's beliefs about their ability to learn also affect their learning. Children who develop perceptions of themselves as academically incompetent and expect

to fail don't exert much effort on school tasks, and they give up as soon as they encounter difficulty. Engagement in academic tasks is also affected by students' sense of personal control. Children enjoy schoolwork less and are less engaged when they feel they are working only because they have to, not because they want to.[5]

Luckily, much is known about practices that foster feelings of competence and expectations for success. These beliefs are not "taught" directly. Rather, they are influenced by the nature and difficulty level of the tasks children are asked to complete and by the kind of evaluation used and the nature of the feedback they receive. Children's self-confidence is maintained by working on tasks that require some effort (so that when they complete them they have a sense of satisfaction and achievement). However, the tasks must not be so difficult that the children cannot complete them even if they try. The huge variability in children's skill levels is why rigidly paced instruction is inappropriate; if all children are asked to do the same task, it will invariably be too easy (and thus boring) for some students or too difficult (and thus discouraging) for others.

Classroom climate is also important. Self-confidence is engendered better in classrooms in which all children's academic achievements are celebrated than in classrooms in which only the best performance is praised, rewarded, or displayed on bulletin boards. Effective teachers encourage and praise children for taking on challenges and persisting when they run into difficulty, and they invoke no negative consequences for failure. ("You didn't get it this time, but I bet if you keep working on these kinds of problems, by lunch, you'll have figured out how to do them.")

The nature of evaluation also matters. Evaluation that tells children what they have learned and mastered and what they need to do next, rather than how their performance compares to that of other children, fosters self-confidence and high expectations. ("You are really good at consonants, but it looks like you need to practice vowels a little more.") All children can learn and will stay motivated if they see their skills developing, but only a few can perform better than their peers, and many will become discouraged if they need to compete for rewards.

We also know how to foster a feeling of autonomy. Clearly children cannot be given carte blanche to engage in any activity they want and be expected to master a set of skills and understandings adults believe to be important. But children can be given choices in what they do and how and when they do it, within a constrained set of alternatives. Even modest choices (whether to use beans or chips for a counting activity; which puzzle to work on) promote interest and engagement in learning.[6]

Emotional well-being and mental health. Children's emotional well-being and mental health (a clear and positive sense of the self; a positive, optimistic mood; the ability to cope with novel and challenging situations) have an enormous impact on how well they learn. Students who are depressed, anxious, or angry are not effective learners. Feeling disrespected, disliked, or disconnected from the social context can also promote disengagement—from academic work in the short term and, eventually for many students, from school altogether. Paying close attention to the social and emotional needs of students and creating a socially supportive environment can go a long way toward promoting social/emotional and mental well-being. It can also reduce the need for special services.

Substantial research suggests that the school social climate is also critical to mental health. A respectful and caring social context that ensures close, personal relationships with adults, that is orderly and predictable, and that promotes feelings of self-determination and autonomy in students can contribute substantially to students' emotional well-being. Peers affect the social context as much as teachers, and thus they have to be taught the effects of their behavior on other children. The "Cool Tools" program, for example, teaches 4-year-olds about "put-ups" and "put-downs," noting that it takes five put-ups to repair one put-down. Children also play games that illustrate how the same comment can be heard differently, depending on the volume and tone of voice and body posture.

Physical development. Lack of exercise and consumption of too much sugar are two behaviors that have immediate negative effects on children's ability to focus on academic work. We need to provide children with opportunities—such as outdoor play time and healthy snacks—to engage in positive behavior while they are at school. And we need to help them develop healthy habits—such as brushing teeth, washing hands, and exercising—that will contribute to their well-being.

Teachers can talk to children about how exercise affects their bodies in the context of a science lesson on physiology. (Why do we need a heart? How are muscles different from fat?) And compelling and visible messages can be given through science experiments, such as observing what happens to two pieces of bread several days after one piece was touched with a dirty hand and the other with a clean one.

Programs serving children from low-income families should also make an effort to work with community agencies to ensure access to dentists and physicians. Even a trip to the doctor or dentist can be used to promote academic skills. Children can develop communication skills by being asked to describe their experience, they can learn vocabulary, and they can develop the cultural knowledge that we now know is necessary for becoming a proficient reader. (It's hard to make sense of a sentence with the word "stethoscope" in it if you've never seen one used.)

Educating Children

Educational leaders need to take seriously the accountability demands made on them. By paying more attention to academic skills in preschool, we can help close the achievement gap, and we can give all children a chance to expand their intellectual skills. But we need to avoid teaching strategies that take all the joy out of learning. This will not, in the end, help students achieve the high standards being set for them.

We also need to resist pressures to prepare children only to perform on tests that assess a very narrow set of academic outcomes. Attention to other domains of development is also important if we want children to be effective learners as well as effective citizens and human beings. Policy makers should demand that if assessments for accountability are to be used in early childhood programs, they measure genuine understanding and the nonacademic skills and dispositions that we want teachers to promote. We have learned from No Child Left Behind that, if the tools used for accountability focus on a narrow set of skills, so will the educational program.

Finally, teaching young children effectively takes a great deal of skill. If we want teachers to promote students' learning and motivation, we need to invest in their training. States vary considerably in their credentialing requirements for early childhood education teachers. Few require a sufficient level of training. On-the-job opportunities for collegial interactions focused on teaching and learning and professional development are also critical. Preschools that are good learning environments for adults are likely to be good learning environments for children.

An investment in preschool education could help us achieve the high academic standards to which we aspire. Let's make sure we provide it in a way that does more good than harm.

Notes

1. Meredith Phillips, James Crouse, and John Ralph, "Does the Black-White Test Score Gap Widen After Children Enter School?," in Christopher Jencks and Meredith Phillips, eds., *The Black-White Test Score Gap* (Washington, D.C.: Brookings Institution Press, 1998), pp. 229–72.

2. A story recounted to me by a researcher who was assessing a young child's reading skill illustrates what can happen if decoding is overemphasized. The child read a brief passage flawlessly but was unable to answer a simple question about what he had read. He complained to the researcher that he had asked him to read the passage, not to understand it. Clearly this child had learned that reading was synonymous with decoding sounds.

3. See, for example, Barbara Bowman, M. Suzanne Donovan, and M. Susan Burns, eds., *Eager to Learn: Educating Our Preschoolers* (Washington, D.C.: National Academy Press, 2001); and Douglas Clements, Julie Sarama, and Ann-Marie DiBiase, *Engaging Young Children in Mathematics: Standards for Early Childhood Mathematics Education* (Mahwah, N.J.: Erlbaum, 2003).

4. See, for example, David Arnold, "Co-Occurrence of Externalizing Behavior Problems and Emergent Academic Difficulties in Young High-Risk Boys: A Preliminary Evaluation of Patterns and Mechanisms," *Journal of Applied Developmental Psychology,* vol. 18, 1997, pp. 317–30; Nancy Eisenberg and Richard A. Fabes, "Prosocial Development," in William Damon and Nancy Eisenberg, eds., *Handbook of Child Psychology,* 5th ed., vol. 3 (New York: Wiley, 1997), pp. 701–78.

5. For a review, see Deborah Stipek, *Motivation to Learn: Integrating Theory and Practice,* 4th ed. (Needham Heights, Mass.: Allyn & Bacon, 2002).

6. See, for example, Leslie Gutman and Elizabeth Sulzby, "The Role of Autonomy-Support Versus Control in the Emergent Writing Behaviors of African-American Kindergarten Children," *Reading Research & Instruction,* vol. 39, 2000, pp. 170–83; and Richard Ryan and Jennifer La Guardia, "Achievement Motivation Within a Pressured Society: Intrinsic and Extrinsic Motivations to Learn and the Politics of School Reform," in Timothy Urdan, ed., *Advances in Motivation and Achievement: A Research Annual,* vol. II (Greenwich, Conn.: JAI Press, 1999), pp. 45–85.

DEBORAH STIPEK is a professor of education and dean of the School of Education at Stanford University, Stanford, Calif.

"Early Sprouts"
Establishing Healthy Food Choices for Young Children

Karrie A. Kalich, Dottie Bauer, and Deirdre McPartlin

Four-year-old Tyler and 5-year-old Cole eagerly tear the shiny green leaves of rainbow chard into small pieces to use in today's recipe: Cheesy Chard Squares. Earlier in the week the children harvested some chard from the play-yard garden and cut up the stalks with scissors. They sampled each of the different colors and talked about the similarities and differences.

It is late in the harvest season, and while they work, Janet, their teacher, discusses plans for next year's garden with the children. Cole wants to plant tomatoes. Tyler suggests cucumbers. Both children agree they want to grow rainbow chard again. They mix together several eggs, grate the cheese, and combine the ingredients in preparation for baking. Tyler announces, "I'm going to eat these squares for dinner!"

The preschool years are a critical period for the development of food preferences and lifelong eating habits. Between the ages of 2 and 5, children become increasingly responsive to external cues, such as television commercials that use popular cartoon characters to advertise foods, candy in supermarket checkout aisles, and fast-food restaurants offering a free toy with the purchase of a kid's meal. These environmental messages influence children's decisions about what and how much they should eat (Birch & Fisher 1995; Fisher & Birch 1999; Rolls, Engell, & Birch 2000). By the age of 5, most children have lost their innate ability to eat primarily in response to hunger (Rolls, Engell, & Birch 2000; Haire-Joshu & Nanney 2002) and have learned to prefer calorie-rich foods (high fat and high sugar)—foods often used as a reward or for comfort in American society.

Some adults offer children healthy foods, such as fruits and vegetables, in a negative or coercive manner. But vegetables become less appealing if children must finish them prior to having dessert or leaving the dinner table (Birch & Fisher 1996). Using a positive approach to foster healthy eating behaviors helps young children develop lifelong habits that decrease the risk of obesity and other related chronic diseases.

Nutrition and Young Children

The current obesity epidemic in the United States is a fast-growing public health concern. For preschool-age children the prevalence of obesity has more than doubled in the past 30 years (CCOR 2006). Traditionally, early childhood educators have focused on the importance of meeting young children's nutritional requirements (Marotz 2009). With the increase in childhood obesity, there is a new call to early childhood educators to guide children and families in developing healthy eating and activity habits.

What we know now is that a diet rich in fruits and vegetables is recommended for achieving or maintaining a healthy body weight. The USDA (U.S. Department of Agriculture) recommends that preschool-age children eat 3 to 5 half-cup servings of vegetables and 2 to 4 half-cup servings of fruit daily (www.mypyramid.gov). However, on the average, preschool children consume approximately 2 servings of vegetables and 1.5 servings of fruit each day. Their diets are typically low in fruits, vegetables, and whole grains and high in saturated fat, sodium, and added sugar (Enns, Mickle, & Goldman 2002; Guenther et al. 2006). In fact, studies have consistently shown that the diets of U.S. children do not meet national dietary recommendations (Gleason & Suitor 2001; U.S. Department of Health and Human Services & U.S. Department of Agriculture 2005). While children ages 2 to 5 have somewhat better diets than older children, their diets still need improvement to meet the 2005 *Dietary Guidelines for Healthy Americans* (Fungwe et al. 2009).

Children's gardens provide an ideal setting for nutrition education by allowing children to observe and care for plants and develop a connection to the natural world.

Role of Early Education in Improving the Diets of Young Children

Early childhood educators have the opportunity to improve children's food choices because they interact with children daily (Birch & Fisher 1998). Family members and teachers can influence the food preferences of young children by providing healthy food choices, offering multiple opportunities to prepare and eat new foods, and serving as positive role models through their own food choices.

Children's preference for vegetables is among the strongest predictors of vegetable consumption (Birch 1979; Domel et al. 1996; Harvey-Berino et al. 1997; Morris & Zidenberg-Cherr 2002). Sullivan and Birch (1994) found that it takes 5 to 10 exposures to a new food for preschool children to become comfortable and familiar with its taste and texture. When children have repeated opportunities to taste a new food, they often change their food reactions from rejection to acceptance (Birch & Marlin 1982; Sullivan & Birch 1994).

Children's gardens provide an ideal setting for nutrition education by allowing children to observe and care for plants and develop a connection to the natural world (Subramaniam 2002; Lautenschlager & Smith 2007). Children exposed to homegrown produce tend to prefer those vegetables (Nanney et al. 2007). Some early childhood garden projects also focus on caring for the environment and science education (Perkins et al. 2005; Nimmo & Hallett 2008). Other nutrition education approaches for young children feature tasting exotic fruits and vegetables (Bellows & Anderson 2006). As more educators bring gardening and nutrition projects into their classrooms, there is a need for additional teacher support and curriculum development (Graham et al. 2005).

The Early Sprouts Program: An Overview

Early Sprouts is a research-based nutrition and gardening curriculum for the preschool years, created by Karrie Kalich and developed in collaboration with the Child Development Center at Keene State College in New Hampshire. We designed the curriculum to encourage children's food preferences for six selected vegetables (bell peppers, butternut squash, carrots, green beans, Swiss rainbow chard, and tomatoes) and increase their consumption of these vegetables (Kalich, Bauer, & McPartlin 2009). The program's scope includes planting raised organic garden beds, sensory and cooking lessons focused on the six vegetables, training and support for classroom teachers, and family involvement.

Through the curriculum we help children overcome an innate food neophobia (*fear of new foods*) through multiple exposures to the six vegetables. Additionally, the Early Sprouts model provides a "seed to table" experience by following the lifespan of the vegetables. The garden features six vegetables that represent a variety of colors and plant parts and are easy to grow in our region (New England), available at farmers' markets, and affordable and available year-round in supermarkets.

One project goal is to expose the children to the six vegetables multiple times over the course of the 24-week curriculum. In preparation for the project, we developed recipes for cooking snacks and meals using the vegetables. The Early Sprouts recipes include a variety of healthy ingredients: low-fat dairy products, healthy fats (canola and olive oils), whole grains (stone-ground cornmeal and whole wheat flours), and reduced amounts of sodium and sugar as compared to commercially available snack products.

Based on feedback from field-testing among teachers and children in our program, we chose 24 recipes (four per vegetable). We adapted the recipes for classroom use and for family use in the Family Recipe Kits component of the project. Each recipe has an accompanying sensory exploration activity that features the same vegetable and involves children in exploring the plant parts by using all of their senses.

We begin the Early Sprouts project at each site by building raised garden beds on the playground and filling them with alternating layers of compost, humus, and topsoil. To ensure children's health and safety, we practice organic gardening techniques, such as using only organic fertilizers and hand-picking garden pests. With the groundwork complete, teachers implement the healthy food curriculum in their preschool classrooms.

How the Early Sprouts Program Works

The program begins when children help plant seeds and seedlings in late May and early June. This is followed by watering, weeding, watching, and waiting. After months of anticipation, the children harvest the vegetables from July through early October; thus they observe the complete growing cycle. The children make many discoveries.

> The children are in the play-yard garden at harvest time. Janet, the preschool teacher, asks Rachel, age 4½, what she thinks the Swiss chard will taste like. Rachel pauses, then she speculates, "It will taste like nachos." She spontaneously takes a bite of the Swiss chard directly from the garden and then corrects herself, proclaiming, "It tastes more like celery!"

Each week the curriculum introduces one of the six vegetables. By the end of the entire curriculum, each vegetable has been featured four times. At the start of the week, the children use their senses to explore the vegetable. This exploration is followed by a cooking activity featuring an Early Sprouts recipe. At the end of the week, the children pack a Family Recipe Kit containing the recipe, tips for cooking with children, and many of the necessary ingredients to take home. The purpose of the kit is to help families reinforce the food preparation and healthy eating experience children have had at preschool. Here is one example:

> Cooper, a cautious 3½-year-old, is hesitant to try any of the Early Sprouts vegetables but thoroughly enjoys all of the sensory and cooking activities. He almost never misses an Early Sprouts activity and spends time in the garden almost daily. His interest in the vegetables continues throughout the 24-week experience, but so does his hesitancy to taste the vegetables. About five weeks before the end of the program, Cooper starts to cautiously lick the vegetables. Three weeks later, he tastes them. By the last two weeks, he has developed into a true vegetable lover. His family says that he requests and eats several vegetables a day.

Sensory Exploration

The sensory exploration experiences safely introduce children to each vegetable. Their familiarity increases as they smell each vegetable, feel the shape and texture, touch its leaves and stalks, shake it and listen for sounds, and notice how it looks before tasting the raw food or the results of the prepared recipe.

Jackson, Caitlin, and José, all enrolled in an older preschool group, enthusiastically gather red, yellow, and green bell peppers. Janet, the teacher, guides each of the children in cutting open their peppers and exploring the seeds. José quickly asks if they can taste them. Each child cuts a piece of pepper and tastes it. Caitlin wants to taste the other colors. The children cut and share pieces of their peppers. Janet and the children discuss the various characteristics of the bell peppers, using vocabulary such as *crunchy, juicy,* and *smooth.* When they finish, the children describe the peppers' characteristics and agree they enjoy all the different colored peppers.

The sensory exploration experiences safely introduce children to each vegetable.

Cooking

After children explore and taste a vegetable in its raw form, most are eager and willing to participate in the cooking and tasting process. Teachers encourage the children to perform each step of the recipe preparation as is developmentally appropriate—measuring, cutting (with safe tools), mixing, and preparing the food for serving.

Children eagerly join Janet at the table after washing their hands. Janet helps them identify all the ingredients for making muffins. They use child-size table knives to dice the peppers and plastic graters to grate the cheese. Janet watches 5-year-old Jermaine as he breaks and mixes the eggs, while guiding 3½-year-old Thomas and 4-year-old Jocelyn in measuring and mixing the dry ingredients. All the children count to 10 as they take turns mixing the wet and dry ingredients.

Cooking experiences connect the Early Sprouts project to other curriculum areas, such as math, science, literacy, and social skills development (Colker 2005).

Two 5-year-olds, Annabelle and Carolyn, are deciding where to place the different colored pegs on the peg board. From across the room, Janet watches the children and admires their cooperative play. After a few minutes, she approaches and sees the girls using many colors. "We're planting a garden," they explain. The orange pegs are carrots; the green pegs are green beans; the red pegs are tomatoes. Janet asks them about the mixed-color assortment of pegs in one of the rows. The children look at her impatiently and exclaim, "Those are rainbow chard, silly!"

Family Involvement

Social modeling by family (as well as peers) plays a particularly large role in the early development of food preferences (Birch & Fisher 1996). The Early Sprouts program supports families in encouraging children to make healthy food choices at home. One parent reports that as a result of the program, her whole family is eating better, even her "I-don't-eat-anything-green" husband.

The Early Sprouts monthly newsletter keeps families well informed of our activities. We also invite families to participate in garden planting; classroom-based sensory and cooking activities; food-based special events, such as the Stone Soup luncheon (made from the Early Sprouts vegetables); and a family nutrition education program. One father comments, "I used to battle with my child about eating vegetables. Now he requests specific vegetables at the store and at mealtimes."

The weekly Family Recipe Kits, which children help to pack, promote family-oriented nutrition education. They contain all needed ingredients and instructions to re-create the week's featured recipe with their child at home. The family experience reinforces the classroom activity and provides another opportunity for the child to taste the vegetable. At the end of the year, families receive a cookbook containing all of the Early Sprouts recipes. Through our weekly program surveys, parents tell us their stories.

Sydney, the mother of two Early Sprouts participants, writes, "On Friday we brought home this week's kit, and, as usual, my oldest child, Ava, excitedly asked about the contents. When I told her it was butternut squash pancakes, she wrinkled her nose and said she would not eat them. Of course Clay, the youngest and a finicky eater, turned his nose up too.

Sunday morning the children begged for "normal pancakes" but I told them that we were making the Early Sprouts pancakes. Three-year-old Clay wanted to help but kept saying he would not eat the squash. As the pancakes were cooking, Ava came to the stove and asked to see what they looked like. I ate the first (Yummy!), put the second on Clay's plate, and kept cooking. Then Ava said she wanted some too. Both children ate the pancakes. Their only comments were, "How soon until the next one?" and "He (she) got more pancakes."

Sydney described the pancakes as "delicious and so easy to make." She wrote, "I did not even serve them with syrup! My only complaint—they were so good I only got two pancakes! I feel good about serving them. I LOVE THIS PROGRAM! These are the only pancakes we will eat from now on!"

Cooking experiences connect the Early Sprouts project to other curriculum areas, such as math, science, literacy, and social skills development.

Involving Teachers and Staff

Training professional and volunteer staff is important to the ongoing success of the Early Sprouts project. Because some adults are unfamiliar with the six vegetables and unsure about how to introduce them to the children, we provide detailed background sheets for each vegetable. We post guidelines in the classrooms to encourage staff and volunteers to serve as positive role models during snack and mealtimes when serving the vegetables and presenting new recipes (see "Early Sprouts Tasting—Suggestions for Teachers and Volunteers"). One experienced teacher even commented, "I know it is important to teach our children about nutrition, but I was never really sure how to do that before Early Sprouts."

Early Sprouts: What We Have Learned

A strong research component supports the Early Sprouts program and has evaluated the impact of the curriculum on the eating habits of young children and their families. At the start, midpoint, and conclusion of the 24 weeks of sensory exploration and vegetable recipes, we measure children's preferences for the program's vegetables as well as dietary changes observed by families at home. At the conclusion of the program, children are more willing to taste the Early Sprouts vegetables and express a greater preference for the six vegetables highlighted. Teachers describe a greater personal confidence in guiding young children in the development of healthy eating behaviors.

Ways to Adapt Early Sprouts at Your Center

The Early Sprouts model can be easily adapted to other geographic regions. When selecting vegetables for your area, consider the available space, the length of the growing season, rainfall levels, and soil type. If outdoor space is limited, try container or window-box gardening, with dwarf cherry tomato plants, greens, or pole beans. Local greenhouses, community garden associations, community-supported agriculture programs, cooperative extension offices, and garden shops have information and are potential partners. There are many ways to engage children and families in a seed-to-table experience that is appropriate for your setting and location. Visit the Early Sprouts website (www.earlysprouts.org) for more information. We encourage you to be creative and innovative in your approach to using the Early Sprouts model. We change and grow ourselves!

Janet has hosted a Stone Soup luncheon for 10 years with children and families during the harvest season. In the past, children brought vegetables from home to contribute to the soup. The luncheon is a great family event. But the downside has been that the children rarely would eat or even taste the soup.

Now, with the Early Sprouts program, Janet notices that the children contribute many more vegetables and

Early Sprouts Tasting— Suggestions for Teachers and Volunteers

- Taste a portion of the Early Sprouts snack. Children will be more willing to try the new snack if you are eating with them and model how to try new foods.
- Invite children to serve themselves from a common bowl, first taking just one helping. Offer a second helping once the children have finished the first one.
- Be a positive role model and adventurous about trying new foods. The goal in providing recipes is to introduce foods creatively and engage all children in trying at least one bite.
- Share your enthusiasm and positive comments if you like the Early Sprouts snack. Even if you do not especially enjoy the snack, let your comments express that it sometimes takes multiple tries to become accustomed to a new food. Explain that we want to give ourselves and the food a chance.
- Compliment the children on their preparation of the snack. Many of them participated in the activity. Thank them for their work and for making delicious food.
- Ask the children to explain how they made the food (the ingredients needed, the stirring, measuring, and so on). They will be eager to talk about what they did to follow the recipe.
- Engage the children in a pleasant conversation about the things they did in cooking, surprises they may have had, and what they'd like to cook next. Discourage negative criticism but invite suggestions for ways to vary the recipe another time. Talk about why we want to respect the feelings of friends and teachers who prepared the food.

are especially focused on bringing in the Early Sprouts vegetables. Families have more interest because they feel involved in the cooking process. At the luncheon, almost all of the children eat the soup, and many request a second and even a third serving. They also eat up all the Confetti Corn Muffins baked to go with it.

References

Bellows, L., & J. Anderson. 2006. The food friends: Encouraging preschoolers to try new foods. *Young Children* 61 (3): 37–39.

Birch, L.L. 1979. Preschool children's food preferences and consumption patterns. *Journal of Nutrition Education* 11: 189–92.

Birch, L.L., & J.A. Fisher. 1995. Appetite and eating behavior in children. *Pediatric Clinical Nutrition America* 42: 931–53.

Birch, L.L., & J.A. Fisher. 1996. Experience and children's eating behaviors. In *Why we eat what we eat,* ed. E.D. Capaldi, 113–41. Washington, DC: American Psychological Association.

Birch L.L., & J.A. Fisher. 1998. Development of eating behaviors among children and adolescents. *Pediatrics* 101: 539–49.

Birch, L.L., & D.W. Marlin. 1982. I don't like it; I never tried it: Effects of exposure to food on two-year-old children's food preferences. *Appetite* 4: 353–60.

CCOR (Center for Childhood Obesity Research). 2006. Over the past 30 years, childhood obesity has doubled for preschool children. website home page at Pennsylvania State University, College of Health & Human Development. www.hhdev.psu.edu/ccor/index.html

Colker, L. 2005. *The cooking book: Fostering young children's learning and delight.* Washington, DC: NAEYC.

Domel, S.B., W.O. Thompson, H.C. Davis, T. Baranowski, S.B. Leonard, & J. Baranowski. 1996. Psychosocial predictors of fruit and vegetable consumption among elementary school children. *Health Education Research* 11 (3): 299–308.

Enns, C.W., S.J. Mickle, & J.D. Goldman. 2002. Trends in food and nutrient intake by children in the United States. *Family Economics and Nutrition Review* 14 (2): 56–69.

Fisher, J.O., & L.L. Birch. 1999. Restricting access to palatable foods affects children's behavioral response, food selection, and intake. *American Journal of Clinical Nutrition* 69: 1264–72.

Fungwe, T., P.M. Guenther, W.W. Juan, H. Hiza, & M. Lino. 2009. Nutrition Insight 43: The quality of children's diets in 2003–04 as measured by the Healthy Eating Index—2005. Alexandria, VA: U.S. Department of Agriculture Center for Nutrition Policy and Promotion.

Gleason, P.M., & C. Suitor. 2001. Children's diets in the mid-1990s: Dietary intake and its relationship with school meal participation. Report no. CN-01-CDI. Alexandria, VA: U.S. Department of Agriculture, Food and Nutrition Service.

Graham, H., D.L. Beall, M. Lussier, P. McLaughlin, & S. Zeidenberg-Cherr. 2005. Use of school gardens in academic instruction. *Journal of Nutrition Education and Behavior* 37 (3): 147–51.

Guenther, P.M., K.W. Dodd, J. Reedy, & S.M. Krebs-Smith. 2006. Most Americans eat much less than recommended amounts of fruits and vegetables. *Journal of the American Dietetic Association* 106 (9): 1371–79.

Haire-Joshu, D., & M.S. Nanney. 2002. Prevention of overweight and obesity in children: Influences on the food environment. *The Diabetes Educator* 28 (3): 415–22.

Harvey-Berino, J., V. Hood, J. Rourke, T. Terrance, A. Dorwaldt, & R. Secker-Walker. 1997. Food preferences predict eating behavior of very young Mohawk children. *Journal of the American Dietetic Association* 97 (7): 750–53.

Kalich, K., D. Bauer, & D. McPartlin. 2009. *Early Sprouts: Cultivating healthy food choices in young children.* St. Paul, MN: Redleaf Press.

Lautenschlager, L., & C. Smith. 2007. Beliefs, knowledge, and values held by inner-city youth about gardening, nutrition, and cooking. *Agriculture and Human Values* 24 (2): 245–58.

Marotz, L. 2009. *Health, safety, and nutrition for the young child.* 7th ed. Clifton Park, NY: Thomson Delmar Learning.

Morris, J., & S. Zidenberg-Cherr. 2002. Garden-enhanced nutrition curriculum improves fourth-grade school children's knowledge of nutrition and preferences for some vegetables. *Journal of the American Dietetic Association* 102 (1): 91–93.

Nanney, M.S., S. Johnson, M. Elliott, & D. Haire-Joshu. 2007. Frequency of eating homegrown produce is associated with higher intake among parents and their preschool-aged children in rural Missouri. *Journal of the American Dietetic Association* 107 (4): 577–84.

Nimmo, J., & B. Hallett. 2008. Childhood in the garden: A place to encounter natural and social diversity. *Young Children* 63 (1): 32–38.

Perkins, D., B. Hogan, B. Hallett, J. Nimmo, C. Esmel, L. Boyer, R. Freyre, & P. Fisher. 2005. *Growing a green generation: A curriculum of gardening activities for preschool and kindergarten children.* Durham: University of New Hampshire, Child Study and Development Center.

Rolls, B.J., D. Engell, & L.L. Birch 2000. Serving portion size influences 5-year-old but not 3-year-old children's food intake. *Journal of the American Dietetic Association* 100: 232–34.

Subramaniam, A. 2002. *Garden-based learning in basic education: A historical review.* 4-H Center for Youth Development Monograph, Summer. University of California, Davis. http://cyd.ucdavis.edu/publications/pubs/focus/pdf/ MO02V8N1.pdf

Sullivan, S.A., & L.L. Birch. 1994. Infant dietary experience and acceptance of solid foods. *Pediatrics* 9: 884–85.

U.S. Department of Health and Human Services & U.S. Department of Agriculture. 2005. *Dietary guidelines for healthy Americans.* 6th ed. Washington, DC: U.S. Government Printing Office.

KARRIE A. KALICH, PhD, RD, is an associate professor of health science and nutrition at Keene State College. Karrie has spent more than 14 years in community-based childhood obesity prevention. kkalich@keene.edu. **DOTTIE BAUER**, PhD, is a professor of early childhood education at Keene State College in Keene, New Hampshire. A former preschool teacher, Dottie now specializes in early childhood curriculum development and teacher preparation. dbauer@keene.edu. **DEIRDRE MCPARTLIN**, MEd, is the associate director at the Child Development Center, the early childhood demonstration site at Keene State College. Deirdre's experience in the field includes preschool and kindergarten teaching, child care administration, and preservice teacher training. dmcpartl@keene.edu. The authors expand the story of their Early Sprouts project in a new book from Redleaf Press, *Early Sprouts: Cultivating Healthy Food Choices in Young Children.*

UNIT 3

Development during Childhood: Cognition and Schooling

Unit Selections

Key Points to Consider

- Would you use a drug or brain implant that would let you think with more clarity?

- Will sophisticated brain studies help us predict the intelligence of children?

- Should schools teach all areas of intelligence or focus on what is required for tests? What are the multiple intelligences?

- Will the constant barrage of digital information entering our brains help or hinder our cognitive processing?

- Should children with attention deficit disorders be given stimulation medications? Why or why not?

- Are achievement tests necessary to make sure first graders acquire sufficient reading and math skills? Should 5- and 6-year-old children be given homework? Should they be tutored if they fall behind their peers? What impact will this have?

- What has the No Child Left Behind (NCLB) legislation done for American education? What are its weaknesses? How can it be improved?

- Are there gender differences in how children learn? Should boys and girls be separated for education?

- Should teachers encourage perfectionistic students to modify their attitudes toward learning? How?

Student Website

www.mhhe.com/cls

Internet References

Children Now
http://www.childrennow.org

Council for Exceptional Children
http://www.cec.sped.org

Educational Resources Information Center (ERIC)
http://www.eric.ed.gov/

Federation of Behavioral, Psychological, and Cognitive Science
http://federation.apa.org

The National Association for the Education of Young Children (NAEYC)
http://www.naeyc.org

Project Zero
http://pzweb.harvard.edu

Teaching Technologies
http://www.inspiringteachers.com/bttindex.html

The mental process of knowing—cognition—includes aspects such as sensing, understanding, associating, and discriminating. Cognitive research has been hampered by the limitations of trying to understand what is happening inside the minds of living persons without doing harm. It has also been challenged by the problem of defining concepts such as intuition, unconsciousness, unawareness, implicit learning, incomprehension, and all the aspects of knowing present behind our sensations and perceptions (metacognition). Many kinds of achievement that require cognitive processes (awareness, perception, reasoning, judgment) cannot be measured with intelligence tests or with achievement tests.

Intelligence is the capacity to acquire and apply knowledge. It is usually assumed that intelligence can be measured. The ratio of tested mental age to chronological age is expressed as intelligence quotient (IQ). For years, schoolchildren have been classified by IQ scores. The links between IQ scores and school achievement are positive, but no significant correlations exist between IQ scores and life success. Consider, for example, the motor coordination and kinesthetic abilities of Hall of Fame baseball player Cal Ripken, Jr. He had a use of his body that surpassed the capacity of most other athletes and nonathletes. Is knowledge of kinesthetics a form of intelligence? Many people believe it is.

Some psychologists have suggested that uncovering more about how the brain processes various types of intelligences will soon be translated into new educational practices. Today's tests of intelligence only measure abilities in the logical/mathematical, spatial, and linguistic areas of intelligence, which is what schools now teach. Jean Piaget, the Swiss founder of cognitive psychology, was involved in the creation of the world's first intelligence test, the Binet-Simon Scale. He became disillusioned with trying to quantify how much children knew at different chronological ages. He was much more intrigued with what they did not know, what they knew incorrectly, and how they came to know the world as they did. He started the Centre for Genetic Epistemology in Geneva, Switzerland, where he began to study the nature, extent, and validity of children's knowledge. He discovered qualitative, rather than quantitative, differences in cognitive processes over the life span. Infants know the world through their senses and their motor responses. After language develops, toddlers and preschoolers know the world through their language/symbolic perspective. Piaget likened early childhood cognitive processes to bad thought, or thought akin to daydreams. By school age, children know things in concrete terms, which allows them to number, seriate, classify, conserve, think backward and forward, and think about their own thinking (metacognition). However, Piaget believed that children do not acquire the cognitive processes necessary to think abstractly and to use clear, consistent, logical patterns of thought until early adolescence. Their moral sense and personal philosophies of behavior are not completed until adulthood.

The first article in this unit, "Get Smart," deals with the information overload children are experiencing with iPods, cell phones, video games, YouTube, Facebook, MySpace, Twitter,

© Corbis/Jupiter Images

and other cyberspace inputs. They are attending to these digital messages while also experiencing real world inputs. The author, Jamais Cascio, suggests that they give only partial attention to each. Will this type of cognitive processing change our brains? Are there cognitive enhancers (drugs, brain implants) which will allow us to focus on multiple sources of information in the future?

The second selection for cognition during childhood, "An Educator's Journey toward Multiple Intelligences," supports the belief that there are many genes and many brain regions involved in many types of intelligences. Each of us may have a unique "general" intelligence. The theory of Howard Gardner on multiple intelligences (MI) is reviewed. Schools tend to focus on math and verbal skills. Should other intelligences (e.g., naturalistic, interpersonal) be augmented with educational curriculum?

Cognitive scientists can study the brain in action today with functional magnetic resonance imaging (fMRI). The article "In Defense of Distraction" by Sam Anderson describes what fMRIs are revealing about multitasking and distraction. Rather than doing two things at once, our brains switch rapidly between two things. Too many distractions result in mistakes and inefficiency. We need to learn to allocate our attention and harness the power of distraction.

The last article on cognition, "Informing the ADHD Debate," gives a comprehensive commentary on the many issues surrounding attention deficit hyperactivity disorder. The authors make clear that ADHD has biological causes. They review new research, which documents that brain differences exist in children with ADHD, as observed using imaging technology. While ADHD has roots in genetic and prenatal development, the environment in childhood also plays a role in ADHD. The use of medication is explained in terms of how and why it helps. The use of behavioral therapy is also strongly recommended.

The first article of the schooling section of this unit, "Ten Big Effects of the No Child Left Behind Act on Public Schools," explains the findings of a four-year, comprehensive review of the implementation of NCLB. The teion effects are broad generalizations drawn from all 50 states. While test scores are rising and low-performing schools are being restructured across the United States, there are problems. Many of these relate to rising costs, staffing, quality teaching, high-stakes testing, and accountability requirements for children with exceptionalities.

"Single-Sex Classrooms Are Succeeding" supports its title. This article by Michael Gurian, Kathy Stevens, and Peggy Daniels describes a variety of schools that have found separate classes for boys and girls to be beneficial to all. Many approaches are depicted and success testimonials from teachers are given. The message is clear: single-sex classes work.

The final article in this unit, "A 'Perfect' Case Study: Perfectionism in Academically Talented Fourth Graders," discusses students who try too hard to be perfect. Their behaviors create unnecessary anxiety about underachievement. Jill Adelson describes five types of perfectionists and suggests ways to support healthy learning behaviors.

Get Smart

Pandemics. Global warming. Food shortages. No more fossil fuels. What are humans to do? The same thing the species has done before: evolve to meet the challenge. But this time we don't have to rely on natural evolution to make us smart enough to survive. We can do it ourselves, right now, by harnessing technology and pharmacology to boost our intelligence. Is Google actually making us smarter?

JAMAIS CASCIO

Seventy-four thousand years ago, humanity nearly went extinct. A super-volcano at what's now Lake Toba, in Sumatra, erupted with a strength more than a thousand times that of Mount St. Helens in 1980. Some 800 cubic kilometers of ash filled the skies of the Northern Hemisphere, lowering global temperatures and pushing a climate already on the verge of an ice age over the edge. Some scientists speculate that as the Earth went into a deep freeze, the population of *Homo sapiens* may have dropped to as low as a few thousand families.

The Mount Toba incident, although unprecedented in magnitude, was part of a broad pattern. For a period of 2 million years, ending with the last ice age around 10,000 B.C., the Earth experienced a series of convulsive glacial events. This rapid-fire climate change meant that humans couldn't rely on consistent patterns to know which animals to hunt, which plants to gather, or even which predators might be waiting around the corner.

How did we cope? By getting smarter. The neurophysiologist William Calvin argues persuasively that modern human cognition—including sophisticated language and the capacity to plan ahead—evolved in response to the demands of this long age of turbulence. According to Calvin, the reason we survived is that our brains changed to meet the challenge: we transformed the ability to target a moving animal with a thrown rock into a capability for foresight and long-term planning. In the process, we may have developed syntax and formal structure from our simple language.

Our present century may not be quite as perilous for the human race as an ice age in the aftermath of a super-volcano eruption, but the next few decades will pose enormous hurdles that go beyond the climate crisis. The end of the fossil-fuel era, the fragility of the global food web, growing population density, and the spread of pandemics, as well as the emergence of radically transformative bio- and nano-technologies—each of these threatens us with broad disruption or even devastation. And as good as our brains have become at planning ahead, we're still biased toward looking for near-term, simple threats. Subtle, long-term risks, particularly those involving complex, global processes, remain devilishly hard for us to manage.

But here's an optimistic scenario for you: if the next several decades are as bad as some of us fear they could be, we can respond, and survive, the way our species has done time and again: by getting smarter. But this time, we don't have to rely solely on natural evolutionary processes to boost our intelligence. We can do it ourselves.

Most people don't realize that this process is already under way. In fact, it's happening all around us, across the full spectrum of how we understand intelligence. It's visible in the hive mind of the Internet, in the powerful tools for simulation and visualization that are jump-starting new scientific disciplines, and in the development of drugs that some people (myself included) have discovered let them study harder, focus better, and stay awake longer with full clarity. So far, these augmentations have largely been outside of our bodies, but they're very much part of who we are today: they're physically separate from us, but we and they are becoming cognitively inseparable. And advances over the next few decades, driven by breakthroughs in genetic engineering and artificial intelligence, will make today's technologies seem primitive. The nascent jargon of the field describes this as "intelligence augmentation." I prefer to think of it as "You+."

Scientists refer to the 12,000 years or so since the last ice age as the Holocene epoch. It encompasses the rise of human civilization and our co-evolution with tools and technologies that allow us to grapple with our physical environment. But if intelligence augmentation has the kind of impact I expect, we may soon have to start thinking of ourselves as living in an entirely new era. The focus of our technological evolution would be less on how we manage and adapt to our physical world, and more on how we manage and adapt to the immense amount of knowledge we've created. We can call it the Nöocene epoch, from Pierre Teilhard de Chardin's concept of the Nöosphere, a collective consciousness created by the deepening interaction of human minds. As that epoch draws closer, the world is becoming a very different place.

Of course, we've been augmenting our ability to think for millennia. When we developed written language, we significantly increased our functional memory and our ability to share insights and knowledge across time and space. The same thing happened with the invention of the printing press, the telegraph, and the radio. The rise of urbanization allowed a fraction of the populace to focus on more-cerebral tasks—a fraction that grew inexorably as more-complex economic and social practices demanded more knowledge work, and industrial technology reduced the demand for manual labor. And caffeine and nicotine, of course, are both classic cognitive-enhancement drugs, primitive though they may be.

With every technological step forward, though, has come anxiety about the possibility that technology harms our natural ability to think. These anxieties were given eloquent expression by Nicholas Carr, whose essay "Is Google Making Us Stupid?" (July/August 2008 *Atlantic*) argued that the information-dense, hyperlink-rich, spastically churning Internet medium is effectively rewiring our brains, making it harder for us to engage in deep, relaxed contemplation.

Carr's fears about the impact of wall-to-wall connectivity on the human intellect echo cyber-theorist Linda Stone's description of "continuous partial attention," the modern phenomenon of having multiple activities and connections under way simultaneously. We're becoming so accustomed to interruption that we're starting to find focusing difficult, even when we've achieved a bit of quiet. It's an induced form of ADD—a "continuous partial attention-deficit disorder," if you will.

There's also just more information out there—because unlike with previous information media, with the Internet, creating material is nearly as easy as consuming it. And it's easy to mistake more voices for more noise. In reality, though, the proliferation of diverse voices may actually improve our overall ability to think. In *Everything Bad Is Good for You*, Steven Johnson argues that the increasing complexity and range of media we engage with have, over the past century, made us smarter, rather than dumber, by providing a form of cognitive calisthenics. Even pulp-television shows and video games have become extraordinarily dense with detail, filled with subtle references to broader subjects, and more open to interactive engagement. They reward the capacity to make connections and to see patterns—precisely the kinds of skills we need for managing an information glut.

Scientists describe these skills as our "fluid intelligence"—the ability to find meaning in confusion and to solve new problems, independent of acquired knowledge. Fluid intelligence doesn't look much like the capacity to memorize and recite facts, the skills that people have traditionally associated with brainpower. But building it up may improve the capacity to think deeply that Carr and others fear we're losing for good. And we shouldn't let the stresses associated with a transition to a new era blind us to that era's astonishing potential. We swim in an ocean of data, accessible from nearly anywhere, generated by billions of devices. We're only beginning to explore what we can do with this knowledge-at-a-touch.

The trouble isn't that we have too much information at our fingertips, but that our tools for managing it are still in their infancy.

Moreover, the technology-induced ADD that's associated with this new world may be a short-term problem. The trouble isn't that we have too much information at our fingertips, but that our tools for managing it are still in their infancy. Worries about "information overload" predate the rise of the Web (Alvin Toffler coined the phrase in 1970), and many of the technologies that Carr worries about were developed precisely to help us get some control over a flood of data and ideas. Google isn't the problem; it's the beginning of a solution.

In any case, there's no going back. The information sea isn't going to dry up, and relying on cognitive habits evolved and perfected in an era of limited information flow—and limited information access—is futile. Strengthening our fluid intelligence is the only viable approach to navigating the age of constant connectivity.

When people hear the phrase *intelligence augmentation,* they tend to envision people with computer chips plugged into their brains, or a genetically engineered race of post-human super-geniuses. Neither of these visions is likely to be realized, for reasons familiar to any Best Buy shopper. In a world of on-going technological acceleration, today's cutting-edge brain implant would be tomorrow's obsolete junk—and good luck if the protocols change or you're on the wrong side of a "format war" (anyone want a Betamax implant?). And then there's the question of stability: Would you want a chip in your head made by the same folks that made your cell phone, or your PC?

Likewise, the safe modification of human genetics is still years away. And even after genetic modification of adult neurobiology becomes possible, the science will remain in flux; our understanding of how augmentation works, and what kinds of genetic modifications are possible, would still change rapidly. As with digital implants, the brain modification you might undergo one week could become obsolete the next. Who would want a 2025-vintage brain when you're competing against hotshots with Model 2026?

Yet in one sense, the age of the cyborg and the super-genius has already arrived. It just involves external information and communication devices instead of implants and genetic modification. The bioethicist James Hughes of Trinity College refers to all of this as "exocortical technology," but you can just think of it as "stuff you already own." Increasingly, we buttress our cognitive functions with our computing systems, no matter that the connections are mediated by simple typing and pointing. These tools enable our brains to do things that would once have been almost unimaginable:

- powerful simulations and massive data sets allow physicists to visualize, understand, and debate models of an 11-dimension universe;
- real-time data from satellites, global environmental databases, and high-resolution models allow geophysicists to recognize the subtle signs of long-term changes to the planet;
- cross-connected scheduling systems allow anyone to assemble, with a few clicks, a complex, multimodal travel itinerary that would have taken a human travel agent days to create.

If that last example sounds prosaic, it simply reflects how embedded these kinds of augmentation have become. Not much more than a decade ago, such a tool was outrageously impressive—and it destroyed the travel-agent industry.

That industry won't be the last one to go. Any occupation requiring pattern-matching and the ability to find obscure connections will quickly morph from the domain of experts to that of ordinary people whose intelligence has been augmented by cheap digital tools. Humans won't be taken out of the loop—in fact, many, many *more* humans will have the capacity to do something that was once limited to a hermetic priesthood. Intelligence augmentation decreases the need for specialization and increases participatory complexity.

As the digital systems we rely upon become faster, more sophisticated, and (with the usual hiccups) more capable, we're becoming more sophisticated and capable too. It's a form of co-evolution: we learn to adapt our thinking and expectations to these digital systems, even as the system designs become more complex and powerful to meet more of our needs—and eventually come to adapt to *us*.

Consider the Twitter phenomenon, which went from nearly invisible to nearly ubiquitous (at least among the online crowd) in early 2007. During busy periods, the user can easily be overwhelmed by the volume of incoming messages, most of which are of only passing interest. But there is a tiny minority of truly valuable posts. (Sometimes they have extreme value, as they did during the October 2007 wildfires in California and the November 2008 terrorist attacks in Mumbai.) At present, however, finding the most-useful bits requires wading through messages like "My kitty sneezed!" and "I hate this taco!"

But imagine if social tools like Twitter had a way to learn what kinds of messages you pay attention to, and which ones you discard. Over time, the messages that you don't really care about might start to fade in the display, while the ones that you do want to see could get brighter. Such attention filters—or focus assistants—are likely to become important parts of how we handle our daily lives. We'll move from a world of "continuous partial attention" to one we might call "continuous augmented awareness."

As processor power increases, tools like Twitter may be able to draw on the complex simulations and massive data sets that have unleashed a revolution in science. They could become individualized systems that augment our capacity for planning and foresight, letting us play "what-if" with our life choices: where to live, what to study, maybe even where to go for dinner.

Initially crude and clumsy, such a system would get better with more data and more experience; just as important, we'd get better at asking questions. These systems, perhaps linked to the cameras and microphones in our mobile devices, would eventually be able to pay attention to what we're doing, and to our habits and language quirks, and learn to interpret our sometimes ambiguous desires. With enough time and complexity, they would be able to make useful suggestions without explicit prompting.

And such systems won't be working for us alone. Intelligence has a strong social component; for example, we already provide crude cooperative information-filtering for each other. In time, our interactions through the use of such intimate technologies could dovetail with our use of collaborative knowledge systems (such as Wikipedia), to help us not just to build better data sets, but to filter them with greater precision. As our capacity to provide that filter gets faster and richer, it increasingly becomes something akin to collaborative intuition—in which everyone is effectively augmenting everyone else.

In pharmacology, too, the future is already here. One of the most prominent examples is a drug called modafinil. Developed in the 1970s, modafinil—sold in the United States under the brand name Provigil—appeared on the cultural radar in the late 1990s, when the American military began to test it for long-haul pilots. Extended use of modafinil can keep a person awake and alert for well over 32 hours on end, with only a full night's sleep required to get back to a normal schedule.

While it is FDA-approved only for a few sleep disorders, like narcolepsy and sleep apnea, doctors increasingly prescribe it to those suffering from depression, to "shift workers" fighting fatigue, and to frequent business travelers dealing with time-zone shifts. I'm part of the latter group: like more and more professionals, I have a prescription for modafinil in order to help me overcome jet lag when I travel internationally. When I started taking the drug, I expected it to keep me awake; I didn't expect it to make me feel smarter, but that's exactly what happened. The change was subtle but clear, once I recognized it: within an hour of taking a standard 200-mg tablet, I was much more alert, and thinking with considerably more clarity and focus than usual. This isn't just a subjective conclusion. A University of Cambridge study, published in 2003, concluded that modafinil confers a measurable cognitive-enhancement effect across a variety of mental tasks, including pattern recognition and spatial planning, and sharpens focus and alertness.

I'm not the only one who has taken advantage of this effect. The Silicon Valley insider webzine *Tech Crunch* reported in July 2008 that some entrepreneurs now see modafinil as an important competitive tool. The tone of the piece was judgmental, but the implication was clear: everybody's doing it, and if you're not, you're probably falling behind.

This is one way a world of intelligence augmentation emerges. Little by little, people who don't know about drugs like modafinil or don't want to use them will face stiffer competition from the people who do. From the perspective of a culture immersed in athletic doping wars, the use of such drugs may seem like cheating. From the perspective of those who find that they're much more productive using this form of enhancement, it's no more cheating than getting a faster computer or a better education.

Modafinil isn't the only example; on college campuses, the use of ADD drugs (such as Ritalin and Adderall) as study aids has become almost ubiquitous. But these enhancements are primitive. As the science improves, we could see other kinds of cognitive-modification drugs that boost recall, brain plasticity, even empathy and emotional intelligence. They would start as therapeutic treatments, but end up being used to make us "better than normal." Eventually, some of these may become over-the-counter products at your local pharmacy, or in the juice and snack aisles at the supermarket. Spam e-mail would be full of offers to make your brain bigger, and your idea production more powerful.

Such a future would bear little resemblance to *Brave New World* or similar narcomantic nightmares; we may fear the idea of a population kept doped and placated, but we're more likely to see a populace stuck in overdrive, searching out the last bits of competitive advantage, business insight, and radical innovation. No small amount of that innovation would be directed toward inventing the next, more powerful cognitive-enhancement technology.

This would be a different kind of nightmare, perhaps, and cause waves of moral panic and legislative restriction. Safety would be a huge issue. But as we've found with athletic doping, if there's a technique for beating out rivals (no matter how risky), shutting it down is nearly impossible. This would be yet another pharmacological arms race—and in this case, the competitors on one side would just keep getting smarter.

The most radical form of superhuman intelligence, of course, wouldn't be a mind augmented by drugs or exocortical technology; it would be a mind that isn't human at all. Here we move from the realm of extrapolation to the realm of speculation, since solid predictions about artificial intelligence are notoriously hard: our understanding of how the brain creates the mind remains far from good enough to tell us how to construct a mind in a machine.

But while the concept remains controversial, I see no good argument for why a mind running on a machine platform instead of a biological platform will forever be impossible; whether one might appear in five years or 50 or 500, however, is uncertain. I lean toward 50, myself. That's enough time to develop computing hardware able to run a high-speed neural network as sophisticated as that of a human brain, and enough time for the kids who will have grown up surrounded by virtual-world software and household robots—that is, the people who see this stuff not as "Technology," but as everyday tools—to come to dominate the field.

Many proponents of developing an artificial mind are sure that such a breakthrough will be the biggest change in human

history. They believe that a machine mind would soon modify itself to get smarter—and with its new intelligence, then figure out how to make itself smarter still. They refer to this intelligence explosion as "the Singularity," a term applied by the computer scientist and science-fiction author Vernor Vinge. "Within thirty years, we will have the technological means to create superhuman intelligence," Vinge wrote in 1993. "Shortly after, the human era will be ended." The Singularity concept is a secular echo of Teilhard de Chardin's "Omega Point," the culmination of the Nöosphere at the end of history. Many believers in Singularity—which one wag has dubbed "the Rapture for nerds"—think that building the first real AI will be the last thing humans do. Some imagine this moment with terror, others with a bit of glee.

My own suspicion is that a stand-alone artificial mind will be more a tool of narrow utility than something especially apocalyptic. I don't think the theory of an explosively self-improving AI is convincing—it's based on too many assumptions about behavior and the nature of the mind. Moreover, AI researchers, after years of talking about this prospect, are already ultra-conscious of the risk of runaway systems.

More important, though, is that the same advances in processor and process that would produce a machine mind would also increase the power of our own cognitive-enhancement technologies. As intelligence augmentation allows us to make *ourselves* smarter, and then smarter still, AI may turn out to be just a sideshow: we could always be a step ahead.

So what's life like in a world of brain doping, intuition networks, and the occasional artificial mind?
Banal.

Not from our present perspective, of course. For us, now, looking a generation ahead might seem surreal and dizzying. But remember: people living in, say, 2030 will have lived every moment from now until then—we won't jump into the future. For someone going from 2009 to 2030 day by day, most of these changes wouldn't be jarring; instead, they'd be incremental, almost overdetermined, and the occasional surprises would quickly blend into the flow of inevitability.

By 2030, then, we'll likely have grown accustomed to (and perhaps even complacent about) a world where sophisticated foresight, detailed analysis and insight, and augmented awareness are commonplace. We'll have developed a better capacity to manage both partial attention and laser-like focus, and be able to slip between the two with ease—perhaps by popping the right pill, or eating the right snack. Sometimes, our augmentation assistants will handle basic interactions on our behalf; that's okay, though, because we'll increasingly see those assistants as extensions of ourselves.

The amount of data we'll have at our fingertips will be staggering, but we'll finally have gotten over the notion that accumulated information alone is a hallmark of intelligence. The power of all of this knowledge will come from its ability to inform difficult decisions, and to support complex analysis. Most professions will likely use simulation and modeling in their day-to-day work, from political decisions to hairstyle options. In a world of augmented intelligence, we will have a far greater appreciation of the consequences of our actions.

This doesn't mean we'll all come to the same conclusions. We'll still clash with each other's emotions, desires, and beliefs. If anything, our arguments will be more intense, buttressed not just by strongly held opinions but by intricate reasoning. People in 2030 will look back aghast at how ridiculously unsubtle the political and cultural disputes of our present were, just as we might today snicker at simplistic advertising from a generation ago.

Conversely, the debates of the 2030s would be remarkable for us to behold. Nuance and multiple layers will characterize even casual disputes; our digital assistants will be there to catch any references we might miss. And all of this will be everyday, banal reality. Today, it sounds mind-boggling; by then, it won't even merit comment.

What happens if such a complex system collapses? Disaster, of course. But don't forget that we already depend upon enormously complex systems that we no longer even think of as technological. Urbanization, agriculture, and trade were at one time huge innovations. Their collapse (and all of them are now at risk, in different ways, as we have seen in recent months) would be an even greater catastrophe than the collapse of our growing webs of interconnected intelligence.

A less apocalyptic but more likely danger derives from the observation made by the science-fiction author William Gibson: "The future is already here, it's just unevenly distributed." The rich, whether nations or individuals, will inevitably gain access to many augmentations before anyone else. We know from history, though, that a world of limited access wouldn't last forever, even as the technology improved: those who sought to impose limits would eventually face angry opponents with newer, better systems.

Even as competition provides access to these kinds of technologies, though, development paths won't be identical. Some societies may be especially welcoming to biotech boosts; others may prefer to use digital tools. Some may readily adopt collaborative approaches; others may focus on individual enhancement. And around the world, many societies will reject the use of intelligence-enhancement technology entirely, or adopt a cautious wait-and-see posture.

The bad news is that these divergent paths may exacerbate cultural divides created by already divergent languages and beliefs. National rivalries often emphasize cultural differences, but for now we're all still standard human beings. What happens when different groups quite literally think in very, very different ways?

The good news, though, is that this diversity of thought can also be a strength. Coping with the various world-histoncal dangers we face will require the greatest possible insight, creativity, and innovation. Our ability to build the future that we want—not just a future we can survive—depends on our capacity to understand the complex relationships of the world's systems, to take advantage of the diversity of knowledge and experience our civilization embodies, and to fully appreciate the implications of our choices. Such an ability is increasingly within our grasp. The Nöocene awaits.

JAMAIS CASCIO is an affiliate at the Institute for the Future and a senior fellow at the Institute for Ethics and Emerging Technologies.

An Educator's Journey toward Multiple Intelligences

Scott Seider

During my first year as a high school English teacher, I got into the habit each Friday afternoon of sitting in the bleachers and grading papers while the players on the freshman football team squared off against their counterparts from nearby towns. I had been assigned four classes of rambunctious freshmen, and several of my most squirrelly students were football players. I hoped that demonstrating my interest in their gridiron pursuits might make them a bit easier to manage in the classroom.

My presence at their games unquestionably helped on the management front, but a second, unexpected benefit emerged as well. A couple of those freshmen—kids in my class who struggled mightily with subject-verb agreement and the function of a thesis statement—had clearly committed several dozen complex plays to memory. During one particularly impressive series of plays, I remember thinking, "These guys are really smart! I'm underestimating what they're capable of!" And over the course of my first year in the classroom, that same thought emerged several more times—at the school musical, visiting the graphic design class, and even just watching a couple of students do their math homework during study hall. Without my realizing it, my relationship with multiple-intelligences (MI) theory had begun.

Rethinking IQ

What has become a powerful force in the world of education all started in 1983, when Harvard University professor Howard Gardner began his book *Frames of Mind: The Theory of Multiple Intelligences* [1] with some simple but powerful questions: Are talented chess players, violinists, and athletes "intelligent" in their respective disciplines? Why are these and other abilities not accounted for on traditional IQ tests? Why is the term *intelligence* limited to such a narrow range of human endeavors?

From these questions emerged multiple-intelligences theory. Stated simply, it challenges psychology's definition of intelligence as a general ability that can be measured by a single IQ score. Instead, MI theory describes eight intelligences (see Howard Gardner's Eight Intelligences) that people use to solve problems and create products relevant to the societies in which they live.

MI theory asserts that individuals who have a high level of aptitude in one intelligence do not necessarily have a similar aptitude in another intelligence. For example, a young person who demonstrates an impressive level of musical intelligence may be far less skilled when it comes to bodily-kinesthetic or logical-mathematical intelligence. Perhaps that seems obvious, but it's important to recognize that this notion stands in sharp contrast to the traditional (and still dominant) view of intelligence as a general ability that can be measured along a single scale and summarized by a single number.

Multiple Misconceptions

During my eight years as a high school English teacher and an administrator, MI theory came up periodically. Colleagues shared assignments with me that sought to tap into the multiple intelligences. At parent-teacher conferences, I fielded questions about whether schools today are too focused (or, alternatively, not focused enough) on verbal-linguistic and logical-mathematical intelligences. In professional-development seminars, I was urged to keep multiple intelligences in mind while developing curriculum.

I also assured my students that everyone is gifted in at least one of the intelligences—a sentiment uttered with the best of intentions, but not entirely accurate.

Not only didn't I fully understand the theory, but when I began teaching at an urban public high school in Boston, I believed I had no time to concern myself with it. I was determined to help my students develop the tools they needed to make it into college: reading comprehension, writing skills, critical thinking, SAT vocabulary. I was certain there simply weren't enough hours in the day to foster students' musical intelligence or bodily-kinesthetic intelligence.

And, then, in 2004, my views began to change. I started working on my doctorate at Harvard University and asked Professor Howard Gardner to be my adviser. My interest in working with Gardner had more to do with his work on ethics than on MI theory, but over the next four years, MI theory was like fluoride in the water. There was a constant clamor from educators across the globe to hear from him about MI theory. Working each day about 20 yards away, I couldn't help overhearing the uproar and, amid that din, I started to pick up on my own misconceptions.

What MI Is—and Is Not

MI theory asserts that, barring cases of severe brain damage, everyone possesses all eight of the intelligences with varying levels of aptitude, giving each person a unique profile. And MI theory makes no claims about everyone being gifted in at least one of the intelligences.

I also discovered that neither Gardner nor MI theory has ever argued that educators should spend equal amounts of time teaching to the eight intelligences, or that every lesson should provide students with eight options for demonstrating their learning. In fact, MI theory offers neither a curriculum nor a goal toward which educators are expected to strive. Rather, MI theory is an *idea* about the concept of intelligence. A psychologist by training, Gardner left it to educators to decide how MI theory can be useful in the particular community and context in which they teach.

Nowadays, as a professor of education myself, when students or colleagues learn that I trained with Gardner, I am often asked facetiously, "How many intelligences is he up to now?" In truth, the original formulation of MI theory included seven intelligences, and Gardner has added just one (naturalistic intelligence) over the past 25 years.

Many other scholars and educators have proposed other intelligences—everything from moral intelligence to cooking intelligence to humor intelligence—but none have provided compelling evidence to justify an addition to the list. That said, advances in fields like neuroscience and genetics may well lead in coming years to the identification of new intelligences or the reorganization of existing intelligences. Ultimately, what is important about MI theory is not the number of identified intelligences, but, rather, its core premise that intelligence is better conceived of as multiple rather than general.

Far-Reaching Impact

Since its inception 26 years ago, thousands of schools, teachers, and researchers across the globe have drawn on MI theory to improve teaching and learning. There are Howard Gardner MI schools in Indiana, Pennsylvania, and Washington State and "multiple intelligences" schools in Bangalore, India, and Quezon City, Philippines. A 2002 conference on MI theory in Beijing attracted 2,500 educators from nine provinces and six neighboring countries. In 2005, a theme park opened in Nordborg, Denmark, that allows Danish children and adults to explore their aptitudes across the intelligences.

Some schools, like Indianapolis's *Key Learning Community*[2], aim to build all eight intelligences for each student. Others, like *New City School*[3], in St. Louis, focus on the two personal intelligences. Both schools are exemplary practitioners of MI theory.

It also happens that MI theory is used in ways that are neither educationally sound nor appropriate. Perhaps the most glaring example has been a state ministry in Australia that compiled a list of ethnic groups within the state as well as the particular intelligences that each group supposedly possessed and lacked—a practice Gardner has denounced as a perversion of his theory.

In Gardner's view, MI theory is used most effectively by educators who have a particular goal they are seeking to achieve and who conceive of the theory as a tool for achieving this goal. For instance, at the start of the school year, an elementary school teacher might want to identify students' strengths and weaknesses among the eight intelligences. That teacher might carefully observe the students' activities and interactions on the playground during recess or, alternatively, ask both students and parents to fill out a short survey identifying what they believe to be their (or their child's) strengths among the eight intelligences. Such information can facilitate lesson and unit planning down the road.

Or perhaps a school leader or department head seeks to improve communication among faculty about student achievement. For this objective, MI theory could serve as a framework or common language for discussing the strengths and challenges of individual students. In this instance, the concept of multiple intelligences may not even be raised directly with students, but, rather, may serve as a tool for fostering dialogue and collaboration among their teachers.

The irony of MI theory's tremendous impact on the educational community is that the theory was not developed with educators in mind. Rather, Gardner wrote his 1983 book, *Frames of Mind,* with the goal of inciting debate among psychologists about the nature of intelligence. By and large, such a debate did not occur. The psychology community has demonstrated relatively little interest in Gardner's theory, perhaps because, in sharp contrast to the traditional IQ test, it offers no easy scale for measuring aptitude across the various intelligences.

In what amounted to a sort of grassroots uprising, however, educators at all grade levels in many types of communities have embraced MI theory with a genuine passion. In describing this groundswell of support, Gardner has often speculated that MI theory provided empirical and conceptual support for what educators had known all along: that the notion of a single, general intelligence does not accurately depict the children that educators see in their classrooms each day.

Perhaps it is for this reason that the earliest groups of educators to embrace MI theory were teachers whose daily work entailed supporting students with learning disabilities. Even more so than their general-ed colleagues, special educators see firsthand that youth who struggle with, say, language can simultaneously possess a strong aptitude for numbers or music or graphic design, and vice-versa. These teachers knew intuitively that IQ tests were not measuring what they purported to measure.

A Broader View

Perhaps the greatest contribution of MI theory, I would argue, has been its role over the past decade as a counterbalance to an educational climate increasingly focused on high-stakes testing, such as the IQ test, the SAT, and the various state assessments that have emerged from the No Child Left Behind Act.

Howard Gardner's Eight Intelligences

- Verbal-linguistic intelligence refers to an individual's ability to analyze information and produce work that involves oral and written language, such as speeches, books, and memos.
- Logical-mathematical intelligence describes the ability to develop equations and proofs, make calculations, and solve abstract problems.
- Visual-spatial intelligence allows people to comprehend maps and other types of graphical information.
- Musical intelligence enables individuals to produce and make meaning of different types of sound.
- Naturalistic intelligence refers to the ability to identify and distinguish among different types of plants, animals, and weather formations found in the natural world.
- Bodily-kinesthetic intelligence entails using one's own body to create products or solve problems.
- Interpersonal intelligence reflects an ability to recognize and understand other people's moods, desires, motivations, and intentions.
- Intrapersonal intelligence refers to people's ability to recognize and assess those same characteristics within themselves.

Source URL: http://www.edutopia.org/multiple-intelligences-theory-teacher

Even if one believes that these assessments have contributions to offer to the practice of teaching and learning, it seems equally true that these tests have presented new challenges to the educational world as well. The IQ test and the SAT, two assessments unquestionably correlated with an individual's class status and schooling opportunities, have been utilized to declare some children intrinsically "smarter" than others and more deserving of seats in gifted-and-talented programs, magnet schools, and elite universities. Particularly in urban schools, the pressure from testing has narrowed the curriculum to focus on those subjects on which graduation and accreditation rest—at the expense of art, music, theater, physical education, foreign language, and even science and social studies.

In the face of these powerful forces, MI theory has served as a reminder to educators to focus on the strengths and weaknesses of the individual child and has also offered conceptual support for educators seeking to prevent individual students from being stigmatized by a low score on one of these standardized tests. On a schoolwide scale, administrators contemplating eliminating or reducing funding for the subjects not covered by state assessments are likely to hear protests (from parents, teachers, students, and even internally) about neglecting children's multiple intelligences. I would argue that MI theory has offered an important check on the standards-based reform movement that has dominated American education for the past decade.

Or, put more simply, MI theory has helped facilitate in the heads of thousands of educators the same sort of appreciation I experienced while watching my students march down the football field: "These guys are really smart! I'm underestimating what they're capable of!" MI theory is neither a curriculum nor a goal nor an endpoint, but it remains, 26 years after its birth, a powerful tool for helping educators to teach more effectively and students to learn more deeply and enduringly.

Links

1. http://www.perseusbooksgroup.com/basic/book_detail.jsp?isbn=0465025102
2. http://www.616.ips.k12.in.us
3. http://www.newcityschool.org
4. http://www.ribasassociates.com/books.htm

SCOTT SEIDER, a former public school teacher, is an assistant professor of curriculum and teaching at Boston University. He is coauthor of *Instructional Practices That Maximize Student Achievement*[4].

In Defense of Distraction

Twitter, Adderall, lifehacking, mindful jogging, power browsing, Obama's BlackBerry, and the benefits of overstimulation.

SAM ANDERSON

I. The Poverty of Attention

I'm going to pause here, right at the beginning of my riveting article about attention, and ask you to please get all of your precious 21st-century distractions out of your system now. Check the score of the Mets game; text your sister that pun you just thought of about her roommate's new pet lizard ("iguana hold yr hand LOL get it like Beatles"); refresh your work e-mail, your home e-mail, your school e-mail; upload pictures of yourself reading this paragraph to your "me reading magazine articles" Flickr photostream; and alert the fellow citizens of whatever Twittertopia you happen to frequent that you will be suspending your digital presence for the next twenty minutes or so (I know that seems drastic: Tell them you're having an appendectomy or something and are about to lose consciousness). Good. Now: Count your breaths. Close your eyes. Do whatever it takes to get all of your neurons lined up in one direction. Above all, resist the urge to fixate on the picture, right over there, of that weird scrambled guy typing. Do not speculate on his ethnicity (German-Venezuelan?) or his backstory (Witness Protection Program?) or the size of his monitor. Go ahead and cover him with your hand if you need to. There. Doesn't that feel better? Now it's just you and me, tucked like fourteenth-century Zen masters into this sweet little nook of pure mental focus. (Seriously, stop looking at him. I'm over here.)

Over the last several years, the problem of attention has migrated right into the center of our cultural attention. We hunt it in neurology labs, lament its decline on op-ed pages, fetishize it in grassroots quality-of-life movements, diagnose its absence in more and more of our children every year, cultivate it in yoga class twice a week, harness it as the engine of self-help empires, and pump it up to superhuman levels with drugs originally intended to treat Alzheimer's and narcolepsy. Everyone still pays some form of attention all the time, of course—it's basically impossible for humans not to—but the currency in which we pay it, and the goods we get in exchange, have changed dramatically.

Back in 1971, when the web was still twenty years off and the smallest computers were the size of delivery vans, before the founders of Google had even managed to get themselves born, the polymath economist Herbert A. Simon wrote maybe the most concise possible description of our modern struggle: "What information consumes is rather obvious: It consumes the attention of its recipients. Hence a wealth of information creates a poverty of attention, and a need to allocate that attention efficiently among the overabundance of information sources that might consume it." As beneficiaries of the greatest information boom in the history of the world, we are suffering, by Simon's logic, a correspondingly serious poverty of attention.

If the pundits clogging my RSS reader can be trusted (the ones I check up on occasionally when I don't have any new e-mail), our attention crisis is already chewing its hyperactive way through the very foundations of Western civilization. Google is making us stupid, multitasking is draining our souls, and the "dumbest generation" is leading us into a "dark age" of bookless "power browsing." Adopting the Internet as the hub of our work, play, and commerce has been the intellectual equivalent of adopting corn syrup as the center of our national diet, and we've all become mentally obese. Formerly well-rounded adults are forced to MacGyver worldviews out of telegraphic blog posts, bits of YouTube videos, and the first nine words of *Times* editorials. Schoolkids spread their attention across 30 different programs at once and interact with each other mainly as sweatless avatars. (One recent study found that American teenagers spend an average of 6.5 hours a day focused on the electronic world, which strikes me as a little low; in South Korea, the most wired nation on earth, young adults have actually died from exhaustion after multiday online-gaming marathons.) We are, in short, terminally distracted. And *distracted,* the alarmists will remind you, was once a synonym for *insane.* (Shakespeare: "poverty hath distracted her.")

The most advanced Budhist monks become world-class multitaskers. Meditation might speed up their mental processes enough to handle information overload.

This doomsaying strikes me as silly for two reasons. First, conservative social critics have been blowing the apocalyptic bugle at every large-scale tech-driven social change since Socrates' famous complaint about the memory-destroying properties of that new-fangled technology called "writing." (A complaint we remember, not incidentally, because it was written down.) And, more practically, the virtual horse has already left the digital barn. It's too late to just retreat to a quieter time. Our jobs depend on connectivity. Our pleasure-cycles—no trivial matter—are increasingly tied to it. Information rains down faster and thicker every day, and there are plenty of non-moronic reasons for it to do so. The question, now, is how successfully we can adapt.

Although attention is often described as an organ system, it's not the sort of thing you can pull out and study like a spleen. It's a complex process that shows up all over the brain, mingling inextricably with other quasi-mystical processes like emotion, memory, identity, will, motivation, and mood. Psychologists have always had to track attention second-hand. Before the sixties, they measured it through easy-to-monitor senses like vision and hearing (if you listen to one voice in your right ear and another in your left, how much information can you absorb from either side?), then eventually graduated to PET scans and EEGs and electrodes and monkey brains. Only in the last ten years—thanks to neuroscientists and their functional MRIs—have we been able to watch the attending human brain in action, with its coordinated storms of neural firing, rapid blood surges, and oxygen flows. This has yielded all kinds of fascinating insights—for instance, that when forced to multitask, the overloaded brain shifts its processing from the hippocampus (responsible for memory) to the striatum (responsible for rote tasks), making it hard to learn a task or even recall what you've been doing once you're done.

When I reach David Meyer, one of the world's reigning experts on multitasking, he is feeling alert against all reasonable odds. He has just returned from India, where he was discussing the nature of attention at a conference with the Dalai Lama (Meyer gave a keynote speech arguing that Buddhist monks multitask during meditation), and his trip home was hellish: a canceled flight, an overnight taxi on roads so rough it took thirteen hours to go 200 miles. This is his first full day back in his office at the University of Michigan, where he directs the Brain, Cognition, and Action Laboratory—a basement space in which finger-tapping, card-memorizing, tone-identifying subjects help Meyer pinpoint exactly how much information the human brain can handle at once. He's been up since 3 A.M. and has by now goosed his attention several times with liquid stimulants: a couple of cups of coffee, some tea. "It does wonders," he says.

My interaction with Meyer takes place entirely via the technology of distraction. We scheduled and rescheduled our appointment, several times, by e-mail. His voice is now projecting, tinnily, out of my cell phone's speaker and into the microphone of my digital recorder, from which I will download it, as soon as we're done, onto my laptop, which I currently have open on my desk in front of me, with several windows spread across the screen, each bearing nested tabs, on one of which I've been reading, before Meyer even had a chance to tell me about it, a blog all about his conference with the Dalai Lama, complete with RSS feed and audio commentary and embedded YouTube videos

and pictures of His Holiness. As Meyer and I talk, the universe tests us with a small battery of distractions. A maximum-volume fleet of emergency vehicles passes just outside my window; my phone chirps to tell us that my mother is calling on the other line, then beeps again to let us know she's left a message. There is, occasionally, a slight delay in the connection. Meyer ignores it all, speaking deliberately and at length, managing to coordinate tricky subject-verb agreements over the course of multi-clause sentences. I begin, a little sheepishly, with a question that strikes me as sensationalistic, nonscientific, and probably unanswerable by someone who's been professionally trained in the discipline of cautious objectivity: Are we living through a crisis of attention?

Before I even have a chance to apologize, Meyer responds with the air of an Old Testament prophet. "Yes," he says. "And I think it's going to get a lot worse than people expect." He sees our distraction as a full-blown epidemic—a cognitive plague that has the potential to wipe out an entire generation of focused and productive thought. He compares it, in fact, to smoking. "People aren't aware what's happening to their mental processes," he says, "in the same way that people years ago couldn't look into their lungs and see the residual deposits."

I ask him if, as the world's foremost expert on multitasking and distraction, he has found his own life negatively affected by the new world order of multitasking and distraction.

"Yep," he says immediately, then adds, with admirable (although slightly hurtful) bluntness: "I get calls all the time from people like you. Because of the way the Internet works, once you become visible, you're approached from left and right by people wanting to have interactions in ways that are extremely time-consuming. I could spend my whole day, my whole night, just answering e-mails. I just can't deal with it all. None of this happened even ten years ago. It was a lot calmer. There was a lot of opportunity for getting steady work done."

Over the last twenty years, Meyer and a host of other researchers have proved again and again that multitasking, at least as our culture has come to know and love and institutionalize it, is a myth. When you think you're doing two things at once, you're almost always just switching rapidly between them, leaking a little mental efficiency with every switch. Meyer says that this is because, to put it simply, the brain processes different kinds of information on a variety of separate "channels"—a language channel, a visual channel, an auditory channel, and so on—each of which can process only one stream of information at a time. If you overburden a channel, the brain becomes inefficient and mistake-prone. The classic example is driving while talking on a cell phone, two tasks that conflict across a range of obvious channels: Steering and dialing are both manual tasks, looking out the windshield and reading a phone screen are both visual, etc. Even talking on a hands-free phone can be dangerous, Meyer says. If the person on the other end of the phone is describing a visual scene—say, the layout of a room full of furniture—that conversation can actually occupy your visual channel enough to impair your ability to see what's around you on the road.

The only time multitasking does work efficiently, Meyer says, is when multiple simple tasks operate on entirely separate channels—for example, folding laundry (a visual-manual task) while listening to a stock report (a verbal task). But real-world scenarios that fit those specifications are very rare.

This is troubling news, obviously, for a culture of BlackBerrys and news crawls and Firefox tabs—tools that, critics argue, force us all into a kind of elective ADHD. The tech theorist Linda Stone famously coined the phrase "continuous partial attention" to describe our newly frazzled state of mind. American office workers don't stick with any single task for more than a few minutes at a time; if left uninterrupted, they will most likely interrupt themselves. Since every interruption costs around 25 minutes of productivity, we spend nearly a third of our day recovering from them. We keep an average of eight windows open on our computer screens at one time and skip between them every twenty seconds. When we read online, we hardly even read at all—our eyes run down the page in an *F* pattern, scanning for keywords. When you add up all the leaks from these constant little switches, soon you're hemorrhaging a dangerous amount of mental power. People who frequently check their e-mail have tested as less intelligent than people who are actually high on marijuana. Meyer guesses that the damage will take decades to understand, let alone fix. If Einstein were alive today, he says, he'd probably be forced to multitask so relentlessly in the Swiss patent office that he'd never get a chance to work out the theory of relativity.

II. The War on the Poverty of Attention

For Winifred Gallagher, the author of *Rapt,* a new book about the power of attention, it all comes down to the problem of jackhammers. A few minutes before I called, she tells me, a construction crew started jackhammering outside her apartment window. The noise immediately captured what's called her bottom-up attention—the broad involuntary awareness that roams the world constantly looking for danger and rewards: shiny objects, sudden movements, pungent smells. Instead of letting this distract her, however, she made a conscious choice to go into the next room and summon her top-down attention—the narrow, voluntary focus that allows us to isolate and enhance some little slice of the world while ruthlessly suppressing everything else.

This attentional self-control, which psychologists call executive function, is at the very center of our struggle with attention. It's what allows us to invest our focus wisely or poorly. Some of us, of course, have an easier time with it than others.

Gallagher admits that she's been blessed with a naturally strong executive function. "It sounds funny," she tells me, "but I've always thought of paying attention as a kind of sexy, visceral activity. Even as a kid, I enjoyed focusing. I could feel it in almost a mentally muscular way. I took a lot of pleasure in concentrating on things. I'm the sort of irritating person who can sit down to work at nine o'clock and look up at two o'clock and say, 'Oh, I thought it was around 10:30.'"

Gallagher became obsessed with the problem of attention five years ago, when she was diagnosed with advanced and aggressive breast cancer. She was devastated, naturally, but then realized, on her way out of the hospital, that even the cancer could be seen largely as a problem of focus—a terrifying, deadly, internal jackhammer. It made her realize, she says, that attention was "not just a latent ability, it was something you could marshal and use as a tool." By the time she reached her subway station, Gallagher had come up with a strategy: She would make all the big pressing cancer-related decisions as quickly as possible, then, in order to maximize whatever time she had left, consciously shift her attention to more positive, productive things.

One of the projects Gallagher worked on during her recovery (she is now cancer free) was *Rapt,* which is both a survey of recent attention research and a testimonial to the power of top-down focus. The ability to positively wield your attention comes off, in the book, as something of a panacea; Gallagher describes it as "the sine qua non of the quality of life and the key to improving virtually every aspect of your experience." It is, in other words, the Holy Grail of self-help: the key to relationships and parenting and mood disorders and weight problems. (You can apparently lose seven pounds in a year through the sheer force of paying attention to your food.)

"You can't be happy all the time," Gallagher tells me, "but you can pretty much focus all the time. That's about as good as it gets."

The most promising solution to our attention problem, in Gallagher's mind, is also the most ancient: meditation. Neuroscientists have become obsessed, in recent years, with Buddhists, whose attentional discipline can apparently confer all kinds of benefits even on non-Buddhists. (Some psychologists predict that, in the same way we go out for a jog now, in the future we'll all do daily 20- to 30-minute "secular attentional workouts.") Meditation can make your attention less "sticky," able to notice images flashing by in such quick succession that regular brains would miss them. It has also been shown to elevate your mood, which can then recursively stoke your attention: Research shows that positive emotions cause your visual field to expand. The brains of Buddhist monks asked to meditate on "unconditional loving-kindness and compassion" show instant and remarkable changes: Their left prefrontal cortices (responsible for positive emotions) go into overdrive, they produce gamma waves 30 times more powerful than novice meditators, and their wave activity is coordinated in a way often seen in patients under anesthesia.

Gallagher stresses that because attention is a limited resource—one psychologist has calculated that we can attend to only 110 bits of information per second, or 173 billion bits in an average lifetime—our moment-by-moment choice of attentional targets determines, in a very real sense, the shape of our lives. *Rapt's* epigraph comes from the psychologist and philosopher William James: "My experience is what I agree to attend to." For Gallagher, everything comes down to that one big choice: investing your attention wisely or not. The jackhammers are everywhere—iPhones, e-mail, cancer—and Western culture's attentional crisis is mainly a widespread failure to ignore them.

It's possible that we're evolving toward a new techno-cognitive nomadism, in which restlessness will be an advantage.

"Once you understand how attention works and how you can make the most productive use of it," she says, "if you continue to just jump in the air every time your phone rings or pounce on those buttons every time you get an instant message, that's not the machine's fault. That's your fault."

Making the responsible attention choice, however, is not always easy. Here is a partial list, because a complete one would fill the entire magazine, of the things I've been distracted by in the course of writing this article: my texting wife, a very loud seagull, my mother calling from Mexico to leave voice mails in terrible Spanish, a man shouting "Your weed-whacker fell off! Your weed-whacker fell off!" at a truck full of lawn equipment, my *Lost*-watching wife, another man singing some kind of Spanish ballad on the sidewalk under my window, streaming video of the NBA playoffs, dissertation-length blog breakdowns of the NBA playoffs, my toenail spontaneously detaching, my ice-cream-eating wife, the subtly shifting landscapes of my three different e-mail in-boxes, my Facebooking wife, infinite YouTube videos (a puffin attacking someone wearing a rubber boot, Paul McCartney talking about the death of John Lennon, a chimpanzee playing Pac-Man), and even more infinite, if that is possible, Wikipedia entries: puffins, *MacGyver*, Taylorism, the phrase "bleeding edge," the Boston Molasses Disaster. (If I were going to excuse you from reading this article for any single distraction, which I am not, it would be to read about the Boston Molasses Disaster.)

When the jackhammers fire up outside my window, in other words, I rarely ignore them—I throw the window open, watch for a while, bring the crew sandwiches on their lunch break, talk with them about the ins and outs of jackhammering, and then spend an hour or two trying to break up a little of the sidewalk myself. Some of my distractions were unavoidable. Some were necessary work-related evils that got out of hand. Others were pretty clearly inexcusable. (I consider it a victory for the integrity of pre-web human consciousness that I was able to successfully resist clicking on the first "related video" after the chimp, the evocatively titled "Guy shits himself in a judo exhibition.") In today's attentional landscape, it's hard to draw neat borders.

I'm not ready to blame my restless attention entirely on a faulty willpower. Some of it is pure impersonal behaviorism. The Internet is basically a Skinner box engineered to tap right into our deepest mechanisms of addiction. As B. F. Skinner's army of lever-pressing rats and pigeons taught us, the most irresistible reward schedule is not, counterintuitively, the one in which we're rewarded constantly but something called "variable ratio schedule," in which the rewards arrive at random. And that randomness is practically the Internet's defining feature: It dispenses its never-ending little shots of positivity—a life-changing e-mail here, a funny YouTube video there—in gloriously unpredictable cycles. It seems unrealistic to expect people to spend all day clicking reward bars—searching the web, scanning the relevant blogs, checking e-mail to see if a co-worker has updated a project—and then just leave those distractions behind, as soon as they're not strictly required, to engage in "healthy" things like books and ab crunches and undistracted deep conversations with neighbors. It would be like requiring employees to take a few hits of opium throughout the day, then being surprised when it becomes a problem. Last year, an editorial in the *American Journal of Psychiatry* raised the prospect of adding "Internet addiction" to the *DSM,* which would make it a disorder to be taken as seriously as schizophrenia.

A quintessentially Western solution to the attention problem—one that neatly circumvents the issue of willpower—is to simply

dope our brains into focus. We've done so, over the centuries, with substances ranging from tea to tobacco to NoDoz to Benzedrine, and these days the tradition seems to be approaching some kind of zenith with the rise of neuroenhancers: drugs designed to treat ADHD (Ritalin, Adderall), Alzheimer's (Aricept), and narcolepsy (Provigil) that can produce, in healthy people, superhuman states of attention. A grad-school friend tells me that Adderall allowed him to squeeze his mind "like a muscle." Joshua Foer, writing in *Slate* after a weeklong experiment with Adderall, said the drug made him feel like he'd "been bitten by a radioactive spider"—he beat his unbeatable brother at Ping-Pong, solved anagrams, devoured dense books. "The part of my brain that makes me curious about whether I have new e-mails in my in-box apparently shut down," he wrote.

Although neuroenhancers are currently illegal to use without a prescription, they're popular among college students (on some campuses, up to 25 percent of students admitted to taking them) and—if endless anecdotes can be believed—among a wide spectrum of other professional focusers: journalists on deadline, doctors performing high-stakes surgeries, competitors in poker tournaments, researchers suffering through the grind of grant-writing. There has been controversy in the chess world recently about drug testing at tournaments.

In December, a group of scientists published a paper in *Nature* that argued for the legalization and mainstream acceptance of neuroenhancers, suggesting that the drugs are really no different from more traditional "cognitive enhancers" such as laptops, exercise, nutrition, private tutoring, reading, and sleep. It's not quite that simple, of course. Adderall users frequently complain that the drug stifles their creativity—that it's best for doing ultra-rational, structured tasks. (As Foer put it, "I had a nagging suspicion that I was thinking with blinders on.") One risk the scientists do acknowledge is the fascinating, horrifying prospect of "raising cognitive abilities beyond their species-typical upper bound." Ultimately, one might argue, neuroenhancers spring from the same source as the problem they're designed to correct: our lust for achievement in defiance of natural constraints. It's easy to imagine an endless attentional arms race in which new technologies colonize ever-bigger zones of our attention, new drugs expand the limits of that attention, and so on.

One of the most exciting—and confounding—solutions to the problem of attention lies right at the intersection of our willpower and our willpower-sapping technologies: the grassroots Internet movement known as "lifehacking." It began in 2003 when the British tech writer Danny O'Brien, frustrated by his own lack of focus, polled 70 of his most productive friends to see how they managed to get so much done; he found that they'd invented all kinds of clever little tricks—some high-tech, some very low-tech—to help shepherd their attention from moment to moment: ingenious script codes for to-do lists, software hacks for managing e-mail, rituals to avoid sinister time-wasting traps such as "yak shaving," the tendency to lose yourself in endless trivial tasks tangentially related to the one you really need to do. (O'Brien wrote a program that prompts him every ten minutes, when he's online, to ask if he's procrastinating.) Since then, lifehacking has snowballed into a massive self-help program, written and revised constantly by the online global hive mind, that seeks to help you allocate your attention efficiently. Tips range from time-management habits (the 90-second shower) to note-taking techniques (mind mapping) to software shortcuts (how to turn your Gmail into a to-do list) to delightfully retro tech solutions (turning an index card into a portable dry-erase board by covering it with packing tape).

When I call Merlin Mann, one of lifehacking's early adopters and breakout stars, he is running late, rushing back to his office, and yet he seems somehow to have attention to spare. He is by far the fastest-talking human I've ever interviewed, and it crosses my mind that this too might be a question of productivity—that maybe he's adopted a time-saving verbal lifehack from auctioneers. He talks in the snappy aphorisms of a professional speaker ("Priorities are like arms: If you have more than two of them, they're probably make-believe") and is always breaking ideas down into their atomic parts and reassessing the way they fit together: "What does it come down to?" "Here's the thing." "So why am I telling you this, and what does it have to do with lifehacks?"

Mann says he got into lifehacking at a moment of crisis, when he was "feeling really overwhelmed by the number of inputs in my life and managing it very badly." He founded one of the original lifehacking websites, 43folders.com (the name is a reference to David Allen's Getting Things Done, the legendarily complex productivity program in which Allen describes, among other things, how to build a kind of "three-dimensional calendar" out of 43 folders) and went on to invent such illustrious hacks as "in-box zero" (an e-mail-management technique) and the "hipster PDA" (a stack of three-by-five cards filled with jotted phone numbers and to-do lists, clipped together and tucked into your back pocket). Mann now makes a living speaking to companies as a kind of productivity guru. He Twitters, podcasts, and runs more than half a dozen websites.

Despite his robust web presence, Mann is skeptical about technology's impact on our lives. "Is it clear to you that the last fifteen years represent an enormous improvement in how everything operates?" he asks. "Picasso was somehow able to finish the *Desmoiselles of Avignon* even though he didn't have an application that let him tag his to-dos. If John Lennon had a BlackBerry, do you think he would have done everything he did with the Beatles in less than ten years?"

One of the weaknesses of lifehacking as a weapon in the war against distraction, Mann admits, is that it tends to become extremely distracting. You can spend solid days reading reviews of filing techniques and organizational software. "On the web, there's a certain kind of encouragement to never ask yourself how much information you really need," he says. "But when I get to the point where I'm seeking advice twelve hours a day on how to take a nap, or what kind of notebook to buy, I'm so far off the idea of lifehacks that it's indistinguishable from where we started. There are a lot of people out there that find this a very sticky idea, and there's very little advice right now to tell them that the only thing to do is action, and everything else is horseshit. My wife reminds me sometimes: 'You have all the information you need to do *something* right now.'"

For Mann, many of our attention problems are symptoms of larger existential issues: motivation, happiness, neurochemistry.

"I'm not a physician or a psychiatrist, but I'll tell you, I think a lot of it is some form of untreated ADHD or depression," he says. "Your mind is not getting the dopamine or the hugs that it needs to keep you focused on what you're doing. And any time your work gets a little bit too hard or a little bit too boring, you allow it to catch on to something that's more interesting to you." (Mann himself started getting treated for ADD a year ago; he says it's helped his focus quite a lot.)

Mann's advice can shade, occasionally, into Buddhist territory. "There's no shell script, there's no fancy pen, there's no notebook or nap or Firefox extension or hack that's gonna help you figure out why the fuck you're here," he tells me. "That's on you." This makes me sound like one of those people who swindled the Beatles, but if you are having attention problems, the best way to deal with it is by admitting it and then saying, 'From now on, I'm gonna be in the moment and more cognizant.' I said not long ago, I think on Twitter—God, I quote myself a lot, what an asshole—that really all self-help is Buddhism with a service mark.

"Where you allow your attention to go ultimately says more about you as a human being than anything that you put in your mission statement," he continues. "It's an indisputable receipt for your existence. And if you allow that to be squandered by other people who are as bored as you are, it's gonna say a lot about who you are as a person."

III. Embracing the Poverty of Attention

Sometimes I wonder if the time I'm wasting is actually being wasted. Isn't blowing a couple of hours on the Internet, in the end, just another way of following your attention? My life would be immeasurably poorer if I hadn't stumbled a few weeks ago across the Boston Molasses Disaster. (Okay, seriously, forget it: I hereby release you to go look up the Boston Molasses Disaster. A giant wave of molasses destroyed an entire Boston neighborhood 90 years ago, swallowing horses and throwing an elevated train off its track. It took months to scrub all the molasses out of the cobblestones! The harbor was brown until summer! The world is a stranger place than we will ever know.)

The prophets of total attentional melt-down sometimes invoke, as an example of the great culture we're going to lose as we succumb to e-thinking, the canonical French juggernaut Marcel Proust. And indeed, at seven volumes, several thousand pages, and 1.5 million words, *Á la Recherche du Temps Perdu* is in many ways the anti-Twitter. (It would take, by the way, exactly 68,636 tweets to reproduce.) It's important to remember, however, that the most famous moment in all of Proust, the moment that launches the entire monumental project, is a moment of pure distraction: when the narrator, Marcel, eats a spoonful of tea-soaked madeleine and finds himself instantly transported back to the world of his childhood. Proust makes it clear that conscious focus could never have yielded such profound magic: Marcel has to abandon the constraints of what he calls "voluntary memory"—the kind of narrow, purpose-driven attention that Adderall, say, might have allowed him to harness—in order to get to the deeper truths available only by distraction. That famous cookie is a kind of hyperlink: a little blip that launches an associative cascade of a million other subjects. This sort of free-associative wandering is essential to the creative process; one moment of judicious unmindfulness can inspire thousands of hours of mindfulness.

My favorite focusing exercise comes from William James: Draw a dot on a piece of paper, then pay attention to it for as long as you can. (Sitting in my office one afternoon, with my monkey mind swinging busily across the lush rain forest of online distractions, I tried this with the closest dot in the vicinity: the bright-red mouse-nipple at the center of my laptop's keyboard. I managed to stare at it for 30 minutes, with mixed results.) James argued that the human mind can't actually focus on the dot, or any unchanging object, for more than a few seconds at a time: It's too hungry for variety, surprise, the adventure of the unknown. It has to refresh its attention by continually finding new aspects of the dot to focus on: subtleties of its shape, its relationship to the edges of the paper, metaphorical associations (a fly, an eye, a hole). The exercise becomes a question less of pure unwavering focus than of your ability to organize distractions around a central point. The dot, in other words, becomes only the hub of your total dot-related distraction.

This is what the web-threatened punditry often fails to recognize: Focus is a paradox—it has distraction built into it. The two are symbiotic; they're the systole and diastole of consciousness. Attention comes from the Latin "to stretch out" or "reach toward," distraction from "to pull apart." We need both. In their extreme forms, focus and attention may even circle back around and bleed into one other. Meyer says there's a subset of Buddhists who believe that the most advanced monks become essentially "world-class multitaskers"—that all those years of meditation might actually speed up their mental processes enough to handle the kind of information overload the rest of us find crippling.

The truly wise mind will harness, rather than abandon, the power of distraction. Unwavering focus—the inability to be distracted—can actually be just as problematic as ADHD. Trouble with "attentional shift" is a feature common to a handful of mental illnesses, including schizophrenia and OCD. It's been hypothesized that ADHD might even be an advantage in certain change-rich environments. Researchers have discovered, for instance, that a brain receptor associated with ADHD is unusually common among certain nomads in Kenya, and that members who have the receptor are the best nourished in the group. It's possible that we're all evolving toward a new techno-cognitive nomadism, a rapidly shifting environment in which restlessness will be an advantage again. The deep focusers might even be hampered by having too much attention: Attention Surfeit Hypoactivity Disorder.

I keep returning to the parable of Einstein and Lennon— the great historical geniuses hypothetically ruined by modern distraction. What made both men's achievements so groundbreaking, though, was that they did something modern technology is getting increasingly better at allowing us to do: They very powerfully linked and synthesized things that had previously been unlinked—Newtonian gravity and particle physics, rock and blues and folk and doo-wop and bubblegum pop and psychedelia. If Einstein and Lennon were growing up today, their natural genius might be so pumped up on the possibilities of the new technology they'd be doing even more dazzling things. Surely Lennon would find a way to manipulate his BlackBerry to his own ends, just like he did with all the new technology of the sixties—he'd harvest spam and text messages and web snippets and build them into a new kind of absurd poetry. The Beatles would make the best viral videos of all time, simultaneously addictive and artful, disposable and forever. All of those canonical songs, let's remember, were created entirely within a newfangled mass genre that was widely considered to be an assault on civilization and the sanctity of deep human thought. Standards change. They change because of great creations in formerly suspect media.

Which brings me, finally, to the next generation of attenders, the so-called "net-gen" or "digital natives," kids who've grown up with the Internet and other time-slicing technologies. There's been lots of hand-wringing about all the skills they might lack, mainly the ability to concentrate on a complex task from beginning to end, but surely they can already do things their elders can't—like conduct 34 conversations simultaneously across six different media, or pay attention to switching between attentional targets in a way that's been considered impossible. More than any other organ, the brain is designed to change based on experience, a feature called neuroplasticity. London taxi drivers, for instance, have enlarged hippocampi (the brain region for memory and spatial processing)—a neural reward for paying attention to the tangle of the city's streets. As we become more skilled at the 21st-century task Meyer calls "flitting," the wiring of the brain will inevitably change to deal more efficiently with more information. The neuroscientist Gary Small speculates that the human brain might be changing faster today than it has since the prehistoric discovery of tools. Research suggests we're already picking up new skills: better peripheral vision, the ability to sift information rapidly. We recently elected the first-ever BlackBerry president, able to flit between sixteen national crises while focusing at a world-class level. Kids growing up now might have an associative genius we don't—a sense of the way ten projects all dovetail into something totally new. They might be able to engage in seeming contradictions: mindful web-surfing, mindful Twittering. Maybe, in flights of irresponsible responsibility, they'll even manage to attain the paradoxical, Zenlike state of focused distraction.

Informing the ADHD Debate

The latest neurological research has injected much needed objectivity into the disagreement over how best to treat children with attention-deficit disorders.

Aribert Rothenberger and Tobias Banaschewski

From the moment Julia entered first grade, she appeared to spend most of her time daydreaming. She needed more time to complete assignments than the other children did. As she moved through elementary school, her test scores deteriorated. She felt increasingly unable to do her homework or follow the teacher's instructions in class. She made few real friends and said her teachers got on her nerves. She complained that her parents pressured her all day long and that nothing she did was right.

Julia was actually very friendly and talkative, but a lack of self-control made others feel uneasy around her. By age 14, she found that concentrating on assignments seemed impossible. She constantly lost her belongings. Neuropsychological exams showed Julia was of average intelligence but repeatedly interrupted the tests. She was easily distracted and seemed to expect failure in everything she did. So she just gave up. Ultimately Julia was diagnosed with attention-deficit hyperactivity disorder (ADHD) and was treated with methylphenidate, one of the standard drugs for her condition. The medication helped Julia organize her life and tackle her schoolwork more readily. She says she now feels better and is much more self-confident.

Julia's symptoms constitute just one profile of a child with ADHD. Other girls and boys exhibit similar yet varied traits, and whereas medication has helped in many cases, for just as many it provides no relief. With the number of cases increasing every year, debate over basic questions has heightened: Is ADHD overdiagnosed? Do drugs offer better treatment than behavior modification? Recent progress in understanding how brain activity differs in ADHD children is suggesting answers.

What Causes ADHD?

ADHD is diagnosed in 2 to 5 percent of children between the ages of six and 16; approximately 80 percent are boys. The typical symptoms of distractibility, hyperactivity and agitation occur at all ages, even in adults who have the condition, but with considerable disparity. Children often seem forgetful or impatient, tend to disturb others and have a hard time observing limits. Poor impulse control manifests itself in rash decision making, silly antics and rapid mood swings. The child acts before thinking. And yet ADHD children often behave perfectly

normally in new situations, particularly those of short duration that involve direct contact with individuals or are pleasurable or exciting, like watching TV or playing games.

Precursor behaviors such as a difficult temperament or sleep and appetite disorders have often been found in children younger than three who were later diagnosed with ADHD, but no definitive diagnosis can be made in those first three years. Physical restlessness often diminishes in teenagers, but attention failure continues and can often become associated with aggressive or antisocial behavior and emotional problems, as well as a tendency toward drug abuse. Symptoms persist into adulthood in 30 to 50 percent of cases.

Longitudinal epidemiological studies demonstrate that ADHD is no more common today than in the past. The apparent statistical rise in the number of cases may be explained by increased public awareness and improved diagnosis. The condition can now be reliably identified according to a set of characteristics that differentiate it from age-appropriate behavior. Nevertheless, debates about overdiagnosis, as well as preferred treatments, are sharper than ever.

Neurologists are making headway in informing these debates. For starters, researchers using state-of-the-art imaging techniques have found differences in several brain regions of ADHD and non-ADHD children of similar ages. On average, both the frontal lobe and the cerebellum are smaller in ADHD brains, as are the parietal and temporal lobes. ADHD seems to be the result of abnormal information processing in these brain regions, which are responsible for emotions and control over impulses and movements.

Yet these variations do not indicate any basic mental deficiency. Currently physicians see the disorder as an extreme within the natural variability of human behavior. On neuropsychological tests such as letter-sequence recognition on a computer, ADHD children have varied but frequently slower reaction times. The reason, experts now believe, is that neural information processing—the foundation of experience and behavior—may break down, especially when many competing demands suddenly flood the brain. In this circumstance or when faced with tasks requiring speed, thoroughness or endurance, the performance of ADHD brains decreases dramatically compared with the brains of other children. A lack of stimulation, on the other hand, quickly leads to boredom.

The attention deficit is particularly evident whenever children are asked to control their behavior—stopping an impulsive action or maintaining a high level of performance in a given task. The problem is not so much a lack of attention per se but a rapid drop in the ability to continually pay attention.

A different phenomenon, however, gives hyperactive children the uncontrollable urge to move. Together with the cerebellum, which coordinates movement, various control systems within and underneath the cerebral cortex are responsible for motor functions. This region is where the neurons of the motor cortex, the basal ganglia and the thalamus come together. The motor cortex represents the final stage of neural processing, after which motor impulses are sent to muscles. When activity in these regions is not balanced, children have difficulty preparing for, selecting and executing movements because they cannot adequately control or inhibit their motor system. Complex movements that require precise sequencing are initiated too early and then overshoot their target. Hyperactivity also often goes hand in hand with deficits in fine-motor coordination and an inability of children to stop speech from bursting forth uncontrollably.

In general, the underlying trait of impulsivity is linked to the development of the brain's so-called executive function: the ability to plan and to monitor working memory. Executive function develops over time as the brain matures. In children with ADHD, however, it tends to remain rudimentary. Anatomically, the executive function stems from neural networks in the prefrontal cortex—the so-called anterior attentional system. Together with the posterior attentional system, located largely in the parietal lobes, it tracks and regulates behavior.

While trying to navigate life without a strong ability to monitor and plan, ADHD children are often in constant battle with their emotions. They are barely able to control their feelings, and they do not endure frustration well. They easily become excited and impatient and tend toward hostility. They also find it hard to motivate themselves for certain tasks. And they are apt to grasp at the first reward that comes their way, no matter how small, rather than wait for a larger, more attractive payoff.

Dopamine plays an important role in the limbic system, which addresses emotional challenges, and ADHD children typically have low levels of this neurotransmitter. Normally, for example, dopamine release strengthens the neural connections that lead to a desired behavior when a reward stimulus is presented. But when dopamine is absent, rewards that are minor or presented at the wrong time have no effect.

Genes or Environment

One question that arises from all these findings is why specific brain regions are smaller than others and why certain brain functions are weak or unbalanced. Genes may play a considerable role. Comprehensive metastudies of parents and children and identical and fraternal twins, such as those conducted by Anita Thapar, then at the University of Manchester in England, in 1999, Philip Asherson of King's College in London in 2001, and Susan Sprich of Massachusetts General Hospital in 2001, show that heredity greatly influences the occurrence of ADHD. For example, children of parents who have had ADHD are far more likely to suffer similar symptoms. The studies indicate that approximately 80 percent of ADHD cases can be traced to genetic factors.

As a result, researchers have been busily trying to identify which genes might be different in ADHD children. High on the suspect list are genes involved in transferring information between neurons. This group includes genes for proteins that influence the circulation of dopamine at the synapses between neurons—for example, proteins that clear away old messenger molecules so new ones can come through. So far researchers have found that receptor mediation of the dopamine signal is too weak in some patients, and dopamine reuptake is too rapid in others.

The genetics work seems to indicate that behavior problems are associated with insufficient regulation of dopamine metabolism, which derails neural information processing. The neurotransmitter norepinephrine may play a role, too. Although the genetic links between norepinephrine and its receptors and transporters are not as clearly understood as those for dopamine, medications such as atomoxetine that inhibit norepinephrine reuptake by neurons do improve symptoms.

When coupled, the neurotransmitter and brain-imaging evidence imply that the brains of ADHD children may be organized and function differently from an early age. These organic disparities may actually be the cause of behavioral changes and not a consequence of them, as has sometimes been suggested. Another piece of evidence is that in some cases, as children mature, certain physiological peculiarities—such as the size of the corpus striatum—become normal, and ADHD fades.

Still, ADHD cannot yet be tied neatly to known physical, genetic factors. Experts believe that the gene loci discovered to date explain at most 5 percent of problematic behaviors. If more fundamental gene variations are at fault, they have not yet been found. The probability of developing a hyperactivity disorder depends on a combination of many different genes.

Furthermore, there is wide variability in the degree to which these genetic factors are expressed. That means environmental influences must certainly play a role. For example, alcohol and nicotine consumption by a mother during pregnancy tend to increase the risk of ADHD in offspring, much the same way they contribute to extreme prematurity, low birth weight and food allergies.

On the other hand, it is also true that mothers with a genetic predisposition to ADHD have a propensity to smoke and drink during pregnancy. They tend to make basic child-rearing errors, too, such as failing to establish clear rules and effective limits. A chaotic household can strengthen biological ADHD tendencies, leading to a vicious cycle.

Other psychosocial factors, including a non-supportive school environment, marital crises or psychological problems arising between parents, and poor parent-child attachment can also transform a latent tendency into a full-blown disorder.

Medication Dispute

Recent findings about deficits in brain function and neurotransmitters make it clear why certain drugs are likely treatments. And yet the role of environment suggests that behavioral therapy can also be effective. Today uncertainty surrounds both options, and the increasing use of medication has proved divisive. Opinion runs from euphoric endorsement to outright rejection.

The body of evidence suggests that neurotransmitter systems need to be targeted. Psycho-stimulants such as amphetamine sulfates and methylphenidate, marketed under such names as Ritalin, have had widespread success. Numerous clinical studies show that these medications can decrease or eliminate behavioral disorders in 70 to 90 percent of patients.

Administering stimulants to hyperactive children might seem counterintuitive. Yet these substances fix the genetically based dopamine imbalance in the parts of the brain responsible for self-regulation, impulse control and perception. In effect, they prevent the overly rapid reuptake of dopamine at synapses. Other substances with similar modes of action, such as the norepinephrine reuptake inhibitor atomoxetine, work equally well.

Many parents are understandably nervous about subjecting their children to a long-term regimen of medication. News that Ritalin use may be implicated in Parkinson's disease, a dopamine deficiency illness, has added to the worry. Such a connection was suspected because rats that received methylphenidate before sexual maturity exhibited fewer than normal dopamine transporters in their striatum. But to date, not a single case of Parkinson's has been attributed to the use of Ritalin during childhood, and on average Parkinson's patients do not have a history of taking psychostimulants more frequently than other people. Nevertheless, many parents may fear that long-term treatment with psychoactive drugs could leave their child vulnerable to drug or medication abuse in the future.

In 2003, however, Timothy E. Wilens and his colleagues at Harvard Medical School laid these concerns to rest with a large-scale metastudy. It turns out that the use of psychostimulants significantly reduces the risk of future abuse. In comparing ADHD adults with comparable symptoms, those who had not received ADHD medications as children were three times more likely to succumb to drug addiction later in life than those who had received medication.

Drugs Plus Behavior

This does not mean that physicians should prescribe drugs lightly. And under no circumstances should doctors, parents or patients rely exclusively on medication. Studies show that adding behavioral therapy greatly enhances improvements. It also can teach children how to overcome any kind of problematic behavior that might arise in their lifetime. Children learn how to observe and control themselves. Unless ADHD erupts in its most extreme form, behavioral therapy should be the initial treatment of choice. If a child shows no significant signs of improvement after several months, a drug regimen can then be considered.

For the youngest children—those of preschool age—psychostimulants should generally be avoided. Parents should instead try to work daily with their children on their behavior. They would also do well to draw on the expertise of preschool teachers, who see many different children with a wide range of challenges.

A comprehensive examination conducted in 2000 by the National Institute of Mental Health rated the effectiveness of medical and behavioral treatments of ADHD. Conducted over two years, the Multimodal Treatment Study of Children with ADHD included 579 ADHD children at six different university medical centers. The principal investigators divided the test subjects, all of whom were between the ages of seven and nine, into four groups that had different treatment plans. The results strongly suggest that a combination of drug and behavioral therapies leads to the highest success:

- Routine daily treatment with prescribed medication normalized behavior in 25 percent of children treated.
- Intensive behavioral therapy without medication ended with 34 percent of patients exhibiting no further remarkable symptoms.
- Carefully tailored medical treatment with accompanying counseling for the child and parents helped 56 percent of the children.
- A combination of medication and behavioral therapy resulted in a success rate of 68 percent.

Always Count to 10

These findings allow us to draw concrete conclusions about how parents and educators might best help ADHD children. With or without drugs, it is imperative that children be taught how to handle tasks with more organization and less impulsivity. One common tool, for example, is teaching them to count to 10 before carrying out an impulse, such as jumping up from a table at school. Wall posters or cards shaped like stop signs can remind children to use the various devices they have learned in the heat of a moment. Older children and teenagers can learn how to make detailed plans and how to follow through when complicated tasks threaten to shut them down—for example, when they must straighten a messy bedroom.

Parents also need aids for dealing with trying situations. They can receive guidance in parent training programs that focus on their child-rearing skills as well as their child's interactions within the family. One common recommendation is to set up written schedules with children so that getting ready for school, for example, does not turn into a contest every morning. Clear rules, specific expectations and known consequences as well as reward points for desired behaviors can all be effective. Particularly with teenagers, parents and even siblings should be included in family therapy.

As neuroscience progresses, therapists continue to try to refine which mixes of drugs and behavioral therapy are best for which types of ADHD. More work is needed. Little is known, for example, about what occurs in the brains of ADHD children between birth and the time they enter school. One conclusion has become increasingly clear, however: the varying combinations of behaviors cannot be grouped into a picture of a single disorder. Researchers are now trying to define subgroups that are more coherent in terms of symptoms and neurological causes. To this end, they are looking at other disturbances

Latest Leap

Neurofeedback is the newest treatment alternative that therapists are exploring to combat ADHD. It is based on the finding that the electrical brain activity of ADHD children often differs from that of their peers. In this scheme, children play special computer games to learn how to consciously influence their brain waves—and therefore their behavior. For example, they can make themselves calmer and more attentive by strengthening certain electrical activity and decreasing other activity. Sounds, music or movie clips reward them when they can elicit a desired change.

In one game, a child wearing electrodes watches a cartoon of a pole-vaulting mouse. The mouse can only clear the bar when the pole turns red. This feat occurs when the child concentrates, but the pole turns blue when the child does not.

Children in neurofeedback therapy usually undergo three or four 30- to 40-minute sessions a week for six to 10 weeks. Attention, concentration, impulsivity and mild forms of hyperactivity frequently improve. A child's feelings of self-esteem also improve because he sees that he can control his own behavior. Many succeed in transferring the concentration skills they develop to their schoolwork.

—A.R. and T.B.

that are often associated with attention deficit or hyperactivity; approximately 80 percent of ADHD children suffer from at least one other challenge, such as nervous tics, antisocial behavior, anxiety, or reading and spelling problems.

In the meantime, as parents and teachers do the best they can, they must remember that ADHD children possess many positive traits. They tend to be free-spirited, inquisitive, energetic and funny, as well as intelligent and creative. Their behavior is often spontaneous, helpful and sensitive. Many ADHD children are talented multitaskers, last-minute specialists and improvisationalists. Parents and educators should encourage these strengths and let their children know whenever possible that these qualities are highly valued. That will help them feel less under attack, a relief that all by itself can help them begin to turn the corner.

Further Readings

Driven to Distraction: Recognizing and Coping with Attention Deficit Disorder from Childhood through Adulthood. Reprint edition. Edward M. Hallowell and John J. Ratey. Touchstone, 1995.

Does Stimulant Therapy of Attention-Deficit/Hyperactivity Disorder Beget Later Substance Abuse? A Meta-Analytic Review of the Literature. T. E. Wilens, S. V. Faraone, J. Biederman and S. Gunawardene in *Pediatrics,* Vol. 111, pages 179–185; January 2003.

ARIBERT ROTHENBERGER and **TOBIAS BANASCHEWSKI** are both in the clinic for child and *adolescent* psychiatry at the University of Goettingen in Germany. Rothenberger is a professor and director of the clinic. Banaschewski is the clinic's chief physician.

Ten Big Effects of the No Child Left behind Act on Public Schools

The Center on Education Policy has been carefully monitoring the implementation of NCLB for four years. Now Mr. Jennings and Ms. Rentner consider the comprehensive information that has been gathered and present their conclusions about the law's impact thus far.

JACK JENNINGS AND DIANE STARK RENTNER

Test-driven accountability is now the norm in public schools, a result of the No Child Left Behind (NCLB) Act, which is the culmination of 15 years of standards-based reform. Many state and local officials believe that this reliance on tests is too narrow a measure of educational achievement, but NCLB has directed greater attention to low-achieving students and intensified efforts to improve persistently low-performing schools.

For the past four years, the Center on Education Policy (CEP), an independent nonprofit research and advocacy organization, has been conducting a comprehensive and continuous review of NCLB, producing the annual reports contained in the series *From the Capital to the Classroom* as well as numerous papers on specific issues related to the law.[1] Each year, the CEP gathers information for this review by surveying officials in all the state departments of education, administering a questionnaire to a nationally representative sample of school districts, conducting case studies of individual school districts and schools, and generally monitoring the implementation of this important national policy.

Ten Effects

Ten major effects of NCLB on American education are evident from this multi-year review and analysis. We describe these effects broadly, because our purpose is to assess the overall influence of this policy on public schools. The effects on particular schools and districts may be different.

1. State and district officials report that student achievement on state tests is rising, which is a cause for optimism. It's not clear, however, that students are really gaining as much as rising percentages of proficient scores would suggest. Scores on state tests in reading and mathematics that are used for

NCLB purposes are going up, according to nearly three-fourths of the states and school districts, and the achievement gaps on these same tests are generally narrowing or staying the same. States and districts mostly credit their own policies as important in attaining these results, although they acknowledge that the "adequate yearly progress" (AYP) requirements of NCLB have also contributed. However, under NCLB, student achievement is equated with the proportion of students who are scoring at the proficient level on state tests, and states have adopted various approaches in their testing programs, such as the use of confidence intervals, that result in more test scores being counted as proficient. In addition, some national studies support our survey findings of increased student achievement, while others do not.

2. Schools are spending more time on reading and math, sometimes at the expense of subjects not tested. To find additional time for reading and math, the two subjects that are required to be tested under NCLB and that matter for accountability purposes, 71% of districts are reducing time spent on other subjects in elementary schools—at least to some degree. The subject most affected is social studies, while physical education is least affected. In addition, 60% of districts require a specific amount of time for reading in elementary schools. Ninety-seven percent of high-poverty districts have this requirement, compared to 55%–59% of districts with lower levels of poverty.

3. Schools are paying much more attention to the alignment of curriculum and instruction and are analyzing test score data much more closely. Changes in teaching and learning are occurring in schools that have not made AYP for two years. The most common improvements are greater alignment of curriculum and instruction with standards and assessments, more use of test data to modify instruction, use of research to inform decisions about improvement strategies, improvement in the quality and quantity of professional development for teachers, and the provision of more intensive instruction to low-achieving students.

4. Low-performing schools are undergoing makeovers rather than the most radical kinds of restructuring. More intensive changes are taking place in schools that have not made AYP for five consecutive years and thus must be "restructured" under NCLB. Greater efforts to improve curriculum, staffing, and leadership are the most common changes, but very few of these restructured schools have been taken over by the states, dissolved, or made into charter schools. Though only about 3% of all schools were in restructuring during the 2005–06 school year, the number may increase in the current year. The longer the law is in effect, the more likely it is that some schools will not make AYP for five years.

5. Schools and teachers have made considerable progress in demonstrating that teachers meet the law's academic qualifications—but many educators are skeptical this will really improve the quality of teaching. With regard to teacher quality, 88% of school districts reported that by the end of the 2005–06 school year all their teachers of core academic subjects would have met the NCLB definition of "highly qualified." Problems persist, however, for special education teachers, high school math and science teachers, and teachers in rural areas who teach multiple subjects. Despite this general compliance with NCLB's provisions, most districts expressed skepticism that this requirement will improve the quality of teaching.

6. Students are taking a lot more tests. Students are taking many more tests as a result of NCLB. In 2002, 19 states had annual reading and mathematics tests in grades 3–8 and once in high school; by 2006, every state had such testing. In the 2007–08 school year, testing in science will be required under NCLB (although the results need not be used for NCLB's accountability requirements), leading to a further increase in the number of assessments.

7. Schools are paying much more attention to achievement gaps and the learning needs of particular groups of students. NCLB's requirement that districts and schools be responsible for improving not only the academic achievement of students as a whole but also the achievement of each subgroup of students is directing additional attention to traditionally underperforming groups of students, such as those who are from low-income families or ethnic and racial minorities, those who are learning English, or those who have a disability. States and school districts have consistently praised NCLB's requirement for the disaggregation of test data by subgroups of students, because it has shone a light on the poor performance of students who would have gone unnoticed if only general test data were considered.

For the past three years, though, states and districts have repeatedly identified as NCLB problem areas the law's testing and accountability provisions for students with disabilities and students learning English. State and district officials have voiced frustration with requirements to administer state exams to students with disabilities because, for disabled students with cognitive impairments, the state test may be inappropriate and serve no instructional purpose. Similarly, officials don't see the merit in administering an English/language arts test to students who speak little or no English. The U.S. Department of Education (ED) has made some administrative changes in those areas, but, in the view of state officials and local educators, these modifications have not been enough.

8. The percentage of schools on state "needs improvement" lists has been steady but is not growing. Schools so designated are subject to NCLB sanctions, such as being required to offer students public school choice or tutoring services. Over the past several years, there has been a leveling off in the number of schools not making AYP for at least two years. About 10% of all schools have been labeled as "in need of improvement" for not making AYP, though these are not always the same schools every year. Urban districts, however, report greater proportions of their schools in this category than do suburban and rural districts. Earlier predictions had been that by this time there would be a very large number of U.S. schools not making AYP. A major reason for the overall stabilization in numbers of such schools is that, as already noted, test scores are increasing. Another reason is that ED has permitted states to modify their NCLB accountability systems so that it is easier for schools and districts to make AYP.

In the last four years, about 2% of eligible students each year have moved from a school not making AYP for at least two years to another school, using the "public school choice" option. Approximately 20% of eligible students in each of the last two years have taken advantage of additional tutoring (called "supplemental educational services") that must be offered to students from low-income families in schools not making AYP for at least three consecutive years. Although student participation in tutoring has been stable, the number of providers of supplemental services has grown dramatically in the last two years, with more than half of the providers now being for-profit entities. Lower proportions of urban and suburban school districts report that they are providing these services than in the past. School districts are skeptical that the choice option and tutoring will lead to increases in academic achievement, though they are somewhat less skeptical about tutoring than they are about choice. (This month's *Kappan* includes a Special Section on Supplemental Educational Services.)

9. The federal government is playing a bigger role in education. Because of NCLB, the federal government is taking a much more active role in public elementary and secondary education than in the past. For example, ED must approve the testing programs states use to carry out NCLB as well as the accountability plans that determine the rules for how schools make AYP. In CEP surveys for the last three years, the states have judged ED's enforcement of many of the key features of the law as being strict or very strict, even while ED was granting some changes in state accountability plans. More states in 2005 than in 2004 reported that ED was strictly or very strictly enforcing the provisions for AYP, supplemental services, public school choice, and highly qualified teachers.

10. NCLB requirements have meant that state governments and school districts also have expanded roles in school operations, but often without adequate federal funds to carry out their duties. State governments are also taking a much more active role in public education, because they must carry out NCLB provisions that affect all their public schools. These state responsibilities include creating or expanding testing programs for grades 3–8 and one year of high school, setting minimum testing goals that all schools must achieve in general and also for their various groups of students, providing assistance to schools in need of improvement, certifying supplemental service providers and then evaluating the quality of their programs, and establishing criteria to determine whether current teachers meet NCLB's teacher-quality requirements. Most state departments of education do not have the capacity to carry out all these duties. Last year, 36 of the 50 states reported to CEP that they lacked sufficient staff to implement NCLB's requirements.

Local school districts must also assume more duties than before because of NCLB. More tests must be administered to students, more attention must be directed to schools in need of improvement, and judgments must be made about whether teachers of core academic subjects are highly qualified. In carrying out these responsibilities, 80% of districts have reported for two years in a row that they are absorbing costs that federal funds are not covering. Overall, federal funding for NCLB has stagnated for several years. Provisions of the law have resulted in a shift of funds so that, in school year 2005–06, two-thirds of school districts in the country received no increases or lost funds compared to the previous year.

NCLB's Future

NCLB is clearly having a major impact on American public education. There is more testing and more accountability. Greater attention is being paid to what is being taught and how it is being taught. Low-performing schools are also receiving greater attention. The qualifications of teachers are coming under greater scrutiny. Concurrently with NCLB, scores on state reading and mathematics tests have risen.

Yet some provisions of the act and of its administration are causing persistent problems. State and local officials have identified the testing and accountability requirements for students with disabilities and for students learning English as troublesome, and other requirements—such as the one to offer a choice of another public school to students in schools needing improvement—have caused administrative burdens with little evidence that they have raised student achievement.

The lack of capacity of state departments of education could undercut the effective administration of NCLB. ED cannot deal with all school districts in the country and so must rely on state agencies to assist in that task. Yet these agencies are under great strain, with little relief in sight. Local school districts must also carry out additional tasks, and they must dig into their own pockets to do so.

The U.S. Congress has begun hearings on the effects of NCLB to prepare for its reauthorization in the new Congress that will assemble in 2007. The key question is whether the strengths of this legislation can be retained while its weaknesses are addressed.

Note

1. For more information on NCLB, including the four annual reports and special papers, go to www.cep-dc.org, the website for the Center on Education Policy.

Jack Jennings is president of the Center on Education Policy, Washington, D.C., where Diane Stark Rentner is director of national programs.

Article 19

Single-Sex Classrooms Are Succeeding

MICHAEL GURIAN, KATHY STEVENS, AND PEGGY DANIELS

Educators at single-sex schools already get it: equality is the goal, and there may be more than one path to the destination.

—Karen Stabiner, journalist and author

Over the past decade, the Gurian Institute has trained more than forty thousand teachers in more than two thousand schools and districts, both coed and single-sex. Our trainers have worked with public and private schools, Montessori schools, and a variety of charter and independent schools in fifteen countries; we have therefore been able to see what is working and not working around the globe. In this essay, we will feature some of the schools and communities that have utilized our resources to help set up and maintain their successful single-sex programs.

The resurgence of single-sex instruction is one of the most powerful educational innovations of the past decade (also one with a long history across the globe). People who advocate for single-sex instruction do not generally claim it to be the only successful way to teach boys and girls, and they are very clear on its mission: gender equality. As they employ this innovation, they often find that it can be an effective way to teach many boys and girls in certain subjects or in certain communities, and that it is especially effective as a response to the ongoing cultural need to discover measurable and substantial achievement gains for both genders.

A Short History of the "New" Single-Sex Option

Broad-based single-sex programs have been available in independent schools, unrestricted by federal regulation, for centuries. From those schools, many with long-established programs, a number of single-sex instructional models have been maintained, many using the same instructional strategies for years. Day schools have offered single-sex classes schoolwide, or in particular divisions (usually lower or middle school), or only in specific grades. Some boarding schools serve only boys or girls; others may serve both boys and girls, but in separate facilities.

Prior to 2006, single-sex classes in public schools were generally limited to physical education and sex education classes, but a growing gender gap in performance and achievement has led public schools to reexamine single-sex possibilities. As public schools looked at piloting single-sex classes, legal challenges

arose. Schools and districts, such as Southside Junior High School in Denham Springs, Louisiana, were taken to court. With the support of the ACLU, a parent legally challenged Southside's plan to implement single-sex classes in fall 2006, delaying the program a year.

In October 2006, the U.S. Department of Education announced changes in Title IX regulations, expanding opportunities for public schools to legally offer the option of single-sex instruction. Within certain parameters set out in the final Title IX single-sex amended regulations, public schools are now allowed to include single-sex classes as a part of their educational program, if they believe those classes will improve student learning and achievement. (Document 34 CFR Part 106, the complete Title IX regulations, is available and may be downloaded directly from the Department of Education website: www.ed.gov/index.jhtml.)

Today, in increasing numbers, public and independent schools are investigating the option of single-sex instruction to further support and improve the educational growth of boys and girls. This option is proving to be an exciting alternative for improving academic performance and for creating classrooms that are more boy- and girl-friendly.

Helping Boys and Girls Succeed—The Logic of Single-Sex Instruction

At the classroom level, single-sex instruction offers specific gender-friendly opportunities for enhancing learning by directly addressing many of the challenges and stressors in boys' and girls' educational and personal lives.

Single-sex programs, whatever their scope or size in a school, have pursued those potential outcomes and collected success data. Some of the schools and teachers who have utilized Gurian Institute resources and training in *Boys and Girls Learn Differently* have shared their success data with us so that we could share it with educators who consider the single-sex option, make your case for the option in your community, or continue to maintain your already-vital program.

Different Approaches and Success Data from a Variety of Schools

No two school districts or schools are the same; thus there are many approaches to creating single-sex environments in schools. Some districts choose to start single-sex academies; some public schools decide to implement single-sex programs only in their core classes; some private schools are already single-sex or, if coed, decide to implement single-sex classes in certain grades.

Here are examples of success in these different modalities. Readers can view other schools and districts that have had success in different single-sex modalities on www.gurianinstitute.com/Success, or on the National Association for Single-Sex Public Education (NASSPE) website, www.singlesexschools.org.

A Public School District in Atlanta: Two Single-Sex Academies

After several years of planning, the Atlanta Public Schools transformed a struggling middle school into two single-sex academies. The B.E.S.T. Academy at Benjamin Carson, the boys' school, and the Coretta Scott King Young Women's Leadership Academy both opened on separate campuses in fall 2007, initially serving sixth-graders, with a plan to expand through twelfth grade. The B.E.S.T. Academy was championed by Robert Haley, at the time president of The 100 Black Men of Atlanta, which committed support and mentoring for the school, its students, and their families. Five Atlanta chapters of The Links, Incorporated—one of the oldest and largest volunteer service organizations of women committed to enriching, sustaining, and ensuring the culture and economic survival of African Americans and other persons of African ancestry—partnered with the girls' school, providing similar support. Both organizations provided substantial assistance, including purchasing uniforms for the charter class of 2007–2008. Many other community organizations also partnered with the Atlanta Public Schools to support the initiative.

The staff of the boys' school focused on closing the achievement gap in literacy, recognizing that reading skills would affect every content area for their students from sixth grade through high school graduation and into college. Implementing best-practice single-sex strategies proven to help boys succeed, the teachers and administrators at the boys' school are excited about the strides their students have already made and will make in the future.

The staff of the girls' school focused on increasing the girls' use of technology. The teachers used Promethean Boards in the areas of math and science, overhead projectors, thin client computers, digital cameras, iPods for podcasting, and LCD projectors. In addition, students created PowerPoint presentations and podcasts for social studies units and concept-based units. Daily, students gathered in the media center, doing research for an event, a project, or a debate.

The struggling students have used the Internet daily to participate in the Achieve 3000 program, a content-based reading program. Principal Melody Morgan said, "I boast that several of the students entered the program as nonreaders and have made significant gains this year. We projected gains of 25 percent in this program, and the students actually had an achievement gain of 74.2 percent. They are proud!"

The use of technology is crucial in the global market; encouraging girls' engagement in technology will prepare them to be part of the future economy. A single-sex environment can greatly increase girls' desired participation.

As the schools enter their second year and expand to grades 6 and 7, many lessons learned will help make the second year an even greater success.

A Statewide Initiative: South Carolina

The South Carolina Department of Education was the first to create a state-level position to lead a statewide single-sex initiative. In July 2007, David Chadwell was appointed director of single-gender initiatives. Chadwell is responsible for facilitating the development of single-sex programs across South Carolina, including training teachers; advising program creation; facilitating implementation; hosting informational sessions for faculty, parents, and community members; and maintaining a network of people interested in or already working in single-gender education.

As of April 2008, there were 97 schools in South Carolina offering some form of single-sex programs across the age levels, with another 214 schools exploring single-sex options. Seventy school districts and nearly 30 percent of the schools in South Carolina are involved in the program, the highest percentage (59 percent) being in middle schools.

Researchers nationwide are watching South Carolina's initiative; it is a great opportunity to learn about the success of single-sex programs as the schools collect and evaluate their data.

A Public, Coed Elementary School: Woodward Avenue Elementary

In 2003 Jo Anne Rodkey, now-retired principal of Woodward Avenue Elementary School in DeLand, Florida, began an opt-in experiment in single-sex instruction, primarily because the boys in her school were lagging significantly behind the girls in reading. The boys were also, by far, the predominant sex in the school's special education classes.

Rodkey began the process by training her teachers, sending them to related professional development workshops and conferences, and supplying them with the latest research on gender learning differences. They started the program in their kindergarten, second, and fourth grades. As an opt-in program, teachers were able to volunteer to teach in the single-sex classes. To be selected, they had to agree to be purposeful as they planned for instruction, making sure they were using practices suggested from research on brain and gender learning differences. Parents could also choose the program for their children, but it was a guided choice, because Rodkey wanted to maintain a heterogeneous balance of race and academic ability in the classroom.

Woodward now has optional single-sex classes in grades K–5. The program is successful: individual student gains are noticeable for both boys' and girls' single-sex classes, and both groups do as well or better than the school's regular coed classes. Academic progress being made by the boys includes learning the fundamentals, the basic skills, to help them become good readers. Rodkey adds that although improving discipline was not a reason Woodward chose to implement its program, she saw fewer problems, especially with boys-only groups. There were fewer office referrals, and she credited this to the fact that the boys' teachers were able to be much more tolerant of boy energy and boy behavior without girls in the classroom.

A Public Middle School: Roosevelt Middle School

Roosevelt Middle School in Oklahoma City, Oklahoma, serves nine hundred students in grades 6–8. One hundred percent of Roosevelt's students qualify for free lunch and 75 percent are minority. In 2005, Roosevelt had a gender gap of 17 percent in reading achievement; 72 percent of Roosevelt's eighth-grade girls scored satisfactory on their state assessment tests, but only 55 percent of eighth-grade boys scored satisfactory.

Principal Marilyn Vrooman began looking for alternatives that would correct the problem. After researching single-sex options, she determined the strategy should be given serious consideration. The teachers agreed, the parents agreed, and after appropriate professional development for all teachers, Roosevelt separated the boys and girls in language arts, math, and technology education.

At the end of the 2005–2006 school year, Roosevelt's boys scored 71 percent satisfactory on the reading CRT and the girls scored 80 percent, narrowing the achievement gap to 9 percent in one year. The 2006–2007 school year was the first year Roosevelt had been off the state's "at risk" list in four years.

A Public Middle School: Wolfe Middle School

Wolfe Middle School in the Center Line School District in Center Line, Michigan, implemented single-sex core courses for sixth-graders in language arts, math, social studies, and science during the 2007–2008 school year. They began by receiving training in how boys and girls learn differently (the subject of one chapter in *Successful Single-Sex Classrooms,* and a crucial starting place for any efforts to close gender and achievement gaps). After one year of single-sex classes, they determined that the significant improvements of both boys and girls in language arts and social studies justified a continuation of single-sex classes in those content areas for 2008–2009. They further decided to move sixth-grade single-sex teachers with their students for seventh grade, a practice known as "looping."

A Public High School: Hope High School

Hope High School in Hope, Arkansas, is a school of approximately eight hundred students in grades 9–12. Assistant Principal Renee Parker works specifically with the ninth and tenth grades, and she saw her ninth-grade students, especially the males, struggling with the transition to high school—failing course after course and spending numerous days in the detention room for immature behavior that disrupted classes.

Hope operates on a straight 4 × 4 block schedule in which all students have four ninety-minute-long courses per semester. At the end of the semester, students change to a new set of four courses and have the potential of earning eight credits per year.

In January 2006 Parker looked at her data and found that 12 percent of students in the ninth grade, primarily males, had failed all four courses for the fall semester. Those students had placed themselves in serious jeopardy of not graduating with their class, and Parker knew that there had to be some way of making this transition from junior high to high school more successful.

Parker and her colleagues researched gender and learning and obtained professional development for all faculty and staff. Hope High School piloted single-sex classes in the ninth grade in 2006. In January 2007, when the data on student achievement were next gathered, there were no ninth-grade students who failed all four courses, only two had failed two courses, and only eleven had failed one course. Furthermore, discipline referrals for the ninth-graders had decreased by 35 percent from the previous fall and the attendance rate had increased by 15 percent.

A Boys' School: Crespi Carmelite High School

Crespi Carmelite High School in Encino, California, is a nonprofit, Catholic, four-year, college preparatory school for young men. In 2005, looking at their performance data and seeking ways to increase student achievement, Father Paul Henson, Crespi's principal, began a two-year process that greatly enhanced the school's ability to establish and maintain a boy-friendly environment. He designed and implemented a two-year professional development plan that included both on-site training for all faculty and staff and sending designated faculty to intensive summer training, thus developing in-house expertise.

Although Crespi had been focused on teaching boys since its founding in 1959, the school was committed to incorporating the latest research on gender and learning into every classroom in the school. Adding to their already-deep knowledge base of how to educate boys in a single-sex environment, Crespi's commitment to training has allowed them to increase performance scores to higher levels than before and to decrease discipline referrals even further.

Crespi, like many boys' schools, approaches developmental issues from a boy-friendly perspective and implements schoolwide strategies that constantly enhance students' level of success.

A Coed Independent School: Carolina Day School

Carolina Day School is an independent, college-preparatory school serving grades Pre-K–12 in Asheville, North Carolina. In fall 2004, Carolina Day engaged in a spirited discussion regarding the possibility of implementing single-sex education in the middle school. School administrators listened carefully to parents, students, and faculty; they reviewed research on the topic; they consulted with experts and practitioners. There were differing opinions of considerable merit and, in the end, the community was convinced that Carolina Day should implement single-sex classes in the sixth grade for fall and winter 2004–2005, then expand the program to include sixth and seventh grades in 2005–2006.

Research convinced Carolina Day that the best advantage would come from having this program for their younger middle school students. They continued coed classes for eighth grade to provide "transitional experiences in preparation for the upper school." Dr. Beverly Sgro, Head of School, supported the administration's efforts to provide initial intensive onsite training for teachers in grades 5–8 and follow-up training for all lower and upper school faculty.

The middle school of Carolina Day School implemented single-sex instruction in its core classes for sixth and seventh grades in fall 2004. Faculty and administrators have stayed current with their training, which began in spring 2004.

The single-sex program has been very successful, producing positive academic results for both gender populations, as well as significantly better dynamics and less social anxiety.

After four years, the middle school at Carolina Day reports these key outcomes:

- Stronger mentoring relationships
- An environment that promotes greater trust and sense of belonging among students
- Teachers who feel more connected with students and with each other
- A greater understanding of how boys and girls learn differently and an emphasis on providing instruction that supports these differences
- More direct ways to deal with students' social and emotional pressures
- Classroom instruction that provides for more teaching and quality learning experiences
- A new energy that causes teachers to be more creative with their ideas and more reflective with their practice

As these and other schools succeed in providing single-sex instruction, their staffs have shared testimonials with us. Following are some powerful testimonials of the kind of immediate shifts in student learning and teacher enjoyment that can occur in single-sex classes.

Success Testimonials from Teachers

During the 2007–2008 school year at Winder-Barrow Middle School, a math teacher, Michael Lofton, piloted a single-sex math class for boys and Erica Boswell piloted a single-sex math class for girls. Lofton told us,

Since I have been teaching an all-boy math class this year the experience has been very different from my mixed-gender classes. One of the first things that stand out is the camaraderie of the class. I was quick to recognize this because of my coaching experience. In the beginning we discussed the need for the students to be successful in the math class this year due to the pass/fail criteria of the state standardized test CRCT (Criterion-Referenced Competency Test). We also discussed the need for the class as a whole to be successful.

To meet our goals, we bonded as a team. Early on the boys started encouraging each other. We created teams among

our team and had inner competition with study games and activities. The groups changed often so everyone helped and encouraged each other to work harder and study more. We made a phone list so anyone in the class could call another student if they need any help with homework or studying. We also spent a few days in the computer lab learning how to use our textbook online resources. Students with computers and online access helped others without online ability.

It wasn't long before I noticed that grades and comprehension of skills were on the rise. Parents stopped me at football or basketball games telling *me* how much their son loved the class and was really trying to do well in math.

One student in Lofton's class shared, "The difference between last year and this is that he doesn't yell at us as much as we got yelled at last year." This student is making B's in Lofton's class after a long year of D's in 2006–2007.

"They feel free to make mistakes, and they feel free not to make mistakes," Boswell said of her female students. "A lot of time girls don't want to look too smart. It's a shame that girls have to feel that way at all, but they do. In here, they can feel free to raise their hand for every single question and no one's going to look at them funny."

Dave Curtis, a fifth-grade teacher at Kenowa Hills Public Schools in Michigan, reports:

We have a grade 5–6 building. Each grade has ten classrooms and last year we turned two of the fifth grades into single-gender classrooms, leaving eight others for coed classes. Those students moved up to sixth grade and as a result of parent and student requests, this year our building has four single-gender classrooms in sixth grade and two in fifth. . . . From the onset we heard comments like, "My son finally likes going to school" or "He finally comes home happy and discusses his day." The same was true for the girls' classrooms and we knew we had provided something desirable for our students and parents.

This letter was sent to co-author Peggy Daniels by Blake Smith, a high school counselor, several weeks after her school incorporated single-sex education:

Dear Peggy,

Just wanted you all in the middle school to know that if you could step back from all the action and see/hear what is happening in the middle school this year—there is something incredible taking place. Parents at the upper school parents' night program commented on the fantastic atmosphere in the middle school this year, and upper school teachers have been talking about what a fun-loving group of teachers the middle school has. The students who roll through the Nash Athletic Center and pass by my office are energized and obviously loving the year so far. It is like we are on a month-long pep rally or spirit day.

I think this is a reflection of several things (single-sex classes, single-sex advisory, efforts with differentiation and vertical teaming), but mostly a result of the teachers' creativity and enthusiasm, which has been encouraged and supported by the middle school leadership to a degree that I haven't seen in another school yet. By taking some new chances (especially the single-sex instruction), risking long debates with parents, and asking teachers what they think about policy, planning, and pedagogy, there is a contagious excitement in the air that gets passed down to our students. It's not just me—I am hearing it across divisions—and I'm glad to be a part of it too. I don't know if all of you in the middle school can see it as much because you're in it all day—but I suspect you can sense the great energy happening this year.

At Woodward Elementary in DeLand, Florida, a wife and husband, Deborah and Jim Roberts, teach together and separately in coed and single-sex classes. In the first year of single-sex classes at Woodward, they co-taught a full-inclusion, single-sex class of fourth-grade boys. The class included 40 percent minority students, 23 percent general education students, and 12 percent exceptional education students. It was a challenging group, but by the end of the year the test scores for this group of boys were outstanding. On the Florida Writes test, they had some of the highest scores in the district, even outperforming many girls.

The following year, Deborah and Jim Roberts looped with this group to fifth grade, and in the third year of the program, Deborah was asked to teach a group of fifth-grade girls while her husband kept the boys. This, too, worked well for both teachers and students. Deborah said, "The changes in the boys and girls, and the challenges for us as teachers, have been very positive. It would be hard to go back to coed classes for these students."

Piri Taborosi, a teacher in New York, shared this story:

In 2002, when a new charter school opened in Syracuse, New York, I was its first principal. During the first three days of school, our fifth-grade numbers stabilized into a group of six girls and twenty-two boys. All of these students were at-risk; many had failed grades before; most of them had behavior problems; with the exception of two or three, all of them were reading significantly below grade level. As I contemplated what to do with this group, I made a decision which the company backed me in.

We had two third-grade rooms and had hired two teachers; unfortunately, we only had a total of twenty-two students. I combined the two classes and assigned a full-time teacher assistant to work with the teacher. The other teacher who had been hired to teach third grade was a male, a military man. He was willing to teach fifth grade. Rather than separating the six girls into two groups, with parental support, I kept the girls together and added a few boys. The other class was totally boys and was taught by the male teacher.

All students were tested at the beginning of the year and near the end of the year. Teacher and principal bonuses and pay raises were tied to student achievement. All our students did very well in the school, but we were not prepared for the phenomenal growth of the boys who were in the single-sex class. This group was also monitored by a local newspaper reporter, who eventually wrote a five-page article about the boys and their class.

Those are just a few of the individual testimonials we are hearing from professionals and parents who are opting to innovate in single-sex instruction. Students themselves also speak up about what they are experiencing. Here are examples from a boy and a girl.

In science we talk more this year because the boys aren't there. I like it when we [girls] get to talk things out. I understand things better when we can talk and share. (Sophie, middle school girl)

We are not distracted by girls and we don't feel so self-conscious. If I say something a little "off," I don't feel as stupid as I would in front of girls. (Nathan, middle school boy)

Single-Sex Classrooms Can Really Work!

We hope this essay has provided you with data and testimonials you can use to gain support for single-sex classes in your school or community. As you make your case for single-sex instruction, you may find that resistance lessens when clear data are shown. Data can be a first major tool of persuasion, as well as a real confidence builder for you as a teacher or parent, as you move through the steps to establish a single-sex program.

The second major tool of persuasion, and an important confidence builder, is an understanding of how boys and girls learn differently. Teachers in coed classes who gain training in male-female brain differences report that both their boys and girls are learning and performing better. Teachers in single-sex classes generally find themselves better able to focus on the brain-gender spectrum for their specific students, giving both girls and boys more of the brain-friendly environment in which they can thrive.

MICHAEL GURIAN, the author of twenty-five books, is the co-founder of the Gurian Institute. **KATHY STEVENS,** the co-author of several books, is the executive director of the institute. **PEGGY DANIELS,** an educator for more than thirty years, is a master trainer at the institute.

From *Educational Horizons,* quarterly journal of Pi Lambda Theta Inc., International Honor Society and Professional Association in Education, Summer 2009, pp. 234–245. Adapted by permission of the authors from chapter 1 of *Successful Single-Sex Classrooms: A Practical Guide to Teaching Boys & Girls Separately,* Copyright © 2009 by Michael Gurian and published by Jossey-Bass.

A "Perfect" Case Study
Perfectionism in Academically Talented Fourth Graders

Jill L. Adelson

"Perfectionism must be seen as a potent force capable of bringing either intense frustration and paralysis or intense satisfaction and creative contribution, depending on how it is channeled."

—Schuler, 2002, p. 71

The topic of perfectionism is bound to surface when discussing the social and emotional development of gifted children and adolescents (Davis & Rimm, 1994; Greenspon, 1998; Kerr, 1991; Parker & Adkins, 1995; Silverman, 1990, 1993a; Schuler, 2002). Whereas Greenspon (2000) asserts that "perfectionism is a wound; it is never healthy" (p. 208), others in the field assert that children with perfectionistic qualities are faced with a double-edged sword that can manifest itself either in a healthy or unhealthy manner. For instance, Silverman (1999) asserts that healthy expressions of perfectionism can lead to achievement, self-confirmation, high self-esteem, responsibility, and "unparalleled greatness" (p. 216). On the other hand, perfectionistic qualities that are exhibited in an unhealthy way may result in procrastination, avoidance, anxiety, a self-defeated attitude, and underachievement (Hamachek, 1978; Reis, 2002; Schuler, 1997, 2002; Silverman, 1993a, 1999).

As a teacher in a self-contained gifted and talented fourth-grade classroom for several years, I observed many students who exhibited perfectionism in a myriad of unhealthy ways, and several findings emerged from my observations of these children. First, across differing rates of development, both mental and physical manifestations of perfectionism abounded. Regardless of group size (e.g., individual, small group, or whole class) or type of activity (e.g., art, music tryouts, recess, math, language arts, or social studies), at least one child exhibited unhealthy perfectionistic behaviors. My observations of the students across various contexts enabled me to document a range of manifestations of perfectionism, suggesting ways in which perfectionism can affect gifted children in schools. I found that these manifestations could be categorized, and the following case studies represent the different types of unhealthy manifestations of perfectionism that emerged in my observations.

The Academic Achiever— "Must Achieve 110%"

Elena[1] was a student academically accelerated in mathematics. When she was first asked to take a diagnostic test, she would become frustrated and would say, "I can't leave it blank!" She believed she should know how to solve every problem, whether or not she had ever been exposed to the concepts tested. Despite the diagnostic nature of the test, she would struggle with the idea of skipping a problem.

Ivan worked diligently on his math practice. He was not satisfied with anything less than 100% correct. If he missed a single problem, he did not believe he was ready for a test of the material. He would continue to do extra practice, even if he only missed one problem due to a "careless" mistake.

While playing a review game in social studies, Sherman became frustrated. For each question asked, he expected himself to remember every detail about the event, person, or place and would become very frustrated if he could not, even resorting to pounding on his head trying to remember. This attitude also affected Sherman's participation in math games. He expected to solve every puzzle and to solve it immediately, or he would become discouraged and upset with himself.

Cho came to the United States when she was in kindergarten. She was identified for the self-contained gifted and talented class and worked very hard to earn top grades. Math and science came easily to her. Although she was reading above grade level in English, her second language, her language arts average was a low A. She was distraught about "not being good" at reading and did extra work each weekend to try to improve. Her parents also were worried about her reading ability and would request extra assignments for Cho.

The Academic Achievers, students exhibiting negative perfectionism in academic pursuits, had unrealistically high expectations for their own performance and were not satisfied with a score of 100, literally pushing for extra credit on everything they did because a score of 100 was not enough for them. If they did not earn the top grade or could not remember the answer word-for-word on every assessment (formal or informal) in every subject, they became upset with themselves. Due to the extremely high standards they imposed on themselves, they put forth more effort than was required to master the material and achieve at the top level. Typically, these students were high achievers and earned very high grades, but they would become disappointed with themselves when they earned anything less and were never satisfied with the achievements and grades they had earned; they wanted to earn all of the extra credit points and obtain the highest possible score for each assessment. Even though they had high grades in all academic subjects, they often completed extra credit projects and assignments and did so with as much energy and effort as they put into their required work. These students focused heavily on their mistakes, and even when they met the expectations of the task at hand, they rarely were satisfied with their performance. Their focus was on the end product or grade, and they judged themselves on that alone. In some cases, like that of Cho, the students had family pressures, as well as their own pressure for perfection. As Davis and Rimm (1994) noted, gifted students may have pressures that arise from their family, their peers, or themselves for "perfect" work.

As an educator, it is important to become aware of these students. Although it is easy to praise students for high grades, it is much more important to praise them for their efforts. Educators need to put more emphasis on effort and strategies and much less on grades and on "personal traits (like being smart)" (Dweck, 1999, p. 3). Furthermore, these students need guidance in taking pride in the process and in using mistakes as learning experiences. For example, Elena learned to take diagnostic tests with less anxiety because she understood the need to identify areas of strength and weaknesses and learn the material she does not know. I had Ivan correct his mistakes and write "WIMI's" ("why I missed it"), leading to a focus on learning from the mistakes instead of on looking at the grade. Despite his competitive nature and tendency to strive for perfection, Sherman learned to identify his mistakes and weaknesses in the math game, and when he was eliminated from the classroom tournament, he focused on learning from the mistakes he made instead of berating himself for them. Despite the completion of the tournament, he took a box of cards home to practice and to improve his own performance for next year. Cho continued to work on her language arts skills, but she learned to focus on improvement rather than the grade. She needed encouragement to recognize and celebrate her strengths rather than focusing solely on her "weakness" and comparing it to the abilities of her peers.

The Risk Evader—"All or Nothing"

Despite the art teacher's compliments of Kathleen's artistic ability and winning a schoolwide artistic contest, she did not think she could draw. In art class, if the task was to draw, Kathleen did not want to participate and only did so reluctantly.

Brandon wanted a major role in the school musical, and he had the singing ability to earn that role. Unfortunately, shortly before the try-outs, Brandon became ill, leaving him with little voice or energy on audition day. He chose not to try out that day and did not request to audition on a different day.

Risk Evaders are plagued by the impact of asynchronous development or physical limitations on their pursuits, and they will avoid allowing their weaknesses to be exposed. When they encounter a task that requires both their mind and their body, gifted children often are faced with asynchrony—their mind has developed faster than their body—which affects perfectionistic behaviors (Morelock, 1992; Silverman, 1993a, 1993b; Tannenbaum, 1992). Although their mind may see ideals and hold high standards, they cannot always meet those expectations in their performance. Fearing this failure to achieve their standards and ideals, they may decide not to even attempt the task, just as Kathleen did in art. In her mind, she could see the intricate details that a botanist sees in a flower

and even noticed the pollen on the stamen, but she feared that her hands, which had the dexterity and precision of a 9-year-old, could not produce the image from her mind.

> **As an educator, developing a safe classroom environment that encourages risk-taking is essential. Children who exhibit perfectionism must feel supported within their classroom, so the entire class must make a commitment to this safe environment.**

Brandon also faced a situation in which he was afraid his body would not be able to perform to his mind's ideal. Students like Brandon are afraid of failure and cannot stand the idea that they may not meet their own expectations. They do not take delight in the process or in their attempts, and they do not even want to try because they fear they will not succeed at a level that meets their personal standards. This is similar to Adderholdt-Elliott's (1987) paralyzed perfectionist, who rationalizes that if he never performs, then he doesn't have to risk being rejected or criticized.

As an educator, developing a safe classroom environment that encourages risk-taking is essential. Children who exhibit perfectionism must feel supported within their classroom, so the entire class must make a commitment to this safe environment. Without it, students may fear not only their own rejection of their work, but also ridicule from their peers. The focus should continue to be placed on the process and revisions. Students should be encouraged to try new and different experiences that may seem challenging. Challenges should be regarded as adventurous and exciting instead of daunting. Students should be applauded for efforts to tackle something new rather than always being judged for their final products.

The Aggravated Accuracy Assessor—"Exactness and Fixation on 'Redos'"

Carlos worked meticulously during several art classes on his drawing of a Confederate soldier for an art gallery focusing on Virginia. Whenever he was nearly done, he decided to redo the drawing because it was not precise enough. He constantly took the drawing up to the art teacher and to his classroom teacher for reassurance.

When taking notes in class, most students appreciate the opportunity to use shorthand and not have to have everything in final copy form. However, Jodie was not this way. When the class period was over, she still would be copying notes. She painstakingly wrote each letter of each word, taking extra time and effort in making her notes as neat as possible, even rewriting her notes if given the opportunity.

Curtis had been working on a drawing for the art gallery for several weeks. His drawing was almost complete when he decided to throw it away. When questioned about his decision, he replied, "But I colored his hair black!" Because he had envisioned the drawing differently but only had a black marker instead of a brown one available to him at the time, Curtis literally threw away his hard work.

Asynchronous development of the gifted child in areas such as writing or artistic expression can result in two different types of unhealthy perfectionists. Students may become Risk Evaders, like Kathleen, and choose an all-or-nothing approach, or they may become Aggravated Accuracy Assessors, like Carlos and Jodie, and attempt the task but become frustrated with their inability to meet their mind's ideal. Likewise, physical limitations, such as the accessibility (or lack thereof) of materials, can result in a final product that does not meet perfectionists' standards, and they can become very frustrated with their efforts and products. They may choose to redo the same work over and over, may look frantically for ways to "fix" their work or find the necessary materials, or may become disappointed in their own work and give up trying.

The key to helping students like these is to recognize their standards as valuable and acceptable as long-term goals and have faith in their vision and their ability to meet their expectations through effort and revision. These students need help modifying their immediate goals or standards and making their unrealistic ones more realistic by setting them as long-term goals. All students could benefit from reading about and discussing people who revised their works multiple times. For example, Thomas Edison did not invent a successful light bulb until after almost 2 years of failed attempts and more than 6,000 different carbonized plant fibers (Grace Products Corporation, 1998), and two young Detroit scientists did not create their famous kitchen-cleaning formula until their 409th attempt (hence the name Formula 409). Because many students struggle in art, examples of famous artists' works, revisions, their biographies, and their autobiographies that illustrate the amount of time devoted to their masterpieces would be beneficial to share.

Students also should have opportunities to critique one another's work, pointing out aspects that they admire and offering constructive suggestions for improvement. This will help students learn to examine their artwork and writing more critically and identify not only weaknesses, but also strengths.

For students like Jodie whose handwriting slows down their ability to participate in class discussions and activities, some prioritizing may be necessary. Younger students may not recognize when "perfect" handwriting is unnecessary or the difference between "perfect" and "legible," and they may need help distinguishing between those times. These students benefit from being forced to create "sloppy copies" that have a stipulation of no eraser marks allowed—they have to write as they think and cross or scribble out, add above and below lines, and draw arrows instead of erasing. This needs to be followed by opportunities to use their "perfect" handwriting and publish the work.

The Controlling Image Manager— "I Could Have Won if I Wanted To"

Brandon not only decided not to audition for the school musical (even though he "could have" gotten the part if he had tried out), but he also "wanted to" be "It." While playing tag on the playground, Brandon ran and yelled, "You can't catch me!" However, as soon as the person who was It got near him, he jumped out of bounds and declared, "I wanted to be It!"

Misty competed in a classroom tournament with great intensity and skill, and she easily won against her classmates. After competing against older students and winning the schoolwide tournament, she contemplated intentionally getting penalties to disqualify herself from the district tournament.

Controlling Image Managers like Brandon and Misty not only want to be perfect, but they also want others to regard them as perfect. If they are afraid they cannot reach their expectations or others' expectations, instead of choosing to not participate, they may intentionally choose to eliminate themselves. This still gives them the opportunity to think—and to say—that they *could have* won and been perfect.

Other children in the class may get frustrated with these students because they either win or give up. The other children never have a chance to fairly win against these students in competitive situations. Role-playing may help these children to better understand others' feelings in competitive situations. They also benefit from reading and discussing other people's losses in competitive situations or having guest speakers talk about their personal defeats, particularly in the sports arena and other competitive situations.

Controlling Image Managers fail to understand the pleasure of competition and of trying to do one's own personal best because they focus too much on winning and being the best. They should be helped to set personal goals before a competitive event so they can strive for a standard based on their personal performance and not that of others. Using these strategies has a positive impact on students and encourages them to compete. For example, setting personal goals helped Misty to decide to take the tournament game home and practice instead of committing to her plan to disqualify herself.

The Procrastinating Perfectionist—"If It Stays in My Mind, Then I Can't Fail"

The class was given the task of creating a social studies review board game over a period of several weeks. Jade excitedly shared her intricate vision. However, just days before the project was due, Jade still had not started working and did not have a plan to create it.

When the class found out they would be competing in a national vocabulary contest, Micah was very excited and announced that he would earn a perfect score. The day before the contest, Micah admitted that he had not begun studying. When asked why not, he just shrugged his shoulders. That night, he stayed up late studying. After he finished the contest the next day, he announced, "I didn't have enough time to study, so I couldn't get them all right."

When assigned an extensive project, some gifted children, like Jade, will plan elaborate, creative projects. They become excited about the project and about sharing their ideas but are not as excited to get started on the project itself for fear of it not turning out the way they imagine it or because they are intimidated by the formidable tasks ahead. Procrastinating Perfectionists have a perfect vision in their mind, but the fear of their inability to achieve that vision causes them to procrastinate, paralyzing them from taking action. They may think, "If I never complete that project, I don't have to risk getting a bad grade" (Adderholdt-Elliott, 1987, p. 27) or even, "If I never complete that project, I don't have to be disappointed that the final project didn't turn out like I wanted it to."

Some Procrastinating Perfectionists, like Micah, are paralyzed by their fear of failure and not meeting their mind's ideal, and they also use their procrastination as a way to control their image. Like Jade, Micah had a vision of perfection in his mind. However, his fear that he could not achieve it lead him to procrastinate. His procrastination also allowed him to preserve his ego and gave him an excuse for not being perfect. Addressing the fear of failure and the tendency to procrastinate will help alleviate the ego-saving behavior that some students use along with procrastination.

Procrastinating Perfectionists need help prioritizing and breaking down a large task into smaller subtasks. In working with a Procrastinating Perfectionist who has great vision but not the steps to commence work on the project, educators need to recognize the need for assistance. Together, the student and teacher can create a plan to break the larger task into smaller segments and identify goals. The student still can have high standards and expectations for the final product, but now he or she has a process to focus on and standards to meet along the way. This helps the student's focus shift from the product to the process and from the outcome to the effort. In designing a schedule, it is important to build in buffers so that when something does not go as planned, the student does not have to feel that he or she already has failed and that there is no need to continue.

Furthermore, all children need help prioritizing at some point. They may need to examine their schedule and see when other tests and projects are due and determine what is most important to them. If they have an elaborate project or challenging goal in mind, they may not be able to put as much effort and focus on their math or social studies test as they normally do—something has to give. Teachers of gifted and talented students need to help them realize that they cannot be perfect at everything and that when they have too much to accomplish they must sacrifice a little of one thing to do well at something else. When discussing these issues with students, it is important to examine the entire picture and what currently requires their attention.

Take Action in Your Classroom

Although it manifests itself in different ways, perfectionism is a strong trait in many gifted children. In a classroom that has gifted children, instances of perfectionism are exhibited every day and in every context. Educators must help students use perfectionism in a positive manner and transform it for future work. Some specific strategies to help each type of perfectionist accomplish this are illustrated in Table 1.

Table 1 Encouraging Healthy Perfectionism in the Classroom

Type of Perfectionist	Defining Characteristics	Action to Take in the Classroom
Academic Achievers	Hold unrealistically high expectations for their performance in academic pursuits and focus on the final grade and on mistakes made	Praise them for their efforts, emphasizing students' hard work rather than their grades Guide students in taking pride in the process and their efforts and using mistakes as learning experiences
Risk Evaders	Fear failure to achieve their standards and ideals due to asynchronous development or physical limitations, so choose no to attempt the task	Develop a safe environment that encourages risk-taking Emphasize process and revisions rather than end products Encourage students to try experiences that are new, different, and challenging Encourage students to look at challenges as adventurous and exciting rather than daunting Applaud students for their efforts to tackle something new
Aggravated Accuracy Assessors	Attempt the task but become frustrated with their inability to meet their mind's ideal due to asynchronous development or physical limitations May choose to redo the same work over and over to try to make it more like their mind's ideal, may look frantically for ways to fix their work or find the necessary materials, or may become disappointed and give up trying	Recognize their standards as valuable and acceptable Have faith in their vision and ability to meet their expectations through effort and revision Read and discuss stories of people who revised their works multiple times Give students opportunities to critique one another's work Have students create "sloppy copies" and also give them opportunities to revise and produce a finished product
Controlling Image Managers	Want others to regard them as perfect If they fear they are unable to meet expectations in competitive situations, choose to eliminate themselves intentionally and say they could have been perfect	Role-play so children understand others' feelings Read and discuss losses in competitive situations Have students set personal goals based on their own performance before a competition
Procrastinating Perfectionists	Plan an extensive project but fail to start it for fear of their inability to achieve their perfect vision	Help students break larger tasks into smaller segments and goals Have students develop a schedule with buffer time Help students prioritize and recognize that they cannot be perfect at everything at every moment

You Can Make a Difference

Using these strategies with gifted students like Judy can help them to pursue work in a healthy manner, resulting in creative contribution and intense satisfaction. Judy, an academically talented fourth grader, grew up in a large family with older and younger siblings who also had been identified for gifted services. She demonstrated many of the types of unhealthy manifestations of perfectionism. Above all else, she was an Academic Achiever. Prior to fourth grade, she had not been challenged sufficiently in the classroom and had channeled her perfectionism in a way that led to being a Risk Evader and, at times, a Procrastinating Perfectionist. During her time in my classroom, I helped her gradually shift her focus from grades to effort and provided her with increasingly challenging academic opportunities, which helped her begin to take more risks in and out of the classroom. Judy had an interest in writing, and focusing on the writing process and revisions helped her learn from her mistakes, as did diagnostic testing and analyzing the problems she had missed in mathematics. She began swimming competitively and would set personal time goals rather than goals of placing first.

During the second semester, Judy accepted a personal challenge and decided to complete an independent study project. This project involved her reading, taking notes, organizing, prioritizing, and presenting. We frequently met to plan the stages of the project, set intermediary goals, analyze her progress, and adjust the timeline as necessary. After completing her research and creating a final product, Judy presented to multiple groups, giving her the opportunity to learn from her experiences and revise her presentation. Finally, Judy reflected in writing about what she learned from the experience, both academically and personally, and what she will do differently the next time she attempts a similar project.

Judy moved to middle school and has continued to channel her perfectionism in a healthy way. She appears to be satisfied in her pursuits (academically, athletically, and artistically) and is making creative contributions in and out of her classrooms. Despite not having exceptional athletic talent, Judy continues to swim and now plays softball. She frequently e-mails me to tell how she increased in the number of hits she had in a game or had a new personal best time in a swim meet, demonstrating her focus on personal performance goals. Judy continues to love to write. She has learned to focus her writing on her ideas and then to revise for grammar and spelling so that she can concentrate on one aspect of the process at a time. Although she still occasionally finds herself procrastinating on studying challenging material for a test or agonizing over an A- rather than an A, Judy has learned to focus on effort, enjoy the process of learning, and accept new challenges.

The story of Judy is one of many stories of gifted students who exhibit unhealthy perfectionistic behaviors in the classroom. By recognizing these behaviors and using strategies like those listed in Table 1, teachers and parents can make a difference and help these students use perfectionism in a positive manner now and in the future.

Note

1. Student names have been changed.

References

Adderholdt-Elliott, M. (1987). *Perfectionism: What's bad about being too good.* Minneapolis, MN: Free Spirit.

Davis, G. A., & Rimm, S. B. (1994). *Education of the gifted and talented* (3rd ed.). Boston: Allyn & Bacon.

Dweck, C. S. (1999). Caution—Praise can be dangerous. *American Educator, 23*(1), 4–9.

Grace Products Corporation. (1998). *The life of Thomas Edison.* Retrieved November 6, 2006, from http://www.graceproducts .com/edison/life.html

Greenspon, T. S. (1998). The gifted self: Its role in development and emotional health. *Roeper Review, 20,* 162–167.

Greenspon, T. S. (2000). "Healthy perfectionism" is an oxymoron! Reflections on the psychology of perfectionism and the sociology of science. *Journal of Secondary Gifted Education, 11,* 197–208.

Hamachek, D. E. (1978). Psychodynamics of normal and neurotic perfectionism. *Psychology, 15,* 27–33.

Kerr, B. A. (1991). *A handbook for counseling the gifted and talented.* Alexandria, VA: American Association for Counseling and Development.

Morelock, M. J. (1992). Giftedness: The view from within. *Understanding Our Gifted, 4*(3), 1, 11–15.

Parker, W. D., & Adkins, K. K. (1995). Perfectionism and the gifted. *Roeper Review, 17,* 173–176.

Reis, S. M. (2002). Internal barriers, personal issues, and decisions faced by gifted and talented females. *Gifted Child Today, 25*(1), 14–28.

Schuler, P. (2002). Perfectionism in gifted children and adolescents. In M. Neihart, S. M. Reis, N. M. Robinson, & S. M. Moon (Eds.), *The social and emotional development of gifted children: What do we know?* (pp. 71–79). Waco, TX: Prufrock Press.

Schuler, P. A. (1997). *Characteristics and perceptions of perfectionism in gifted adolescents in a rural school environment.* Unpublished doctoral dissertation, University of Connecticut, Storrs.

Silverman, L. K. (1990). Issues in affective development of the gifted. In J. VanTassel–Baska (Ed.), *A practical guide to counseling the gifted in a school setting* (pp. 15–30). Reston, VA: Council for Exceptional Children.

Silverman, L. K. (1993a). A developmental model for counseling the gifted. In L. K. Silverman (Ed.), *Counseling the gifted and talented* (pp. 51–78). Denver, CO: Love.

Silverman, L. K. (1993b). The gifted individual. In L. K. Silverman (Ed.), *Counseling the gifted and talented* (pp. 3–28). Denver, CO: Love.

Silverman, L. K. (1999). Perfectionism. *Gifted Education International, 13,* 216–225.

Tannenbaum, A. J. (1992). Early signs of giftedness: Research and commentary. *Journal for the Education of the Gifted, 13,* 22–36.

From *Gifted Child Today,* Fall 2007, pp. 14–20. Copyright © 2007 by Prufrock Press. Reprinted by permission.

UNIT 4

Development during Childhood: Family and Culture

Unit Selections

Key Points to Consider

- Should unconventional children be labeled as having disorders . . . or called what they seem, quirky and unique?

- How should parents respond to children with passive aggressive behaviors?

- How can childrearing practices come to terms with genetic potentialities to maximize development?

- Can bad behavior in children be blamed on bad parenting? Are good behaviors the result of good parenting? What roles do genetic factors play in behaviors?

- How common is domestic abuse? What are the effects on children and families?

- Are we raising a generation of prosti-tots who idolize pop culture's bad girls?

- Do our young people have good ideas for reforming their academic and social cultures? Do we listen to them? If not, why not?

- Do men prefer younger, fertile women? Do women prefer older, richer men? Is this programmed in our genes?

- We live in a multicultural society; how do you self-identify?

Student Website

www.mhhe.com/cls

Internet References

Harborview Injury Prevention and Research Center
   http://depts.washington.edu/hiprc/
Families and Work Institute
   http://www.familiesandwork.org/index.html
Village Pregnancy and Parenting
   http://parenting.ivillage.com
Parentsplace.com: Single Parenting
   http://www.parentsplace.com
Passive Aggressive Diaries
   http://www.PassiveAggressiveDiaries.com

Families and cultures have substantial effects on child outcomes. How? New interpretations of behavioral genetic research suggest that genetically predetermined child behaviors may have substantial effects on how families parent, how children react, and how cultures evolve. Nature and nurture are very interactive. Is it possible that there is a genetic predisposition toward more warlike, aggressive, and violent behaviors in some children? Do some childrearing practices suppress this genetic trait? Do others aggravate it? Are some children predisposed to care for others? The answers are not yet known.

If parents and societies have a significant impact on child outcomes, is there a set of universal family values? Does one culture have more success than another culture? Laypersons often assume that children's behaviors and personalities have a direct correlation with the behaviors and personality of the person or persons who provided their socialization during infancy and childhood. Have Americans become paranoid about terrorist intentions? Do we try to justify our culture's flaws by claims that other cultures are worse? Do we teach our children this fear? Conversely, do other cultures try to hide their atrocities behind the screen that Americans are worse?

Are you a mirror image of the person or persons who raised you? How many of their beliefs, preferences, and virtuous behaviors do you reflect? Did you learn their hatreds and vices as well? Do you model your family, your peers, your culture, all of them, or none of them? If you have a sibling, are you alike because the same person or persons raised you? What accounts for all the differences between people with similar genes, similar parenting, and the same cultural background? These and similar questions are fodder for future research.

During childhood, a person's family values are compared to and tested against the values of schools, community, and culture. Peers, schoolmates, teachers, neighbors, extracurricular activity leaders, religious leaders, and even shopkeepers play increasingly important roles. Culture influences children through holidays, styles of dress; music; television; the Internet; world events; movies; slang; games; parents' jobs; transportation; exposure to sex, drugs, and violence; and many other variables. The ecological theorist Urie Bronfenbrenner called these cultural variables exosystem and macrosystem influences. The developing personality of a child has multiple interwoven influences: from genetic potentialities through family values and socialization practices to community and cultural pressures for behaviors.

The first article in this unit, "The Angry Smile," suggests that having a passive resistance to demands and a pervasive negative attitude is not only troubling and destructive in family interactions, but is also fairly common. It is not a behavior that is genetically preprogrammed. It is learned. It can be unlearned. The author, Signe Whitson, explains how parents can help their children learn assertive expression by both modeling it and encouraging assertion.

The second article cautions that parents are not the only force shaping behavior in children. Many behaviors are inherent in human nature, predetermined by genetic factors. They are found in peoples of every culture, regardless of parenting

© PhotoAlto/Picture Quest

practices. Parents are important and good parenting is vital to a civilized society. Parents, however, should not be blamed or credited for every action taken by normally behaving members of the human race in their childhoods.

The third article in this unit, "The Blank Slate," suggests that family forces and cultural factors (e.g., fast foods full of fats and empty calories, Mozart CDs for babies) always interact with genetic potentialities. Parents and society cannot always be credited or blamed for every outcome in a developing child. Advice on how to raise happy, achieving children, and how to keep children healthy, physically fit, and well-nourished, is slavishly adhered to by many parents and caregivers. However, some children will simply not turn out as prescribed by the formulas. Our younglings cannot be molded like lumps of clay. Steven Pinker suggests that social progress proceeds with the inherent natures (both good and bad) of all humans. Blaming and/or crediting amounts to empty vocalizing. Working with our offsprings' genes makes more sense. Can we decipher what that is?

Unit 4, subsection B (Culture), emphasizes our increasing population diversity. It is imperative that time and effort be spent to avoid life-threatening misunderstandings.

The first article, "Girls Gone Bad?," decries the influence of female sex symbols of pop culture who are adored by young teenagers. While parents denounce the behavior of these divas, adolescent girls are infatuated. They want to dress, talk, and act like their heroines. The author, Kathleen Deveny, reminds readers that parents also criticized the sex goddesses of the past (e.g., Marilyn Monroe, Liz Taylor, Madonna), and their daughters turned out well. The difference today is the power and pervasiveness of the media, which reports on celebrity antics 24/7. This essay, and the next one, are effective together in portraying the paradox of social forces on our youth.

The cultural commentary, "Disrespecting Childhood," presents evidence that America is not a child-loving nation. Our media overwhelmingly sputter about what is wrong with our juveniles ("Girls Gone Bad?"). Our childrearing practices and educational policies are directed more at fixing what is wrong than with reinforcing what is right. The authors report on a project called What Kids Can Do, Inc., which respects and listens to the voices of young Americans and celebrates their strengths. It inspires hope for our future.

The third article in the Culture subsection, "Don't Blame the Caveman," questions the often repeated myth that men are genetically programmed to sleep around and take sex forcefully from women through rape. The author, Sharon Begley, presents statistics which demonstrate that the likelihood of rape being beneficial is extremely low. A myth that stepfathers abuse stepchildren is also debunked. Stepfathers who are kind to their partner's children get more marital benefits.

The last selection for the Culture subsection, "The End of White America?," asks "What is twenty first century mainstream America?" Children born today will not live in a predominantly Caucasian/European American population. Many aspects of contemporary life already transcend ethnicity, race, and religion. Will rapid demographic changes create new ways to self-identify (e.g., lifestyle choices)?

The Angry Smile

Recognizing and responding to your child's passive aggressive behaviors.

SIGNE L. WHITSON, LSW

Amber had been giving her mother the silent treatment all week. She was angry about not being allowed to sleep over at a friend's house. Late Thursday night, she left a note on her mother's pillow, asking her mom to wash her uniform before Friday's soccer game. When Amber returned home from school on Friday, in a rush to pack her gear, she looked all over for her uniform. She finally found it in the washer—perfectly clean, as per her request—but still soaking wet! Amber was late for her game and forced to ride the bench.

When all was un-said and done, Amber's mother felt defeated. Having one-upped her daughter in the conflict, it was clear to her that she had lost by winning. As parents, most of us have been in situations where traveling the low road is irresistible and we become temporarily reckless in our driving. But anytime we mirror a child's poor behavior instead of modeling a healthier way to behave, our victories add up to long-term relationship damage and lasting hostilities.

So, what could Amber's mother have done differently in this hostile un-confrontation? What can any parent do to avoid the agony of victory and the defeat of healthy communication? The following guidelines offer parents strategies for maintaining their calm in a passive aggressive storm and responding in ways that lay the groundwork for less conflictual relationships with their children and adolescents.

1. Know What You Are Dealing With

Amber's silent treatment is a classic example of passive aggressive behavior, a deliberate and masked way of expressing feelings of anger. Common passive aggressive behaviors in young people include:

- Verbally denying feelings of anger (*"I'm fine. Whatever!"*)
- Verbally complying but behaviorally delaying (*"I'll clean my room after soccer."*)
- Shutting down conversations (*"Fine." and "Whatever."*)
- Intentional inefficility (*"I did make my bed. I didn't know you meant all of the blankets had to be pulled up!"*)

- "Forgetting" or "misplacing" important items (*"I don't know where your car keys are."*)
- Avoiding responsibility for tasks (*"I didn't know you wanted me to do it. Putting away the clean dishes is his chore!"*)

Parents who are familiar with these typical patterns are able to respond directly to their children's underlying anger and to avoid misbehaving in counter-passive aggressive ways!

2. Consult the Mirror on the Wall

Passive aggressive persons master concealing their anger, and are expert at getting unsuspecting others to act it out in one of two ways. Many respond with an outburst of anger and frustration—yelling, finger wagging, threatening punishment—then feel guilty and embarrassed for having lost control. Others keep the tension low, but turn up the heat on the simmering conflict by mirroring the passive aggression. When Amber's mother purposely left the soccer uniform in the washer, she mirrored the anger that Amber had been feeling all week long. What's more, her counter-passive aggression ensured that the anger between mother and daughter would linger, fester, and grow more intense over time in its buried, unaddressed form! The second step in effectively confronting passive aggression is to refuse to act out the anger for the other person. Helping Amber learn to express her anger assertively is one of this mother's most valuable parenting opportunities!

3. Say Yes to Anger

Anger is a basic, spontaneous, neurophysiological part of the human condition. As such, it is neither good nor bad. It just is. Too often young people are held to an unrealistic social standard about what it takes to be "good." From a very early age, they begin to associate having angry feelings with being bad. Like Amber, our children perceive anger as taboo and take steps to suppress angry feelings.

When parents teach their children to say "yes" to the presence of anger and "no" to the expression of anger through aggressive or passive aggressive behaviors, they build a foundation for lifelong emotional intelligence and strong relationships.

4. Be the Change You Want to See

Each time passive aggressive behavior is answered with a mirrored counter-passive aggressive response, the hidden means of expressing anger is reinforced and an opportunity for direct emotional expression is lost. On the other hand, each time passive aggressive behavior is confronted assertively, the hidden anger is weakened.

The most effective way for our kids to learn to acknowledge and accept angry feelings is to role model this for them on a daily basis. As parents, this can be a real challenge since we, too, may have faced stringent socializing forces regarding the expression of our anger. It's never too late to learn to express anger in emotionally honest, direct ways, however, and the stakes have never been so high!

5. Allow It, Tolerate It, Encourage It, Even!

The final essential angle to confronting passive aggressive behavior in our kids is our willingness to receive their anger when they test out their new voice. If you are going to guide your child to be more open and direct with his anger, then you must also be willing to accept his anger when he expresses it. For many, this is truly difficult. But for lasting change to take hold for Amber and other young people, they must know that the assertive expression of their anger will be tolerated, respected and even honored!

SIGNE WHITSON is a co-author of the book, *"The Angry Smile: The Psychology of Passive Aggressive Behavior in Families, Schools, and Workplaces, 2nd edition."* She is also the creator of the website www .PassiveAggressiveDiaries.com. Signe is a licensed social worker and therapist who has developed and delivered numerous training programs around the country in areas related to child and adolescent mental health. Copies of *The Angry Smile,* as well as information on Angry Smile seminars, can be found at www.Isci.org.

Where Personality Goes Awry

A multifaceted research approach is providing more clues to the origins of personality disorders.

CHARLOTTE HUFF

Over the years, few large-scale prospective studies have targeted the causes of personality disorders (PDs). But recently, a new body of research has begun to explore the potential influences of several factors, from genetics and parenting to peer influences, and even the randomness of life events.

Indeed, says Patricia Hoffman Judd, PhD, clinical professor of psychiatry at the University of California, San Diego, research into the origins of PDs is just beginning to take off. "I think for years people thought, 'It's just personality—you can't do anything about it,'" she explains. "There's also been moralism [that people with such disorders] are evil, that they are lazy," adds Judd, author of "A Developmental Model of Borderline Personality Disorder" (American Psychiatric Publishing, 2003).

But research is helping to turn such misconceptions around. Genetics researchers, for example, are closer to identifying some of the biological underpinnings that may influence PDs. Last year, for example, a team located—and described in *Molecular Psychiatry* (Vol, 8. No. 11)—a malfunctioning gene they believe may be a factor in obsessive-compulsive disorder. Other researchers are investigating genetic links to aggression, anxiety and fear—traits that could be influential in the later development of a personality disorder.

However, genetics don't work in a vacuum. Studies continue to indicate that abuse, even verbal abuse, can amplify the risk of developing a personality disorder.

For some disorders, such as antisocial PD, the evidence suggests that genetic factors play a significant role, while others, such as dependent personality disorder, appear to be more environmentally influenced, says longtime PD researcher Theodore Millon, PhD, DSc, editor of an ongoing book series, "Personality-guided Psychology" (APA).

But regardless of the specific disorder, researchers increasingly observe a back-and-forth interplay between genetic and environmental influences.

"We see a paradigm shift taking place in the field now toward a more interactionist perspective," says Jeffrey G. Johnson, PhD, associate professor of clinical psychology in Columbia University's psychiatry department. "I think the field is getting away from genetics versus environment—it's a major change."

The Genetic/Environmental Convergence

One of the largest efforts to look at PDs, the Collaborative Longitudinal Personality Disorders Study (CLPS), is attempting to gain insight into a cross-section of the disorders' characteristics, stability and progression. The multisite study, funded by the National Institute of Mental Health until 2005, has since 1996 enrolled 668 people with the diagnoses of avoidant, borderline, obsessive-compulsive or schizotypal personality disorders. A summary of the study's aims appeared in the *Journal of Personality Disorders* (Vol. 14. No. 4).

Although the study is not looking directly at causes, it's collecting historical information that may one day provide some insights, says Tracie Shea, PhD, associate professor in the department of psychiatry and human behavior at Brown Medical School and one of CLPS's principal investigators. "I like to think of it as generating hypotheses that can be tested," she says.

Shea co-authored a 2002 study in the *Journal of Nervous and Mental Disease* (Vol. 190, No. 8) that looked at CLPS data and found an association between the severity of specific PDs and the number and type of childhood traumas. In particular, people with borderline PDs reported particularly high rates of childhood sexual trauma—55 percent detailing physically forced, unwanted sexual contact. The researchers note, however, that the type of analysis couldn't determine if the personality adaptations occurred in response to the trauma or whether the individuals' underlying character pathology predisposed them.

Among those exploring the genetic and environmental influences linking normal and abnormal personality is Robert Krueger, PhD, associate professor of psychology at the University of Minnesota. In 2002, Krueger co-authored a study in the *Journal of Personality* (Vol. 70, No. 5) that looked at the personality traits of 128 twin pairs who had been raised apart. The study found that the identical twins were more similar in personality traits than the fraternal twins.

Thus, although both genetics and environment contributed to the association between normal and abnormal personality, genetics appeared to play the greater role overall, Krueger says. "The predominant reason normal and abnormal personality are linked to each other is because they are linked to the same underlying genetic mechanisms," he explains.

With borderline PD, for example, ongoing research indicates that there may be a genetic base for the problems with impulsivity and aggression, says the University of California's Judd. But environmental influences are significant and can extend deep into childhood, even infancy, Judd adds.

"There is a pretty high prevalence of maltreatment by caregivers across all personality disorders," she notes. "One of the key problems appears to be neglect. Probably more of an emotional neglect—more of a lack of attention to a child's emotional needs."

Judd points to several studies by Johnson, including one published in 1999 in the *Archives of General Psychiatry* (Vol. 56, No. 7) that followed 639 New York state families and their children for nearly two decades. Children with documented instances of childhood abuse or neglect were more than four times as likely to develop a PD in early adulthood, according to the research.

Another study, led by Johnson and published in 2001 in *Comprehensive Psychiatry* (Vol. 42, No. 1), came to a similar conclusion when examining maternal verbal abuse in the same New York group of families, involving this time 793 mothers and their children. The prospective study asked mothers a variety of questions, including whether they had screamed at their children in the previous month and whether they had told their child they didn't love them or would send them away. Offspring who experienced verbal abuse in childhood—compared with those who didn't—were more than three times as likely to be diagnosed as adults with borderline, narcissistic, obsessive-compulsive and paranoid PDs.

Shea cautions, though, that at this point research into childhood neglect and abuse, albeit intriguing, has largely been suggestive because prospective studies remain limited.

"It's likely that these childhood abuse factors do play an important role," he explains. "It's hard to say what and how big that role is, more specifically."

The Parent-Blame Problem

The role of abuse is particularly controversial among family members of people with a borderline disorder, who say they are being unfairly blamed—similar to what happened in the early days of schizophrenia research. Emphasizing maltreatment and abuse is misleading and has a devastating effect on families, says Valerie Porr, president of a New York-based nonprofit group, Treatment and Research Advancements National Association for Personality Disorder (www.tara4bpd.org/tara.html).

Porr doesn't deny that parental behavior can play a role in borderline PD. "But it's not like it's the evil mother beating her children," she says. Rather, she explains, the child's "behavior is so off the wall [that] the family's responses are off the wall."

Porr, who has a family member with borderline personality disorder, points to emerging research, including that of Harvard University-based psychologist Jerome Kagan, PhD, identifying the high sensitivity to outside stimuli of some children as significant. Family members of people with borderline PD report unusual responses even in the first months of life, Porr says, noting that, "They say, 'The light bothers them. They are sensitive to noise. Texture bothers them.'"

But Kagan, in a 2002 *Dialogues in Clinical Neuroscience* article (Vol. 4, No. 3), says that the role of high reactivity in infancy is far from clear-cut. It's true, he says, that highly reactive infants are more likely to develop shy, timid or anxious personalities. Still, there are puzzling questions, including the significant gap between the percentage of children—20 percent—who are highly reactive infants and the prevalence—less than 10 percent—of those who develop social phobias.

"This fact suggests that many high reactives find an adaptive niche in their society that allows them to titer unpredictable social encounters," Kagan writes.

In the end, says Johnson, the goal of research into environmental influences is not to blame, but to help parents. "We must understand what parenting behaviors are associated with greater risk to the child," he says. "When we identify those parenting behaviors, we can use them to design intervention."

The Role of Peers

Psychologists' findings also suggest that caregivers, teachers and even peers may play a role in PDs—both in positive as well as negative ways. Even a single strong positive relationship—say a close bond with a grandmother—can offset negative influences in a dysfunctional household.

"The child with a predisposition toward developing a personality disorder doesn't need the perfect teacher or the perfect friends to not develop the disorder," says Judith Beck, PhD, director of the Beck Institute for Cognitive Therapy and Research in suburban Philadelphia. "If the child is in an extreme environment, such as abuse or neglect, that may make the difference in terms of developing a personality disorder."

And life events can help tip the balance, Beck says. For example, a child with obsessive-compulsive tendencies who has alcoholic parents may assume the responsibility of caring for his younger siblings—a move that may amplify his propensities until he meets the diagnosis of a disorder. "It's the fit between your environment and your personality," Beck explains.

Over time, researchers will continue probing that fit and will likely identify more than a few causes even for a single personality disorder, says Millon, dean of the Florida-based Institute for Advanced Studies in Personology and Psychopathology. Narrowing down potential causes will help psychologists more quickly isolate what might be influencing a particular patient, he says.

Millon explains: "Once you identify the one cause that seems most probable and most significant, then you can design your therapy in order to unlearn what seemed most problematic for that individual."

CHARLOTTE HUFF is a freelance writer in Fort Worth, Texas.

The Blank Slate

The long-accepted theory that parents can mold their children like clay has distorted choices faced by adults trying to balance their lives, multiplied the anguish of those whose children haven't turned out as hoped, and mangled the science of human behavior.

STEVEN PINKER

If you read the pundits in newspapers and magazines, you may have come across some remarkable claims about the malleability of the human psyche. Here are a few from my collection of clippings:

- Little boys quarrel and fight because they are encouraged to do so.
- Children enjoy sweets because their parents use them as rewards for eating vegetables.
- Teenagers get the idea to compete in looks and fashion from spelling bees and academic prizes.
- Men think the goal of sex is an orgasm because of the way they were socialized.

If you find these assertions dubious, your skepticism is certainly justified. In all cultures, little boys quarrel, children like sweets, teens compete for status, and men pursue orgasms, without the slightest need of encouragement or socialization. In each case, the writers made their preposterous claims without a shred of evidence—without even a nod to the possibility that they were saying something common sense might call into question.

Intellectual life today is beset with a great divide. On one side is a militant denial of human nature, a conviction that the mind of a child is a blank slate that is subsequently inscribed by parents and society. For much of the past century, psychology has tried to explain all thought, feeling, and behavior with a few simple mechanisms of learning by association. Social scientists have tried to explain all customs and social arrangements as a product of the surrounding culture. A long list of concepts that would seem natural to the human way of thinking—emotions, kinship, the sexes—are said to have been "invented" or "socially constructed."

At the same time, there is a growing realization that human nature won't go away. Anyone who has had more than one child, or been in a heterosexual relationship, or noticed that children learn language but house pets don't, has recognized that people are born with certain talents and temperaments. An acknowledgment that we humans are a species with a timeless and universal psychology pervades the writings of great political thinkers, and without it we cannot explain the recurring themes of literature, religion, and myth. Moreover, the modern sciences of mind, brain, genes, and evolution are showing that there is something to the commonsense idea of human nature. Although no scientist denies that learning and culture are crucial to every aspect of human life, these processes don't happen by magic. There must be complex innate mental faculties that enable human beings to create and learn culture.

Sometimes the contradictory attitudes toward human nature divide people into competing camps. The blank slate camp tends to have greater appeal among those in the social sciences and humanities than it does among biological scientists. And until recently, it was more popular on the political left than it was on the right.

But sometimes both attitudes coexist uneasily inside the mind of a single person. Many academics, for example, publicly deny the existence of intelligence. But privately, academics are *obsessed* with intelligence, discussing it endlessly in admissions, in hiring, and especially in their gossip about one another. And despite their protestations that it is a reactionary concept, they quickly invoke it to oppose executing a murderer with an IQ of 64 or to support laws requiring the removal of lead paint because it may lower a child's IQ by five points. Similarly, those who argue that gender differences are a reversible social construction do not treat them that way in their advice to their daughters, in their dealings with the opposite sex, or in their unguarded gossip, humor, and reflections on their lives.

No good can come from this hypocrisy. The dogma that human nature does not exist, in the face of growing evidence from science and common sense that it does, has led to contempt among many scholars in the humanities for the concepts of evidence and truth. Worse, the doctrine of the blank slate often distorts science itself by making an extreme position—that culture alone determines behavior—seem moderate, and by making the moderate position—that behavior comes from an interaction of biology and culture—seem extreme.

Although how parents treat their children can make a lot of difference in how happy they are, placing a stimulating mobile over a child's crib and playing Mozart CDs will not shape a child's intelligence.

For example, many policies on parenting come from research that finds a correlation between the behavior of parents and of their children. Loving parents have confident children, authoritative parents (neither too permissive nor too punitive) have well-behaved children, parents who talk to their children have children with better language skills, and so on. Thus everyone concludes that parents should be loving, authoritative, and talkative, and if children don't turn out well, it must be the parents' fault.

Those conclusions depend on the belief that children are blank slates. It ignores the fact that parents provide their children with genes, not just an environment. The correlations may be telling us only that the same genes that make adults loving, authoritative, and talkative make their children self-confident, well-behaved, and articulate. Until the studies are redone with adopted children (who get only their environment from their parents), the data are compatible with the possibility that genes make all the difference, that parenting makes all the difference, or anything in between. Yet the extreme position—that parents are everything—is the only one researchers entertain.

The denial of human nature has not just corrupted the world of intellectuals but has harmed ordinary people. The theory that parents can mold their children like clay has inflicted child-rearing regimes on parents that are unnatural and sometimes cruel. It has distorted the choices faced by mothers as they try to balance their lives, and it has multiplied the anguish of parents whose children haven't turned out as hoped. The belief that human tastes are reversible cultural preferences has led social planners to write off people's enjoyment of ornament, natural light, and human scale and forced millions of people to live in drab cement boxes. And the conviction that humanity could be reshaped by massive social engineering projects has led to some of the greatest atrocities in history.

The phrase "blank slate" is a loose translation of the medieval Latin term tabula rasa—scraped tablet. It is often attributed to the 17th-century English philosopher John Locke, who wrote that the mind is "white paper void of all characters." But it became the official doctrine among thinking people only in the first half of the 20th century, as part of a reaction to the widespread belief in the intellectual or moral inferiority of women, Jews, nonwhite races, and non-Western cultures.

Part of the reaction was a moral repulsion from discrimination, lynchings, forced sterilizations, segregation, and the Holocaust. And part of it came from empirical observations.

Waves of immigrants from southern and eastern Europe filled the cities of America and climbed the social ladder. African Americans took advantage of "Negro colleges" and migrated northward, beginning the Harlem Renaissance. The graduates of women's colleges launched the first wave of feminism. To say that women and minority groups were inferior contradicted what people could see with their own eyes.

Academics were swept along by the changing attitudes, but they also helped direct the tide. The prevailing theories of mind were refashioned to make racism and sexism as untenable as possible. The blank slate became sacred scripture. According to the doctrine, any differences we see among races, ethnic groups, sexes, and individuals come not from differences in their innate constitution but from differences in their experiences. Change the experiences—by reforming parenting, education, the media, and social rewards—and you can change the person. Also, if there is no such thing as human nature, society will not be saddled with such nasty traits as aggression, selfishness, and prejudice. In a reformed environment, people can be prevented from learning these habits.

In psychology, behaviorists like John B. Watson and B. F. Skinner simply banned notions of talent and temperament, together with all the other contents of the mind, such as beliefs, desires, and feelings. This set the stage for Watson's famous boast: "Give me a dozen healthy infants, well-formed, and my own specified world to bring them up in, and I'll guarantee to take any one at random and train him to become any type of specialist I might select—doctor, lawyer, artist, merchant-chief, and yes, even beggar-man and thief, regardless of his talents, penchants, tendencies, abilities, vocations, and race of his ancestors."

Watson also wrote an influential child-rearing manual recommending that parents give their children minimum attention and love. If you comfort a crying baby, he wrote, you will reward the baby for crying and thereby increase the frequency of crying behavior.

In anthropology, Franz Boas wrote that differences among human races and ethnic groups come not from their physical constitution but from their *culture*. Though Boas himself did not claim that people were blank slates—he only argued that all ethnic groups are endowed with the same mental abilities—his students, who came to dominate American social science, went further. They insisted not just that *differences* among ethnic groups must be explained in terms of culture (which is reasonable), but that *every aspect* of human existence must be explained in terms of culture (which is not). "Heredity cannot be allowed to have acted any part in history," wrote Alfred Kroeber. "With the exception of the instinctoid reactions in infants to sudden withdrawals of support and to sudden loud noises, the human being is entirely instinctless," wrote Ashley Montagu.

In the second half of the 20th century, the ideals of the social scientists of the first half enjoyed a well-deserved victory. Eugenics, social Darwinism, overt expressions of racism and sexism, and official discrimination against women and minorities were on the wane, or had been eliminated, from the political and intellectual mainstream in Western democracies.

At the same time, the doctrine of the blank slate, which had been blurred with ideals of equality and progress, began to show cracks. As new disciplines such as cognitive science, neuroscience, evolutionary psychology, and behavioral genetics flourished, it became clearer that thinking is a biological process, that the brain is not exempt from the laws of evolution, that the sexes differ above the neck as well as below it, and that people are not psychological clones. Here are some examples of the discoveries.

Hundreds of traits, from romantic love to humorous insults, can be found in every society ever documented.

Natural selection tends to homogenize a species into a standard design by concentrating the effective genes and winnowing out the ineffective ones. This suggests that the human mind evolved with a universal complex design. Beginning in the 1950s, linguist Noam Chomsky of the Massachusetts Institute of Technology argued that a language should be analyzed not in terms of the list of sentences people utter but in terms of the mental computations that enable them to handle an unlimited number of new sentences in the language. These computations have been found to conform to a universal grammar. And if this universal grammar is embodied in the circuitry that guides babies when they listen to speech, it could explain how children learn language so easily.

Similarly, some anthropologists have returned to an ethnographic record that used to trumpet differences among cultures and have found an astonishingly detailed set of aptitudes and tastes that all cultures have in common. This shared way of thinking, feeling, and living makes all of humanity look like a single tribe, which the anthropologist Donald Brown of the University of California at Santa Barbara has called the universal people. Hundreds of traits, from romantic love to humorous insults, from poetry to food taboos, from exchange of goods to mourning the dead, can be found in every society ever documented.

One example of a stubborn universal is the tangle of emotions surrounding the act of love. In all societies, sex is at least somewhat "dirty." It is conducted in private, pondered obsessively, regulated by custom and taboo, the subject of gossip and teasing, and a trigger for jealous rage. Yet sex is the most concentrated source of physical pleasure granted by the nervous system. Why is it so fraught with conflict? For a brief period in the 1960s and 1970s, people dreamed of an erotopia in which men and women could engage in sex without hang-ups and inhibitions. "If you can't be with the one you love, love the one you're with," sang Stephen Stills. "If you love somebody, set them free," sang Sting.

But Sting also sang, "Every move you make, I'll be watching you." Even in a time when, seemingly, anything goes, most people do not partake in sex as casually as they partake in food or conversation. The reasons are as deep as anything in biology. One of the hazards of sex is a baby, and a baby is not just any seven-pound object but, from an evolutionary point of view, our reason for being. Every time a woman has sex with a man, she is taking a chance at sentencing herself to years of motherhood, and she is forgoing the opportunity to use her finite reproductive output with some other man. The man, for his part, may be either implicitly committing his sweat and toil to the incipient child or deceiving his partner about such intentions.

On rational grounds, the volatility of sex is a puzzle, because in an era with reliable contraception, these archaic entanglements should have no claim on our feelings. We should be loving the one we're with, and sex should inspire no more gossip, music, fiction, raunchy humor, or strong emotions than eating or talking does. The fact that people are tormented by the Darwinian economics of babies they are no longer having is testimony to the long reach of human nature.

Although the minds of normal human beings work in pretty much the same way, they are not, of course, identical. Natural selection reduces genetic variability but never eliminates it. As a result, nearly every one of us is genetically unique. And these differences in genes make a difference in mind and behavior, at least quantitatively. The most dramatic demonstrations come from studies of the rare people who *are* genetically identical, identical twins.

Identical twins think and feel in such similar ways that they sometimes suspect they are linked by telepathy. They are similar in verbal and mathematical intelligence, in their degree of life satisfaction, and in personality traits such as introversion, agreeableness, neuroticism, conscientiousness, and openness to experience. They have similar attitudes toward controversial issues such as the death penalty, religion, and modern music. They resemble each other not just in paper-and-pencil tests but in consequential behavior such as gambling, divorcing, committing crimes, getting into accidents, and watching television. And they boast dozens of shared idiosyncrasies such as giggling incessantly, giving interminable answers to simple questions, dipping buttered toast in coffee, and, in the case of Abigail van Buren and the late Ann Landers, writing indistinguishable syndicated advice columns. The crags and valleys of their electroencephalograms (brain waves) are as alike as those of a single person recorded on two occasions, and the wrinkles of their brains and the distribution of gray matter across cortical areas are similar as well.

Identical twins (who share all their genes) are far more similar than fraternal twins (who share just half their genes). This is as true when the twins are separated at birth and raised apart as when they are raised in the same home by the same parents. Moreover, biological siblings, who also share half their genes, are far more similar than adoptive siblings, who share no more genes than strangers. Indeed, adoptive siblings are barely similar at all. These conclusions come from massive studies employing the best instruments known to psychology. Alternative explanations that try to push the effects of the genes to zero have by now been tested and rejected.

People sometimes fear that if the genes affect the mind at all they must determine it in every detail. That is wrong, for two reasons. The first is that most effects of genes are probabilistic. If one identical twin has a trait, there is often no more than an even chance that the other twin will have it, despite having a complete genome in common (and in the case of twins raised together, most of their environment in common as well).

The second reason is that the genes' effects can vary with the environment. Although Woody Allen's fame may depend on genes that enhance a sense of humor, he once pointed out that "we live in a society that puts a big value on jokes. If I had been an Apache Indian, those guys didn't need comedians, so I'd be out of work."

Studies of the brain also show that the mind is not a blank slate. The brain, of course, has a pervasive ability to change the strengths of its connections as the result of learning and experience—if it didn't, we would all be permanent amnesiacs. But that does not mean that the structure of the brain is mostly a product of experience. The study of the brains of twins has shown that much of the variation in the amount of gray matter in the prefrontal lobes is genetically caused. And these variations are not just random differences in anatomy like fingerprints; they correlate significantly with differences in intelligence.

People born with variations in the typical brain plan can vary in the way their minds work. A study of Einstein's brain showed that he had large, unusually shaped inferior parietal lobules, which participate in spatial reasoning and intuitions about numbers. Gay men are likely to have a relatively small nucleus in the anterior hypothalamus, a nucleus known to have a role in sex differences. Convicted murderers and other violent, antisocial people are likely to have a relatively small and inactive prefrontal cortex, the part of the brain that governs decision making and inhibits impulses. These gross features of the brain are almost certainly not sculpted by information coming in from the senses. That, in turn, implies that differences in intelligence, scientific genius, sexual orientation, and impulsive violence are not entirely learned.

The doctrine of the blank slate had been thought to undergird the ideals of equal rights and social improvement, so it is no surprise that the discoveries undermining it have often been met with fear and loathing. Scientists challenging the doctrine have been libeled, picketed, shouted down, and subjected to searing invective.

This is not the first time in history that people have tried to ground moral principles in dubious factual assumptions. People used to ground moral values in the doctrine that Earth lay at the center of the universe, and that God created mankind in his own image in a day. In both cases, informed people eventually reconciled their moral values with the facts, not just because they had to give a nod to reality, but also because the supposed connections between the facts and morals—such as the belief that the arrangement of rock and gas in space has something to do with right and wrong—were spurious to begin with.

We are now living, I think, through a similar transition. The blank slate has been widely embraced as a rationale for morality, but it is under assault from science. Yet just as the supposed foundations of morality shifted in the centuries following Galileo and Darwin, our own moral sensibilities will come to terms with the scientific findings, not just because facts are facts but because the moral credentials of the blank slate are just as spurious. Once you think through the issues, the two greatest fears of an innate human endowment can be defused.

One is the fear of inequality. Blank is blank, so if we are all blank slates, the reasoning goes, we must all be equal. But if the slate of a newborn is not blank, different babies could have different things inscribed on their slates. Individuals, sexes, classes, and races might differ innately in their talents and inclinations. The fear is that if people do turn out to be different, it would open the door to discrimination, oppression, or eugenics.

But none of this follows. For one thing, in many cases the empirical basis of the fear may be misplaced. A universal human nature does not imply that *differences* among groups are innate. Confucius could have been right when he wrote, "Men's natures are alike; it is their habits that carry them far apart."

Regardless of IQ or physical strength, all human beings can be assumed to have certain traits in common.

More important, the case against bigotry is not a factual claim that people are biologically indistinguishable. It is a moral stance that condemns judging an *individual* according to the average traits of certain *groups* to which the individual belongs. Enlightened societies strive to ignore race, sex, and ethnicity in hiring, admissions, and criminal justice because the alternative is morally repugnant. Discriminating against people on the basis of race, sex, or ethnicity would be unfair, penalizing them for traits over which they have no control. It would perpetuate the injustices of the past and could rend society into hostile factions. None of these reasons depends on whether groups of people are or are not genetically indistinguishable.

Far from being conducive to discrimination, a conception of human nature is the reason we oppose it. Regardless of IQ or physical strength or any other trait that might vary among people, all human beings can be assumed to have certain traits in common. No one likes being enslaved. No one likes being humiliated. No one likes being treated unfairly. The revulsion we feel toward discrimination and slavery comes from a conviction that however much people vary on some traits, they do not vary on these.

Parents often discover that their children are immune to their rewards, punishments, and nagging. Over the long run, a child's personality and intellect are largely determined by genes, peer groups, and chance.

A second fear of human nature comes from a reluctance to give up the age-old dream of the perfectibility of man. If we are forever saddled with fatal flaws and deadly sins, according to this fear, social reform would be a waste of time. Why try to make the world a better place if people are rotten to the core and will just foul it up no matter what you do?

But this, too, does not follow. If the mind is a complex system with many faculties, an antisocial desire is just one component among others. Some faculties may endow us with greed or lust or malice, but others may endow us with sympathy, foresight, self-respect, a desire for respect from others, and an ability to learn from experience and history. Social progress can come from pitting some of these faculties against others.

For example, suppose we are endowed with a conscience that treats certain other beings as targets of sympathy and inhibits us from harming or exploiting them. The philosopher Peter Singer of Princeton University has shown that moral improvement has proceeded for millennia because people have expanded the mental dotted line that embraces the entities considered worthy of sympathy. The circle has been poked outward from the family and village to the clan, the tribe, the nation, the race, and most recently to all of humanity. This sweeping change in sensibilities did not require a blank slate. It could have arisen from a moral gadget with a single knob or slider that adjusts the size of the circle embracing the entities whose interests we treat as comparable to our own.

Some people worry that these arguments are too fancy for the dangerous world we live in. Since data in the social sciences are never perfect, shouldn't we err on the side of caution and stick with the null hypothesis that people are blank slates? Some people think that even if we were certain that people differed genetically, or harbored ignoble tendencies, we might still want to promulgate the fiction that they didn't.

This argument is based on the fallacy that the blank slate has nothing but good moral implications and a theory that admits a human nature has nothing but bad ones. In fact, the dangers go both ways. Take the most horrifying example of all, the abuse of biology by the Nazis, with its pseudoscientific nonsense about superior and inferior races. Historians agree that bitter memories of the Holocaust were the main reason that human nature became taboo in intellectual life after the Second World War.

But historians have also documented that Nazism was not the only ideologically inspired holocaust of the 20th century. Many atrocities were committed by Marxist regimes in the name of egalitarianism, targeting people whose success was taken as evidence of their avarice. The kulaks ("bourgeois peasants") were exterminated by Lenin and Stalin in the Soviet Union. Teachers, former landlords, and "rich peasants" were humiliated, tortured, and murdered during China's Cultural Revolution. City dwellers and literate professionals were worked to death or executed during the reign of the Khmer Rouge in Cambodia.

And here is a remarkable fact: Although both Nazi and Marxist ideologies led to industrial-scale killing, *their biological and psychological theories were opposites.* Marxists had no use for the concept of race, were averse to the notion of genetic inheritance, and were hostile to the very idea of a human nature rooted in biology. Marx did not explicitly embrace the blank slate, but he was adamant that human nature has no enduring properties: "All history is nothing but a continuous transformation of human nature," he wrote. Many of his followers did embrace it. "It is on a blank page that the most beautiful poems are written," said Mao. "Only the newborn baby is spotless," ran a Khmer Rouge slogan. This philosophy led to persecution of the successful and of those who produced more crops on their private family plots than on communal farms. And it made these regimes not just dictatorships but totalitarian dictatorships, which tried to control every aspect of life, from art and education to child rearing and sex. After all, if the mind is structureless at birth and shaped by its experience, a society that wants the right kind of minds must control the experience.

None of this is meant to impugn the blank slate as an evil doctrine, any more than a belief in human nature is an evil doctrine. Both are separated by many steps from the evil acts committed under their banners, and they must be evaluated on factual grounds. But the fact that tyranny and genocide can come from an anti-innatist belief system as readily as from an innatist one does upend the common misconception that biological approaches to behavior are uniquely sinister. And the reminder that human nature is the source of our interests and needs as well as our flaws encourages us to examine claims about the mind objectively, without putting a moral thumb on either side of the scale.

Girls Gone Bad?

Paris, Britney, Lindsay & Nicole: They seem to be everywhere and they may not be wearing underwear. Tweens adore them and teens envy them. But are we raising a generation of 'prosti-tots'?

KATHLEEN DEVENY WITH RAINA KELLEY

My 6-year-old daughter loves Lindsay Lohan. Loves, loves, *loves* her. She loves Lindsay's hair; she loves Lindsay's freckles. She's seen "The Parent Trap" at least 10 times. I sometimes catch her humming the movie's theme song, Nat King Cole's "Love." She likes "Herbie Fully Loaded" and now we're cycling through "Freaky Friday." So when my daughter spotted a photo of Lindsay in the New York Post at the breakfast table not long ago, she was psyched. "That's Lindsay Lohan," she said proudly. "What's she doing?"

I couldn't tell her, of course. I didn't want to explain that Lindsay, who, like Paris Hilton and Britney Spears, sometimes parties pantyless, was taking pole-dancing lessons to prepare for a movie role. Or that her two hours of research left her bruised "everywhere." Then again, Lindsay's professional trials are easy to explain compared with Nicole Richie's recent decision to stop her car in the car-pool lane of an L.A. freeway. Or Britney Spears's "collapse" during a New Year's Eve party in Las Vegas. Or the more recent report that Lindsay had checked into rehab after passing out in a hotel hallway, an item that ran on the Post's Page Six opposite a photo of Kate Moss falling down a stairway while dressed in little more than a fur jacket and a pack of cigarettes.

Something's in the air, and I wouldn't call it love. Like never before, our kids are being bombarded by images of oversexed, underdressed celebrities who can't seem to step out of a car without displaying their well-waxed private parts to photographers. Videos like "Girls Gone Wild on Campus Uncensored" bring in an estimated $40 million a year. And if US magazine, which changed the rules of mainstream celebrity journalism, is too slow with the latest dish on "Brit's New Man," kids can catch up 24/7 with hugely popular gossip blogs like perezhilton.com, tmz.com or defamer.com.

Allow us to confirm what every parent knows: kids, born in the new-media petri dish, are well aware of celebrity antics. But while boys are willing to take a peek at anyone showing skin, they're baffled by the feuds, the fashions and faux pas of the Brit Pack. Girls, on the other hand, are their biggest fans. A recent NEWSWEEK Poll found that 77 percent of Americans believe that Britney, Paris and Lindsay have too much influence on young girls. Hardly a day passes when one of them isn't making news. Paris Hilton "was always somewhere, doing something," says Melissa Monaco, an 18-year-old senior at Oldfield's boarding school for girls in Maryland, who describes herself as a recovered Paris Hilton addict. "I loved everything from her outfits to her attitude," she says. And it's not just teenagers. Julie Seborowski, a first-grade teacher at Kumeyaay Elementary School in San Diego, says she sees it in her 7-year-old students: girls using words like "sexy," singing pop songs with suggestive lyrics and flirting with boys.

That's enough to make any parent cringe. But are there really harmful long-term effects of overexposure to Paris Hilton? Are we raising a generation of what one L.A. mom calls "prosti-tots," young girls who dress like tarts, live for Dolce & Gabbana purses and can neither spell nor define such words as "adequate"? Or does the rise of the bad girl signal something more profound, a coarsening of the culture and a devaluation of sex, love and lasting commitment? We're certainly not the first generation of parents to worry about such things, nor will we be the last. Many conservative thinkers view our sex-drenched culture as dangerous; liberals are more prone to wave off fears about the chastity of our daughters as reactionary. One thing is not in doubt: a lot of parents are wondering about the effect our racy popular culture may have on their kids and the women they would like their girls to become. The answers are likely to lie in yet another question: where do our children learn values?

Here's a radical idea—at home, where they always have. Experts say attentive parents, strong teachers and nice friends are an excellent counterbalance to our increasingly sleazy culture. Statistical evidence indicates that our girls are actually doing pretty well, in spite of Paris Hilton and those like her: teen pregnancy, drinking and drug use are all down, and there is no evidence that girls are having intercourse at a younger age. And in many ways it's a great time to be a girl: women are excelling in sports, academics and the job market. It's just that the struggle to impart the right values to our kids is a 24/7 proposition. It can be done, but an ancient rule of warfare applies: first, know thy enemy.

I didn't want to explain to my 6-year-old that Lindsay was taking pole dancing to prepare for a movie role.

"It takes a very strong adolescent to know what's right and what's wrong and not get sucked into all this stuff," says Emily Waring, 40, a paralegal from San Diego and mother of two girls, ages 9 and 2. Waring says her "mom radar" is always on because she believes negative influences, including entertainers like Britney Spears, are everywhere. "Kids can so easily stray," she says.

Nobody wants her bright, innocent girls to grow up believing "hard-partying heiress" is a job title to which they can aspire. But does dressing like Paris or slavishly following the details of Britney's love life make kids more likely to stray? Educators say they don't believe most girls in middle school wear short skirts or midriff shirts to attract the attention of older men, or even boys. (High school is, granted, a different story.) Sixth graders dress to fit in with other girls and for acceptance in social groups. "They dress that way because that's what they see in the media," says Nancy T. Mugele, who works in communications at Roland Park Country School in Baltimore. "They don't want to be different."

Which is not to say that hearing about Lindsay Lohan's, um, "fire crotch" doesn't affect the way kids think about sex. A study published last year in the journal *Pediatrics* concluded that for white teens, repeated exposure to sexual content in television, movies and music increases the likelihood of becoming sexually active at an earlier age. (Black teens appear less influenced by media, and more by their parents' expectations and their friends' sexual behavior; those who had the least exposure to sexual content were also less likely to have intercourse.) Specifically, the study found that 55 percent of teens who were exposed to a lot of sexual material had intercourse by 16, compared with only 6 percent of teens who rarely saw sexual imagery in the media. That jibes with what many Americans fear: 84 percent of adults in the NEWSWEEK Poll said sex plays a bigger role in popular culture than it did 20 or 30 years ago, and 70 percent said that was a bad influence on young people.

Many factors affect kids' sexual behavior, and it may be that kids who are already considering sex are more likely to seek out sexy shows and music. But researchers say one of the strongest predictors of early intercourse is the impression—real or imagined—that everybody else is doing it. For some teens, especially those who aren't getting strong messages about abstinence from their parents, the media can become a sort of "sexual superpeer," according to

Jane D. Brown, a journalism professor at UNC Chapel Hill, and an author of the *Pediatrics* study. The message, says Brown, is that "you can walk around with no clothes on, you can have sex with whoever shows up, you can have a baby and not be married."

Some observers think the real effect of the Brit Pack on our culture is more subtle, but no less negative. Rather than instantly inspiring kids to rush and have sex, out-of-control celebs create a sense of normalcy about behavior—drinking, smoking, casual sex—that is dangerous for teens. Britney, Paris and Lindsay have no shortage of "boyfriends" but seem to have few real relationships. "It creates a general sense that life is about being crazy, being kooky, having fun and not carrying on serious relationships," says Christian Smith, professor of sociology at Notre Dame. But the really insidious consequence is that teenagers often consider themselves immune to these influences. "They don't have enough perspective on how they are being formed by the world around them—and when they don't realize it, it can be more powerful," he says.

Eighty-four percent of adults say sex plays a bigger role in popular culture than it did 20 or 30 years ago.

Still, this seems like a lot to place on the slender shoulders of Nicole Richie and her frenemies. That some girls dress like Paris/Britney/Lindsay is empirically true. But it's difficult to draw a straight line between the behavior of celebrities and the behavior of real girls. "We certainly don't see our girls clamoring to get to downtown Chicago to the clubs," says Mark Kuzniewski, principal of Aptakisic Junior High in Buffalo Grove, Ill. And while girls may admire Britney's clothes and dance moves, her students "can't understand why Britney would wear no underwear," says Michelle Freitag, fifth-grade teacher in suburban Chicago. Their verdict: Britney is a "hootch," which is a polite way of saying "slut."

Our anxiety about girls and sex is growing just as the statistics seem to be telling as different story. Sex surveys are notoriously unreliable, but the best available data show that the average age of first sexual intercourse for girls is 17, according to the Guttmacher Institute, and hasn't changed by more than a few months in 20 years. The overall teenage pregnancy rate in 2002, the most recent available, was down 35 percent from 1990, according to the Centers for Disease Control. And while celebrity idols stumble in and out of rehab, the rates of drinking, smoking and overall drug use among teenage girls have declined in recent years, says the Institute for Social Research at the University of Michigan.

Girls born after 1990 live in a world where they have ready access to organized sports, safe contraception and Ivy League colleges. Yale didn't admit women until 1969; its freshman class is currently half female. In the 2004–2005 school year, women earned 57 percent of all bachelor's degrees awarded and 59 percent of master's degrees. The Congress now has 90 female members—the highest in history—with 16 in the Senate and 74 in the House, including Speaker Nancy Pelosi. Hillary Clinton, our first viable female presidential candidate, has thrown her hat into the ring.

Dan Kindlon, a professor of child psychology at Harvard and author of "Alpha Girls," calls these girls the daughters of the revolution, the first generation that is reaping the full benefit of the women's movement. "Sure, there are plenty of girls with big problems out there," he says. "Like the 'Girls Gone Wild' videos. But what percentage of the college population is that?" There is still plenty of pressure to be beautiful and thin, he adds, but now there are more options. Girls can define themselves as athletes or good students. For better or for worse, it may also be that they now feel entitled to dress as crassly as they choose, date unwisely and fall down drunk, the way men have since the dawn of time.

Plenty of high-school bad girls (us, for instance!) grow up to be successful people with happy home lives.

That's at least how long parents have worried about how their children would turn out. The text on a Sumerian tablet from the village of Ur (located in modern-day Iraq) says: "If the unheard-of actions of today's youth are allowed to continue, then we are doomed." Certainly, queens and noblewomen have long gotten away with behaving badly: in the early 16th century, Anne Boleyn not only had an affair with the King of England, Henry VIII, but helped persuade him to throw the Roman Catholic Church out of the country (although we all know how that ended). Their daughter, Elizabeth I, was the "virgin queen" who slept around.

But for most of history, average women who had sex outside the vows of marriage were subject to banishment, beating or death. When Jesus said, "If any of you is without sin, let him be the first to throw a stone at her," he was protecting a woman caught in adultery. In her book "Promiscuities," Naomi Wolf recalls a searing image she came across in her research: a photo of the mummified remains of a 14-year-old German girl from the first century A.D.: "Her right arm still clutched the garrote that had been used to twist the rope around her neck. Her lips were open in an 'O' of surprise or pain . . ." Historians had concluded that the girl had been blindfolded, strangled and drowned, most likely as retribution for "adultery," or what we would now call premarital sex.

Until after the Civil War, women didn't have enough freedom to create much of a public scandal. By the turn of the century, however, the Industrial Revolution had transformed the lives of adolescent daughters of working-class families. Once confined to home, young white women could now work in offices, stores and factories, where they enjoyed unprecedented social freedoms—much to the chagrin of their parents and social critics. Young African-American women didn't have the same economic opportunities, but did gain new autonomy as they fled farms in the South to live and work in Northern cities.

Meanwhile, improved literacy along with technological advances like the wireless telegraph and radio gave rise to a national media. By 1900, there were more than 16,000 newspapers in the United States; circulation numbers at the biggest topped 1 million. Keeping a dirty little secret had become much, much harder. By the time the 1920s rolled around, bad girls could grow up to become not just the destroyers of men (in the tradition of Salome and Delilah), but also to be rich and famous.

Mae West, best remembered for one-liners like "If you don't like my peaches, why do you shake my tree," may have been the original bad girl of the 20th century. Born in Brooklyn in 1893, she wrote and starred in bawdy theatrical productions, delighting and scandalizing audiences. She went too far, however, when she wrote a play called "Sex," about waterfront hookers and pimps, which became a national hit. In 1927, the New York production was raided and she was arrested, convicted of a performance that "tended to corrupt the morals of youth and others," and sentenced to 10 days in jail, according to *The New York Times*. Seven years later she was featured on the cover of NEWSWEEK for a story titled "The Churches Protest," which called her the "personification of Hollywood's sins."

Gypsy Rose Lee, born in 1914, followed closely on Mae West's spike heels. A burlesque superstar, Lee's shows at Minsky's Winter Garden in New York in the 1930s were a sensation. Before a congressional committee in 1937, Herbert Minsky, who co-owned the theater, called Lee "one of the most highly publicized stars in the country." According to a *Washington Post* account, "A momentary hush fell on the hearings . . . The name of Gypsy Rose Lee had been mentioned." Despite her fame—and $2,000-a-week salary—Lee was arrested numerous times by the NYPD for public indecency, once allegedly protesting, "I wasn't naked. I was completely covered by a blue spotlight."

By the '50s, both Hollywood and the public took a harsh view of female stars' off-screen indiscretions. In 1950, Ingrid Bergman was America's sweetheart, having starred in "The Bells of St. Mary's" and "Notorious." But when Bergman, then married, had an affair with director Roberto Rossellini, who was also married, and gave birth to their child, she was shunned by Hollywood and called "a powerful influence for evil" on the floor of the Senate. (Hollywood "forgave" Bergman a few years later by giving her an Oscar for "Anastasia.") After news broke that Marilyn Monroe would be featured in a nude calendar, Hollywood proclaimed her career DOA. (She was on the cover of Life magazine a month later, and went on to the biggest roles of her career.)

America was scandalized in 1962 when Elizabeth Taylor cheated on Eddie Fisher with Richard Burton during the filming of "Cleopatra." The Vatican denounced her as "a woman of loose morals." When "Dickenliz," as they were known, checked into a Toronto hotel, protesters marched outside with signs that read DRINK NOT THE WINE OF ADULTERY, according to a 1964 NEWSWEEK article. But soon America's priorities shifted. The Vietnam War was on television; the civil-rights movement was in the streets, and the national mood had been sobered by the assassinations of John F. Kennedy, Martin Luther King Jr. and Robert Kennedy. The '60s also brought reliable contraception in the form of the birth-control pill and ushered in the sexual revolution. We no longer needed to look to Hollywood for bad influences; the girl next door, the one with birth-control pills and a couple of joints tucked into her fringed purse, became the new object of our anxiety.

America had become harder to shock—until 1984, that is, when Madonna showed up in a wedding dress at the first MTV Video Music Awards and sang "Like a Virgin" while writhing on the floor. When her "Virgin" tour opened a year later, parents fretted over the hordes of Madonna wannabes who thronged her concerts dressed in tatty lace, spandex and armfuls of black rubber bracelets. The Material Girl went on to outrage both Planned Parenthood and the Catholic Church in 1986 with her single "Papa Don't Preach," about a pregnant teenager. The 1992 coffee-table book called "Sex," which glorified nearly every sexual fetish you can think of, cemented her title as the Queen of Bad Girls. Eleven years later she passed on her crown to Britney with a lingering French kiss on the stage of yet another MTV Video Music Awards ceremony.

And Brit, as we know, has run with it. One-day marriages aside, why wouldn't girls be fascinated by her and her celebrity pals? These 21st-century "bad influences" are young, beautiful and rich, unencumbered by school, curfews or parents. "They've got great clothes and boyfriends. They seem to have a lot of fun," explains Emma Boyce, a 17-year-old junior at Louise S. McGehee School in New Orleans. But fascination and admiration are two very different things. As they get arrested for driving drunk and feuding with their former BFFs, the Brit Pack makes it easy for young women like Boyce, a top student and accomplished equestrian, to feel superior to them. "My friends and I look at them to laugh at them," adds Boyce. "Our lives seem pretty good by comparison. We're not going to rehab like Lindsay."

Boyce says she and her friends have simply outgrown their devotion to celebrities. Twelve- to 14-year-olds are probably the most vulnerable to stars' influence. "Clearly it is at this age for girls that they are trying to find an identity to associate with," says Kuzniewski, the junior-high principal from Buffalo Grove, Ill. "It seems desirable to be Lindsay Lohan." Now that's a legitimate cause for parental concern. But it may very well be fleeting. After all, have you read your junior-high journals lately? Like us, you were probably obsessed with trivial things that had little bearing on the person you became at 24 or 34. Even if your daughter does dress like Paris or behave like Lindsay, that doesn't mean she's doomed to a life on the pole. Plenty of high-school bad girls (us, for instance!) grow up to be successful professionals with happy home lives.

And as much as we hate to admit it, we grown-ups are complicit. We're uncomfortable when kids worship these girls, yet we also love US magazine; we can't get enough of YouTube videos or "E! True Hollywood Stories." So rather than wring our hands over an increase in 17-year-olds getting breast implants,

what if we just said no? They're minors, right? And while we worry that middle-schoolers are dressing like hookers, there are very few 11-year-olds with enough disposable income to keep Forever 21 afloat. The greatest threat posed by these celebrity bad girls may be that they're advertising avatars, dressed by stylists and designers, who seem to live only to consume: clothes, cell phones, dogs and men. But there's good news: that problem is largely under the control of we who hold the purse strings.

And even if our adolescents pick up a few tricks from the Brit Pack, we have a big head start on them. We begin to teach our kids values while they're still in diapers. "Kids learn good morals and values by copying role models who are close to them," says Michele Borba, author of "Teaching Moral Intelligence."

Good Times, Bad Apples

By the 20th century, women had freedom enough to cause public scandals. Social critics have been wringing their hands ever since.

1. Ingrid Bergman — The married star had an affair in 1950 with Roberto Rossellini, who was also married, and Bergman gave birth to their child. She was denounced on the floor of the Senate.

2. Mae West — The vaudeville performer spent 10 days in jail for the 1927 play 'Sex.'

3. Marilyn Monroe — Long before she purred 'Happy Birthday' to JFK, she appeared in a calendar in her birthday suit. Hollywood called her career DOA.

4. Monica Lewinsky — The former intern helped create myriad teaching moments about oral sex after her liaison with President Clinton.

5. Madonna — Parents flipped in '85 when girls showed up at her concerts dressed in spandex and black rubber bracelets.

6. Kate Moss — Photos of her apparently using coke showed up in a British tab in 2005. She went to rehab, and has regained her status as a fashion icon.

7. Liz Taylor — She had an affair with Richard Burton in 1962 during the filming of 'Cleopatra'; the Vatican called her 'a woman of loose morals.'

8. Gypsy Rose Lee — A burlesque superstar in the '30s, she was arrested numerous times for taking it almost all off.

9. Nicole Richie — She was arrested last fall for parking on an L.A. freeway.

Experts say that even the most withdrawn teens scrutinize their parents for cues on how to act. So watch your behavior; don't gossip with your friends in front of the kids and downplay popularity as a lifetime goal. Parents need to understand and talk about the things that interest their kids—even if it's what Paris is wearing—without being judgmental. That makes it easier for kids to open up. "The really subtle thing you have to do is hear where they are coming from, and gently direct them into thinking about it," says Borba. That means these celebrities gone wild and all their tabloid antics can be teachable moments. Lesson No. 1: wear underwear.

With Jamie Reno, in San Diego; Karen Springen in Chicago and Susannah Meadows, Anne Underwood and Julie Scelfo in New York.

Disrespecting Childhood

Although Americans see ours as a child-loving nation, the authors present evidence of policies and practices that are not respectful of children or childhood. They call on us to question the assumptions about our young people that form the basis for our teaching, research, and policies.

CURT DUDLEY-MARLING, JANICE JACKSON, AND LISA PATEL STEVENS

What I discovered in Spain was a culture that held children to be its meringues and eclairs. My own culture . . . tended to regard children as a sort of toxic waste.[1]

In the popular imagination, Americans are a child-loving people. Across the land, selfless parents take classes, read books, create playgroups, and exchange the latest information about how to ensure safe, contented, and productive childhoods. Thousands of contemporary American families indulge their children materially to a degree that may be unparalleled in the world and in our own history. As a society, we have enacted a range of laws designed to protect children from physical and psychological abuse and economic and sexual exploitation. We have legions of pediatricians specially trained to attend to the physical and mental well-being of our children. Even the presence of metal detectors at the entrances of our schools can be taken as emblematic of our collective desire to protect the nation's children.

The range of public programs and policies benefiting children, directly or indirectly, offers further evidence of the high regard Americans have for their children. Tax credits for children and child care, child nutrition and health-care programs, preschool programs like Head Start, and billions of dollars spent each year to support elementary, secondary, and postsecondary education all demonstrate the desire of federal, state, and local governments to look after the physical, emotional, and intellectual well-being of the young. The prominence we give to educational issues in local, state, and federal elections further supports the assertion that children are indeed a high priority for Americans.

More than 133,000 children are in juvenile or adult correctional facilities on any given day.

While these commonly held beliefs communicate a consistent and shared regard for children, when we dig beneath the platitudes,

we find a far messier and more complex set of assumptions, beliefs, and challenges to this inspiring image of the United States as a child-loving society. Writing over 20 years ago, Letty Pogrebin argued that "America is a nation fundamentally ambivalent about its children, often afraid of its children, and frequently punitive towards its children."[2] Pogrebin cited attacks on the cost of public education and child health and nutrition programs, along with an inclination to pathologize an entire period in children's lives—that is, adolescence—to support her contention that the country was afflicted by what she called "an epidemic of pedophobia."[3]

Novelist Barbara Kingsolver has observed that children have come to hold an increasingly negative position in the economy.[4] Children are spoken of as a responsibility, a legal liability, and an encumbrance[5]—or they are seen in terms of potential profits. Today's children and adolescents, weaned on images of McDonald's and toy companies, are targeted as a ripe segment of the market for building powerful brand loyalty for everything from video games to prescriptions for drugs to treat attention deficit disorders.[6] And, if Pogrebin, writing in the early Reagan years, saw child-focused government programs under attack, then Kingsolver, writing 14 years later, had seen many of these same programs ravaged. Funding for virtually every program that benefits children in this country, Kingsolver writes—from "Sesame Street" to free school lunches—has been cut back in the past decade, in many cases cut to nothing.[7] Indeed, programs that support children in the U.S. are, in Kingsolver's words, the hands-down worst in the industrialized world.[8]

The Kingsolver quote that serves as epigraph to this article is disturbing. After all, it is a rare parent who does not put the needs of his or her children first, and Americans generally do care about *their own* children. But the evidence suggests that Americans are not consistent in caring for other people's children, especially children from marginalized populations. Nearly one in six children in the U.S. lives in poverty, a rate as much as two to three times higher than that in other industrialized nations.[9] The data for children of color are even more distressing, as black (32%) and Hispanic (29%) children are far more likely than white children (14%) to live in poverty. And many of these same children attend deteriorating, underfunded schools.[10] Here are some additional statistics from

116

The State of America's Children: more than 133,000 children are in juvenile or adult correctional facilities on any given day; children under 18 are increasingly incarcerated in adult facilities (more than 21,000 youths under 18 are being held in adult correctional facilities); in 2003, youth jobless rates for ages 16–19 reached nearly 60%, as compared to the 6% unemployment rate for all ages; in 2002, nearly 9.3 million American children were not covered by health insurance; also in 2003, 2,911 children and teens were killed by gunfire; and in 2002, an estimated three million children in the U.S. were reported as suspected cases of child abuse or neglect.[11] While these statistics arise from a complex set of social and economic circumstances, taken together, they challenge the image of America as a child-loving society.

Additional evidence of America's antipathy toward its youths comes from a Public Agenda survey of the attitudes of adult Americans toward the next generation.[12] Only 23% of the respondents had anything positive to say about children and adolescents, while just 37% of the adults surveyed thought that today's children would grow up to make the world a better place; 61% believed that many young people were failing to learn such values as honesty, respect, and responsibility; and just 12% thought it was common for children and adolescents to treat people with respect. Writing in *The Nation,* Annette Fuentes observed that policies like zero tolerance really mean that "to be young is to be suspect,"[13] and a 1995 U.S. Supreme Court ruling supports the notion that simply being an adolescent is reasonable cause for authorities to suspect drug abuse and demand urine samples.[14] Massachusetts is one of a number of jurisdictions proposing widespread "voluntary" drug testing of high school students.[15] This negative assessment of the nation's youths undoubtedly lies behind the willingness of the American public to support a range of "get tough on kids" policies.

America's ambivalence toward young people manifests itself in the suspicion and fear of adolescents. Although we see children largely as burdens of responsibility, we nonetheless romanticize younger children as pliable potential citizens in need of close adult guidance and care. Various public policies seek to preserve their perceived innocence. Indeed, some have argued that an overly myopic focus on children is an attempt to defer—and potentially avoid—"dealing with" the miscreant tendencies of adolescence.[16]

Children under 18 are increasingly incarcerated in adult facilities (more than 21,000 youths under 18 are being held in adult correctional facilities).

The nation's low opinion of its youths is also apparent in the frequent media campaigns that link young people to a host of social "crises," including youth violence, teen pregnancy, violent and sexually explicit movies and video games, offensive lyrics in popular music, drug and alcohol abuse, smoking, and suicide. Underlying the critiques of the American Decency Association and others who blame popular culture for many of the problems of adolescence are two sets of assumptions. First, young people are assumed to mediate their senses of self through the popular culture of music and films. (Arguably, anyone living in this Information Age engages in that kind of identity work, finding and creating images, sounds, and messages that resonate with a sense of self.) However, the

association between young people and the texts of popular culture all but equates the two. This is a misuse and confusion of the terms and concepts of popular culture, youth subculture, and mass-mediated culture. In truth, the variety, breadth, and seemingly endless choices of mass-mediated texts are pervasive throughout the lives of citizens today.

The second assumption underlying the critiques of popular culture's impact on youths is that young people are so impressionable and shallow that a movie scene, rock lyric, or T-shirt slogan will lead them to violence, promiscuity, or drug addiction. While it is not our purpose here to explore the hotly debated relationships between images, beliefs, and behaviors, we simply note that it is taken for granted that youths in general cannot discriminate, be critical, or add perspectives to these media-based practices. In fact, the disregard of young people has begun to affect even those youths who are largely considered to be fortunate, supported, and well loved: the middle class. As sociologist and journalist Elliott Currie argues, the very culture of middle-class materialism and individualism has all but ensured a context of disconnection and stripped-down communities for young people.[17]

Fear, suspicion, and resentment toward the nation's young have led to the appearance of groups of child-free adults, such as No Kidding!, that challenge "family-friendly" public policies seen to (unfairly) favor people with children.[18] Advocacy groups for childless adults seek the creation of child-free zones in such public spaces as restaurants, supermarkets, and health clubs.[19] If it takes a village to raise a child, many villagers are abdicating their responsibilities.

In the face of such examples, we would do well to reconsider our sense of ourselves as a child-loving people. Examining the policies, discourses, and practices that surround children and adolescents sheds light on our ambivalence toward them, at best, and a profound mistrust and disrespect of our youngest charges, at worst. As educators, we have the responsibility to care for and guide our nation's young people, and so we must be prepared to challenge the policies that frame our work with them. Just as the kind of marketing directed toward adolescents tells us something about how certain economic sectors see them, so does the language of our education policies reveal our societal attitudes. Underlying education reform proposals are sets of assumptions about children and adolescents and about childhood and adolescence as stages of life. Underpinning child-centered and back-to-basics reforms, for example, are fundamentally different beliefs about how children learn and about the nature of childhood. Below, we examine some of the dominant themes underlying two strands of education reform—standards and accountability and safe schools—to see what we can learn about the nation's respect for its young people and for childhood and adolescence as special times of life. Then we briefly discuss an alternative and, we believe, more respectful vision of school reform that seeks to engage students in the process.

Standards and Accountability

Former *New York Times* education columnist Richard Rothstein distinguishes two meanings for standards-based reform:

> Standards-based reform has two contradictory meanings. Some policy makers want minimum standards representing what all students must know for promotion or graduation. Others want high standards as goals toward which all

students should strive but not all may achieve. Schools need both, but one standard cannot do both jobs.[20]

The first of these two strands of standards-based reform, which emphasizes high expectations for all students regardless of who they are or where they live, demonstrates respect for students by assuming that all children can (and should) learn. The second, as Rothstein observes, sets up high expectations by requiring that all students achieve the highest standards in all subjects. We argue below that this version of standards-based reform, which has come to dominate today's landscape of reform, is not respectful of children or of childhood and adolescence.

High stakes. Many education reformers assume that the failures of American education alleged in *A Nation at Risk* can be remedied only by high standards tied to sanctions. Presumably, because they lack the intrinsic motivation to excel in school, students can be motivated by the desire to avoid such sanctions as grade retention, the threat of failing courses, and the withholding of high school diplomas. But the desire to get tough on kids through high-stakes decisions is not supported by research. Neither grade retention nor course failure, for example, appears to be related to improved academic performance; grade retention does, however, increase the chances students will drop out of school.[21] Increased dropout rates may also be one of the principal effects of linking high school diplomas to the results of high-stakes tests.[22]

In 2003, youth jobless rates for ages 16–19 reached nearly 60%, as compared to the 6% unemployment rate for all ages.

Education reformers who demand that *all students* be held accountable to the highest standards often argue that they are motivated by faith in the ability of all children to learn challenging academic material. This logic sits uncomfortably beside the underlying assumption that extrinsic retribution is needed to motivate learning. Furthermore, the evidence indicates that *high standards* enforced through grade retention, failing grades, and high school exit exams are diminishing the life chances of significant numbers of students, especially poor and minority students, who are more likely to be retained or drop out of school.[23]

Intensification of schooling. Working from assumptions about needing extrinsic goals to motivate learners, the education reform of "getting tough on kids" has led to an intensification of schooling. Political platforms of more homework, longer school days, and longer school years imply that children need to be pushed to do more of what they've been asked to do in the past. Former Republican leader of the U.S. House of Representatives Newt Gingrich asserted that "every child . . . should be required to do at least two hours of homework a night, or they're being cheated for the rest of their lives."[24]

School districts across the country have taken up this challenge as elementary and secondary students in the U.S. are doing more homework than ever.[25] In some school districts, even kindergartners are doing up to 30 minutes of homework each night and working toward academic report cards.[26] But using intensified homework as a means of increasing academic achievement, especially for elementary students, is unsupported by research.[27] Nonetheless, for many children the increased homework demands, by extending the reach of schooling into children's homes, have

significantly reduced the time available for leisure and recreational opportunities.[28]

Schooling is also being intensified by cutting back on recess for elementary students, as up to 40% of the nation's school districts have either curtailed or eliminated recess.[29] A former superintendent of the Atlanta Public Schools defended the elimination of recess in his district by arguing that academic performance cannot be improved by having kids hanging on the monkey bars.[30] Similar reasoning has been used to justify cutting such educational "frills" as art and music. Of course, recess, art, and music are far more likely to be cut in urban schools—populated disproportionately by children of color and children living in poverty—than in suburban schools, suggesting that, as a nation, we believe that art, music, and play time are more important for some children than for others.

In 2002, nearly 9.3 million American children were not covered by health insurance.

Standardization. Enforcing standards through high-stakes testing demands standards that are specific, measurable, and uniform across jurisdictions.[31] Arguably, such uniform standards lead to a focus on those aspects of learning that can most easily be standardized and, inevitably, create a one-size-fits-all curriculum in which students are processed like so many widgets. Put in raw material at one end, treat it all in exactly the same way, and there will emerge at the other end a predictable and standardized product.[32]

Relegating students to such a passive role—treating them as objects—reveals a fundamental lack of respect for children and adolescents as rational, thoughtful, varied, and interesting people.[33] The expectation that standardized approaches to education can lead to "predictable and standardized" products assumes that, at some level, children (the raw material) are, essentially, all the same. This view of learning, which renders differences in students' learning opportunities, abilities, development levels, background knowledge, and experience irrelevant and even problematic, respects neither children and adolescents nor the homes, neighborhoods, and cultures from which they come.

Focusing relentlessly on academic achievement, as determined by high-stakes tests,[34] has turned many American classrooms into dreary workplaces where the basics are translated into worksheets while art, music, and recess games are seen as unnecessary distractions. High standards and high stakes are creating high-stress environments that leave little room for the playful and aesthetic pursuits of children—in or out of school. David Elkind's words echo across the decades:

> The concept of childhood, so vital to the traditional American way of life, is threatened with extinction in the society we have created. Today's child has become the unwilling, unintended victim of overwhelming stress—the stress born of rapid, bewildering social change and constantly rising expectations.[35]

Safe Schools

As a society, we love children—when they are under control. We hate children who defy us, children who are independent, quirky, free-thinking, nonconforming, idiosyncratic, precocious, or critical of adults.[36]

Despite evidence of a slight decline in violence in our schools,[37] Americans continue to identify lack of discipline, fighting, violence, and substance abuse as serious problems in our schools.[38] Certainly, official data on the decreasing incidence of violence in schools have not been as readily available to the public as media reports on school shootings, infighting among adolescent females, or violent plots in New Bedford, Massachusetts. Influenced by sensational reports in the media, most Americans would probably agree that the gravity of youth violence has increased dramatically in recent years.[39] Conflicts that used to result in fist fights and end with bloody noses, black eyes, and the occasional chipped tooth are now said to result in the drawing of weapons and to end with life-threatening lacerations and occasional gunshot wounds.

Whatever the actual rate of violence in our schools, no one would dispute that all students are entitled to safe, secure learning environments. There is, however, strong disagreement over the means by which safe schools might be best achieved. Social scientists and professional educators tend to prefer approaches to safe schools that focus on improving the school climate through expanded curricular offerings, decreased school and class size, increased staffing, and teaching the skills of conflict resolution.[40] Underlying these initiatives is an assumption that, given an environment that is respectful of their social, emotional, and intellectual needs, children and adolescents will be generally respectful of the needs of teachers and other students. From this perspective, respect begets respect.

Legislators, media pundits, and some segments of the public, on the other hand, are disposed to embrace politically expedient, get-tough-on-kids policies that play on the nation's generally low opinion and fear of its youths. The surveillance cameras, random locker searches, drug testing, and zero tolerance policies that characterize safe school efforts in many states reinforce the impression of youths as "savage beasts," a provocative phrase used by Lilia Bartolome in 1994 and a sentiment that is still common in contemporary circles.[41] The phrase invokes the image of young people who require nearly constant surveillance and control and justifies denying students any right to privacy or due process.

In the absence of data on the efficacy of various get-tough-on-youth policies, it could easily be concluded that the desire to enact these policies is motivated by a general loathing of youths, especially minority youths. The degree to which such policies predominate in urban schools, which are disproportionately populated by students of color, signals a national fear of minority youths out of control. The desire to control children of color may also underlie the proliferation of heavily scripted learning programs that effectively control the bodies and minds of students in urban schools.[42] Whatever the means, control is a quintessentially disrespectful act.

All children and adolescents are entitled to safe schools and challenging curricula. All too often, however, the impulse to create safe and challenging schools is underpinned by an antipathy toward children and adolescents that has resulted in policies and practices that are fundamentally disrespectful of American youths. While the effectiveness of these policies is debatable, they are rarely evaluated at all on the basis of their underlying regard for children and young people. Indeed, a recent book by two fellows at the conservative American Enterprise Institute ridicules school-based practices that attend to students' emotional well-being because they have no demonstrable link to academic achievement[43]—as if

students' psychological and emotional health are beyond the purview of schooling. Other conservative scholars have challenged the efficacy of health and dental care and hot lunch programs because they don't affect measures of academic achievement.[44] Examining the assumptions about our young people that pervade schooling is one way of taking an important step back to consider matters that are often drowned out by the cacophony of agendas, reforms, and platforms.

Including Student Voices: A Demonstration of Respect

I'm not adult enough to get a job and have my own apartment, but I'm adult enough to make decisions on my own, know right from wrong, have ideas about the world. That's why it's hard to be a teenager—it's like a middle stage. . . . To a certain extent [teachers] have to have a personality that students respond to. But that doesn't mean you have to be our best friend, because that will cause our education to suffer. I hate to admit it, but respect and authority are a part of the job. Kids expect adults to give us directions and boundaries, but it's a balance.[45]

The debate about reforming schools to make them better places to prepare young people to participate fully in the life of the community has been raging at least since the 1996 *Breaking Ranks* report from the National Association of Secondary School Principals. In particular, there has been great attention given to redesigning high schools into places that will improve student learning. There have been two main approaches: a policy-oriented, managerial approach and a student-centered approach.[46] The former advocates the alignment of standards, curriculum, and assessment. The latter advocates a cultural change in schools that creates an environment supportive of students' academic and social/emotional development.

Though there is much conversation about improving the relationships between adults and students, neither approach has advocated for including students' ideas as an essential element in a successful reform strategy. Many policy makers and school personnel believe that students lack the ability to be thoughtful about their own circumstances; therefore, little attention is paid to the knowledge and perspectives that students bring with them to the classroom. The students of What Kids Can Do, Inc. (WKCD) call the adults' mistrust into question. Vance, quoted above, was a member of a project to listen to students' thoughts about high school. Their work culminated in the book *Fires in the Bathroom: Advice for Teachers from High School Students,* from which Vance's words are taken. As this work demonstrates, young people are quite articulate about their experience of schooling, and they could make meaningful contributions to conversations regarding the reform of school culture, school governance, curriculum, and pedagogy.

The inclusion of the student voice could provide insights that would help policy makers and school personnel understand students' disengagement from school and how it leads to an increase in the dropout rate. It could provide adults with better insights into the various youth subcultures and young peoples' varied responses to them. "Meaningful and sustained school reform has at its core the involvement and engagement of students. Student voice can be a powerful mechanism for building school morale, improving school climate, and creating demand for high quality instruction," according to students in the Boston project Student Researchers for High School Renewal.[47]

Another WKCD project was the Students-as-Allies Initiative, which was designed to help students and teachers become allies in solving the problems arising in their school communities. In collaboration with the MetLife Foundation, WKCD selected five cities to participate in the project: Chicago, Houston, Oakland, Philadelphia, and St. Louis. WKCD identified local nonprofit organizations in each city to guide the process. The goals of the initiative were to support student voice, to strengthen the relationships between students and teachers in order to bolster school improvement efforts, to provide opportunities for students to serve as resources to their schools and communities, and to model relationship building. The nonprofit partners set the criteria for the development of teams made up of students and teachers to conduct research about their particular schools, to analyze the data, to engage in dialogue, to make recommendations for action, and, finally, to take action.[48]

One objective was to enlist students who were not usually recognized in their schools as leaders. In Houston, teachers wove the project into their writing classes so that all the students they taught could participate. In St. Louis, teachers recruited students in order to build a team that was representative of the many cliques in the school. In Oakland, students were enrolled in a special class designed to cultivate nontraditional leaders.

The participants decided that surveys would be the best tools for gathering information, and each team designed its own survey after looking at a common core of questions derived from a review of teacher and student surveys that had been conducted by MetLife. The focus was on "areas where knowing the thoughts of students and teachers would help students become actors in improving their schools." The teams were taught principles of survey research and guided through an analysis of the data. They learned to present the data and to host dialogues in their schools and communities.

The final phase of the project is to engage students in making recommendations for solutions and in taking appropriate actions. Each of the partnerships is in the early stages of taking action. Detailed information about the initiative can be found on the website of What Kids Can Do, Inc. (www.whatkidscando.org/index.asp).

The work of this group of students demonstrates that many young people care deeply about their own education and are capable of contributing to the reform of high schools in ways that could make deep and long-lasting changes for themselves and their teachers. These examples are not intended to serve as simplistic recommendations of actions to be taken at all levels and in all contexts. Rather, we offer them as examples of the kinds of initiatives that can be entertained when children and adolescents are treated as thoughtful participants in the enterprise of American education and not as problems to be overcome—in short, if they are treated with respect.

When we look past the naive belief that we treat our children with undying care, we find a disconcerting mix of policies and practices that are not respectful of children or of childhood. Examining these platforms and actions is far from a simple matter. We must move beyond simple quantitative tally sheets of how much money is devoted to education and the care of our young. We must also ask what kind of institutional spaces are created for children, what we expect from them, and what we have assumed about them that may in fact restrict their abilities to thrive.

In reform after reform, the lens has not been widened enough to consider underlying assumptions about children. In the application of NCLB to students, younger and older, a consistent set of mistakes marks the policy territory: a fundamental lack of explicit, evidence-based knowledge and respect for students coupled with an overwhelming emphasis on control and singular measurements. We must learn to question what forms the basis for our teaching, research, and policy. And in reviewing our practices, necessarily a discursive and recursive process, we must also consider the ways in which we represent, understand, and listen to our children and young people.

How then do we begin the considerable work of truly valuing and respecting our nation's young? Education is just one institutional site for the enactment, performance, and mediation of values, but it is a multifaceted one. Thus the efforts to reconfigure our beliefs and practices must affect the daily lives of students, teachers, researchers, and policy makers. All of these groups can take the same first step: examining the assumptions we hold about our young.

Notes

1. Barbara Kingsolver, *High Tide in Tucson: Essays from Now or Never* (New York: HarperPerennial, 1996), p. 100.

2. Letty Cottin Pogrebin, *Family Politics: Love and Power on an Intimate Frontier* (New York: McGraw-Hill, 1983), p. 42.

3. Ibid., p. 46.

4. Kingsolver, p. 102.

5. Ibid.

6. Alissa Quart, *Branded: The Buying and Selling of Teenagers* (Cambridge, Mass.: Perseus, 2003).

7. Kingsolver, p. 102.

8. Kingsolver, p. 101.

9. *The State of America's Children, 2004* (Washington, D.C.: Children's Defense Fund, 2004), p. 3; and "Young Children in Poverty Fact Sheet," National Center for Children in Poverty, 1999, available at www.nccp.org, click on Fact Sheets.

10. Jonathan Kozol, *Savage Inequalities: Children in America's Schools* (New York: Crown, 1991).

11. *The State of America's Children, 2004.*

12. Ann Duffet, Jean Johnson, and Steve Farkas, *Kids These Days: What Americans Really Think About the Next Generation* (Washington, D.C.: Public Agenda, 1999).

13. Annette Fuentes, "The Crackdown on Kids," *The Nation,* 15/22 June 1998, pp. 20–22.

14. Mike A. Males, *The Scapegoat Generation: America's War on Adolescents* (Monroe, Me.: Common Courage Press, 1996).

15. John R. Knight, "An F for School Drug Tests," *Boston Globe,* 13 June 2005, p. 15.

16. Allan Luke and Carmen Luke, "Adolescence Lost and Childhood Regained," *Australian Journal of Language and Literacy,* July 2001, pp. 91–120.

17. Elliott Curie, *The Road to Whatever: Middle-Class Culture and the Crisis of Adolescence* (New York: Henry Holt, 2005).

18. Scott Lehigh, "No Kidding," *Boston Globe,* 21 May 2000, pp. E-1, E-5.

19. Elinor Burkett, *The Baby Boon: How Family-Friendly America Cheats the Childless* (New York: Free Press, 2000).

20. Richard Rothstein, "In Judging Schools, One Standard Doesn't Fit All," *New York Times,* 8 December 1999, p. A-20.

21. See, for example, Eugene R. Johnson et al., "The Effects of Early Grade Retention on the Academic Achievement of Fourth-Grade Students," *Psychology in the Schools,* October 1990, pp. 333–38; William A. Owings and Susan Magliaro, "Grade Retention: A History of Failure," *Educational Leadership,* September 1998, pp. 86–88; Melissa Roderick, "Grade Retention and School Dropout: Investigating the Association," *American Educational Research Journal,* Winter 1994, pp. 729–59; Melissa Roderick and Eric Camburn, "Risk and Recovery from Course Failure in the Early Years of High School," *American Educational Research Journal,* Summer 1999, pp. 303–43; Lorrie A. Shepard and Mary L. Smith, "Synthesis of Research on Grade Retention," *Educational Leadership,* May 1999, pp. 84–88; and C. Kenneth Tanner and F. Edward Combs, "Student Retention Policy: The Gap Between Research and Practice," *Journal of Research in Childhood Education,* Fall/Winter 1993, pp. 69–77.

22. Walt Haney, "The Myth of the Texas Miracle in Education," *Education Policy Analysis Archives,* August 2000, available at http://epaa.asu.edu/epaa/v8n41.

23. Ibid.

24. Joel H. Spring, *Political Agendas for Education: From the Christian Coalition to the Green Party* (Mahwah, N.J.: Erlbaum, 1997), p. 16.

25. Sandra Hofferth, "Healthy Environments, Healthy Children: Children in Families," University of Michigan Institute for Social Research, ERIC ED 426779, 1998.

26. Diane Loupe, "Value of Homework Comes Under Question," *Atlanta Constitution,* 22 April 1999, p. 5JA.

27. Harris Cooper, *Homework* (New York: Longman, 1989).

28. Etta Kralovec and John Buell, *The End of Homework: How Homework Disrupts Families, Overburdens Children, and Limits Learning* (Boston, Mass.: Beacon Press, 2000).

29. Donald B. Gratz, "High Standards for Whom?," *Phi Delta Kappan,* May 2000, pp. 681–87; and Anthony D. Pellegrini and Catherine M. Bohn, "The Role of Recess in Children's Cognitive Performance and School Adjustment," *Educational Researcher,* January/February 2005, pp. 13–19.

30. Susan Ohanian, *One Size Fits Few: The Folly of Educational Standards* (Portsmouth, N.H.: Heinemann, 2000), pp. 13-14.

31. Anne T. Lockwood, *Standards: From Policy to Practice* (Thousand Oaks, Calif.: Corwin, 2000).

32. Frank Smith, *The Book of Learning and Forgetting* (New York: Teachers College Press, 1998).

33. Alfie Kohn, *The Schools Our Children Deserve: Moving Beyond Traditional Classrooms and "Tougher Standards"* (Boston: Houghton Mifflin, 1999).

34. Marc S. Tucker and Judy B. Codding, *Standards for Our Schools: How to Set Them, Measure Them, and Reach Them* (San Francisco, Calif.: Jossey-Bass, 1998).

35. David Elkind, *The Hurried Child: Growing Up Too Fast, Too Soon,* rev. ed. (Reading, Mass.: Addison-Wesley, 1988), p. 3.

36. Pogrebin, op. cit.

37. Michael F. Heaney and Robert J. Michela, "Safe Schools: Hearing Past the Hype," *High School Magazine,* May/June 1999, pp. 14–17.

38. Lowell C. Rose and Alec M. Gallup, "The 37th Annual Phi Delta Kappa/ Gallup Poll of the Public's Attitudes Toward the Public Schools," *Phi Delta Kappan,* September 2005, p. 44.

39. Paul M. Kingery, Mark B. Coggeshall, and Aaron A. Alford, "Weapon Carrying by Youth: Risk Factors and Prevention," *Education and Urban Society,* May 1999, pp. 309–33.

40. James A. Fox and Jack Levin, "The Hard (but Doable) Job of Making Schools Safe," *Boston Globe,* 22 August 1999, pp. F-1, F-3.

41. Lilia I. Bartolome, "Beyond the Methods Fetish: Toward a Humanizing Pedagogy," *Harvard Educational Review,* Summer 1994, pp. 173–94; and Nancy Lesko, *Act Your Age! A Cultural Construction of Adolescence* (New York: Routledge, 2001).

42. Jonathan Kozol, "Confections of Apartheid: A Stick-and-Carrot Pedagogy for the Children of Our Inner-City Poor," *Phi Delta Kappan,* December 2005, pp. 264–75.

43. Christina Hoff Sommers and Sally Satel, *One Nation Under Therapy: How the Helping Culture Is Eroding Self-Reliance* (New York: St. Martin's Press, 2005).

44. Gary L. Adams and Siegfried Engelmann, *Research on Direct Instruction: 25 Years Beyond DISTAR* (Seattle: Educational Achievement Systems, 1996).

45. Kathleen Cushman, *Fires in the Bathroom: Advice for Teachers from High School Students* (New York: New Press, 2003).

46. Lynn Olson, "Report Points Out Lack of Clarity for High School Reforms," *Education Week,* 19 May 2004.

47. *School Climate in Boston's High Schools: What Students Say* (Boston, Mass.: Boston Plan for Excellence, 2004).

48. Students as Allies, *Breaking Ranks: Changing an American Institution* (Reston, Va.: National Association of Secondary School Principals, 1996).

CURT DUDLEY-MARLING is a professor of education at the Lynch School of Education, Boston College, Chestnut Hill, Mass., where **JANICE JACKSON** and **LISA PATEL STEVENS** are assistant professors.

From *Phi Delta Kappan,* June 2006, pp. 748–755. Copyright © 2006 by Phi Delta Kappan. Reprinted by permission of Phi Delta Kappan and Curt Dudley-Marling, Janice Jackson, and Lisa Patel Stevens.

Don't Blame the Caveman

Why do we rape, kill and sleep around? The fault, dear Darwin, lies not in our ancestors, but in ourselves.

SHARON BEGLEY

Among Scientists at the University of New Mexico that spring, rape was in the air. One of the professors, biologist Randy Thornhill, had just coauthored *A Natural History of Rape: Biological Bases of Sexual Coercion,* which argued that rape is (in the vernacular of evolutionary biology) an adaptation, a trait encoded by genes that confers an advantage on anyone who possesses them. Back in the late Pleistocene epoch 100,000 years ago, the 2000 book contended, men who carried rape genes had a reproductive and evolutionary edge over men who did not: they sired children not only with willing mates, but also with unwilling ones, allowing them to leave more offspring (also carrying rape genes) who were similarly more likely to survive and reproduce, unto the nth generation. That would be us. And that is why we carry rape genes today. The family trees of prehistoric men lacking rape genes petered out.

The argument was well within the bounds of evolutionary psychology. Founded in the late 1980s in the ashes of sociobiology, this field asserts that behaviors that conferred a fitness advantage during the era when modern humans were evolving are the result of hundreds of genetically based cognitive "modules" pre-programmed in the brain. Since they are genetic, these modules and the behaviors they encode are heritable—passed down to future generations—and, together, constitute a universal human nature that describes how people think, feel and act, from the nightclubs of Manhattan to the farms of the Amish, from the huts of New Guinea aborigines to the madrassas of Karachi. Evolutionary psychologists do not have a time machine, of course. So to figure out which traits were adaptive during the Stone Age, and therefore bequeathed to us like a questionable family heirloom, they make logical guesses. Men who were promiscuous back then were more evolutionarily fit, the researchers reasoned, since men who spread their seed widely left more descendants. By similar logic, evolutionary psychologists argued, women who were monogamous were fitter; by being choosy about their mates and picking only those with good genes, they could have healthier children. Men attracted to young, curvaceous babes were fitter because such women were the most fertile; mating with dumpy, barren hags is not a good way to grow a big family tree. Women attracted to high-status, wealthy males were fitter; such men could best provide for the kids, who, spared starvation, would grow up to have many children of their own. Men who neglected or even murdered their stepchildren (and killed their unfaithful wives) were fitter because they did not waste their resources on non-relatives. And so on, to the fitness-enhancing value of rape. We in the 21st century, asserts evo psych, are operating with Stone Age minds.

Over the years these arguments have attracted legions of critics who thought the science was weak and the message (what philosopher David Buller of Northern Illinois University called "a get-out-of-jail-free card" for heinous behavior) pernicious. But the reaction to the rape book was of a whole different order. Biologist Joan Roughgarden of Stanford University called it "the latest 'evolution made me do it' excuse for criminal behavior from evolutionary psychologists." Feminists, sex-crime prosecutors and social scientists denounced it at rallies, on television and in the press.

Among those sucked into the rape debate that spring was anthropologist Kim Hill, then Thornhill's colleague at UNM and now at Arizona State University. For decades Hill has studied the Ache, hunter-gatherer tribesmen in Paraguay. "I saw Thornhill all the time," Hill told me at a barbecue at an ASU conference in April. "He kept saying that he thought rape was a special cognitive adaptation, but the arguments for that just seemed like more sloppy thinking by evolutionary psychology." But how to test the claim that rape increased a man's fitness? From its inception, evolutionary psychology had warned that behaviors that were evolutionarily advantageous 100,000 years ago (a sweet tooth, say) might be bad for survival today (causing obesity and thence infertility), so there was no point in measuring whether that trait makes people more evolutionarily fit today. Even if it doesn't, evolutionary psychologists argue, the trait might have been adaptive long ago and therefore still be our genetic legacy. An unfortunate one, perhaps, but still our legacy. Short of a time machine, the hypothesis was impossible to disprove. Game, set and match to evo psych.

Or so it seemed. But Hill had something almost as good as a time machine. He had the Ache, who live much as humans

---

Rape

Old Thinking

Men who rape produce more offspring, ensuring the survival of their DNA—including the rape gene.

New Thinking

Rapists were often ostracized or killed and their offspring abandoned.

Lust

Old Thinking

Men desire women with an hourglass figure.

New Thinking

Only in cultures where women are economically dependent does the 36-25-38 ideal prevail.

---

did 100,000 years ago. He and two colleagues therefore calculated how rape would affect the evolutionary prospects of a 25-year-old Ache. (They didn't observe any rapes, but did a what-if calculation based on measurements of, for instance, the odds that a woman is able to conceive on any given day.) The scientists were generous to the rape-as-adaptation claim, assuming that rapists target only women of reproductive age, for instance, even though in reality girls younger than 10 and women over 60 are often victims. Then they calculated rape's fitness costs and benefits. Rape costs a man fitness points if the victim's husband or other relatives kill him, for instance. He loses fitness points, too, if the mother refuses to raise a child of rape, and if being a known rapist (in a small hunter-gatherer tribe, rape and rapists are public knowledge) makes others less likely to help him find food. Rape increases a man's evolutionary fitness based on the chance that a rape victim is fertile (15 percent), that she will conceive (a 7 percent chance), that she will not miscarry (90 percent) and that she will not let the baby die even though it is the child of rape (90 percent). Hill then ran the numbers on the reproductive costs and benefits of rape. It wasn't even close: the cost exceeds the benefit by a factor of 10. "That makes the likelihood that rape is an evolved adaptation extremely low," says Hill. "It just wouldn't have made sense for men in the Pleistocene to use rape as a reproductive strategy, so the argument that it's preprogrammed into us doesn't hold up."

These have not been easy days for evolutionary psychology. For years the loudest critics have been social scientists, feminists and liberals offended by the argument that humans are preprogrammed to rape, to kill unfaithful girlfriends and the like. (This was a reprise of the bitter sociobiology debates of the 1970s and 1980s. When Harvard biologist Edward O. Wilson proposed that there exists a biologically based human nature, and that it included such traits as militarism and male domination of women, left-wing activists—including eminent biologists in his own department—assailed it as an attempt "to provide a genetic justification of the status quo and of existing privileges for certain groups according to class, race, or sex" analogous to the scientific justification for Nazi eugenics.) When Thornhill appeared on the *Today* show to talk about his rape book, for instance, he was paired with a sex-crimes prosecutor, leaving the impression that do-gooders might not like his thesis but offering no hint of how scientifically unsound it is.

That is changing. Evo psych took its first big hit in 2005, when NIU's Buller exposed flaw after fatal flaw in key studies

underlying its claims, as he laid out in his book *Adapting Minds.* Anthropological studies such as Hill's on the Ache, shooting down the programmed-to-rape idea, have been accumulating. And brain scientists have pointed out that there is no evidence our gray matter is organized the way evo psych claims, with hundreds of specialized, preprogrammed modules. Neuroscientist Roger Bingham of the University of California, San Diego, who describes himself as a once devout "member of the Church of Evolutionary Psychology" (in 1996 he created and hosted a multimillion-dollar PBS series praising the field) has come out foursquare against it, accusing some of its adherents of an "evangelical" fervor. Says evolutionary biologist Massimo Pigliucci of Stony Brook University, "evolutionary stories of human behavior make for a good narrative, but not good science."

Like other critics, he has no doubt that evolution shaped the human brain. How could it be otherwise, when evolution has shaped every other human organ? But evo psych's claims that human behavior is constrained by mental modules that calcified in the Stone Age make sense "only if the environmental challenges remain static enough to sculpt an instinct over evolutionary time," Pigliucci points out. If the environment, including the social environment, is instead dynamic rather than static—which all evidence suggests—then the only kind of mind that makes humans evolutionarily fit is one that is flexible and responsive, able to figure out a way to make trade-offs, survive, thrive and reproduce in whatever social and physical environment it finds itself in. In some environments it might indeed be adaptive for women to seek sugar daddies. In some, it might be adaptive for stepfathers to kill their stepchildren. In some, it might be adaptive for men to be promiscuous. But not in all. And if that's the case, then there is no universal human nature as evo psych defines it.

That is what a new wave of studies has been discovering, slaying assertions about universals right and left. One evopsych claim that captured the public's imagination—and a 1996 cover story in Newsweek—is that men have a mental module that causes them to prefer women with a waist-to-hip ratio of 0.7 (a 36-25-36 figure, for instance). Reprising the rape debate, social scientists and policymakers who worried that this would send impressionable young women scurrying for a measuring tape and a how-to book on bulimia could only sputter about how pernicious this message was, but not that it was scientifically wrong. To the contrary, proponents of this idea had gobs of data in their favor. Using their favorite guinea pigs—American college students—they found that men, shown pictures of different female body types, picked Ms. 36-25-36 as their sexual ideal. The studies, however, failed to rule out the possibility that the preference was not innate—human nature—but, rather, the product of exposure to mass culture and the messages it sends about what's beautiful. Such basic flaws, notes Bingham, "led to complaints that many of these experiments seemed a little less than rigorous to be underpinning an entire new field."

Later studies, which got almost no attention, indeed found that in isolated populations in Peru and Tanzania, men consider hourglass women sickly looking. They prefer 0.9s—heavier women. And last December, anthropologist Elizabeth Cashdan of the University of Utah reported in the journal *Current Anthropology* that men now prefer this non-hourglass shape in countries where women tend to be economically independent (Britain and Denmark) and in some non-Western societies where women bear the responsibility for finding food. Only in countries where women are economically dependent on men (such as Japan, Greece and Portugal) do men have a strong preference for Barbie. (The United States is in the middle.) Cashdan puts it this way: which body type men prefer "should *depend on* [italics added] the degree to which they want their mates to be strong, tough, economically successful and politically competitive."

Depend on? The very phrase is anathema to the dogma of a universal human nature. But it is the essence of an emerging, competing field. Called behavioral ecology, it starts from the premise that social and environmental forces select for various behaviors that optimize people's fitness in a given environment. Different environment, different behaviors—and different human "natures." That's why men prefer Ms. 36-25-36 in some cultures (where women are, to exaggerate only a bit, decorative objects) but not others (where women bring home salaries or food they've gathered in the jungle).

And it's why the evo-psych tenet that men have an inherited mental module that causes them to prefer young, beautiful women while women have one that causes them to prefer older, wealthy men also falls apart. As 21st-century Western women achieve professional success and gain financial independence, their mate preference changes, scientists led by Fhionna Moore at Scotland's University of St Andrews reported in 2006 in the journal *Evolution and Human Behaviour*. The more financially independent a woman is, the more likely she is to choose a partner based on looks more than bank balance—kind of like (some) men. (Yes, growing sexual equality in the economic realm means that women, too, are free to choose partners based on how hot they are, as the cougar phenomenon suggests.) Although that finding undercuts evo psych, it supports the "it depends" school of behavioral ecology, which holds that natural selection chose general intelligence and flexibility, not mental modules preprogrammed with preferences and behaviors. "Evolutionary psychology ridicules the notion that the brain could have evolved to be an all-purpose fitness-maximizing mechanism," says Hill. "But that's exactly what we keep finding."

One of the uglier claims of evo psych is that men have a mental module to neglect and even kill their stepchildren. Such behavior was adaptive back when humans were evolving, goes the popular version of this argument, because men who invested

---

Infanticide

Old Thinking

Men are predisposed to kill their stapchildren rather than waste precious resources on another man's DNA.

New Thinking

A man who supports his stepchildren improves his chances of mating with their mother, and the kids themselves can become a valuable source of labor.

---

in stepchildren wasted resources they could expend on their biological children. Such kindly stepfathers would, over time, leave fewer of their own descendents, causing "support your stepchildren" genes to die out. Men with genes that sculpted the "abandon stepchildren" mental module were evolutionarily fitter, so their descendants—us—also have that preprogrammed module. The key evidence for this claim comes from studies showing that stepchildren under the age of 5 are 40 times more likely to be abused than biological children.

Those studies have come under fire, however, for a long list of reasons. For instance, many child-welfare records do not indicate who the abuser was; at least some abused stepchildren are victims of their mother, not the stepfather, the National Incidence Study of Child Abuse and Neglect reported in 2005. That suggests that records inflate the number of instances of abuse by stepfathers. Also, authorities are suspicious of stepfathers; if a child living in a stepfamily dies of maltreatment, they are nine times more likely to record it as such than if the death occurs in a home with only biological parents, found a 2002 study led by Buller examining the records of every child who died in Colorado from 1990 to 1998. That suggests that child-abuse data undercount instances of abuse by biological fathers. Finally, a 2008 study in Sweden found that many men who kill stepchildren are (surprise) mentally ill. It's safe to assume that single mothers do not exactly get their pick of the field when it comes to remarrying. If the men they wed are therefore more likely to be junkies, drunks and psychotic, then any additional risk to stepchildren reflects that fact, and not a universal mental module that tells men to abuse their new mate's existing kids. Martin Daly and Margo Wilson of Canada's McMaster University, whose work led to the idea that men have a mental module for neglecting stepchildren, now disavow the claim that such abuse was ever adaptive. But, says Daly, "attempts to deny that [being a stepfather] is a risk factor for maltreatment are simply preposterous and occasionally, as in the writings of David Buller, dishonest."

If the data on child abuse by stepfathers seem inconsistent, that's exactly the point. In some circumstances, it may indeed be adaptive to get rid of the other guy's children. In other circumstances, it is more adaptive to love and support them. Again, it depends. New research in places as different as American cities and the villages of African hunter-gatherers shows that it's common for men to care and provide for their stepchildren. What seems to characterize these situations, says Hill, is marital instability: men and women pair off, have children, then break up. In such a setting, the flexible human mind finds ways "to attract or maintain mating access to the mother," Hill explains. Or, more crudely, be nice to a woman's kids and she'll sleep with you, which maximizes a man's fitness. Kill her kids and she's likely to take it badly, cutting you off and leaving your sperm unable to fulfill their Darwinian mission. And in societies that rely on relatives to help raise kids, "it doesn't make sense to destroy a 10-year-old stepkid since he could be a helper," Hill points out. "The fitness cost of raising a stepchild until he is old enough to help is much, much less than evolutionary biologists have claimed. Biology is more complicated than these simplistic scenarios saying that killing stepchildren is an adaptation that enhances a man's fitness."

Even the notion that being a brave warrior helps a man get the girls and leave many offspring has been toppled. Until missionaries moved in in 1958, the Waorani tribe of the Ecuadoran Amazon had the highest rates of homicide known to science: 39 percent of women and 54 percent of men were killed by other Waorani, often in blood feuds that lasted generations. "The conventional wisdom had been that the more raids a man participated in, the more wives he would have and the more descendants he would leave," says anthropologist Stephen Beckerman of Pennsylvania State University. But after painstakingly constructing family histories and the raiding and killing records of 95 warriors, he and his colleagues reported last month in *Proceedings of the National Academy of Sciences,* they turned that belief on its head. "The badass guys make terrible husband material," says Beckerman. "Women don't prefer them as husbands and they become the targets of counterraids, which tend to kill their wives and children, too." As a result, the über-warriors leave fewer descendants—the currency of evolutionary fitness—than less aggressive men. Tough-guy behavior may have conferred fitness in some environments, but not in others. It depends. "The message for the evolutionary-psychology guys," says Beckerman, "is that there was no single environment in which humans evolved" and therefore no single human nature.

I can't end the list of evo-psych claims that fall apart under scientific scrutiny without mentioning jealousy. Evo psych argues that jealousy, too, is an adaptation with a mental module all its own, designed to detect and thwart threats to reproductive success. But men's and women's jealousy modules supposedly differ. A man's is designed to detect sexual infidelity: a woman who allows another man to impregnate her takes her womb out of service for at least nine months, depriving her mate of reproductive opportunities. A woman's jealousy module is tuned to emotional infidelity, but she doesn't much care if her mate is unfaithful; a man, being a promiscuous cad, will probably stick with wife No. 1 and their kids even if he is sexually unfaithful, but may well abandon them if he actually falls in love with another woman.

Let's not speculate on the motives that (mostly male) evolutionary psychologists might have in asserting that their wives are programmed to not really care if they sleep around, and turn instead to the evidence. In questionnaires, more men than women say they'd be upset more by sexual infidelity than emotional

---

Lust

Old Thinking
Women are attracted to alpha males.

New Thinking
Warring types make terrible mates: they leave behind widows and orphans who are often the target of rivals' counterattacks.

---

infidelity, by a margin of more than 2-to-1, David Buss of the University of Texas found in an early study of American college students. But men are evenly split on which kind of infidelity upsets them more: half find it more upsetting to think of their mate falling in love with someone else; half find it more upsetting to think of her sleeping with someone else. Not very strong evidence for the claim that men, as a species, care more about sexual infidelity. And in some countries, notably Germany and the Netherlands, the percentage of men who say they find sexual infidelity more upsetting than the emotional kind is only 28 percent and 23 percent. Which suggests that, once again, it depends: in cultures with a relaxed view of female sexuality, men do not get all that upset if a woman has a brief, meaningless fling. It does not portend that she will leave him. It is much more likely that both men and women are wired to detect behavior that threatens their bond, but what that behavior is depends on culture. In a society where an illicit affair portends the end of a relationship, men should indeed be wired to care about that. In a society where that's no big deal, they shouldn't—and, it seems, don't. New data on what triggers jealousy in women also undercut the simplistic evo-psych story. Asked which upsets them more—imagining their partner having acrobatic sex with another woman or falling in love with her—only 13 percent of U.S. women, 12 percent of Dutch women and 8 percent of German women chose door No. 2. So much for the handy "she's wired to not really care if I sleep around" excuse.

Critics of evo psych do not doubt that men and women are wired to become jealous. A radar for infidelity would indeed be adaptive. But the evidence points toward something gender-neutral. Men and women have both evolved the ability to distinguish between behavior that portends abandonment and behavior that does not, and to get upset only at the former. Which behavior is which depends on the society.

Evolutionary psychology is not going quietly. It has had the field to itself, especially in the media, for almost two decades. In large part that was because early critics, led by the late evolutionary biologist Stephen Jay Gould, attacked it with arguments that went over the heads of everyone but about 19 experts in evolutionary theory. It isn't about to give up that hegemony. Thornhill is adamant that rape is an adaptation, despite Hill's results from his Ache study. "If a particular trait or behavior is organized to do something," as he believes rape is, "then it is an adaptation and so was selected for by evolution," he told me. And in the new book *Spent,* evolutionary psychologist Geoffrey

Infidelity

Old Thinking

Men prize sexual fidelity, while women prefer emotional constancy.

New Thinking

Both men and women are concerned with threats to their bond, which vary greatly by culture: one country's harmless tryst is another's irreconcilable differences.

Miller of the University of New Mexico reasserts the party line, arguing that "males have much more to gain from many acts of intercourse with multiple partners than do females," and there is a "universal sex difference in human mate choice criteria, with men favoring younger, fertile women, and women favoring older, higher-status, richer men."

On that point, the evidence instead suggests that both sexes prefer mates around their own age, adjusted for the fact that men mature later than women. If the male mind were adapted to prefer the most fertile women, then AARP-eligible men should marry 23-year-olds, which—Anna Nicole Smith and J. Howard Marshall not-withstanding—they do not, instead preferring women well past their peak fertility. And, interestingly, when Miller focuses on the science rather than tries to sell books, he allows that "human mate choice is much more than men just liking youth and beauty, and women liking status and wealth," as he told me by e-mail.

Yet evo psych remains hugely popular in the media and on college campuses, for obvious reasons. It addresses "these very sexy topics," says Hill. "It's all about sex and violence," and has what he calls "an obsession with Pleistocene just-so stories." And few people—few scientists—know about the empirical data and theoretical arguments that undercut it. "Most scientists are too busy to read studies outside their own narrow field," he says.

Far from ceding anything, evolutionary psychologists have moved the battle from science, where they are on shaky ground, to ideology, where bluster and name-calling can be quite successful. UNM's Miller, for instance, complains that critics "have convinced a substantial portion of the educated public that evolutionary psychology is a pernicious right-wing conspiracy," and complains that believing in evolutionary psychology is seen "as an indicator of conservatism, disagreeableness and selfishness." That, sadly, is how much too much of the debate has gone. "Critics have been told that they're just Marxists motivated by a hatred of evolutionary psychology," says Buller. "That's one reason I'm not following the field anymore: the way science is being conducted is more like a political campaign."

Where, then, does the fall of evolutionary psychology leave the idea of human nature? Behavioral ecology replaces it with "it depends"—that is, the core of human nature is variability and flexibility, the capacity to mold behavior to the social and physical demands of the environment. As Buller says, human variation is not noise in the system; it *is* the system. To be sure, traits such as symbolic language, culture, tool use, emotions and emotional expression do indeed seem to be human universals. It's the behaviors that capture the public imagination—promiscuous men and monogamous women, stepchild-killing men and the like—that turn out not to be. And for a final nail in the coffin, geneticists have discovered that human genes evolve much more quickly than anyone imagined when evolutionary psychology was invented, when everyone assumed that "modern" humans had DNA almost identical to that of people 50,000 years ago. Some genes seem to be only 10,000 years old, and some may be even younger.

That has caught the attention of even the most ardent proponents of evo psych, because when the environment is changing rapidly—as when agriculture was invented or city-states arose—is also when natural selection produces the most dramatic changes in a gene pool. Yet most of the field's leaders, admits UNM's Miller, "have not kept up with the last decade's astounding progress in human evolutionary genetics." The discovery of genes as young as agriculture and city-states, rather than as old as cavemen, means "we have to rethink to foundational assumptions" of evo psych, says Miller, starting with the claim that there are human universals and that they are the result of a Stone Age brain. Evolution indeed sculpted the human brain. But it worked in malleable plastic, not stone, bequeathing us flexible minds that can take stock of the world and adapt to it.

With Jeneen Interlandi.

The End of White America?

The election of Barack Obama is just the most startling manifestation of a larger trend: the gradual erosion of "whiteness" as the touchstone of what it means to be American. If the end of white America is a cultural and demographic inevitability, what will the new mainstream look like—and how will white Americans fit into it? What will it mean to be white when whiteness is no longer the norm? And will a post-white America be less racially divided—or more so?

HUA HSU

"Civilization's Going To Pieces," he remarks. He is in polite company, gathered with friends around a bottle of wine in the late-afternoon sun, chatting and gossiping. "I've gotten to be a terrible pessimist about things. Have you read *The Rise of the Colored Empires* by this man Goddard?" They hadn't. "Well, it's a fine book, and everybody ought to read it. The idea is if we don't look out the white race will be—will be utterly submerged. It's all scientific stuff; it's been proved."

He is Tom Buchanan, a character in F. Scott Fitzgerald's *The Great Gatsby,* a book that nearly everyone who passes through the American education system is compelled to read at least once. Although *Gatsby* doesn't gloss as a book on racial anxiety—it's too busy exploring a different set of anxieties entirely—Buchanan was hardly alone in feeling besieged. The book by "this man Goddard" had a real-world analogue: Lothrop Stoddard's *The Rising Tide of Color Against White World-Supremacy,* published in 1920, five years before *Gatsby.* Nine decades later, Stoddard's polemic remains oddly engrossing. He refers to World War I as the "White Civil War" and laments the "cycle of ruin" that may result if the "white world" continues its infighting. The book features a series of foldout maps depicting the distribution of "color" throughout the world and warns, "Colored migration is a universal peril, menacing every part of the white world."

As briefs for racial supremacy go, *The Rising Tide of Color* is eerily serene. Its tone is scholarly and gentlemanly, its hatred rationalized and, in Buchanan's term, "scientific." And the book was hardly a fringe phenomenon. It was published by Scribner, also Fitzgerald's publisher, and Stoddard, who received a doctorate in history from Harvard, was a member of many professional academic associations. It was precisely the kind of book that a 1920s man of Buchanan's profile—wealthy, Ivy League-educated, at once pretentious

and intellectually insecure—might have been expected to bring up in casual conversation.

As white men of comfort and privilege living in an age of limited social mobility, of course, Stoddard and the Buchanans in his audience had nothing literal to fear. Their sense of dread hovered somewhere above the concerns of everyday life. It was linked less to any immediate danger to their class's political and cultural power than to the perceived fraying of the fixed, monolithic identity of whiteness that sewed together the fortunes of the fair-skinned.

From the hysteria over Eastern European immigration to the vibrant cultural miscegenation of the Harlem Renaissance, it is easy to see how this imagined worldwide white kinship might have seemed imperiled in the 1920s. There's no better example of the era's insecurities than the 1923 Supreme Court case *United States v. Bhagat Singh Thind,* in which an Indian American veteran of World War I sought to become a naturalized citizen by proving that he was Caucasian. The Court considered new anthropological studies that expanded the definition of the Caucasian race to include Indians, and the justices even agreed that traces of "Aryan blood" coursed through Thind's body. But these technicalities availed him little. The Court determined that Thind was not white "in accordance with the understanding of the common man" and therefore could be excluded from the "statutory category" of whiteness. Put another way: Thind was white, in that he was Caucasian and even Aryan. But he was not *white* in the way Stoddard or Buchanan were white.

The '20s debate over the definition of whiteness—a legal category? a commonsense understanding? a worldwide civilization?—took place in a society gripped by an acute sense of racial paranoia, and it is easy to regard these episodes as evidence of how far we have come. But consider that these anxieties surfaced when whiteness was synonymous with the

American mainstream, when threats to its status were largely imaginary. What happens once this is no longer the case—when the fears of Lothrop Stoddard and Tom Buchanan are realized, and white people actually become an American minority?

Whether you describe it as the dawning of a post-racial age or just the end of white America, we're approaching a profound demographic tipping point. According to an August 2008 report by the U.S. Census Bureau, those groups currently categorized as racial minorities—blacks and Hispanics, East Asians and South Asians—will account for a majority of the U.S. population by the year 2042. Among Americans under the age of 18, this shift is projected to take place in 2023, which means that every child born in the United States from here on out will belong to the first post-white generation.

Obviously, steadily ascending rates of interracial marriage complicate this picture, pointing toward what Michael Lind has described as the "beiging" of America. And it's possible that "beige Americans" will self-identify as "white" in sufficient numbers to push the tipping point further into the future than the Census Bureau projects. But even if they do, whiteness will be a label adopted out of convenience and even indifference, rather than aspiration and necessity. For an earlier generation of minorities and immigrants, to be recognized as a "white American" whether you were an Italian or a Pole or a Hungarian, was to enter the mainstream of American life; to be recognized as something else, as the *Thind* case suggests, was to be permanently excluded. As Bill Imada, head of the IW Group, a prominent Asian American communications and marketing company, puts it: "I think in the 1920s, 1930s, and 1940s, [for] anyone who immigrated, the aspiration was to blend in and be as American as possible so that white America wouldn't be intimidated by them. They wanted to imitate white America as much as possible: learn English, go to church, go to the same schools."

Today, the picture is far more complex. To take the most obvious example, whiteness is no longer a precondition for entry into the highest levels of public office. The son of Indian immigrants doesn't have to become "white" in order to be elected governor of Louisiana. A half-Kenyan, half-Kansan politician can self-identify as black and be elected president of the United States.

As a purely demographic matter, then, the "white America" that Lothrop Stoddard believed in so fervently may cease to exist in 2040, 2050, or 2060, or later still. But where the culture is concerned, it's already all but finished. Instead of the long-standing model of assimilation toward a common center, the culture is being remade in the image of white America's multiethnic, multicolored heirs.

For some, the disappearance of this centrifugal core heralds a future rich with promise. In 1998, President Bill Clinton, in a now-famous address to students at Portland State University, remarked:

Today, largely because of immigration, there is no majority race in Hawaii or Houston or New York City. Within five years, there will be no majority race in our largest state, California. In a little more than 50 years, there will be no majority race in the United States. No other nation in history has gone through demographic change of this magnitude in so short a time . . . [These immigrants] are energizing our culture and broadening our vision of the world. They are renewing our most basic values and reminding us all of what it truly means to be American.

Not everyone was so enthused. Clinton's remarks caught the attention of another anxious Buchanan—Pat Buchanan, the conservative thinker. Revisiting the president's speech in his 2001 book, *The Death of the West,* Buchanan wrote: "Mr. Clinton assured us that it will be a better America when we are all minorities and realize true 'diversity.' Well, those students [at Portland State] are going to find out, for they will spend their golden years in a Third World America."

Today, the arrival of what Buchanan derided as "Third World America" is all but inevitable. What will the new mainstream of America look like, and what ideas or values might it rally around? What will it mean to be white after "whiteness" no longer defines the mainstream? Will anyone mourn the end of white America? Will anyone try to preserve it?

Another moment from *The Great Gatsby:* as Fitzgerald's narrator and Gatsby drive across the Queensboro Bridge into Manhattan, a car passes them, and Nick Carraway notices that it is a limousine "driven by a white chauffeur, in which sat three modish negroes, two bucks and a girl." The novelty of this topsy-turvy arrangement inspires Carraway to laugh aloud and think to himself, "Anything can happen now that we've slid over this bridge, anything at all . . ."

For a contemporary embodiment of the upheaval that this scene portended, consider Sean Combs, a hip-hop mogul and one of the most famous African Americans on the planet. Combs grew up during hip-hop's late-1970s rise, and he belongs to the first generation that could safely make a living working in the industry—as a plucky young promoter and record-label intern in the late 1980s and early 1990s, and as a fashion designer, artist, and music executive worth hundreds of millions of dollars a brief decade later.

In the late 1990s, Combs made a fascinating gesture toward New York's high society. He announced his arrival into the circles of the rich and powerful not by crashing their parties, but by inviting them into his own spectacularly over-the-top world. Combs began to stage elaborate annual parties in the Hamptons, not far from where Fitzgerald's novel takes place. These "white parties"—attendees are required to wear white—quickly became legendary for their opulence (in 2004, Combs showcased a 1776 copy of the Declaration of Independence) as well as for the cultures-colliding quality of Hamptons elites paying their respects to someone so comfortably nouveau riche. Prospective business partners angled to get close to him and praised him as a guru of the lucrative "urban" market, while grateful partygoers hailed him as a modern-day Gatsby.

"Have I read *The Great Gatsby?*" Combs said to a London newspaper in 2001. "I am the Great Gatsby."

Yet whereas Gatsby felt pressure to hide his status as an arriviste, Combs celebrated his position as an outsider-insider—someone who appropriates elements of the culture he seeks to join without attempting to assimilate outright. In a sense, Combs was imitating the old WASP establishment; in another sense, he was subtly provoking it, by over-enunciating its formality and never letting his guests forget that there was something slightly off about his presence. There's a silent power to throwing parties where the best-dressed man in the room is also the one whose public profile once consisted primarily of dancing in the background of Biggie Smalls videos. ("No one would ever expect a young black man to be coming to a party with the Declaration of Independence, but I got it, and it's coming with me," Combs joked at his 2004 party, as he made the rounds with the document, promising not to spill champagne on it.)

In this regard, Combs is both a product and a hero of the new cultural mainstream, which prizes diversity above all else, and whose ultimate goal is some vague notion of racial transcendence, rather than subversion or assimilation. Although Combs's vision is far from representative—not many hip-hop stars vacation in St. Tropez with a parasol-toting manservant shading their every step—his industry lies at the heart of this new mainstream. Over the past 30 years, few changes in American culture have been as significant as the rise of hip-hop. The genre has radically reshaped the way we listen to and consume music, first by opposing the pop mainstream and then by becoming it. From its constant sampling of past styles and eras—old records, fashions, slang, anything—to its mythologization of the self-made black antihero, hip-hop is more than a musical genre: it's a philosophy, a political statement, a way of approaching and remaking culture. It's a lingua franca not just among kids in America, but also among young people worldwide. And its economic impact extends beyond the music industry, to fashion, advertising, and film. (Consider the producer Russell Simmons—the ur-Combs and a music, fashion, and television mogul—or the rapper 50 Cent, who has parlayed his rags-to-riches story line into extracurricular successes that include a clothing line; book, video-game, and film deals; and a startlingly lucrative partnership with the makers of Vitamin Water.)

But hip-hop's deepest impact is symbolic. During popular music's rise in the 20th century, white artists and producers consistently "mainstreamed" African American innovations. Hip-hop's ascension has been different. Eminem notwithstanding, hip-hop never suffered through anything like an Elvis Presley moment, in which a white artist made a musical form safe for white America. This is no dig at Elvis—the constrictive racial logic of the 1950s demanded the erasure of rock and roll's black roots, and if it hadn't been him, it would have been someone else. But hip-hop—the sound of the post-civil-rights, post-soul generation—found a global audience on its own terms.

Today, hip-hop's colonization of the global imagination, from fashion runways in Europe to dance competitions in Asia, is Disney-esque. This transformation has bred an unprecedented cultural confidence in its black originators. Whiteness is no longer a threat, or an ideal: it's kitsch to be appropriated, whether with gestures like Combs's "white parties" or the trickle-down epidemic of collared shirts and cuff links currently afflicting rappers. And an expansive multiculturalism is replacing the us-against-the-world bunker mentality that lent a thrilling edge to hip-hop's mid-1990s rise.

Peter Rosenberg, a self-proclaimed "nerdy Jewish kid" and radio personality on New York's Hot 97 FM—and a living example of how hip-hop has created new identities for its listeners that don't fall neatly along lines of black and white—shares another example: "I interviewed [the St. Louis rapper] Nelly this morning, and he said it's now very cool and *in* to have multicultural friends. Like you're not really considered hip or 'you've made it' if you're rolling with all the same people."

Just as Tiger Woods forever changed the country-club culture of golf, and Will Smith confounded stereotypes about the ideal Hollywood leading man, hip-hop's rise is helping redefine the American mainstream, which no longer aspires toward a single iconic image of style or class. Successful network-television shows like *Lost, Heroes,* and *Grey's Anatomy* feature wildly diverse casts, and an entire genre of half-hour comedy, from *The Colbert Report* to *The Office,* seems dedicated to having fun with the persona of the clueless white male. The youth market is following the same pattern: consider the Cheetah Girls, a multicultural, multi-platinum, multiplatform trio of teenyboppers who recently starred in their third movie, or Dora the Explorer, the precocious bilingual 7-year-old Latina adventurer who is arguably the most successful animated character on children's television today. In a recent address to the Association of Hispanic Advertising Agencies, Brown Johnson, the Nickelodeon executive who has overseen Dora's rise, explained the importance of creating a character who does not conform to "the white, middle-class mold." When Johnson pointed out that Dora's wares were outselling Barbie's in France, the crowd hooted in delight.

Pop culture today rallies around an ethic of multicultural inclusion that seems to value every identity—except whiteness. "It's become harder for the blond-haired, blue-eyed commercial actor," remarks Rochelle Newman-Carrasco, of the Hispanic marketing firm Enlace. "You read casting notices, and they like to cast people with brown hair because they could be Hispanic. The language of casting notices is pretty shocking because it's so specific: 'Brown hair, brown eyes, could look Hispanic.' Or, as one notice put it: 'Ethnically ambiguous.'"

"I think white people feel like they're under siege right now—like it's not okay to be white right now, especially if you're a white male," laughs Bill Imada, of the IW Group. Imada and Newman-Carrasco are part of a movement within advertising, marketing, and communications firms to reimagine the profile of the typical American consumer. (Tellingly, every person I spoke with from these industries knew the Census Bureau's projections by heart.)

"There's a lot of fear and a lot of resentment," Newman-Carrasco observes, describing the flak she caught after writing an article for a trade publication on the need for more-diverse hiring practices. "I got a response from a friend—he's, like, a 60-something white male, and he's been involved with multicultural recruiting," she recalls. "And he said, 'I really feel like the hunted. It's a hard time to be a white man in America right now, because I feel like I'm being lumped in with all white males in America, and I've tried to do stuff, but it's a tough time.'"

"I always tell the white men in the room, 'We need you,'" Imada says. "We cannot talk about diversity and inclusion and engagement without you at the table. It's okay to be white!

"But people are stressed out about it. 'We used to be in control! We're losing control!'"

If they're right—if white America is indeed "losing control," and if the future will belong to people who can successfully navigate a post-racial, multicultural landscape—then it's no surprise that many white Americans are eager to divest themselves of their whiteness entirely.

For some, this renunciation can take a radical form. In 1994, a young graffiti artist and activist named William "Upski" Wimsatt, the son of a university professor, published *Bomb the Suburbs,* the spiritual heir to Norman Mailer's celebratory 1957 essay, "The White Negro." Wimsatt was deeply committed to hip-hop's transformative powers, going so far as to embrace the status of the lowly "wigger," a pejorative term popularized in the early 1990s to describe white kids who steep themselves in black culture. Wimsatt viewed the wigger's immersion in two cultures as an engine for change. "If channeled in the right way," he wrote, "the wigger can go a long way toward repairing the sickness of race in America."

Wimsatt's painfully earnest attempts to put his own relationship with whiteness under the microscope coincided with the emergence of an academic discipline known as "whiteness studies." In colleges and universities across the country, scholars began examining the history of "whiteness" and unpacking its contradictions. Why, for example, had the Irish and the Italians fallen beyond the pale at different moments in our history? Were Jewish Americans *white?* And, as the historian Matthew Frye Jacobson asked, "Why is it that in the United States, a white woman can have black children but a black woman cannot have white children?"

Much like Wimsatt, the whiteness-studies academics—figures such as Jacobson, David Roediger, Eric Lott, and Noel Ignatiev—were attempting to come to terms with their own relationships with whiteness, in its past and present forms. In the early 1990s, Ignatiev, a former labor activist and the author of *How the Irish Became White,* set out to "abolish" the idea of the white race by starting the New Abolitionist Movement and founding a journal titled *Race Traitor.* "There is nothing positive about white identity," he wrote in 1998. "As James Baldwin said, 'As long as you think you're white, there's no hope for you.'"

Although most white Americans haven't read *Bomb the Suburbs* or *Race Traitor,* this view of whiteness as something to be interrogated, if not shrugged off completely, has migrated to less academic spheres. The perspective of the whiteness-studies academics is commonplace now, even if the language used to express it is different.

"I get it: as a straight white male, I'm the worst thing on Earth," Christian Lander says. Lander is a Canadian-born, Los Angeles-based satirist who in January 2008 started a blog called Stuff White People Like (stuffwhitepeoplelike.com), which pokes fun at the manners and mores of a specific species of young, hip, upwardly mobile whites. (He has written more than 100 entries about whites' passion for things like bottled water, "the idea of soccer," and "being the only white person around.") At its best, Lander's site—which formed the basis for a recently published book of the same name (reviewed in the October 2008 *Atlantic*)—is a cunningly precise distillation of the identity crisis plaguing well-meaning, well-off white kids in a post-white world.

"Like, I'm aware of all the horrible crimes that my demographic has done in the world," Lander says. "And there's a bunch of white people who are desperate—*desperate*—to say, 'You know what? My skin's white, but I'm not one of the white people who's destroying the world.'"

For Lander, whiteness has become a vacuum. The "white identity" he limns on his blog is predicated on the quest for authenticity—usually other people's authenticity. "As a white person, you're just desperate to find something else to grab onto. You're jealous! Pretty much every white person I grew up with wished they'd grown up in, you know, an ethnic home that gave them a second language. White culture is *Family Ties* and Led Zeppelin and Guns N' Roses—like, this is white culture. This is all we have."

Lander's "white people" are products of a very specific historical moment, raised by well-meaning Baby Boomers to reject the old ideal of white American gentility and to embrace diversity and fluidity instead. ("It's strange that we are the kids of Baby Boomers, right? How the hell do you rebel against that? Like, your parents will march against the World Trade Organization next to you. They'll have bigger white dreadlocks than you. What do you do?") But his lighthearted anthropology suggests that the multicultural harmony they were raised to worship has bred a kind of self-denial.

> **One sociologist observes that his white students are plagued by a racial-identity crisis. "They care about culture. And to be white is to be culturally broke."**

Matt Wray, a sociologist at Temple University who is a fan of Lander's humor, has observed that many of his white students are plagued by a racial-identity crisis: "They don't care about socioeconomics; they care about culture. And to be white is to be culturally broke. The classic thing white students say when you ask them to talk about who they are is, 'I don't have a culture.' They might be privileged, they might be loaded socioeconomically, but they feel bankrupt when it comes to culture . . . They feel disadvantaged, and they feel marginalized. They don't have a culture that's cool or oppositional." Wray says that this feeling of being culturally bereft often prevents students from recognizing what it means to be a child of privilege—a strange irony that the first wave of whiteness-studies scholars, in the 1990s, failed to anticipate.

Of course, the obvious material advantages that come with being born white—lower infant-mortality rates and easier-to-acquire bank loans, for example—tend to undercut any sympathy that this sense of marginalization might generate. And in the right context, cultural-identity crises can turn well-meaning whites into instant punch lines. Consider *ego trip's The (White) Rapper Show,* a brilliant and critically acclaimed reality show that VH1 debuted in 2007. It depicted 10 (mostly hapless) white rappers living together in a dilapidated house—dubbed "Tha White House"—in the South Bronx. Despite the contestants' best intentions, each one seemed like a profoundly confused caricature, whether it was the solemn graduate student committed to fighting racism or the ghetto-obsessed suburbanite who had, seemingly by accident, named himself after the abolitionist John Brown.

Similarly, Smirnoff struck marketing gold in 2006 with a viral music video titled "Tea Partay," featuring a trio of strikingly bad, V-neck-sweater-clad white rappers called the Prep Unit. "Haters like to clown our Ivy League educations/But they're just jealous 'cause our families run the nation," the trio brayed, as a pair of bottle-blond women in spiffy tennis whites shimmied behind them. There was no nonironic way to enjoy the video; its entire appeal was in its self-aware lampooning of WASP culture: verdant country clubs, "old money," croquet, popped collars, and the like.

"The best defense is to be constantly pulling the rug out from underneath yourself," Wray remarks, describing the way self-aware whites contend with their complicated identity. "Beat people to the punch. You're forced as a white person into a sense of ironic detachment. Irony is what fuels a lot of white subcultures. You also see things like Burning Man, when a lot of white people are going into the desert and trying to invent something that is entirely new and not a form of racial mimicry. That's its own kind of flight from whiteness. We're going through a period where whites are really trying to figure out: Who are we?"

The "Flight from Whiteness" of urban, college-educated, liberal whites isn't the only attempt to answer this question. You can flee *into* whiteness as well. This can mean pursuing the authenticity of an imagined past: think of the deliberately white-bread world of Mormon America, where the '50s never ended, or the anachronistic WASP entitlement flaunted in books like last year's *A Privileged Life: Celebrating WASP Style,* a handsome coffee-table book compiled by Susanna Salk, depicting a world of seersucker blazers, whale pants, and deck shoes. (What the book celebrates is the "inability to be outdone," and the "self-confidence and security that comes with it," Salk tells me. "That's why I call it 'privilege.' It's this privilege of time, of heritage, of being in a place longer than anybody else?'") But these enclaves of preserved-in-amber whiteness are likely to be less important to the American future than the construction of whiteness as a somewhat pissed-off minority culture.

This notion of a self-consciously white expression of minority empowerment will be familiar to anyone who has come across the comedian Larry the Cable Guy—he of "Farting Jingle Bells"—or witnessed the transformation of Detroit-born-and-bred Kid Rock from teenage rapper into "American Bad Ass" southern-style rocker. The 1990s may have been a decade when multiculturalism advanced dramatically—when American culture became "colorized," as the critic Jeff Chang put it—but it was also an era when a very different form of identity politics crystallized. Hip-hop may have provided the decade's soundtrack, but the highest-selling artist of the '90s was Garth Brooks. Michael Jordan and Tiger Woods may have been the faces of athletic superstardom, but it was NASCAR that emerged as professional sports' fastest-growing institution, with ratings second only to the NFL's.

As with the unexpected success of the apocalyptic Left Behind novels, or the Jeff Foxworthy—organized Blue Collar Comedy Tour, the rise of country music and auto racing took place well off the American elite's radar screen. (None of Christian Lander's white people would be caught dead at a NASCAR race.) These phenomena reflected a growing sense of cultural solidarity among lower-middle-class whites—a solidarity defined by a yearning for American "authenticity," a folksy realness that rejects the global, the urban, and the effete in favor of nostalgia for "the way things used to be."

Like other forms of identity politics, white solidarity comes complete with its own folk heroes, conspiracy theories (Barack Obama is a secret Muslim! The U.S. is going to merge with Canada and Mexico!), and laundry lists of injustices. The targets and scapegoats vary—from multiculturalism and affirmative action to a loss of moral values,

131

from immigration to an economy that no longer guarantees the American worker a fair chance—and so do the political programs they inspire. (Ross Perot and Pat Buchanan both tapped into this white identity politics in the 1990s; today, its tribunes run the ideological gamut, from Jim Webb to Ron Paul to Mike Huckabee to Sarah Palin.) But the core grievance, in each case, has to do with cultural and socioeconomic dislocation—the sense that the system that used to guarantee the white working class some stability has gone off-kilter.

Wray is one of the founders of what has been called "white-trash studies," a field conceived as a response to the perceived elite-liberal marginalization of the white working class. He argues that the economic downturn of the 1970s was the pre-condition for the formation of an "oppositional" and "defiant" white-working-class sensibility—think of the rugged, anti-everything individualism of 1977's *Smokey and the Bandit*. But those anxieties took their shape from the aftershocks of the identity-based movements of the 1960s. "I think that the political space that the civil-rights movement opens up in the mid-1950s and '60s is the transformative thing," Wray observes. "Following the black-power movement, all of the other minority groups that followed took up various forms of activism, including brown power and yellow power and red power. Of course the problem is, if you try and have a 'white power' movement, it doesn't sound good."

One can imagine white identity politics growing more potent and forthright as the soon-to-be white minority's sense of being besieged and disdained increases.

The result is a racial pride that dares not speak its name, and that defines itself through cultural cues instead—a suspicion of intellectual elites and city dwellers, a preference for folksiness and plainness of speech (whether real or feigned), and the association of a working-class white minority with "the real America." (In the Scots-Irish belt that runs from Arkansas up through West Virginia, the most common ethnic label offered to census takers is "American.") Arguably, this white identity politics helped swing the 2000 and 2004 elections, serving as the powerful counterpunch to urban white liberals, and the McCain-Palin campaign relied on it almost to the point of absurdity (as when a McCain surrogate dismissed Northern Virginia as somehow not part of "the real Virginia") as a bulwark against the threatening multiculturalism of Barack Obama. Their strategy failed, of course, but it's possible to imagine white identity politics growing more potent and more forthright in its racial identifications in the future, as "the real America" becomes an ever-smaller portion of, well, the real America, and as the soon-to-be white minority's sense of being besieged and disdained by a multicultural majority grows apace.

This vision of the aggrieved white man lost in a world that no longer values him was given its most vivid expression in the 1993 film *Falling Down*. Michael Douglas plays Bill Foster, a downsized defense worker with a buzz cut and a pocket protector who rampages through a Los Angeles over-run by greedy Korean shop-owners and Hispanic gangsters, railing against the eclipse of the America he used to know. (The film came out just eight years before California became the nation's first majority-minority state.) *Falling Down* ends with a soulful police officer apprehending Foster on the Santa Monica Pier, at which point the middle-class vigilante asks, almost innocently: "*I'm* the bad guy?"

But this is a nightmare vision. Of course most of America's Bill Fosters aren't the bad guys—just as civilization is not, in the words of Tom Buchanan, "going to pieces" and America is not, in the phrasing of Pat Buchanan, going "Third World." The coming white minority does not mean that the racial hierarchy of American culture will suddenly become inverted, as in 1995's *White Man's Burden,* an awful thought experiment of a film, starring John Travolta, that envisions an upside-down world in which whites are subjugated to their high-class black oppressors. There will be dislocations and resentments along the way, but the demographic shifts of the next 40 years are likely to reduce the power of racial hierarchies over everyone's lives, producing a culture that's more likely than any before to treat its inhabitants as individuals, rather than members of a caste or identity group.

Consider the world of advertising and marketing, industries that set out to mold our desires at a subconscious level. Advertising strategy once assumed a "general market"—"a code word for 'white people,' " jokes one ad executive—and smaller, mutually exclusive, satellite "ethnic markets." In recent years, though, advertisers have begun revising their assumptions and strategies in anticipation of profound demographic shifts. Instead of herding consumers toward a discrete center, the goal today is to create versatile images and campaigns that can be adapted to highly individualized tastes. (Think of the dancing silhouettes in Apple's iPod campaign, which emphasizes individuality and diversity without privileging—or even representing—any specific group.)

At the moment, we can call this the triumph of multi-culturalism, or post-racialism. But just as *whiteness* has no inherent meaning—it is a vessel we fill with our hopes and anxieties—these terms may prove equally empty in the long run. Does being post-racial mean that we are past race completely, or merely that race is no longer essential to how we identify ourselves? Karl Carter, of Atlanta's youth-oriented GTM Inc. (Guerrilla Tactics Media), suggests that marketers and advertisers would be better off focusing on matrices like "lifestyle" or "culture" rather than race or ethnicity. "You'll have crazy in-depth studies of the white consumer or the

Latino consumer," he complains. "But how do skaters feel? How do hip-hoppers feel?"

The logic of online social networking points in a similar direction. The New York University sociologist Dalton Conley has written of a "network nation," in which applications like Facebook and MySpace create "crosscutting social groups" and new, flexible identities that only vaguely overlap with racial identities. Perhaps this is where the future of identity after whiteness lies—in a dramatic departure from the racial logic that has defined American culture from the very beginning. What Conley, Carter, and others are describing isn't merely the displacement of whiteness from our cultural center; they're describing a social structure that treats race as just one of a seemingly infinite number of possible self-identifications.

The problem of the 20th century, W. E. B. DuBois famously predicted, would be the problem of the color line. Will this continue to be the case in the 21st century, when a black president will govern a country whose social networks increasingly cut across every conceivable line of identification? The ruling of *United States v. Bhagat Singh Thind* no longer holds weight, but its echoes have been inescapable: we aspire to be post-racial, but we still live within the structures of privilege, injustice, and racial categorization that we inherited from an older order. We can talk about defining ourselves by lifestyle rather than skin color, but our lifestyle choices are still racially coded. We know, more or less, that race is a fiction that often does more harm than good, and yet it is something we cling to without fully understanding why—as a social and legal fact, a vague sense of belonging and place that we make solid through culture and speech.

But maybe this is merely how it used to be—maybe this is already an outdated way of looking at things. "You have a lot of young adults going into a more diverse world" Carter remarks. For the young Americans born in the 1980s and 1990s, culture is something to be taken apart and remade in their own image. "We came along in a generation that didn't have to follow that path of race," he goes on. "We saw something *different*." This moment was not the end of white America; it was not the end of anything. It was a bridge, and we crossed it.

Hua Hsu teaches at Vassar College.

UNIT 5

Development during Adolescence and Young Adulthood

Unit Selections

Key Points to Consider

- What parental behaviors help ensure a peaceful adolescence?

- Do teachers and administrators have a duty to intervene when sexual harassment occurs in school?

- What are the effects of sleep deprivation? Why do so many adolescents fail to get enough sleep?

- Do adolescents who play violent video games engage in more real life aggression, hostility, and violence?

- Should incarcerated adolescents continue their education in jail? What would a jail school teach?

- What education and experiences are the best preparation for twenty-first-century employment?

- Why is touch important to emotional connection?

- Is sexual pleasure a lifelong pursuit? Can it get better, healthier, and happier?

- Are men with depression underdiagnosed or misdiagnosed? Will improvement in treating male depression reduce drug abuse and/or suicide?

Student Website

www.mhhe.com/cls

Internet References

Alcohol & Drug Addiction Resource Center
   http://www.addict-help.com/
ADOL: Adolescent Directory On-Line
   http://site.educ.indiana.edu/aboutus/AdolescenceDirectoryonLineADOL/tabid/4785/Default.aspx
AMA—Adolescent Health On-Line
   http://www.ama-assn.org/ama/pub/category/1947.html
American Academy of Child and Adolescent Psychiatry
   http://www.aacap.org/
Depression
   http://www.depression-primarycare.org

The term "adolescence" was coined in 1904 by G. Stanley Hall, one of the world's first psychologists. He saw adolescence as a discrete stage of life that bridges the gap between sexual maturity (puberty) and socioemotional and cognitive maturity. He believed it to be characterized by "storm and stress." At the beginning of the twentieth century, it was typical for young men to begin working in middle childhood (there were no child labor laws), and for young women to work as wives and mothers as soon as they were fertile and/or spoken for. At the turn of the twenty-first century, the beginning of adolescence was marked by the desire to be independent of parental control. The end of adolescence, which once coincided with the age of legal maturity (usually 16 or 18, depending on local laws), has now been extended upwards. Although legal maturity is now 18 (voting, enlisting in the armed services, owning property, marrying without permission), the social norm is to consider persons in their late teens as adolescents, not adults. The years between 18 and 21 are often problematic for youth tethered between adult and not-adult status. They can be married, with children, living in homes of their own, running their own businesses, yet not be able to drive their cars in certain places or at certain times. They can go to college and participate in social activities, but they cannot legally drink. Often the twenty-first birthday is viewed as a rite of passage into adulthood in the United States because it signals the legal right to buy and drink alcoholic beverages. "Maturity" is usually reserved for those who have achieved full economic as well as socioemotional independence as adults.

Erik Erikson, the personality theorist, marked the passage from adolescence to young adulthood by a change in the nuclear conflicts of two life stages: identity versus role confusion and intimacy versus isolation. Adolescents struggle to answer the question, "Who am I?" Young adults struggle to find a place within the existing social order where they can feel intimacy rather than isolation. In the 1960s, Erikson wrote that females resolved both their conflicts of identity and intimacy by living vicariously through their husbands, an unacceptable idea to many females today.

As adolescence has been extended, so too has young adulthood. One hundred years ago, life expectancy did not extend too far beyond menopause for women and retirement for men. Young adulthood began when adolescents finished puberty. Parents of teenagers were middle-aged, between 35 and 55. Later marriages and delayed childbearing have redefined the line between young adulthood and middle age. Many people today consider themselves young adults well into their 40s.

Jean Piaget, the cognitive theorist, marked the end of the development of mental processes with the end of adolescence. Once full physical maturity, including brain maturity, was achieved, one reached the acme of his or her abilities to assimilate, accommodate, organize, and adapt to sensations, perceptions, associations, and discriminations. Piaget did not feel cognitive processing of information ceased with adulthood. He believed, however, that cognitive judgments would not reach a stage higher than the abstract, hypothetical, logical reasoning of formal operations. Today many cognitive theorists believe postformal operations are possible.

© Getty Images/Digital Vision

The first article, "A Peaceful Adolescence," addresses the G. Stanley Hall belief that adolescence was a stage of life marked by "storm and stress." While some teenagers do have conflicts with their parents, new research documents that many teenagers have peaceful passages through adolescence. The authors of this article, Barbara Kantrowitz and Karen Springen, report on what adults do to nurture successful teen years.

The second selection for Unit 5, Part A, "Adolescence," tells a true story about a homosexual adolescent murdered in school because of his sexual orientation. The author, Ramin Setoodeh, questions the role of school personnel in loco parentis (in the role of parent). Should schools have a "don't ask, don't tell" policy? If self-identification as gay, lesbian, or bisexual (GLB) is allowed, should schools assure that the rights of GLB students are protected? What are the parameters of tolerance?

The third article about adolescents deals with video game violence. The authors report conflicting research data about the correlation between heavy, brutal game playing and real-world violence. The United States does not restrict violent video games, as do most other industrialized nations. Future longitudinal studies may be able to demonstrate that violence in games does (or does not) predict more hostile acts in life.

The fourth selection, "Jail Time Is Learning Time," describes efforts to help jailed youth acquire GED instruction and earn high school equivalency diplomas. The program described also teaches anger management and vocational/job skills. Many adolescents are incarcerated in the United States every year. They should not be forgotten.

The first article in the Young Adulthood portion of this unit, "Finding a Job in the 21st Century," predicts that knowledge of other countries and expertise in information technology are keys to good employment opportunities. John Challenger also advocates being flexible and mobile over looking for 9-to-5 stay-in-place jobs. He lists both jobs with projected increases and projected decreases in the next five years.

The second Young Adulthood selection, "Hold Me Tight," addresses the concerns of Erik Erikson in his life stage of intimacy versus isolation. Intimacy is emotional connection. Isolation is traumatic aloneness for young adults. Evidence suggests that the brain codes a lack of emotional connection as danger. Sue Johnson writes that touch is healing. Regular holding, soothing, caressing, hugging, and kissing primes young adults to develop and keep intimacy in their lives.

A Peaceful Adolescence

The teen years don't have to be a time of family storm and stress. Most kids do just fine and now psychologists are finding out why that is.

BARBARA KANTROWITZ AND KAREN SPRINGEN

At 17, Amanda Hund is a straight-A student who loves competing in horse shows. The high school junior from Willmar, Minn., belongs to her school's band, orchestra and choir. She regularly volunteers through her church and recently spent a week working in an orphanage in Jamaica. Usually, however, she's closer to home, where her family eats dinner together every night. She also has a weekly breakfast date with her father, a doctor, at a local coffee shop. Amanda credits her parents for her relatively easy ride through adolescence. "My parents didn't sweat the small stuff," she says. "They were always very open. You could ask any question."

Is the Hund family for real? Didn't they get the memo that says teens and their parents are supposed to be at odds until . . . well, until forever? Actually, they're very much for real, and according to scientists who study the transition to adulthood, they represent the average family's experience more accurately than all those scary TV movies about out-of-control teens. "Research shows that most young people go through adolescence having good relationships with their parents, adopting attitudes and values consistent with their parents' and end up getting out of the adolescent period and becoming good citizens," says Richard Lerner, Bergstrom chair of applied developmental science at Tufts University. This shouldn't be news—but it is, largely because of widespread misunderstanding of what happens during the teen years. It's a time of transition, just like the first year of parenthood or menopause. And although there are dramatic hormonal and physical changes during this period, catastrophe is certainly not preordained. A lot depends on youngsters' innate natures combined with the emotional and social support they get from the adults around them. In other words, parents do matter.

The roots of misconceptions about teenagers go back to the way psychologists framed the field of adolescent development a century ago. They were primarily looking for explanations of why things went wrong. Before long, the idea that this phase was a period of storm and stress made its way into the popular consciousness. But in the last 15 years, developmental scientists have begun to re-examine these assumptions. Instead of focusing on kids who battle their way through the teen years, they're studying the dynamics of success.

At the head of the pack are Lerner and his colleagues, who are in the midst of a major project that many other researchers are following closely. It's a six-year longitudinal study of exactly what it takes to turn out OK and what adults can do to nurture those behaviors. "Parents and sometimes kids themselves often talk about positive development as the absence of bad," says Lerner. "What we're trying to do is present a different vision and a different vocabulary for young people and parents."

The first conclusions from the 4-H Study of Positive Youth Development, published in the February issue of *The Journal of Early Adolescence,* show that there are quantifiable personality traits possessed by all adolescents who manage to get to adulthood without major problems. Psychologists have labeled these traits "the 5 Cs": competence, confidence, connection, character and caring. These characteristics theoretically lead to a sixth C, contribution (similar to civic engagement). The nomenclature grows out of observations in recent years by a number of clinicians, Lerner says, but his study is the first time researchers have measured how these characteristics influence successful growth.

The 5 Cs are interconnected, not isolated traits, Lerner says. For example, competence refers not just to academic ability but also to social and vocational skills. Confidence includes self-esteem as well as the belief that you can make a difference in the world. The value of the study, Lerner says, is that when it is completed next year, researchers will have a way to quantify these characteristics and eventually determine what specific social and educational programs foster them.

During these years, parents should stay involved as they help kids move on.

In the meantime, parents can learn a lot from this rethinking of the teen years. Don't automatically assume that your kids become alien beings when they leave middle school. They still care what their parents think and they still need love and guidance—although in a different form. Temple University psychology professor Laurence Steinberg, author of "The Ten Basic Principles of Good Parenting," compares raising kids to building a boat that you eventually launch. Parents have to build a strong underpinning so their kids are equipped to face whatever's ahead. In the teen years, that means staying involved as you slowly let go. "One of the things that's natural in adolescence is that kids are going to pull away from their parents as they become increasingly interested in peers," says Steinberg. "It's important for parents to hang in there, for them not to pull back in response to that."

Communication is critical. "Stay in touch with your kids and make sure they feel valued and appreciated," advises Suniya Luthar, professor of clinical and developmental psychology at Columbia University. Even if they roll their eyes when you try to hug them, they still need direct displays of affection, she says. They also need help figuring out goals and limits. Parents should monitor their kids' activities and get to know their friends. Luthar says parents should still be disciplinarians and set standards such as curfews. Then teens need to know that infractions will be met with consistent consequences.

Adolescents are often critical of their parents but they're also watching them closely for clues on how to function in the outside world. Daniel Perkins, associate professor of family and youth resiliency at Penn State, says he and his wife take their twins to the local Ronald McDonald House and serve dinner to say thank you for time the family spent there when the children had health problems after birth. "What we've done already is set up the notion that we were blessed and need to give back, even if it's in a small way." That kind of example sets a standard youngsters remember, even if it seems like they're not paying attention.

Parents should provide opportunities for kids to explore the world and even find a calling. Teens who have a passion for something are more likely to thrive. "They have a sense of purpose beyond day-to-day teenage life," says David Marcus, author of "What It Takes to Pull Me Through." Often, he says, kids who were enthusiastic about something in middle school lose enthusiasm in high school because the competition gets tougher and they're not as confident. Parents need to step in and help young people find other outlets. The best way to do that is to regularly spend uninterrupted time with teens (no cell phones). Kids also need to feel connected to other adults they trust and to their communities. Teens who get into trouble are "drifting," he says. "They don't have a web of people watching out for them."

Teens should build support webs of friends and adults.

At some point during these years, teen-agers should also be learning to build their own support networks—a skill that will be even more important when they're on their own. Connie Flanagan, a professor of youth civic development at Penn State, examines how kids look out for one another. "What we're interested in is how they help one another avoid harm," she says. In one of her focus groups, some teenage girls mentioned that they decided none would drink from an open can at a party because they wouldn't know for sure what they were drinking. "Even though you are experimenting, you're essentially doing it in a way that you protect one another," Flanagan says. Kids who don't make those kinds of connections are more likely to get in trouble because there's no one their own age or older to stop them from going too far. Like any other stage of life, adolescence can be tough. But teens and families can get through it—as long as they stick together.

With Julie Scelfo

Young, Gay, and Murdered

Kids are coming out younger, but are schools ready to handle the complex issues of identity and sexuality? For Larry King, the question had tragic implications.

RAMIN SETOODEH

At 15, Lawrence King was small—5 feet 1 inch—but very hard to miss. In January, he started to show up for class at Oxnard, Calif.'s E. O. Green Junior High School decked out in women's accessories. On some days, he would slick up his curly hair in a Prince-like bouffant. Sometimes he'd paint his fingernails hot pink and dab glitter or white foundation on his cheeks. "He wore makeup better than I did," says Marissa Moreno, 13, one of his classmates. He bought a pair of stilettos at Target, and he couldn't have been prouder if he had on a varsity football jersey. He thought nothing of chasing the boys around the school in them, teetering as he ran.

But on the morning of Feb. 12, Larry left his glitter and his heels at home. He came to school dressed like any other boy: tennis shoes, baggy pants, a loose sweater over a collared shirt. He seemed unhappy about something. He hadn't slept much the night before, and he told one school employee that he threw up his breakfast that morning, which he sometimes did because he obsessed over his weight. But this was different. One student noticed that as Larry walked across the quad, he kept looking back nervously over his shoulder before he slipped into his first-period English class. The teacher, Dawn Boldrin, told the students to collect their belongings, and then marched them to a nearby computer lab, so they could type out their papers on World War II. Larry found a seat in the middle of the room. Behind him, Brandon McInerney pulled up a chair.

Brandon, 14, wasn't working on his paper, because he told Mrs. Boldrin he'd finished it. Instead, he opened a history book and started to read. Or at least he pretended to. "He kept looking over at Larry," says a student who was in the class that morning. "He'd look at the book and look at Larry, and look at the book and look at Larry." At 8:30 A.M., a half hour into class, Brandon quietly stood up. Then, without anyone's noticing, he removed a handgun that he had somehow sneaked to school, aimed it at Larry's head, and fired a single shot. Boldrin, who was across the room looking at another student's work, spun around. "Brandon, what the hell are you doing!" she screamed. Brandon fired at Larry a second time, tossed the gun on the

ground and calmly walked through the classroom door. Police arrested him within seven minutes, a few blocks from school. Larry was rushed to the hospital, where he died two days later of brain injuries.

Poster Boy: Larry has become a gay-rights icon, but the reason he died isn't as clear-cut as many people think.

The Larry King shooting became the most prominent gay-bias crime since the murder of Matthew Shepard 10 years ago. But despite all the attention and outrage, the reason Larry died isn't as clear-cut as many people think. California's Supreme Court has just legalized gay marriage. There are gay characters on popular TV shows such as "Gossip Girl" and "Ugly Betty," and no one seems to notice. Kids like Larry are so comfortable with the concept of being openly gay that they are coming out younger and younger. One study found that the average age when kids self-identify as gay has tumbled to 13.4; their parents usually find out a year later.

What you might call "the shrinking closet" is arguably a major factor in Larry's death. Even as homosexuality has become more accepted, the prospect of being openly gay in middle school raises a troubling set of issues. Kids may want to express who they are, but they are playing grown-up without fully knowing what that means. At the same time, teachers and parents are often uncomfortable dealing with sexual issues in children so young. Schools are caught in between. How do you protect legitimate, personal expression while preventing inappropriate, sometimes harmful, behavior? Larry King was, admittedly, a problematical test case: he was a troubled child who flaunted his sexuality and wielded it like a weapon—it was often his first line of defense. But his story sheds light on the difficulty of defining the limits of tolerance. As E. O. Green found, finding that balance presents an enormous challenge.

Larry's life was hard from the beginning. His biological mother was a drug user; his father wasn't in the picture. When Greg and Dawn King took him in at age 2, the family was told he wasn't being fed regularly. Early on, a speech impediment made Larry difficult to understand, and he repeated first grade because he had trouble reading. He was a gentle child who loved nature and crocheting, but he also acted out from an early age. "We couldn't take him to the grocery store without him shoplifting," Greg says. "We couldn't get him to clean up his room. We sent him upstairs—he'd get a screwdriver and poke holes in the walls." He was prescribed ADHD medication, and Greg says Larry was diagnosed with reactive attachment disorder, a rare condition in which children never fully bond with their caregivers or parents.

Kids started whispering about Larry when he was in third grade at Hathaway Elementary School. "In a school of 700 students, you'd know Larry," says Sarah Ranjbar, one of Larry's principals. "He was slightly effeminate but very sure of his personality." Finally, his best friend, Averi Laskey, pulled him aside one day at the end of class. "I said, 'Larry, are you gay?' He said, 'Yeah, why?' " He was 10. Averi remembers telling Larry she didn't care either way, but Larry started telling other students, and they did. They called him slurs and avoided him at recess. One Halloween, someone threw a smoke bomb into his house, almost killing the family's Jack Russell terrier. In the sixth grade, a girl started a "Burn Book"—an allusion to a book in the movie "Mean Girls," where bullies scribble nasty rumors about the people they hate—about Larry. The Larry book talked about how he was gay and falsely asserted that he dressed in Goth and drag. And it ended with a threat: "I hate Larry King. I wish he was dead," according to one parent's memory of the book. "The principal called my wife on the phone and she was crying," Greg says. "She found the book, and said we needed to do something to help protect Larry." His parents transferred him to another elementary school, hoping he could get a fresh start before he started junior high.

E. O. Green is a white slab of concrete in a neighborhood of pink and yellow homes. In the afternoons, SUVs roll down the street like gumballs, the sound of hip-hop music thumping. Once the students leave the campus, two blue gates seal it shut, and teachers are told not to return to school after dark, because of gang violence. Outside, there's a worn blue sign that greets visitors: this was a California distinguished school in 1994. The school is under a different administration now.

'Random people would come up to Larry and start laughing,' Moreno says. 'I thought that was very rude.'

E. O. Green was a comfortable place for Larry when he arrived as a seventh grader. He hung out with a group of girls who, unlike in elementary school, didn't judge him. But that didn't mean he was entirely accepted. In gym class, some of his friends say that the boys would shove him around in the locker room. After he started dressing up, he was ridiculed even more. He lost a high heel once and the boys tossed it around at lunch like a football. "Random people would come up to him and start laughing," Moreno says. "I thought that was very rude." One day, in science class, he was singing "Somewhere Over the Rainbow" to himself. Kids nearby taunted him for being gay. "He said to me, 'It's OK'," says Vanessa Castillo, a classmate. " 'One day, they'll regret it. One day, I'll be famous'."

Larry's home life wasn't getting any better. At 12, he was put on probation for vandalizing a tractor with a razor blade, and he entered a counseling program, according to his father. One therapist said Larry might be autistic. At 14, Larry told Greg he thought he was bisexual. "It wouldn't matter either way to me," Greg says. "I thought maybe some of the problems would go away if we supported him." But the therapist told Greg he thought that Larry was just trying to get attention and might not understand what it meant to be gay. Larry began telling his teachers that his father was hitting him. Greg says he never harmed Larry; still, the authorities removed Larry from his home in November 2007. He moved to Casa Pacifica, a group home and treatment center in Camarillo, five miles away from Oxnard.

Larry seemed to like Casa Pacifica—"peaceful home" in Spanish. The 23-acre facility—more like a giant campground, with wooden cottages, a basketball court and a swimming pool—has 45 beds for crisis kids who need temporary shelter. Every day a driver would take Larry to school, and some weeks he went to nearby Ventura, where he attended gay youth-group meetings. "I heard this was the happiest time of his life," says Vicki Murphy, the center's director of operations. For Christmas, the home gave Larry a $75 gift card for Target. He spent it on a pair of brown stiletto shoes.

In January, after a few months at Casa Pacifica, Larry decided to dress like a girl. He went to school accessorized to the max, and his already colorful personality got louder. He accused a girl to her face of having breast implants. Another girl told him she didn't like his shoes. "I don't like your necklace," Larry snapped back. Larry called his mom from Casa Pacifica to tell her that he wanted to get a sex-change operation. And he told a teacher that he wanted to be called Leticia, since no one at school knew he was half African-American. The teacher said firmly, "Larry, I'm not calling you Leticia." He dropped the idea without an argument.

The staff at E. O. Green was clearly struggling with the Larry situation—how to balance his right to self-expression while preventing it from disrupting others. Legally, they couldn't stop him from wearing girls' clothes, according to the California Attorney General's Office, because of a state hate-crime law that prevents gender discrimination. Larry, being Larry, pushed his rights as far as he could. During lunch, he'd sidle up to the popular boys' table and say in a high-pitched voice, "Mind if I sit here?" In the locker room, where he was often ridiculed, he got even by telling the boys, "You look hot," while they were changing, according to the mother of a student.

Larry was eventually moved out of the P.E. class, though the school didn't seem to know the extent to which he was clashing with other boys. One teacher describes the gym transfer as more of a "preventative measure," since Larry complained that one student wouldn't stop looking at him. In other classes, teachers were baffled that Larry was allowed to draw so much attention to himself. "All the teachers were complaining, because it was disruptive," says one of them. "Dress code is a huge issue at our school. We fight [over] it every day." Some teachers thought Larry was clearly in violation of the code, which prevents students from wearing articles of clothing considered distracting. When Larry wore lipstick and eyeliner to school for the first time, a teacher told him to wash it off, and he did. But the next day, he was back wearing even more. Larry told the teacher he could wear makeup if he wanted to. He said that Ms. Epstein told him that was his right.

Joy Epstein was one of the school's three assistant principals, and as Larry became less inhibited, Epstein became more a source of some teachers' confusion and anger. Epstein, a calm, brown-haired woman with bifocals, was openly gay to her colleagues, and although she was generally not out to her students, she kept a picture of her partner on her desk that some students saw. While her job was to oversee the seventh graders, she formed a special bond with Larry, who was in the eighth grade. He dropped by her office regularly, either for counseling or just to talk—she won't say exactly. "There was no reason why I specifically started working with Larry," Epstein says. "He came to me." Some teachers believe that she was encouraging Larry's flamboyance, to help further an "agenda," as some put it. One teacher complains that by being openly gay and discussing her girlfriend (presumably, no one would have complained if she had talked about a husband), Epstein brought the subject of sex into school. Epstein won't elaborate on what exactly she said to Larry because she expects to be called to testify at Brandon's trial, but it's certain to become one of the key issues. William Quest, Brandon's public defender, hasn't disclosed his defense strategy, but he has accused the school of failing to intercede as the tension rose between Larry and Brandon. Quest calls Epstein "a lesbian vice principal with a political agenda." Larry's father also blames Epstein. He's hired an attorney and says he is seriously contemplating a wrongful-death lawsuit. "She started to confuse her role as a junior-high principal," Greg King says. "I think that she was asserting her beliefs for gay rights." In a tragedy such as this, the natural impulse is to try to understand why it happened and to look for someone to blame. Epstein won't discuss the case in detail and, until she testifies in court, it's impossible to know what role—if any—she played in the events leading to Larry's death.

Whatever Epstein said to Larry, it's clear that his coming out proved to be a fraught process, as it can often be. For tweens, talking about being gay isn't really about sex. They may be aware of their own sexual attraction by the time they're 10, according to Caitlin Ryan, a researcher at San Francisco State University, but those feelings are too vague and unfamiliar to be their primary motivation. (In fact, Larry told a teacher that he'd never kissed anyone, male or female.) These kids are actually concerned with exploring their identity. "When you're a baby, you cry when you're hungry because you don't know the word for it," says Allan Acevedo, 19, of San Diego, who came out when he was in eighth grade. "Part of the reason why people are coming out earlier is they have the word 'gay,' and they know it explains the feeling." Like older teenagers, tweens tend to tell their friends first, because they think they'll be more accepting. But kids that age often aren't equipped to deal with highly personal information, and middle-school staffs are almost never trained in handling kids who question their sexuality. More than 3,600 high schools sponsor gay-straight alliances designed to foster acceptance of gay students, but only 110 middle schools have them. Often the entire school finds out before either the student or the faculty is prepared for the attention and the backlash. "My name became a punch line very fast," says Grady Keefe, 19, of Branford, Conn., who came out in the eighth grade. "The guidance counselors told me I should not have come out because I was being hurt."

The faculty tried to help Larry as he experimented with his identity, but he liked to talk in a roar.

The staff at E. O. Green tried to help as Larry experimented with his identity, but he liked to talk in a roar. One teacher asked him why he taunted the boys in the halls, and Larry replied, "It's fun to watch them squirm." But Brandon McInerney was different. Larry really liked Brandon. One student remembered that Larry would often walk up close to Brandon and stare at him. Larry had studied Brandon so well, he once knew when he had a scratch on his arm—Larry even claimed that he had given it to Brandon by mistake, when the two were together. Larry told one of his close friends that he and Brandon had dated but had broken up. He also said that he'd threatened to tell the entire school about them, if Brandon wasn't nicer to him. Quest, Brandon's defense attorney, says there was no relationship between Larry and Brandon, and one of Larry's teachers says that Larry was probably lying to get attention.

Like Larry, Brandon had his share of troubles. His parents, Kendra and Bill McInerney, had a difficult, tempestuous relationship. In 1993, Kendra alleged that Bill pointed a .45 handgun at her during a drunken evening and shot her in the arm, according to court records. She and Bill split in 2000, when Brandon was 6. One September morning, a fight broke out after Kendra accused her husband of stealing the ADHD medication prescribed to one of her older sons from her first marriage. Bill "grabbed Kendra by the hair," and "began choking her until she was almost unconscious," according to Kendra's version of the events filed in court documents. He pleaded no contest to corporal injury to a spouse and was sentenced to 10 days in jail. In a December 2001 court filing for a restraining order against Kendra, he claimed that she had turned her home into a "drug house." "I was very functional," Kendra later explained to a local newspaper, in a story about meth addiction. By 2004, she had entered a rehab program, and Brandon went to live with his father. But he spent years caught in the middle of a war.

While his life did seem to become more routine living with his dad, Brandon's troubles resurfaced in the eighth grade. His father was working in a town more than 60 miles away, and he was alone a lot. He began hanging out with a group of misfits on the beach. Although he was smart, he didn't seem to have much interest in school. Except for Hitler—Brandon knew all about the Nuremberg trials and all the names of Hitler's deputies. (When other kids asked him how he knew so much, he replied casually, "Don't you watch the History Channel?" Brandon's father says his son was interested in World War II, but not inappropriately.) By the end of the first semester, as his overall GPA tumbled from a 3.3 to a 1.9, he was kicked out of his English honors class for not doing his work and causing disruptions. He was transferred to Boldrin's English class, where he joined Larry.

Larry's grades were also dropping—he went from having a 1.71 GPA in November to a 1.0 in February, his father says. But he was too busy reveling in the spotlight to care. "He was like Britney Spears," says one teacher who knew Larry. "Everyone wanted to know what's the next thing he's going to do." Girls would take photos of him on their camera phones and discuss him with their friends. "My class was in a frenzy every day with Larry stories," says a humanities teacher who didn't have Larry as one of her students. He wore a Playboy-bunny necklace, which one of his teachers told him to remove because it was offensive to women. But those brown Target stilettos wobbled on.

The commotion over Larry's appearance finally forced the school office to take formal action. On Jan. 29, every teacher received an e-mail with the subject line "Student Rights". It was written by Sue Parsons, the eighth-grade assistant principal. "We have a student on campus who has chosen to express his sexuality by wearing make-up," the e-mail said without mentioning Larry by name. "It is his right to do so. Some kids are finding it amusing, others are bothered by it. As long as it does not cause classroom disruptions he is within his rights. We are asking that you talk to your students about being civil and non-judgmental. They don't have to like it but they need to give him his space. We are also asking you to watch for possible problems. If you wish to talk further about it please see me or Ms. Epstein."

Jerry Dannenberg, the superintendent, says the front office received no complaints about Larry, but according to several faculty members, at least two teachers tried to formally protest what was going on. The first was the same teacher who told Larry to scrub the makeup off his face. She was approached by several boys in her class who said that Larry had started taunting them in the halls—"I know you want me," he'd say—and their friends were calling them gay. The teacher told some of her colleagues that when she went to the office to file a complaint, Epstein said she would take it. "It's about Larry," the teacher said. "There's nothing we can do about that," Epstein replied. (Epstein denies she was ever approached.) A few days later another teacher claims to have gone to the school principal, Joel Lovstedt. The teacher says she told him that she was concerned about Larry and she thought he was a danger to himself—she worried that he might fall in his three-inch stilettos and injure himself. Lovstedt told the teacher that he had directions, though

he wouldn't say from where, that they couldn't intervene with Larry's sexual expression. (Lovstedt denied *Newsweek's* request for an interview.) There was an unusual student complaint, too. Larry's younger brother, Rocky, 12, also attended E. O. Green, and the kids started picking on him the day in January when Larry showed up in hot pink knee-length boots. Rocky says he went to several school officials for help, including Epstein. "I went up to her at lunchtime," he says. "I said, 'Ms. Epstein, can you stop Larry from dressing like a girl? The kids are saying since Larry is gay, I must be gay, too, because I'm his brother'."

As you talk to the teachers, many of them say they tried to support Larry, but they didn't always know how. In blue-collar, immigrant Oxnard, there is no gay community to speak of and generally very little public discussion of gay issues, at least until Larry's murder happened. One teacher was very protective of Larry, his English teacher, Mrs. Boldrin. To help Larry feel better about moving to Casa Pacifica, she brought Larry a present: a green evening dress that once belonged to her own daughter. Before school started, Larry ran to the bathroom to try it on. Then he showed it to some of his friends, telling them that he was going to wear it at graduation.

A nd then there was Valentine's Day. A day or two before the shooting, the school was buzzing with the story about a game Larry was playing with a group of his girlfriends in the outdoor quad. The idea was, you had to go up to your crush and ask them to be your Valentine. Several girls named boys they liked, then marched off to complete the mission. When it was Larry's turn, he named Brandon, who happened to be playing basketball nearby. Larry walked right on to the court in the middle of the game and asked Brandon to be his Valentine. Brandon's friends were there and started joking that he and Larry were going to make "gay babies" together. At the end of lunch, Brandon passed by one of Larry's friends in the hall. She says he told her to say goodbye to Larry, because she would never see him again.

The friend didn't tell Larry about the threat—she thought Brandon was just kidding. There are many rumors of another confrontation between Larry and Brandon, on Feb. 11, the day before the shooting. Several students and teachers said they had heard about a fight between the two but they hadn't actually witnessed it themselves. The next morning a counselor at Casa Pacifica asked Larry what was wrong, and he said, vaguely, "I've had enough." When he got to school, his friends quizzed him about his noticeably unfabulous appearance. He said that he ran out of makeup and hair gel (which wasn't true) and that he had a blister on his ankle (this was true—he'd just bought a new pair of boots). Larry walked alongside Boldrin to the computer class and sat in front of a computer. A few minutes later, a counselor summoned him to her office. She told him that his grades were so low, he was at risk of not graduating from the eighth grade. He went back to his computer. He had written his name on his paper as Leticia King. Most of the campus heard the gunshots. Some described it like a door slammed shut very hard.

On March 7, the school held a memorial service for Larry. Epstein stood at the podium with students who read from notecards about what they liked best about Larry: he was nice, he was unique, he was brave. The band played "Amazing Grace," and two dozen doves were released into the sky. Averi read a poem about how her friend was like a garden seed that grew, and died; Larry's mom wept in the front row. Deep in the audience, an eighth grader turned to one of Brandon's friends and whispered, "That's so gay."

The obvious question now is whether Larry's death could have been prevented. "Absolutely," says Dannenberg. "Why do we have youngsters that have access to guns? Why don't we have adequate funding to pay for social workers at the school to make sure students have resources? We have societal issues." Many teachers and parents aren't content with that answer. For them, the issue isn't whether Larry was gay or straight—his father still isn't convinced his son was gay—but whether he was allowed to push the boundaries so far that he put himself and others in danger. They're not blaming Larry for his own death—as if anything could justify his murder—but their attitude toward his assailant is not unsympathetic. "We failed Brandon," a teacher says. "We didn't know the bullying was coming from the other side—Larry was pushing as hard as he could, because he liked the attention."

Greg King doesn't feel sympathy for Brandon, but he does believe his son sexually harassed him. He's resentful that the gay community has appropriated his son's murder as part of a larger cause. "I think the gay-rights people want it to be a gay-rights issue, because it makes a poster child out of my son," King says. "That bothered me. I'm not anti-gay. I have a lot of co-workers and friends who are gay." That anger was made worse when he heard this summer that Epstein would be promoted to principal of an elementary school. "This is a slap in the face of my family," Greg says. Many teachers wonder if the district moved her because she had become a lightning rod for criticism after Larry's death. Dannenberg, the superintendent, says that she was the most qualified person for the new principal job.

'If we're going to be sure this isn't going to happen again,' says Elaine Garber, 'this has got to be discussed more.'

The school has conducted its own investigation, though its lawyer won't make it public. But it will likely be brought up when Brandon goes to trial. He is charged with first-degree murder and a hate crime, and is scheduled to be arraigned this week. Hundreds of his classmates have signed a petition asking that he be tried in juvenile court. The district attorney wants him tried as an adult, which could result in a prison sentence of 51 years to life. "Brandon was being terrorized," says Bill, who has set up a public defense fund in his son's name. "He was being stalked almost, to the degree of the school should have never let this happen." What happened to Larry and Brandon was certainly extreme, but it has implications for schools across the country. "If we're going to be absolutely sure this isn't going to happen again," says Elaine Garber, 81, who has served on the school's board for 48 years, "this has got to be discussed some more."

As if anyone has stopped talking—and arguing—about Larry King. He had an entire page devoted to him in the E. O. Green yearbook. On the Internet, he's become a gay martyr, and this year's National Day of Silence, an annual event created to raise awareness of homophobia, was dedicated to Larry. And in Averi Laskey's bedroom, she still keeps a handmade purple get-well card she made for Larry on the day after he was shot. At the time, there was still hope he would pull through. He had survived the night, which the doctors said was a good sign. Averi rounded up dozens of teachers and friends between classes to sign messages of encouragement. "Larry, I miss you. Get better," Boldrin wrote in blue ink. "Keep up your spirit. A lot of people are rooting for you to get better," the principal wrote. Some of Larry's classmates apologized for how he had been treated. A few even left their phone numbers, so he could call them if he ever needed to talk to someone. But when Averi got home that day, she learned that Larry had suffered a fatal stroke. Larry was pronounced brain-dead that afternoon, and the family decided to donate his organs. The following day, Feb. 14, doctors harvested his pancreas, liver, lungs and the most important organ of all, which now beats inside the chest of a 10-year-old girl. On Valentine's Day, Larry King gave away his heart, but not in the way he thought he would.

With Andrew Murr and Jennifer Ordoñez.

Interview with Dr. Craig Anderson
Video Game Violence

Dr. Craig Anderson, a leader in the research on the effects of exposure to violent video games on aggressive behavior, was invited to speak at Nebraska Wesleyan University. A group of Nebraska Wesleyan University students interviewed Dr. Anderson. We explored his interest and experiences in this research area.

SARAH HOWE, JENNIFER STIGGE, AND BROOKE SIXTA

Since 1997, Nebraska Wesleyan University (NE) has held an endowed lecture to honor the 40-year career of Dr. Clifford Fawl. The FAWL Lecture Series brings distinguished psychologists to the Wesleyan campus to present their research and interact with undergraduate psychology students. On March 22, 2007, we welcomed Dr. Craig Anderson as the FAWL lecturer to speak on *Violent Video Games: Theory, Research, and Public Policy.*

Dr. Craig Anderson received his bachelors degree at Butler University (IN) in 1976. He earned a masters degree (1978) and PhD (1980) in psychology at Stanford University (CA). He currently is a distinguished professor of psychology at Iowa State University and is widely regarded as the leader in research on the effects of violent video games and other forms of media violence. He has published widely on depression, loneliness, and shyness; attribution processes; social judgment; and human aggression. He has earned recognition as the second most highly cited scholar in social psychology textbooks. He has testified before the U.S. Senate Committee on Commerce, Science and Transportation's hearing on "The Impact of Interactive Violence on Children" and has served on the Media Violence Expert Panel for the Surgeon General.

Dr. Anderson started his visit by discussing the importance of good methodology to a research methods class. He was then interviewed by a small group of Wesleyan students concerning his work on violence and video games.

Student: What was your motivation for starting research on media violence and video games?

Anderson: It originally had to do with working on the General Aggression Model and learning about the media violence literature. There were literally hundreds of studies, but there were still gaps and unanswered questions. I had some students looking for research topics that were interesting and publishable, and then they identified gaps in the research. That was the initial reason. Later they basically extended the research using video games to test some aspects of the General Aggression Model. Next, my research team looked at priming issues, which prior to our work, had never been used in the context of media violence effects. After talking to some colleagues in cognitive psychology and debating about which method to use, we thought of using some cognitive measures such as a modified Stroop test but we chose a reading reaction time task.

Student: Looking back on many of your articles, we noticed you first did a study on video games in 1987 and another in 1995, but the majority of your studies have been since 1999. Did this more recent increase in research on the effects of video games have anything to do with Columbine and other school shootings?

Anderson: No, it had to do with an internal grant I received about 1996. It funded three graduate students and enabled us to start doing research on the effects of violent video games. I had been writing grant proposals on the topic for some time, but this was the first time I had the opportunity to do some of those studies. Then, Columbine came along.

Student: Were you asked to help with any of the Columbine research?

Anderson: No, although I was asked to testify in the U.S. Senate hearing about violent video games some time after the shooting.

Student: What group of people do you think are the most susceptible to the effects of violent video games, and why?

Anderson: Many researchers in the field of media violence think that people who are high on what you would call trait aggression (especially children and adolescents) are going to be more influenced by exposure to media violence than people who are low on trait aggression. In other words, many scholars believe that highly aggressive people are more susceptible to the harmful effects of media violence than are nonaggressive people. However, I think that the research evidence over the years doesn't bear that out, yet. Some studies show this heightened susceptibility of highly aggressive people, but some studies show the opposite including one of my studies (Anderson, 1997). That study found that people who are lowest on trait aggression showed the biggest effect of a violent movie manipulation. Those data yielded a significant interaction between measures of trait aggression and measures of media violence exposure. The nonaggressive people who watched a violent movie clip displayed more aggressive thoughts than nonaggressive people who saw the nonviolent clip, but highly aggressive people were relatively unaffected by the movie clip manipulation. Other researchers have found the opposite type of interaction. For example, in some studies those who score high on trait aggressiveness and have been exposed to a lot of violent media are the ones who are most likely to have, at some time in their lives, been arrested for assault. Well, is that because the media violence effect only operates on high trait-aggressive people? Perhaps low traitaggressive people are equally affected, but because their general level of aggression is low, media violence can't increase their willingness to aggress enough to rise to the level of assaulting someone.

Student: From where do you recruit your participants?

Anderson: Well, very often, it's a convenience sample. However, the present grant research that my colleagues/students and I have been doing allows us to pay participants. So we are able to pay kids to play video games, which they think is great (laughter). Some try to come in two or three times, and we have to tell them they cannot. In these situations, we have to select samples to fit the particular research question or issue.

Student: In your experimental research, how do you account for the participants who regularly play video games from those who have little to no experience?

Anderson: We usually give the participants questionnaires that tell us how much the individuals have played and what kinds of games they play. Prior experience with video games can then figure into the data analysis. We seldom find any kind of difference in our experimental studies between those participants with a lot of experience and those without. The one difference we do find is that participants with a lot of gaming experience really like being in the violent video game condition. Typically, we do not find much of a statistically reliable effect of gaming experience on aggressive thought processes and behavior.

Student: Do you feel that your research has or will have an impact on the video game industry? If so, what impact do you think it will have?

Anderson: Our research has probably had a bigger impact in countries other than in the United States. Almost every other modern country has legal restrictions on violent media including video games. Many of them ban some of the games outright and most have age-based restrictions. Certainly the research that my students and I have done over the years has been used by child advocacy groups and others in these countries to make sure that these ratings are enforced. The research certainly has increased the awareness of the issue in the United States. However, there

are no U.S. laws regarding violent video games. I have never said publicly whether I support a legislative solution, because my political opinion is not relevant to what I regard as my scientific expertise. Even in the court cases with which I have been involved, I say upfront that I will not comment on what I think about the law under judicial review. I will talk about what the science says or what it cannot say. The work and interviews that we've done concerning violence in video games is used to get the word out to parents about the effect of violent video games. Our research has had a big impact on parents, but not as big as it needs to be. There are still people teaching their 2- or 3-year-olds how to shoot a gun in these video games.

Student: What are some of the stronger arguments against your research? How do you counter those arguments?

Anderson: One of the best arguments, until recently, is that there are no longitudinal studies, but we have now published one (Anderson, Gentile, & Buckley, 2007). Previously in my various talks, I had described the lack of longitudinal data on the effects of video games. The paucity of these studies was due to the lack of government support for longitudinal research. The support for the longitudinal study I just mentioned came from non-governmental sources. More recently, we finally got the funding needed to perform a larger, longer-term longitudinal study after being turned down six or seven times. There really aren't any long-term longitudinal studies, such as when you follow the group of individuals and see where these participants end up after several years. Some participants may end up in jail, juvenile detention facilities, or kicked out of school, which makes this an important field of interest. A response to this criticism about the lack of longitudinal studies on violent video games is that such studies have already been done pertaining to television violence, which is the same phenomenon, but some individuals fail to see the similarities between violence on television and violence in video games. People used this lack of a longitudinal study, focusing on violent video games, as a criticism for the evidence found between increased aggression and exposure to violent video games. Of course, they can no longer do this.

Student: Do you have any plans for the future implementation of your research? How should your research be applied to schools, home, everyday life, etc.?

Anderson: We haven't been thinking much about intervention studies, mainly because I don't do intervention studies. There is a group at Iowa State University that does intervention studies, but most of their work focuses on drug use and intervention to reduce kids' use of alcohol, tobacco, and various illegal substances. There have been some TV/video game interventions done in school systems, but intervention as a whole is done by another group of researchers.

Student: Where do you think video game research will go from here?

Anderson: There are two related issues that are going to be big soon. One is the identification of video game addiction or Internet addiction, including text messaging, as a true addiction in need of clinical intervention for some individuals.

The other has to do with attention deficit disorders, executive control, and impulse control. There is potential long-term damage in those brain systems due to extensive viewing of media that flash across the screen and demand constantly shifting attention. Some evidence indicates that extensive use of screening media, whether it is violent or not, leads to attention deficit disorder, especially in very young children who see a lot of TV.

References

Anderson, C. A. (1997). Effects of violent movies and trait irritability on hostile feelings and aggressive thoughts. *Aggressive Behavior, 23*, 161–178.

Anderson, C. A., Gentile, D. A., & Buckley, K. E. (2007). *Violent video game effects on children and adolescents.* New York: Oxford University Press.

SARAH HOWE, a junior at Nebraska Wesleyan University, is a psychology major with a minor in health and human performance. Following graduation, she plans to attend graduate school in counseling. JENNIFER STIGGE, also a junior at Nebraska Wesleyan University, is an industrial-organizational psychology (I/O psychology) major with a business administration minor. She plans to begin graduate school in the fall of 2009 in I/O psychology. BROOKE SIXTA graduated from Nebraska Wesleyan University in December of 2007 with a bachelor's degree in psychology and a minor in business administration. She is currently working; however, plans to also attend I/O psychology graduate school beginning at the fall of 2008.

Author's note—We would like to thank Dr. Anderson for visiting with Nebraska Wesleyan students and faculty, and presenting his research regarding violence and video games. We would also like to give a special thanks to Dr. Marilyn Petro, Dr. Michael Tagler, Allyson Bell, and Amanda Holmgren for their assistance with the process of this interview.

Jail Time Is Learning Time

Signe Nelson and Lynn Olcott

There is excitement in the large, well-lit classroom. Student work, including history posters and artwork, adorn the walls. A polite shuffling of feet can be heard, as names are called and certificates presented. It is the graduation ceremony at the Onondaga County Justice Center in Syracuse, N.Y. The ceremony is held several times a year, recognizing inmates in the Incarcerated Education Program who have passed the GED exam or completed a 108-hour vocational program. The courses in the Incarcerated Education Program are geared to prepare inmates to transition successfully to several different settings.

The Incarcerated Education Program is a joint effort by the Syracuse City School District and the Onondaga County Sheriff's Office, and is housed inside the nine-story Onondaga County Justice Center in downtown Syracuse. The Justice Center is a 250,000 square-foot maximum-security, nonsentenced facility, completed and opened in 1995. The facility was built to contain 616 beds, but currently houses 745 inmates. Between 13,000 and 14,000 inmates passed through booking during 2004. About 2,500 of them were minors.

The Justice Center

The Justice Center is a state-of-the-art facility, designed for and operating on the direct supervision model. Direct supervision is a method of inmate management developed by the federal government in 1974 for presentenced inmates in the Federal Bureau of Prisons. There are about 140 such facilities operating throughout the United States and a few hundred currently under construction. Direct supervision places a single deputy directly in a "housing pod" with between 32 and 64 inmates. Maximum pod capacity in the Onondaga County Justice Center is 56 inmates. Inmates are given either relative freedom of movement within the pod or confined to their cells based on their behavior.

The program has been providing courses and classes at the Justice Center for 10 years, but this partnership between the school district and the sheriff's office began almost 30 years ago with the provision of GED instruction. The Incarcerated Education Program was originally conceived to ensure education for inmates who are minors. The program has grown tremendously and now has more than 20 offerings in academic, vocational and life management areas.

The Syracuse City School District professional staff includes six full-time and 18 part-time teachers and staff members. The program is unique in that there are three Onondaga County Sheriff's sergeants who hold New York State Adult Education certification and who teach classes in the vocational component. An average of 250 inmates, or about one-third of the Justice Center's incarcerated population, are enrolled in day and/or evening classes. There are about 250 hours of class time in the facility per week.

Varied Educational and Training Opportunities

As in the public education sector, vocational programs have evolved with the times. The Basic Office Skills class now offers two sections, and includes computer repair and office production skills. A course in building maintenance can be complemented by a course in pre-application to pre-apprenticeship plumbing, or in painting and surface preparation, a class that includes furniture refinishing. A baking class and nail technology have been added in the past few years. All vocational courses, before implementation, are approved by the New York State Education Department and are designed to be consistent with New York State Department of Labor employment projections for Onondaga County. No vocational programming is implemented without first identifying whether the occupation is an area of growth in the community.

Additionally, a broadly inclusive advisory board, made up of community representatives who are stakeholders in the local economy and in the quality of life in the Syracuse metropolitan area has been established. The Incarcerated Education Advisory Board meets approximately three times a year to discuss the perceived needs of the community and to address strategies for transitioning students into employment. Ongoing topics of study are issues surrounding employment, continuing education and housing.

Incarcerated Education Program planners are very aware that job skills are ineffective without proper work attitudes. Job Readiness Training addresses work ethic, proper work behavior, communication and critical behavior skills. Vocational classes are voluntary for the nonsentenced population. However, because of their popularity, a waiting list is maintained for several courses. Among these popular courses are Basic Office

Skills and Small Engine Repair. An additional section of Small Engine Repair has been added for female inmates in the class to ensure gender equity in this training opportunity.

New York State law requires that incarcerated minors continue their education while incarcerated. The Incarcerated Education Program enrolls inmates, ages 16 to 21, in Adult Basic Education/GED classes and addresses students with special needs. Other adult inmates attend on a voluntary basis. Inmates are given an initial placement test to determine math and reading skill levels. Because inmates work at a wide range of ability levels, instruction is individualized and materials are geared to independent work. English as a second Language and English Literacy/Civics are complementary offerings for inmates who are in need of assistance in English language proficiency and knowledge of American culture and history.

The GED exam is given at the Justice Center every 60 days or more often as needed. In the past three years, 225 students have taken the exam. Passing rates fluctuate between 63 percent and 72 percent. The average passing rate for correctional institutions in New York is about 51 percent. The state average passing rate for the general public in community-based courses is fairly stable at 50 percent.[1]

Of course, not everyone will take the GED. Student turnover is high, as inmates are released, bailed out, sent to treatment centers, or sentenced to county, state and federal correctional facilities. Judy Fiorini is a GED teacher who has been with the program for more than 10 years. "Many go back out into our community. We try to teach them something useful for their lives," Fiorini explains.

Transition services form an integral part of the program. The focus is on minors, but help is available for everyone. Two fulltime staff members assist people upon release, with such important tasks as acquiring a driver's license, seeking housing, reenrolling in high school or preparing for job interviews. A very important part of transition services is helping people acquire birth certificates, social security cards and other documents crucial for identification.

Tackling Cognitive Issues

Corrections professionals and educators are aware that it is not enough to improve the skill base of an inmate. There must be cognitive changes as well. The justice center is not a treatment facility, but it has been evolving into a therapeutic community. As the Incarcerated Education Program has grown, there has been the flexibility to add several important courses dealing with life issues, attitude and decision-making. According to data provided by the justice center, about 80 percent of inmates have substance abuse-related issues at the time of their arrest. To support desired cognitive changes, the justice center began establishing "clean and sober" pods in 2002. Currently, there are several clean and sober pods, including pods for adult men, women and youths. There are waiting lists for placement in the clean and sober pods.

The Incarcerated Education Program has been offering anger management groups for several years. Anger management helps group members deal with compulsive behavior and focus on long-term goals. Other life management offerings include family education, action for personal choice and a course called Parent and Child Together. Most courses of study are developed inhouse by experienced professional faculty. Additionally, the program established gender-specific courses, Men's Issues and Women's Issues, to help inmates become more directly aware of their own responsibilities, separate from the role of a partner or significant other in their lives. The Men's Issues class is led by certified professionals and focuses on actions and their consequences. As in most jails, male inmates significantly outnumber female inmates. Courses and groups continue to be added, though it is sometimes difficult to find space for the abundance of activity in the program.

The program is financially supported, using state and federal funds, via nine carefully coordinated grants. Also significant for the success of the program has been ongoing encouragement and technical assistance from the New York State Education Department, the New York State Association of Incarcerated Education Programs and support from the New York State Sheriffs' Association.[2]

The Incarcerated Education Program continues to encounter challenges. It takes energy and dedication to keep the varied curricula substantial and cohesive, despite high student turnover and complex student needs. With a large civilian staff, the program requires close coordination between security and civilian concerns to help civilian staff work most effectively within the safety and security priorities of the facility. Biweekly meetings facilitate ongoing communication.

Making the Most of Time

Every available square inch of classroom space is in constant use. Classes have exceeded available space and some classes meet in core areas of the justice center as well. Several classes are held in the residence pods, where heavy, white tables are pulled together and portable white-boards are erected to create nomadic classrooms. Overall, the program is succeeding in several ways. Incarcerated minors are directly and meaningfully involved in high school equivalency classes, and inmates older than 21 receive academic and vocational services on a voluntary basis. All inmates are offered the opportunity for life-skills classes and for transitional services upon release. Time served at the Onondaga County Justice Center can also be time used for valuable academic, vocational and life management achievements.

Notes

1. New York State Department of Education maintains statistics for educational activities at correctional facilities in New York state. Patricia Mooney directs the GED Program for the state through the GED Testing Office in the State Department of Education. Greg Bayduss is the State Department of Education coordinator in charge of Incarcerated Education Programs throughout New York state.

2. State Professional Organizations: The New York State Association of Incarcerated Education Programs Inc. is a professional organization for teachers, administrators and security personnel (www.nysaiep.org). Its mission is to

promote excellence in incarcerated education programs in the state, support research in this field and advocate for incarcerated education initiatives through collaboration with other professional organizations. The authors must mention the valuable assistance of the New York State Sheriffs' Association, supporting each county sheriff, as the chief law enforcement officer in his or her county (www.nyssheriffs.org). The association provides valuable information and technical assistance to county sheriffs to help implement programs in their jails.

SIGNE NELSON is the coordinator of the Incarcerated Education Program, and LYNN OLCOTT is a teacher at Auburn Correctional Facility in New York, formerly with the Incarcerated Education Program. The program could not have attained its present strength without the vision and support of law enforcement officials Sheriff Kevin Walsh, Chief Anthony Callisto, and Syracuse City School District administrator Al Wolf. Special thanks to Capt. John Woloszyn, commander of Support Services; Sgt. Joseph Powlina, administrative compliance supervisor; and Deputy Joseph Caruso, photographer. Their assistance in the production of this article was crucial and much appreciated.

Finding a Job in the 21st Century

**Seek training, be flexible, and get hired in the
fast-moving working world of the future.**

JOHN A. CHALLENGER

The current recession, expected to be the worst economic crisis since the Great Depression, will surely put to rest those old concerns about looming labor shortages, right? Probably not. In fact, immigration, globalization, outsourcing, and other trends affecting employment and the workplace will evolve over the next five, 10, and 20 years to change the workplace completely, and well-trained and flexible workers will be at a premium.

More than 5 million layoffs have been announced in the United States since the beginning of 2008. Economists are projecting that U.S. unemployment may top out at 10.5% or over 11% by the middle of 2010.

At Challenger, Gray & Christmas, we look at official unemployment, but we also track job-cut announcements. These provide an indication of where the job market is going in the short term.

We observed in April that the rate of layoffs, while still high, was slowing. The global economy was not entering a roaring recovery, but we were hearing faint signals that the worst of the worst was over. On the one hand, manufacturing jobs in the United States continued to vanish. On the other hand, the layoff rate in the financial sector seemed to have stabilized.

At our firm, we talk to human-resources people around the country on a casual, anecdotal basis; the people we're speaking with are taking whatever measures they can to avoid making further layoffs. They don't want to be short-staffed in the event of a turnaround. The current cycle will surely go down in history as the worst in most people's memory. Fortunately, the future of work looks completely different.

Key Piece of Advice for Job Seekers

As unemployment continues to rise, more people are seeking help to improve their employability. My key piece of advice for job seekers is to get a fast start. Don't let your résumé gather dust. If you've been laid off, use contacts as quickly as possible to uncover new positions and opportunities.

The second piece of advice I offer is to consider changing industries. Look outside your normal boundaries, but look within your job function. You'll want to pursue jobs that correspond to your core competency and that let you do what you do best. Your skills are your best asset; they're what you're selling. Be ready to make the potential customer list for those skills as long as possible. What many people don't realize is the variety of jobs in different fields that may be open in a single industry, requiring people with all sorts of talents and abilities.

Let me give an example: Health care is commonly touted as an industry forever in need of workers. Conversely, the personal computer (PC) market in the United States has been weak of late. Our firm counted layoffs in the computer industry up 75% in 2008 from the year before, and analysts expect PC sales to fall an additional 10% by the end of 2009.

For a qualified IT worker or computer programmer seeking employment, one strategy is to wait for the global PC market to recover. Another strategy is to sell your technical skills to a growing industry like health care.

Most of us assume that growth in health care translates into more competition among employers to find qualified nurses and doctors. Surely, the doctor and nurse shortage will continue and favor qualified candidates for those jobs in the future. But in the years ahead, as baby boomers and the United States spend more money on medical care, the industry will need more computer scientists and database technicians to streamline operations and create new systems.

The coming innovation leap that will sweep the health-care field will extend well beyond simply digitizing medical records. If the industry is to meet rising demands for service from an aging population and contain costs, it will become much more reliant on information technology. The industry will need to reach and train qualified workers wherever they may be through e-learning technologies. Health-care providers will want to automate the delivery of health care as much as possible; they'll want to detect symptoms and diagnose patients remotely through advanced sensing technologies.

This is only one example among many. The health-care industry also needs therapists of all types, business managers,

U.S. Employment Ups and Downs, 2006–2016

The Five Largest Employment Increases

Job	Employees, 2006	Employees, 2016	Percentage Change
Network Systems and Data Communications Analyst	262,000	402,000	53.4%
Personal and Home Care Aide	767,000	1.16 million	50.6%
Home Health Aide	787,000	1.17 million	48.7%
Computer Software Engineer	507,000	733,000	44.6%
Veterinary Technologist/ Technician	71,000	100,000	41.0%

The Five Largest Employment Declines

Job	Employees, 2006	Employees, 2016	Percentage Change
Photographic Processing Machine Operator	49,000	25,000	–49.8%
File Clerk	234,000	137,000	–41.3%
Sewing Machine Operator	233,000	170,000	–27.2%
Electrical and Electronic Equipment Assembler	213,000	156,000	–26.8%
Computer Operator	130,000	98,000	–24.7%

Source: "Employment projections: 2006–2016." U.S. Bureau of labor statistics. Website, www.bls.gov.

human resource professionals, and even journalists and communications workers to track new developments and medical breakthroughs and publicize good work or medical research to the public (and to potential hospital donors). The world still needs journalists, but the information gathering and refinement process that is journalism will, more and more, happen at communications offices or niche-specific publications as opposed to regional or local newspapers. Finding opportunity in the future may mean sacrificing the dream of working for a particular cherished employer or even for a particular type of company. Many industrial titans of the twentieth century won't exist five years from now. That doesn't mean skills won't still be in demand.

The Globalized Workforce

Another question I'm asked frequently is, where are the jobs *going?* Many American workers fret about their jobs moving overseas to China and India. Outsourcing and even immigration have become convenient punching bags for pundits looking to blame someone or something for rising unemployment. But the argument that we can protect jobs by "keeping them at home"

or "not hiring immigrant labor" doesn't reflect the realities of globalization or labor in the twenty-first century.

The global labor market is not a zero-sum game. If U.S. firms are going to reach new customers in China and India—and they will have to in order to grow and be relevant in the twentyfirst century—then they will have to hire workers in those countries. More people in these countries finding work will create bigger markets for U.S. goods. China will continue to build factories and operations in order to put its large population to work; India will grow as a mathematics and engineering center. In the Philippines, a great accounting and health-care center exists; in South Korea, a manufacturing base is flourishing and will continue to do so.

All of these countries will experience employment growth, and yes, some of the growth will be from American firms hiring in those countries partly to better secure access to the Chinese and Indian consumers. There's no getting around it: U.S. companies need to be able to compete in these international markets if they are to expand in the United States.

However, companies from around the world will also have plenty of reasons to hire in the United States, which has a highly skilled labor force and the most diverse population of

Careers for "Re-Careering"

"Retirement years" may be a great time to take up a new line of work. According to a recent study, older workers tend to be more satisfied with their jobs, less stressed, and enjoy more flexible hours.

"Many older workers are ready to give up the long-time grind and look for stimulating jobs with flexible schedules as they begin the process toward retirement," says Susan Reinhard, senior vice president of the AARP's Public Policy Institute. AARP is the official name of the former American Association of Retired Persons.

The study surveyed 1,750 workers ages 55 and older over a period of 14 years. An overwhelming 91% say that they enjoy their current jobs, compared with 79% who said they liked the jobs they had held previously.

There are some tradeoffs, though. Most of the older workers who switched jobs took pay cuts, lost pension or health-care benefits, and forfeited some managerial duties.

Older workers who switch jobs tend to have lower wages than they earned in their previous jobs: $11 per hour versus $17 (36% difference). Older workers also lose pension coverage when they take up a new job, and they are less likely to have health coverage as an employment benefit. Still, Reinhard is optimistic.

"The current downturn presents a real bump in the road," She adds, "but, for the future, the findings are a welcome signal that workers 50 and over can really enjoy themselves while remaining productive in a vibrant economy."

AARP's website lists these as some of the most promising lines of work for adults over 55 to pursue:

- **Nursing.** As populations of elderly adults increase, so will the need for specialists in treating long-term health conditions.
- **Health-care technician.** Workers with training in laboratory operations, radiology, physical therapy, and nursing assistance will be in high demand.

- **Teacher and teaching assistant.** Society needs good teachers, especially given high teacher turnover and retirement rates.
- **Home health aide.** Specialists who can offer personalized care in the comfort of one's home will be in great demand.
- **Massage and yoga practitioner.** Most businesses expect to lose customers when economic times get tough, but not massage therapists or yoga practitioners. Many have seen their customer base expand due to stressed-out adults who need relief.
- **Car service technician.** Consumers are learning to be more frugal. That means maintaining the cars they have instead of buying new ones. Mechanics who can keep cars running are wanted.
- **Shoe worker and repairer.** Frugality applies to apparel as well. Customers are finding that fixing a good pair of shoes that wear out is much more economical than replacing them.
- **Office and administrative assistant.** Staffing agencies can steer skilled retirees to temporary, part-time, and temporary-to-hire administrative and office positions.
- **Health-care administration (nonmedical).** Medical facilities and insurance companies will need employees with general education and skills to handle administrative, clerical, and management responsibilities.
- **General merchandise.** Retirees with management experience may come in handy at department stores in any community.

—Rick Docksai

Source: AARP, www.aarp.org.

any country. The United States is uniquely suited to reach out to a global population.

The strength of the U.S. economy lies in its ability to capture global growth and to collaborate with economies around the planet. In the years ahead, the way that growth occurs will be very different from the past. From the middle of the twentieth century onward, U.S. companies began expanding aggressively into other countries; the pursuit of global growth translated into large U.S. firms cajoling foreign officials for special treatment or special contracts to set up shop. For U.S. employees overseas, a corporate expansion meant higher salaries and more money to live apart from the local community. I call this the colonial corporate expansion model.

IBM is one of the first big companies to transition out of that mode of overseas expansion and into a more community-focused strategy. In February 2009, IBM gave 4,000 laid-off workers the opportunity to move to other countries where the company had positions open (India and Brazil, for example)

through a program called Project Match. IBM was willing to pay for the move and help with visa procurement. The catch? The company told the employees that they would be paid local wages; the employees would live among the population.

Naturally, not every IBMer took to the idea. As originally reported in *Information Week,* one employee group called the Alliance@IBM was furious, complaining that the company was asking employees to "offshore themselves." They had a point; wages in India even for highly skilled IT workers are often a quarter of what they are in the United States.

But many of the employees—those with fewer commitments, who didn't have to worry about paying down a mortgage because they were young and just starting out, or who were looking to do something other than play shuffleboard in retirement— were intrigued by the idea and took the company up on the offer. Arrangements like Project Match may be a wave of the future, exciting and increasingly *de rigueur.* It reminds me of something I heard Larry Summers remark at a Harvard alumni event not long ago. When he was a student, he said, the final requirement to graduate was to swim a lap around the pool. In the future, it will be having spent a semester overseas.

Mobility, Flexibility, and the Workforce of the Future

IBM's Perfect Match program showcases one of the biggest trends to affect the future of work: increased mobility and flexibility. The information-technology revolution, which began with widespread adoption of PCs in the workplace in the 1980s, has changed virtually every aspect of doing business. In the next decade, that trend will accelerate and obliterate many long-held notions of work.

For many, the office of the future will not be an office at all. The mobile workforce will carry their office in their pocket; they'll work when it's most convenient for them or for the client. The U.S. Bureau of Labor Statistics reports that the number of Americans who worked from home or remotely at least one day per month for their employer rose from 12.4 million in 2006 to 17.2 million in 2008. (The trend may slow slightly in 2009.) Telecommuting is an easy way for employers facing tight budgets to give employees something that more and more of them say they want: time. Enhanced mobile flexibility will be a boon to the employers that take advantage of it as well. This will better enable smart companies to place employees where they can be most useful—namely, where customers and clients are located.

Contrary to a lot of popular opinion, face time is still important, but it may be less important within companies than between companies and customers.

Imagine, for instance, a customer walking into a car dealership and being greeted not by a salesperson but by an actual car designer, available to answer any and every technical query a consumer might have, or even design specifications on the spot (for a premium, of course). Many Ferrari buyers already get something like this royal treatment when they buy a new car directly from the factory in Maranello, Italy. For about $3.1 million, wealthy car enthusiasts can, in essence, design their own F430, 612 Scaglietti, or Enzo. What does the famously hobbled U.S. car industry look like when Chevrolet buyers can have the same personalized car-buying experience as someone buying a Ferrari Enzo?

Getting to that future from where we are now doesn't require a tremendous amount of technical IT innovation. What's needed is a little imagination and, again, flexibility. The twenty-somethings will lead this change. Today's younger workers will be the ones who help U.S. companies succeed abroad in the new era of globalization and mobility.

Hopefully, we'll continue to see more examples of the Project Match phenomenon playing with more people from more countries, coming to the United States to work as elements of the economy and to take advantage of U.S. educational opportunities. America's ability to attract these people is one of its key assets.

The U.S. economy will need these highly skilled workers desperately, a fact that underscores why immigration reform is so vital to the future of U.S. business. If the United States cannot remain an attractive destination for talented and well-trained workers from around the world, the country won't grow economically as it did in the past. Also, the U.S. government must find ways to support lifelong education. As new fields grow, education must become a permanent part of every worker's career. Immigration reform and lifelong learning are critical if the United States is to overcome the looming talent shortage. In the years ahead, it will pay dividends not just economically, but also in terms of more-effective foreign policy.

The more people from more places who feel they have a connection to America—either because someone they know has gone to America on a work or student visa or because they had a positive experience with a U.S. worker locally—the more effective the U.S. government will be in marketing its policies abroad. My hope is that people from around the world still want to take part in the U.S. educational experience. But American educational institutions will also expand as global brands with campuses in China, India, Europe, Africa, and Latin America.

The opportunities of the future will go to the best-trained, most-flexible candidates, and they will be spread globally. But opportunity exists and will increase; of that you can be certain.

JOHN A. CHALLENGER, chief executive officer of Challenger, Gray & Christmas, is one of the most quoted labor and employment experts in America. He's become a regular fixture on CNN, CBS, and a host of other networks and is a featured speaker at World-Future 2009, the annual conference of the World Future Society. Website www.challengergray.com.

Originally published in the September/October 2009, vol. 43, no.5, pp. 29–33 issue of *The Futurist*. Copyright © No.5 by World Future Society, 7910 Woodmont Avenue, Suite 450, Bethesda, MD 20814. Telephone: 301/656-8274; Fax: 301/951-0394; http://www.wfs.org. Used with permission from the World Future Society.

Hold Me Tight

Love demands the reassurance of a touch most fights are really protests over emotional disconnection. Underneath the distress, partners are desperate to know: Are you there for me?

SUE JOHNSON

I grew up in my parents' pub in England, where there was always a lot of drama. And all the drama—fights, flirting, tears, tantrums—revolved around love. I also watched my parents destroy their own love for each other. Since that time I've been on a mission to figure out exactly what love is. My mother described it as "a funny five minutes." It's also been called a mysterious mix of sentiment and sex. Or a combination of infatuation and companionship. Well, it's more than that.

My personal insights, gleaned from researching and counseling more than a thousand couples over 35 years, have now merged with a growing body of scientific studies, to the point where I can now say with confidence that we know what love is. It's intuitive and yet not necessarily obvious: It's the continual search for a basic, secure connection with someone else. Through this bond, partners in love become emotionally dependent on each other for nurturing, soothing, and protection.

We have a wired-in need for emotional contact and responsiveness from significant others. It's a survival response, the driving force of the bond of security a baby seeks with its mother. This observation is at the heart of attachment theory. A great deal of evidence indicates that the need for secure attachment never disappears; it evolves into the adult need for a secure emotional bond with a partner. Think of how a mother lovingly gazes at her baby, just as two lovers stare into each other's eyes.

Although our culture has framed dependency as a bad thing, a weakness, it is not. Being attached to someone provides our greatest sense of security and safety. It means depending on a partner to respond when you call, to know that you matter to him or her, that you are cherished, and that he will respond to your emotional needs.

The most basic tenet of attachment theory is that isolation—not just physical isolation but emotional isolation—is traumatizing for human beings. The brain actually codes it as danger. Gloria Steinem once said a woman needs a man like a fish needs a bicycle. That's nonsense.

The drama of love that I saw played out at the bar each night as a child is all about the human hunger for safe emotional connection, a survival imperative we experience from the cradle to the grave. Once we do feel safely linked with our partner, we can tolerate the hurts they will—inevitably—inflict upon us in the course of daily life.

Broken Connections

We start out intensely connected to and responsive to our partners. But our level of attentiveness tends to drop off over time. We then experience moments of disconnection, times when we don't express our needs clearly. He is upset and really wants to be comforted, but she leaves him alone, thinking that he wants solitude. These moments are actually inescapable in a relationship. If you're going to dance with someone, you're going to step on each other's feet once in a while.

Losing the connection with a loved one, however, jeopardizes our sense of security. We experience a primal feeling of panic. It sets off an alarm in the brain's amygdala, our fear center, where we are highly attuned to threats of all kinds. Once the amygdala sends out an alarm, we don't think—we act. The threat can come from the outside world or from our own inner cosmos. It's our perception that counts, not the reality. If we feel abandoned at a moment of need, we are set up to enter a state of panic.

It's what we do next, after those moments of disconnection, that has a huge impact on the shape of our relationship. Can you turn around and reconnect? If not, you'll start engaging in fights that follow a clear pattern. I call these "demon dialogues." If they gain momentum, they start to take over and induce a terrible sense of emotional aloneness. Your relationship feels less and less like a safe place, and it

154

starts to unravel. You start to doubt that your partner is there for you, that he values you. Or that she will put you first.

Consider a couple with their firstborn child. Having a baby is a stressful, sleep-depriving experience. But it's also a time when people's attachment fears and needs are particularly strong. The man might think something like, "I know it's wrong, and I know it's pathetic, but I feel like I've lost my wife to my kid." And the woman might say, "When I had the baby I felt so fragile. I was taking care of this little being, and I just needed extra comfort and caring myself, but he was out working all the time." Their intentions are good—she cares for the infant, he works hard to support his new family—but they fail to give each other what they really need.

Or think of a man who is doing just fine in his job while his wife flies high in a new career. She's spending long hours on exciting projects while he is deprived of affection, attention, and sex. Lying in bed alone each night, waiting for her, he feels like a fool for needing her so much—and also angry that she can't see how deeply her absence affects him.

But we don't talk about these conflicts in terms of deeply rooted attachment needs. We talk about the surface emotions, the ire or indifference, and blame the other. "He's so angry; I feel so attacked," or "She's so cold. I don't think she cares at all!" Each person retreats into a corner, making it harder and harder for the two to express their fundamental attachment needs, foreclosing the ability to gain reassurance from each other.

Women are often more sensitive to the first signs of connection breakdown than men, and their response is often to begin what I call the dance of disconnection. Almost ritualistically they will pursue their partners in a futile attempt to get a comforting response. But they do it in a way that almost guarantees their basic need will not be met—they blame their partner for failing in some essential way.

Men, on the other hand, have been taught to suppress emotional responses and needs, which inclines them to withdraw from the conflict. But her rage and his withdrawal both mask what lies below the surface—an underlying vulnerability and need for connection, now compounded by sadness, shame, and, most of all, fear.

Too often, what couples do not see is that most fights are really protests over emotional disconnection. Underneath all the distress, partners are desperate to know: Are you there for me? Do you need me? Do you rely on me?

Repairing Bonds

For years, therapists have viewed these demon dialogues as power struggles. They've attempted to resolve couples' fights by teaching them problem-solving skills. But this is a little like offering Kleenex as the cure for viral pneumonia. It ignores the attachment issues that underlie the pattern. Rather than conflict or control, the issue, from an attachment perspective, is emotional distance.

And what's frustrating to people is not knowing how to bridge that emotional distance. In my office, men sometimes tell me, "I do all kinds of things to show I care. I mow the lawn, bring in a good salary, solve problems, and I don't play around. Why is it that in the end, these things don't seem to matter, and all that counts with my wife is that we talk about emotional stuff and cuddle?" I tell them, "Because that's just the way we are made. We need someone to pay real attention to us, to hold us tight. Have you forgotten that you need that, too?"

When we fight with our partners, we tend to follow the ball as it goes over the net, paying attention to the last barb lobbed at us—and not whether we even want to be in the game at all. It's possible to break out of the demon dialogues, but the first step is to be aware of the game itself, not just the play-by-play. Once you realize you are latched onto your pattern of arguing, you can agree to put the whole game on hold.

Disappointments are always part of relationships. But you can always choose how you handle them. Will you react defensively, out of fear, or in the spirit of understanding? Let's say your partner says, "I don't feel like having sex tonight." You can take a deep breath and think about how much she loves you, and say, "Gee, that's too bad, I was really looking forward to that." Or you can spit out a sarcastic, "Right! Well, we never make love anymore, do we?"

Of course, you may not feel you really have a choice if your panic button has been pushed and your emotions are boiling over. But just being aware that it has been pushed can help calm you down. You can think to yourself, "What is happening here? I'm yelling. But inside, I'm feeling really small." Then you can tell your partner, "I got really scared there—I'm feeling hurt."

If you take that leap of faith and respond with such a bid for reconnection, you have to hope your partner will, too, instead of saying something hurtful like, "Well, you're being asinine and difficult." That's the tricky part about relationships: To change the dance, both people have to change their steps.

Simply accepting your attachment needs instead of feeling ashamed of them is a big and necessary first step, and it applies to single people as well as to those in relationships. A single person might say, "I'm depressed because I'm lonely, and I know I shouldn't be lonely; I know I should be independent." Well, *of course* you're depressed if you're feeling lonely and then you turn around and beat yourself up for it! When you're ashamed, you tend to hide from others, setting off a vicious cycle that nearly ensures you won't find the social connection you need.

Healing Touches

A man will often say to me, "Even if I do think that she really needs me or is feeling scared, I don't know what to do!" He'll end up making his wife a cup of tea, which is very nice—but it's not what is called for. Had he put his hand on her shoulder and pulled her towards him, however, his bid for connection would have been much more successful.

Men often say they don't know what to do. Yet men do know how to soothe—they do it with their children, tucking them in at night and whispering gently to them. The difference is, they see their children's vulnerability, and respond to it, but when they look at their wives, they see only someone who is judging them. But she feels vulnerable, too.

Touch is the most basic way of connecting. Taking your partner's hand when she is nervous can instantly defuse anxiety and anger.

Touch is the most basic way of connecting with another human being. Taking your partner's hand when she is nervous or touching his shoulder in the middle of an argument can instantly defuse anxiety and anger.

The world of therapy has been obsessed with maintaining boundaries in recent years. I say our problem is just the opposite—we're all cut off from each other.

If you watch two people in love, they touch each other all the time. If you watch two people finding their way back into a love relationship, after falling into demon dialogues, they touch each other more, too. They literally reach for each other; it's a tangible sign of their desire for connection.

Secure (and Saucy) Sex

A big myth about love is that it's got a "best before" date, that passion is a burning fever that must subside. That's pretty silly. I don't see any scientific or human reason why people can't have happy long-term love relationships.

Among people who do have affairs, they don't do so because their sex lives are boring. I've never had anyone come to my office and tell me that they had an affair because they were bored in bed. They have affairs because they're lonely, because they can't emotionally connect with their partner. Then somebody else smiles at them and makes them feel special and valued—and suddenly, they're in this strange situation where they're committed to one person but find themselves responding to another.

Sex is boring if it's cut off from emotional connection. But if you're emotionally involved, sex is play and passion with a hundred dimensions.

Passion is like everything else: It ebbs and flows. But sex is always going to be boring if it's one-dimensional, cut off from emotional connection. On the other hand, if you're

emotionally involved, sex has a hundred dimensions to it, and is as much play as passion.

I call this kind of secure sex "synchrony sex," where emotional openness and responsiveness, tender touch, and erotic exploration all come together. When partners have a secure emotional connection, physical intimacy can retain all of its initial ardor and creativity and then some. Lovers can be tender and playful one moment, fiery and erotic another. Securely attached partners can more openly express their needs and preferences and are more willing to experiment sexually with their lovers.

Excitement comes from the risk involved in staying open in the here and now experience of physical and emotional connection.

In a secure relationship, excitement comes not from trying to resurrect the novel moments of infatuated passion but from the risk involved in staying open in the moment-to-moment, here-and-now experience of physical and emotional connection. With this openness comes the sense that lovemaking with your partner is always a new adventure.

Lasting Love

Once you're reconnected with your partner, and both of you are getting your attachment needs filled, you have to keep working at being emotionally responsive to one another. You can do that by helping each other identify the attachment issues that tend to come up in your recurring arguments.

If, for example, you always erupt over your girlfriend's risky mountain climbingtrips, talk to her about how your anger is born out of a fear of losing her. Figure out how she can take more precautions. Or, if you often feel abandoned when left with the brunt of childcare duties, plan out how you and your husband can be better parents together, so that you won't call him a deadbeat in a moment of pent-up frustration.

You should also celebrate positive moments together, both big and small. Regularly and deliberately hold, hug, and kiss each other when you wake up, leave the house, return, and go to sleep. Recognize special days, anniversaries, and birthdays in very personal ways. These rituals keep your relationship safe in a distracting and chaotic world.

Stories shape our lives, and the stories we tell about our lives shape us in turn. Create a future love story for you and your partner that outlines what your life together will look like five or ten years down the road. It will prime you to keep your bond strong.

Arms Wide Open

Because attachment is a universal need, the attachment view of love can also help parents understand conflicts with their children. I was recently in a café with my teenage son, yelling at him over the roar of the latte machine, while he sulked and huffed. Then suddenly he said, "Mom, we're doing that thing, where I feel like you are criticizing me, and you feel like I don't care what you have to say." We both started laughing and my anger melted away.

Now that we know what love is really about, we know how to sustain it. It's up to us to use that knowledge to nurture it with our partners and families. And then, with the empathy and courage it teaches us, we can search for ways to take it out into the world and make a difference.

SUE JOHNSON is a clinical psychologist and author of *Hold Me Tight*. She lives in Ottawa, Canada, and has been happily married for 20 years. Learn more at www.holdmetight.net.

From *Psychology Today,* January/February 2009, vol. 42, no. 1, pp. 74–75, 78–79. Copyright © by Sussex Publishers, LLC. Reprinted by permission.

UNIT 6

Development during Middle and Late Adulthood

Unit Selections

Key Points to Consider

- How do adults over age 50 view their lives? What changes do they see in themselves?

- Is hormone therapy safe for menopause? What else helps?

- How often do you suffer back pain? Do you know what causes back pain?

- When and how should one begin to plan for retirement?

- Are the over age 65 people in your life hopeful and active or full of self-pity?

- What is a Mediterranean diet? What factors contribute to a long life?

- People with Alzheimer's disease have lost many of their memories. Can new therapies help them rediscover some of their past knowledge?

- What do middle and late adulthood Americans believe about life after death?

- What are the ethics of terminal care? Who should prepare advanced-care directives? When?

Student Website

www.mhhe.com/cls

Internet References

Alzheimer's Disease Research Center
   http://alzheimer.wustl.edu/
American Association of Retired Persons
   http://www.aarp.org
Lifestyle Factors Affecting Late Adulthood
   http://www.school-for-champions.com/health/lifestyle_elderly.htm
National Aging Information and Referral Support Center
   http://www.nausa.org/informationandreferral/index-ir.php
Department of Health and Human Services—Aging
   http://www.hhs.gov/aging/index.html

Joseph Campbell, a twentieth-century sage, said that the privilege of a lifetime is being who you are. This ego-confidence often arrives during middle and late adulthood, even as physical confidence declines. There is a gradual slowing of the rate of mitosis of cells of all the organ systems with age. This gradual slowing of mitosis translates into a slowed rate of repair of cells of all organs. By the 40s, signs of aging can be seen in skin, skeleton, vision, hearing, smell, taste, balance, coordination, heart, blood vessels, lungs, liver, kidneys, digestive tract, immune response, endocrine functioning, and ability to reproduce. To some extent, moderate use of any body part (as opposed to disuse or misuse) helps retain its strength, stamina, and repairability. However, by middle and late adulthood persons become increasingly aware of the effects of aging organ systems on their total physical fitness. A loss of height occurs as spinal disks and connective tissues diminish and settle. Demineralization, especially loss of calcium, causes weakening of bones. Muscles atrophy, and the slowing of cardiovascular and respiratory responses creates a loss of stamina for exercise. All of this may seem cruel, but it occurs very gradually and need not adversely affect a person's enjoyment of life.

Healthful aging, at least in part, seems to be genetically pre-programmed. The females of many species, including humans, outlive the males. The sex hormones of females may protect them from some early aging effects. Males, in particular, experience earlier declines in their cardiovascular system. Diet and exercise can ward off many of the deleterious effects of aging. A reduction in saturated fat (low density lipid) intake coupled with regular aerobic exercise contributes to less bone demineralization, less plaque in the arteries, stronger muscles (including heart and lung muscles), and a general increase in stamina and vitality. An adequate intake of complex carbohydrates, fibrous foods, fresh fruits, fresh vegetables, unsaturated fats (high density lipids), and water also enhances good health.

Cognitive abilities do not appreciably decline with age in healthy adults. Research suggests that the speed with which the brain carries out problems involving abstract (fluid) reasoning may slow but not cease. Complex problems may simply require more time to solve with age. On the other hand, research suggests that the memory banks of older people may have more crystallized (accumulated and stored) knowledge and more insight. Creativity also frequently spurts after age 50. One's ken (range of knowledge) and practical skills (common sense) grow with age and experience. Older human beings also become expert at the cognitive tasks they frequently do. Many cultures celebrate these abilities as the "wisdom of age."

The first article about middle adulthood speaks of the urge to laugh. New brain research reported in "Emotions and the Brain: Laughter" suggests that laughing is a form of instinctive social bonding. We do not make a conscious decision to laugh. We are often unaware that we are laughing. And laughter is contagious. It makes us healthier by enhancing our immune responsivity and reducing our stress hormones. The "wisdom of age" may allow us to be more frivolous, and to take more pleasure in

© Getty Images/Digital Vision

happy friendships within our families and communities. Children laugh freely. Somehow many adults learn to suppress laughter and be more serious. Perhaps some wisdom and maturity is evidenced by not trying to suppress this important biological response.

"Fifty Reasons to Love Being 50+" is a collection of anecdotes from older adults (including B. B. King, Judge Judy, and Martina Navratilova) explaining the joys of seniority. Old age for these respondents represents wisdom, veneration, and autonomy, coupled with new creative outlets and the love of friends and family.

"Are You Ready for Act II?," by Paula Ketter, discusses steps which adults can take before they make a decision about retirement. Planning ahead helps people make more realistic choices about pursuing work they enjoy and in which they find more pleasure. Recommendations include networking, volunteering, and phasing out of one's active working occupation.

The first article selected for the Late Adulthood section of this unit is a positive view of "Healthy Aging in Later Life." Jill Duba Onedera and Fred Stickle review theories of aging and advocate for the activity theory. A case example helps the reader understand why. They give many other criteria for successful aging beyond the active lifestyle including social support, reciprocating to others, and maintaining strong friendship bonds.

The second selection for Late Adulthood, "More Good Years," highlights secrets from the Greek island of Ikaria. There many people reach age 100 in good health. They eat a Mediterranean diet and seem to have endless optimism. Dan Buettner lists 13 likely contributors to Ikarian longevity.

The third late-adulthood selection, "Lost and Found," deals with people with Alzheimer's disease. The author, Barbara Basler, describes new therapeutic methods devised by Cameron Camp, the head of the Myers Research Institute in Ohio. Dr. Camp's methods, deemed valid and reliable by researchers, help draw patients out of their confusion and recapture some of their basic skills and knowledge.

The fourth article deals with life after death. Over 1,000 Americans over age 50 were asked to share their beliefs about God, Heaven, Hell, and/or what they believe happens after death. The author found a surprising lack of fear about death. His results give a fascinating picture of opinions about whether Heaven and Hell are places, or states of being. Many respondents mentioned reincarnation. The author also explains what is known about near-death experiences.

The last article describes end-of-life care. The author, Helen Sorenson, discusses the conflicting opinions that create turmoil for patients, family, friends, and health care professionals when death is imminent. "Navigating Practical Dilemmas in Terminal Care" gives useful information on how to reduce such conflicts. Family conferences should occur well ahead of the end of life to discuss the terms of advanced-care directives. Asking questions and communicating openly can prevent misunderstandings.

Emotions and the Brain: Laughter

If evolution comes down to survival of the fittest, then why do we joke around so much? New brain research suggests that the urge to laugh is the lubricant that makes humans higher social beings.

Steven Johnson

Robert Provine wants me to see his Tickle Me Elmo doll. Wants me to hold it, as a matter of fact. It's not an unusual request for Provine. A professor of psychology and neuroscience at the University of Maryland, he has been engaged for a decade in a wide-ranging intellectual pursuit that has taken him from the panting play of young chimpanzees to the history of American sitcoms—all in search of a scientific understanding of that most unscientific of human customs: laughter.

The Elmo doll happens to incorporate two of his primary obsessions: tickling and contagious laughter. "You ever fiddled with one of these?" Provine says, as he pulls the doll out of a small canvas tote bag. He holds it up, and after a second or two, the doll begins to shriek with laughter. There's something undeniably comic in the scene: a burly, bearded man in his mid-fifties cradling a red Muppet. Provine hands Elmo to me to demonstrate the doll's vibration effect. "It brings up two interesting things," he explains, as I hold Elmo in my arms. "You have a best-selling toy that's a glorified laugh box. And when it shakes, you're getting feedback as if you're tickling."

Provine's relationship to laughter reminds me of the dramatic technique that Bertolt Brecht called the distanciation effect. Radical theater, in Brecht's vision, was supposed to distance us from our too-familiar social structures, make us see those structures with fresh eyes. In his study of laughter, Provine has been up to something comparably enlightening, helping us to recognize the strangeness of one of our most familiar emotional states. Think about that Tickle Me Elmo doll: We take it for granted that tickling causes laughter and that one person's laughter will easily "infect" other people within earshot. Even a child knows these things. (Tickling and contagious laughter are two of the distinguishing characteristics of childhood.) But when you think about them from a distance, they are strange conventions. We can understand readily enough why natural selection would have implanted the fight-or-flight response in us or endowed us with sex drives. But the tendency to laugh when others laugh in our presence or to laugh when someone strokes our belly with a feather—what's the evolutionary advantage of that? And yet a quick glance at the Nielsen ratings or the personal ads will tell you that laughter is one of the most satisfying and sought-after states available to us.

Funnily enough, the closer Provine got to understanding why we laugh, the farther he got from humor. To appreciate the roots of laughter, you have to stop thinking about jokes.

There is a long, semi-illustrious history of scholarly investigation into the nature of humor, from Freud's *Jokes and Their Relation to the Unconscious,* which may well be the least funny book about humor ever written, to a British research group that announced last year that they had determined the World's Funniest Joke. Despite the fact that the researchers said they had sampled a massive international audience in making this discovery, the winning joke revolved around New Jersey residents:

A couple of New Jersey hunters are out in the woods when one of them falls to the ground. He doesn't seem to be breathing; his eyes are rolled back in his head. The other guy whips out his cell phone and calls the emergency services. He gasps to the operator: "My friend is dead! What can I do?"

The operator says: "Take it easy. I can help. First, let's make sure he's dead." There is silence, then a shot is heard. The guy's voice comes back on the line. He says, "OK, now what?"

This joke illustrates that most assessments of humor's underlying structure gravitate to the notion of controlled incongruity: You're expecting x, and you get y. For the joke to work, it has to be readable on both levels. In the hunting joke there are two plausible ways to interpret the 911 operator's instructions—either the hunter checks his friend's pulse or he shoots him. The context sets you up to expect that he'll check his friend's pulse, so the—admittedly dark—humor arrives when he takes the more unlikely path. That incongruity has limits, of course: If the hunter chooses to do something utterly nonsensical—untie his shoelaces or climb a tree—the joke wouldn't be funny.

A number of studies in recent years have looked at brain activity while subjects were chuckling over a good joke—an attempt to locate a neurological funny bone. There is evidence that the frontal lobes are implicated in "getting" the joke while the brain regions associated with motor control execute the physical response of laughter. One 1999 study analyzed patients with damage to the right frontal lobes, an integrative region of the brain where emotional, logical, and perceptual data converge. The brain-damaged patients had far more difficulty than control subjects in choosing the proper punch line to a series of jokes, usually opting for absurdist, slapstick-style endings rather than traditional ones. Humor can often come in coarse,

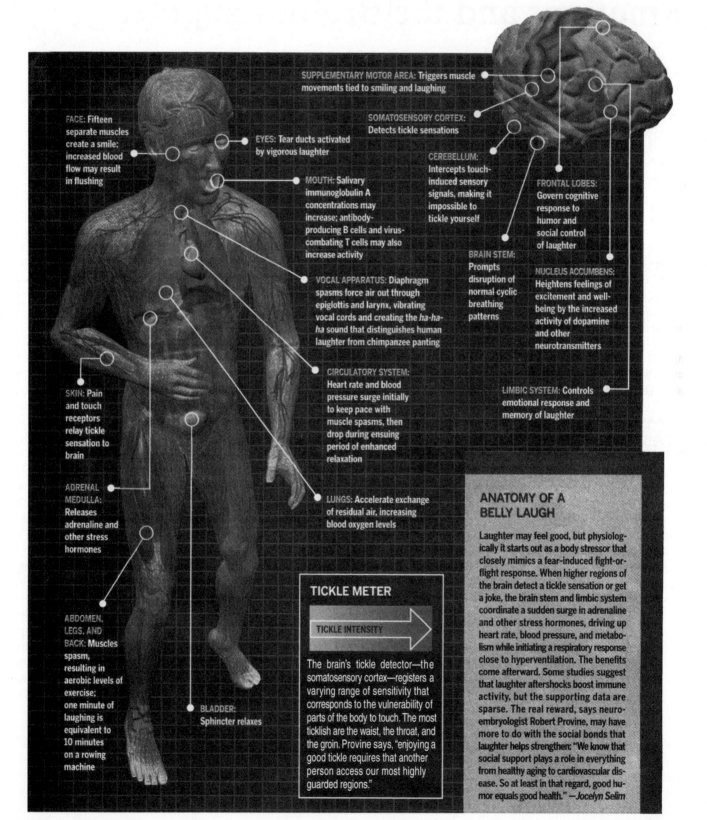

SUPPLEMENTARY MOTOR AREA: Triggers muscle movements tied to smiling and laughing

SOMATOSENSORY CORTEX: Detects tickle sensations

FRONTAL LOBES: Govern cognitive response to humor and social control of laughter

CEREBELLUM: Intercepts touch-induced sensory signals, making it impossible to tickle yourself

BRAIN STEM: Prompts disruption of normal cyclic breathing patterns

NUCLEUS ACCUMBENS: Heightens feelings of excitement and well-being by the increased activity of dopamine and other neurotransmitters

LIMBIC SYSTEM: Controls emotional response and memory of laughter

FACE: Fifteen separate muscles create a smile; increased blood flow may result in flushing

EYES: Tear ducts activated by vigorous laughter

MOUTH: Salivary immunoglobulin A concentrations may increase; antibody-producing B cells and virus-combating T cells may also increase activity

VOCAL APPARATUS: Diaphragm spasms force air out through epiglottis and larynx, vibrating vocal cords and creating the *ha-ha-ha* sound that distinguishes human laughter from chimpanzee panting

CIRCULATORY SYSTEM: Heart rate and blood pressure surge initially to keep pace with muscle spasms, then drop during ensuing period of enhanced relaxation

SKIN: Pain and touch receptors relay tickle sensation to brain

ADRENAL MEDULLA: Releases adrenaline and other stress hormones

LUNGS: Accelerate exchange of residual air, increasing blood oxygen levels

ABDOMEN, LEGS, AND BACK: Muscles spasm, resulting in aerobic levels of exercise; one minute of laughing is equivalent to 10 minutes on a rowing machine

BLADDER: Sphincter relaxes

TICKLE METER

TICKLE INTENSITY

The brain's tickle detector—the somatosensory cortex—registers a varying range of sensitivity that corresponds to the vulnerability of parts of the body to touch. The most ticklish are the waist, the throat, and the groin. Provine says, "enjoying a good tickle requires that another person access our most highly guarded regions."

ANATOMY OF A BELLY LAUGH

Laughter may feel good, but physiologically it starts out as a body stressor that closely mimics a fear-induced fight-or-flight response. When higher regions of the brain detect a tickle sensation or get a joke, the brain stem and limbic system coordinate a sudden surge in adrenaline and other stress hormones, driving up heart rate, blood pressure, and metabolism while initiating a respiratory response close to hyperventilation. The benefits come afterward. Some studies suggest that laughter aftershocks boost immune activity, but the supporting data are sparse. The real reward, says neuro-embryologist Robert Provine, may have more to do with the social bonds that laughter helps strengthen: "We know that social support plays a role in everything from healthy aging to cardiovascular disease. So at least in that regard, good humor equals good health." —*Jocelyn Selim*

Graphics by Don Foley

162

lowest-common-denominator packages, but actually getting the joke draws upon our higher brain functions.

When Provine set out to study laughter, he imagined that he would approach the problem along the lines of these humor studies: Investigating laughter meant having people listen to jokes and other witticisms and watching what happened. He began by simply observing casual conversations, counting the number of times that people laughed while listening to someone speaking. But very quickly he realized that there was a fundamental flaw in his assumptions about how laughter worked. "I started recording all these conversations," Provine says, "and the numbers I was getting—I didn't believe them when I saw them. The speakers were laughing more than the listeners. Every time that would happen, I would think, 'OK, I have to go back and start over again because that can't be right.'"

Speakers, it turned out, were 46 percent more likely to laugh than listeners—and what they were laughing at, more often than not, wasn't remotely funny. Provine and his team of undergrad students recorded the ostensible "punch lines" that triggered laughter in ordinary conversation. They found that only around 15 percent of the sentences that triggered laughter were traditionally humorous. In his book, *Laughter: A Scientific Investigation,* Provine lists some of the laugh-producing quotes:

I'll see you guys later./Put those cigarettes away./I hope we all do well./It was nice meeting you too./We can handle this./I see your point./I should do that, but I'm too lazy./I try to lead a normal life./I think I'm done./I told you so!

The few studies of laughter to date had assumed that laughing and humor were inextricably linked, but Provine's early research suggested that the connection was only an occasional one. "There's a dark side to laughter that we are too quick to overlook," he says. "The kids at Columbine were laughing as they walked through the school shooting their peers."

As his research progressed, Provine began to suspect that laughter was in fact about something else—not humor or gags or incongruity but our social interactions. He found support for this assumption in a study that had already been conducted, analyzing people's laughing patterns in social and solitary contexts. "You're 30 times more likely to laugh when you're with other people than you are when you're alone—if you don't count simulated social environments like laugh tracks on television," Provine says. "In fact, when you're alone, you're more likely to talk out loud to yourself than you are to laugh out loud. Much more." Think how rarely you'll laugh out loud at a funny passage in a book but how quick you'll be to make a friendly laugh when greeting an old acquaintance. Laughing is not an instinctive physical response to humor, the way a flinch responds to pain or a shiver to cold. It's a form of instinctive social bonding that humor is crafted to exploit.

P rovine's lab at the Baltimore county campus of the University of Maryland looks like the back room at a stereo repair store—long tables cluttered with old equipment, tubes and wires everywhere. The walls are decorated with brightly colored pictures of tangled neurons, most of which were painted by Provine. (Add some Day-Glo typography and they might pass for signs promoting a Dead show at the Fillmore.) Provine's old mentor, the neuroembryologist Viktor Hamburger, glowers down from a picture hung above a battered Silicon Graphics workstation. His expression suggests a sense of concerned bafflement: "I trained you as a scientist, and here you are playing with dolls!"

The more technical parts of Provine's work—exploring the neuromuscular control of laughter and its relationship to the human and chimp respiratory systems—draw on his training at Washington University in St. Louis under Hamburger and Nobel laureate Rita Levi-Montalcini. But the most immediate way to grasp his insights into the evolution of laughter is to watch video footage of his informal fieldwork, which consists of Provine and a cameraman prowling Baltimore's inner harbor, asking people to laugh for the camera. The overall effect is like a color story for the local news, but as Provine and I watch the tapes together in his lab, I find myself looking at the laughters with fresh eyes. Again and again, a pattern repeats on the screen. Provine asks someone to laugh, and they demur, look puzzled for a second, and say something like, "I can't just laugh." Then they turn to their friends or family, and the laughter rolls out of them as though it were as natural as breathing. The pattern stays the same even as the subjects change: a group of high school students on a field trip, a married couple, a pair of college freshmen.

At one point Provine—dressed in a plaid shirt and khakis, looking something like the comedian Robert Klein—stops two waste-disposal workers driving a golf cart loaded up with trash bags. When they fail to guffaw on cue, Provine asks them why they can't muster one up. "Because you're not funny," one of them says. They turn to each other and share a hearty laugh.

"See, you two just made each other laugh," Provine says.

"Yeah, well, we're coworkers," one of them replies.

The insistent focus on laughter patterns has a strange effect on me as Provine runs through the footage. By the time we get to the cluster of high school kids, I've stopped hearing their spoken words at all, just the rhythmic peals of laughter breaking out every 10 seconds or so. Sonically, the laughter dominates the speech; you can barely hear the dialogue underneath the hysterics. If you were an alien encountering humans for the first time, you'd have to assume that the laughing served as the primary communication method, with the spoken words interspersed as afterthoughts. After one particularly loud outbreak, Provine turns to me and says, "Now, do you think they're all individually making a conscious decision to laugh?" He shakes his head dismissively. "Of course not. In fact, we're often not aware that we're even laughing in the first place. We've vastly overrated our conscious control of laughter."

The limits of our voluntary control of laughter are most clearly exposed in studies of stroke victims who suffer from a disturbing condition known as central facial paralysis, which prevents them from voluntarily moving either the left side or the right side of their faces, depending on the location of the neurological damage. When these individuals are asked to smile or laugh on command, they produce lopsided grins: One side of the mouth curls up, the other remains frozen. But when they're told a joke or they're tickled, traditional smiles and laughs animate their entire faces. There is evidence that the physical mechanism of laughter itself is generated in the brain stem, the most ancient region of the nervous system, which is also responsible for fundamental functions like breathing. Sufferers of amyotrophic lateral sclerosis—Lou Gehrig's disease—which targets the brain stem, often experience spontaneous bursts of uncontrollable laughter, without feeling mirth. (They often undergo a comparable experience with crying as well.) Sometimes called the reptilian brain because its basic structure dates back to our reptile ancestors, the brain stem is largely devoted to our most primal instincts, far removed from our complex, higher-brain skills in understanding humor. And yet somehow, in this primitive region of the brain, we find the urge to laugh.

We're accustomed to thinking of common-but-unconscious instincts as being essential adaptations, like the startle reflex or the suckling of newborns. Why would we have an unconscious propensity for something as frivolous as laughter? As I watch them on the screen, Provine's teenagers remind me of an old Carl Sagan riff, which begins with his describing "a species of primate" that likes to gather in packs of 50 or 60 individuals, cram together in a darkened cave, and hyperventilate in unison, to the point of almost passing out. The behavior is described in such a way as to make it sound exotic and somewhat foolish, like salmon swimming furiously upstream to their deaths or butterflies traveling thousands of miles to rendezvous once a year. The joke, of course, is that the primate is *Homo sapiens,* and the group hyperventilation is our fondness for laughing together at comedy clubs or theaters, or with the virtual crowds of television laugh tracks.

I'm thinking about the Sagan quote when another burst of laughter arrives through the TV speakers, and without realizing what I'm doing, I find myself laughing along with the kids on the screen, I can't help it—their laughter is contagious.

We may be the only species on the planet that laughs together in such large groups, but we are not alone in our appetite for laughter. Not surprisingly, our near relatives, the chimpanzees, are also avid laughers, although differences in their vocal apparatus cause the laughter to sound somewhat more like panting. "The chimpanzee's laughter is rapid and breathy, whereas ours is punctuated with glottal stops," says legendary chimp researcher Roger Fouts. "Also, the chimpanzee laughter occurs on the inhale and exhale, while ours is primarily done on our exhales. But other than these small differences, chimpanzee laughter seems to me to be just like ours in most respects."

Chimps don't do stand-up routines, of course, but they do share a laugh-related obsession with humans, one that Provine believes is central to the roots of laughter itself: Chimps love tickling. Back in his lab, Provine shows me video footage of a pair of young chimps named Josh and Lizzie playing with a human caretaker. It's a full-on ticklefest, with the chimps panting away hysterically when their bellies are scratched. "That's chimpanzee laughter you're hearing," Provine says. It's close enough to human laughter that I find myself chuckling along.

Parents will testify that ticklefests are often the first elaborate play routine they engage in with their children and one of the most reliable laugh inducers. According to Fouts, who helped teach sign language to Washoe, perhaps the world's most famous chimpanzee, the practice is just as common, and perhaps more long lived, among the chimps. "Tickling... seems to be very important to chimpanzees because it continues throughout their lives," he says. "Even Washoe at the age of 37 still enjoys tickling and being tickled by her adult family members." Among young chimpanzees that have been taught sign language, tickling is a frequent topic of conversation.

Like laughter, tickling is almost by definition a social activity. Like the incongruity theory of humor, tickling relies on a certain element of surprise, which is why it's impossible to tickle yourself. Predictable touch doesn't elicit the laughter and squirming of tickling—it's unpredictable touch that does the trick. A number of tickle-related studies have convincingly shown that tickling exploits the sensorimotor system's awareness of the difference between self and other: If the system orders your hand to move toward your belly, it doesn't register surprise when the nerve endings on your belly report being stroked. But if the touch is being generated by another sensorimotor system, the belly stroking will come as a surprise. The pleasant laughter of tickle is the way the brain responds to that touch. In both human and chimpanzee societies, that touch usually first appears in parent-child interactions and has an essential role in creating those initial bonds. "The reason [tickling and laughter] are so important," Roger Fouts says, "is because they play a role in maintaining the affinitive bonds of friendship within the family and community."

A few years ago, Jared Diamond wrote a short book with the provocative title *Why Is Sex Fun?* These recent studies suggest an evolutionary answer to the question of why tickling is fun: It encourages us to play well with others. Young children are so receptive to the rough-and-tumble play of tickle that even pretend tickling will often send them into peals of laughter. (Fouts reports that the threat of tickle has a similar effect on his chimps.) In his book, Provine suggests that "feigned tickle" can be thought of as the Original Joke, the first deliberate behavior designed to exploit the tickling-laughter circuit. Our comedy clubs and our sitcoms are culturally enhanced versions of those original playful childhood exchanges. Along with the suckling and smiling instincts, the laughter of tickle evolved as a way of cementing the bond between parents and children, laying the foundation for a behavior that then carried over into the social lives of adults. While we once laughed at the surprise touch of a parent or sibling, we now laugh at the surprise twist of a punch line.

Bowling Green State University professor Jaak Panksepp suggests that there is a dedicated "play" circuitry in the brain, equivalent to the more extensively studied fear and love circuits. Panksepp has studied the role of rough-and-tumble play in cementing social connections between juvenile rats. The play instinct is not easily suppressed. Rats that have been denied the opportunity to engage in this kind of play—which has a distinct choreography, as well as a chirping vocalization that may be the rat equivalent of laughter—will nonetheless immediately engage in play behavior given the chance. Panksepp compares it to a bird's instinct for flying. "Probably the most powerful positive emotion of all—once your tummy is full and you don't have bodily needs—is vigorous social engagement among the young," Panksepp says. "The largest amount of human laughter seems to occur in the midst of early childhood—rough-and-tumble play, chasing, all the stuff they love."

Playing is what young mammals do, and in humans and chimpanzees, laughter is the way the brain expresses the pleasure of that play. "Since laughter seems to be ritualized panting, basically what you do in laughing is replicate the sound of rough-and-tumble play," Provine says. "And you know, that's where I think it came from. Tickle is an important part of our primate heritage. Touching and being touched is an important part of what it means to be a mammal."

There is much that we don't know yet about the neurological underpinnings of laughter. We do not yet know precisely why laughing feels so good; one recent study detected evidence that stimulating the nucleus accumbens, one of the brain's pleasure centers, triggered laughter. Panksepp has performed studies that indicate opiate antagonists significantly reduce the urge to play in rats, which implies that the brain's endorphin system may be involved in the pleasure of laughter. Some anecdotal and clinical evidence suggest that laughing makes you healthier by suppressing stress hormones and elevating immune system antibodies. If you think of laughter as a form of behavior that is basically synonymous with the detection of humor, the laughing-makes-you-healthier premise seems bizarre. Why would natural selection make our immune system respond to jokes? Provine's approach helps solve the mystery. Our bodies aren't responding to wisecracks and punch lines; they're responding to social connection.

In this respect, laughter reminds us that our emotional lives are as much outward bound as they are inner directed. We tend to think of emotions as private affairs, feelings that wash over our subjective worlds. But emotions are also social acts, laughter perhaps most of all. It's no accident that we have so many delicately choreographed gestures and facial expressions—many of which appear to be innate to our species—to convey our emotions. Our emotional systems are designed to share our feelings and not just represent them internally—an insight that Darwin first grasped more than a century ago in his book *The Expression of the Emotions in Man and Animals*. "The movements of expression in the face and body, whatever their origin may have been, are in themselves of much importance for our welfare. They serve as the first means of communication between mother and infant; she smiles approval, and thus encourages her child on the right path. . . . The free expression by outward signs of an emotion intensifies it."

And even if we don't yet understand the neurological basis of the pleasure that laughing brings us, it makes sense that we should seek out the connectedness of infectious laughter. We are social animals, after all. And if that laughter often involves some pretty childish behavior, so be it. "I mean, this is why we're not like lizards," Provine says, holding the Tickle Me Elmo doll on his lap. "Lizards don't play, and they're not social the way we are. When you start to see play, you're starting to see mammals. So when we get together and have a good time and laugh, we're going back to our roots. It's ironic in a way: Some of the things that give us the most pleasure in life are really the most ancient."

50 Reasons to Love Being 50+

1 Because you can spoil the grandkids with sweets

It's all about the shamelessness of lots of butter and sugar and eggs. It's about quantity and variety and having things coming warm from the oven when my kids' kids tumble through my kitchen door. It's about gingersnaps and chocolate chips and short-bread. It's about my grandson Ralphie saying, "I want go Nana cookie house."

Twenty-four years ago my first grandchild spackled his mouth with my corn muffins—and two years later, his little brother, when I was showing him a single apple on a tree, held out both hands and said gleefully, "Whole bunch!" I have 12 grandchildren now. They don't all come at the same time, although the two sets of twins born three years ago often show up on the same weekend. Good thing I love to bake.

Living alone, I don't dare bake without kids around. I would never get the cookies into a tin, nor would anything delicious wind up carefully wrapped in the freezer. I'd eat it all. So when the kids come, it is reason for celebration. It's about eating more than is good for you, once in a while.

I was allowed three desserts in a row at my grandmother's house. I like tradition, and I'm passing it on.

Abigail Thomas writes in *Woodstock,* New York.

2 Gray stripes
(Anthony Bourdain, Edward James Olmos, Jay Leno)

3 Wavy gray
(Emmylou Harris, Linda Evans, Cloris Leachman)

4 Gray beards
(Kofi Annan, Willie Nelson, Sean Connery)

5 Gray bangs
(Olympia Dukakis, Paula Deen, Ruby Dee)

6 Solid gray
(Richard Gere, James Earl Jones, Ted Danson)

7 Faux gray
(Santa Claus, Gandalf, Statler and Waldorf)

8 Because sex gets better with age

Too much of a good thing, Mae West told us, can be wonderful, even at this age. Our hormones aren't as abundant as they used to be, but with a little help from our friends—Viagra, Estrace cream, Astroglide—we can still be as bad as we wanna be. When the spirit is willing but the body isn't, we improvise. We're self-confident enough to say what we want, content enough to swap calisthenics for intimacy. More tenderness and less testosterone can be very sexy indeed.

A female friend of mine says her husband used to want sex so often, she felt "dispensable." These days it feels more like a choice. It's different for men, too. "I'm more concerned with making the other person happy," says a male friend. His wife is happy, too: "Who knew we'd be having so much fun?"

Elizabeth Benedict is a novelist who writes frequently about sex (www.elizabethbenedict.com).

9 Because you're more compassionate

You've always been the rightest person in the room—so why did your boss just fire you? You were certain your parents made terrible mistakes raising you—now your own kids say you made the same errors (and they're forwarding their therapy bills to you). You've led a charmed life—but suddenly you know what it's like to live with depression . . . or cancer . . . or losing a spouse . . . or a sudden turn in fortune that's left you wondering how to pay the bills.

By the time we pass the half-century mark, we've all withstood our share of slights, indignities, or outright suffering. Watched our self-image go up in flames. Played a starring role in our own TV version of *When Bad Things Happen to Good People.*

And maybe it's lucky. Lucky because we've seen enough, felt enough, been self-aware enough to learn from our experiences. What we've learned is that all of us are inherently flawed and very, very vulnerable; that this, in part, is what it means to be human; and that—most important—we really are all in this together. It's the reason we treat our fellow humans with a heavy dose of compassion and respect. Okay, so it's taken a handful of decades and some life upheavals to figure this all out. That still puts us in the catbird seat, compared with people who have never learned it at all.

Nancy Wartik is a writer based in New York City.

10 Because men can use "midlife crisis" as an excuse for any embarrassing, highly questionable activity

Including body piercings, bad toupees, love-handle surgery, leather pants (or any wardrobe addition that makes you look like David Hasselhoff), and the purchase of a sports car more expensive than your first house.

11 Because you have the guts to change careers

I look up from a phonics lesson to hear screaming in my classroom. Emmanuel, a sad-eyed first grader who joined our class three days earlier, is hurling books, punching any kids who come near. At least ten children are sobbing and hurt. I call the main office: "I need help in 221—*now!*" Emmanuel hits more children in the seconds I'm on the phone. Another teacher runs into the room and ushers him out. I am the lone adult with 24 traumatized children. Now I do the only thing I can think of to calm everyone down: we sing the class favorite, "If I Had a Hammer."

I had brought in some CDs a few weeks earlier, hoping that deciphering song lyrics would improve my students' ability to listen. After a 20-year career as a magazine editor, I'm teaching at-risk first graders in one of the country's poorest neighborhoods. A large percentage of students at this South Bronx school are borderline autistic, have ADD, or suffer from an array of developmental disorders. Some, like Emmanuel, are shuffled from one foster home to another. Many others have parents who are absent, jailed, unemployed, addicted to drugs, or abusive.

Emmanuel returns after a few days' suspension and mumbles "Sorry" after a brief discussion of the earlier events. Juan, a helpful child who loves Spider-Man and sharks, has a suggestion, "Why don't we make Emmanuel the Student of the Day so we can get to know him better?"

I marvel at Juan's maturity. Maybe his live-in-the-moment attitude, however naive, is the best way to cope. I realize how much I can learn from these kids about forgiveness, and the value of starting anew.

EILEEN GARRED

12 Because you get better at crossword puzzles

It's simple. We know words our kids don't. Studies show that 50-plus folks have larger vocabularies than people in their 20s or 30s do, partly because of the younger generation's more video-obsessed lives, but also because we know more obsolete terms (mimeograph, phonograph . . .). What matters is we can kick serious bahookey—an eight-letter word for *buttocks*—at crossword puzzles. Here's a test. Ask your under-30 family members to define these words: **larder, eight-track, analog, Instamatic.** When they can't answer, just smile and return to your puzzle.

13 Because you know money can buy some happiness

Our dog's name is Lucky. The twins named him. They were seven years old and weren't listening when I said naming anything Lucky is tempting fate. I was perfectly willing to go to the shelter for a cute terrier mix named Peanut, but the hypoallergenic hype on Labradoodles—they don't shed!—and the puppy pictures online won the day. The breeder got $900, and we got Lucky.

There were other costs. To fit him into our life, we bought a minivan, slightly used. Of course Lucky needed schooling—a bargain at $10 a week—and I'm sure it helped give him the discipline to chew up just one household object per day for his

first two years. From an early age Lucky showed us how to get along with less.

Then there are the four vacuum cleaners, each stronger than the last. I can't fault Lucky for taking after his Labrador mother, but, yes, he does shed, prodigiously. At some point I toted up Lucky-related costs and started calling him our $30,000 dog.

One of my jobs at this magazine is encouraging AARP members to be careful with their money. Really, folks, put away whatever you can. Spend only on necessities. But what is a necessity? Last fall Lucky bolted across the street toward a friend and was hit by a speeding SUV. In 12 days we spent $20,000 to save him.

Yes, there went a semester at college, or a new car, or years off the mortgage. There went the emergency fund. But I have no regrets. We could find the money. In good conscience we couldn't not spend it. Love made that a necessity, just as love prompted family to send unsolicited checks.

And now that Lucky is back to rolling in rabbit poop and eating, let's just say, very widely, he's become my daily reminder of what we really can and can't do without.

GEORGE BLOOSTON

14 Because if Keith Richards can make it into his 60s, there's hope for all of us

1965 Knocked out by electric shock onstage after whacking microphone with guitar

1969 Wrecks his 19-foot Nazi staff car, gets it repaired, then wrecks it down embankment

1973 (Or maybe it was '74 . . .) Falls asleep and crashes into speaker, breaking nose

1974 Falls asleep mid-sentence during live television interview

1980 Declares in interview, "I've been drunk for 27 years"

1981 Doesn't recognize title of new Stones album: "What's this Tattoo You?"

1998 While reaching for book in home library, gets pummeled by avalanche of texts. Suffers three broken ribs and punctured lung

2006 Falls out of coconut tree in Fiji

2007 Claims he snorted Dad's ashes (later denies snorting Dad's ashes)

2008 Gives key to his longevity: "I'm doomed to live"
—Alex Kizer

Because You're Free to Do What You Want!

When we asked readers what they like best about being 50-plus, one answer popped up more than others: freedom.

15 "I do things simply because I want. I can go to a movie or a restaurant alone and not worry whether someone thinks I'm a loser."

GAIL PAUL, Los Angeles, California

16 "No one is shocked if I decide the refrigerator looks nice in the living room."

KAREN EDGAR, Olive Branch, Mississippi

17 "I don't give a flip what other people think. I sing at the top of my lungs in the car with the windows down, even at traffic lights."

BARBARA KEETON, Taylors, South Carolina

18 Because our music rocks!

AARP The Magazine's music critic, Richard Gehr, picks five songs music lovers will still be listening to in 100 years.

Angel-voiced Carl Wilson seeks romantic guidance from above in this gorgeous track from brother Brian's 1966 pop masterpiece, *Pet Sounds.* This one will still be on iPods (or implants) in 2108.

The Queen of Soul unforgettably blends stirring gospel and soaring R&B in her first hit single, written by Ronnie Shannon. She'd soon have bigger hits, but this one gives you chills.

Among the world's most memorable riffs—"Sunshine of Your Love," "Smoke on the Water"—this could be the catchiest, courtesy of the instrumental group that launched a thousand Stax R&B hits.

Motherhood, freight trains, prison, and church. Merle Haggard's autobiographical hit sums up the domestic consolations and outlaw impulses of great American country music. It's an underrated classic.

A cool psychedelic breeze blows through John Lennon's nostalgic memories of his Liverpool childhood. The Beatles rarely sounded more revolutionary than on this dreamy slice of genius.

. . . So tell us your picks for the best songs ever. Go to www.aarpmagazine.org/people.

19 Because you've been embarrassed so much, you're all out of chagrin

When I was in second grade I wet my pants.

It was at a rehearsal of the school play, just before I spoke my lines—well, line. But an important line. For, in our version of *Little Red Riding Hood,* the Big Bad Wolf (yours truly) was transformed from predator ("*Grrr*") to protector ("Leave her alone! *Grrr*").

I didn't grasp that symbolism. I just knew the other parts had gone to sixth graders and that I was one of the few Negro children in the school. Motivated by pride, I spent hours practicing my snarling. But the script called for the Big Bad Wolf to appear in nearly every scene, and as rehearsals grew longer, eventually, almost inevitably, I experienced . . . a release of dramatic tension.

In the boys' room, waiting for my mother to fetch fresh pants, I *grr*ed at my own stupidity. Big Bad Wolf? Big, bad disgrace. I cringed recalling how, before exiting, dripping, stage left, I'd actually delivered my line. But the next day the director said that showed "stage presence" and told me not to worry; this was not the most embarrassing thing I'd ever do.

Too right. There was that solo I began as a boy soprano and ended sounding like a bullfrog. There was that jump shot at the buzzer that swished through the wrong net. And after I left home in rural Pennsylvania for college, there were all those city customs I never got right.

I practiced public obtuseness, ignoring astonished looks when my savoir fell behind my faire. But privately I was haunted by echoes of my inanities ("A friend of Bill who?" "Aren't you going to cook that?")

As the years passed, I learned to check my facts, and also my fly—better to be caught at that than with my zipper down. But recently, listening to an old friend introduce me with an exaggerated account of one of my Greatest Misses, it struck me, now that I'm fiftysomething, that the most embarrassing thing I'd ever do was probably something I'd already done.

So I checked my fly and I stepped onstage in a state of grace beyond disgrace, beyond chagrin.

DAVID BRADLEY, author of *The Chaneysville Incident,* teaches creative writing at the University of Oregon.

20 Because you *experienced* the Beatles

I was 13 years old when my best friend, Margo, won tickets to see the Beatles in San Francisco in '65. We'd seen girls scream for the Fab Four on television and vowed we would never act so silly. But when the Beatles arrived onstage, we were swept away by the hysteria. We screamed, we jumped, we cried, we shook—we even tried climbing the chainlink fence that surrounded the stage. We were gasping for breath the entire show, slightly lightheaded, tears streaming down our faces. I've been to other concerts, but none were ever like this.

LIBBY GUTHRIE is an AARP member in Redwood Valley, California.

21 Because we know how to fight—literally

In March 2008, Saoul Mamby, age 60, became the oldest boxer to compete in a pro bout, going ten rounds with 32-year-old fighter Anthony Osborne. Okay, Mamby didn't win. So what. The guy is doing what he loves: punching other guys in the face until they drool. Since turning pro in 1969, the Bronx-born fighter has held the World Boxing Council (WBC) junior-welterweight title, amassed 56 wins (plus 11 grandchildren), and fought on the same card as Muhammad Ali. Now he's training in hopes of another bout. "To be successful at boxing—at anything—it has to become a part of you," says Mamby. "You get out of it what you put in—and I put in 100 percent."

NICK KOLAKOWSKI

22 Because love grows deeper over time

In the early days it was all about him. His favorite foods, favorite color, favorite flavor of ice cream, and whether he liked my hair up or down. I loved to make him laugh, and worked hard not to cry in front of him. I cleaned my house before he came over, always wore mascara, always had champagne in the fridge.

Marriage changes that, of course. Artifice goes, as it should. Love deepens, maybe even relaxes a little. And anyway, who has time to set a scene or arrange the canapés when somebody has to be picked up at soccer practice, or the boss has a fit, or the creek rises (literally) into the cellar an hour before the in-laws are to arrive for Easter brunch? When the dog is throwing up, or your mother breaks her hip, who among us can be bothered to murmur, "Darling, I've always loved that color of blue on you."

We've seen each other at our worst, and that's not an exaggeration. Physically ill, emotionally grief-stunned, job-panicked, or angry enough to throw crockery at the wall (and then do it again). Red-faced, blotchy, hoarse from yelling. Our parents grow old, and ill, or nutty; our children make mistakes that drop us to our knees. Through it all, how on earth can he love me, given what a flawed, messy, moody person I am? The artifice is long gone; he sees me. As my oldest friend said when we were girls, "If Prince Charming loves me, he's probably not really Prince Charming."

Well, as it turns out, maybe he is. Okay, so we won't make love on the kitchen table again (there's not enough ibuprofen and, besides, that's why God invented pillow-top mattresses). But lately, when he puts his arm around me in the movie line, or takes my hand as we cross the street, my heart jumps as it did in the beginning. I'm happy to see him in the morning and blessed to sleep beside him at night; there are even days, in a certain light, that he makes me feel all swoony. He *does* see me, which is why he's still here. And I see him, far more clearly than I did—burnished, like my grandmother's sterling silver, and as grounded as the white oak in our front yard. I couldn't have known that's how it would be, back when I was putting on a show.

LARKIN WARREN lives in Connecticut. She is working on her first novel.

23 Because B. B. King proves the pursuit of perfection never ends

I play "The Thrill Is Gone" every night. But I never do exactly what I did last night or the night before. I tell my band to play it as they feel it each night. I like that. It keeps it fresh.

I have a motto: Always do your best. When I was in grade school there was a poem a teacher used to tell us. It went something like "Be the labor great or small, do it well or not at all." I do the best I can each night. Even though a lot of nights my best is nothing as good as I'd like it to be.

Every day I learn something. I have a computer that's my professor. If I don't learn something every day, it's a day lost.

As told to Richard Gehr. B.B. King's new album is *One Kind Favor.*

Because We Can Live Alone and Not Be Lonely

When I used to get home from work, I'd pull up in the driveway and the front door would fly open and out would shoot my three kids, two dogs, and my husband, Vince. They'd all start talking at once as the dogs barked their welcome. "Just let me get in the house," I'd plead. "Then you can tell me what's going on." Flash forward 25 years. Now I come home to an almost empty house. I say almost because my two cats—a fat tabby named Penny Lane and spunky Jenny Jones—are waiting at the front door. No, it's not the same. But those of us who live alone have come to appreciate some simple truths:

24 You can finally hear yourself think

I remember when I'd long for a quiet house. Even after my divorce, there was always someone around. And there was noise. It was the sound-track of my life. Then one day it stopped and my emptying nest was completely empty. And the quiet was almost deafening. It took a long while before I valued hearing my own thoughts. But I never really got used to the silence. To this day I switch on the stereo when I walk in the house.

25 Good neighbors are a godsend

I never realized how true that was until I had to move cross-country for my work. I knew no one. I bought a great house, but even more important, I got a great bunch of neighbors. Over the years they have helped me when I was sick, watched my house, and invited me to their parties. Because of them, I'm never really alone.

26 Single friends are protective friends

I have many friends. But my closest ones are women like me, who live alone. We have an almost natural tendency to look out for one another. Shortly after I moved, a single neighbor came over with a bottle of wine and a welcome. She introduced me to her women friends. We laugh, we cry, we share our deepest secrets. But most important, we understand one another.

27 You cherish new opportunities

I savor being on my own, doing what I want, when I want. But I wouldn't enjoy this freedom half as much if I hadn't experienced a noisy home full of loved ones. Yes, I'm used to living alone, but my door is always open to future possibilities.

KAREN REYES

28 Because . . . Paul Newman

Back in 1961, I was dumb enough to think *The Hustler* was a Jackie Gleason movie. But then came this upstart pool shark with cobalt-blue eyes (yes, *The Hustler* was in black and white, but somehow the blue still showed). He got into The Great One's face and bragged, "I'm the best you ever seen," and there was no arguing the point.

By the time he turned 50 in 1975, Paul Newman could have coasted. But the actor rewrote his career with one breakaway role after another: there he is barreling across the ice in *Slap*

Shot (1977). Then he solemnly offers a summation to the jury in *The Verdict* (1982). Later there's his Oscar-winning return to the role of *The Hustler*'s Fast Eddie Felson in *The Color of Money* (1986).

A new generation knows Newman more as a racecar driver, or as the voice of an old sedan in the animated *Cars,* or as the face on McDonald's salad dressing packets, than for his turn as Butch Cassidy. But for those who grew up with Paul Newman, he's more than a brand, a voice, or a set of blazing peepers. He's proof you can keep chasing that checkered flag even after you've entered the winner's circle.

Read Bill Newcott's Movies for Grownups® reviews at www .aarpmagazine.org.

29 Because your spiritual side grows stronger

The older I get, the more I realize I don't know everything. And that makes me spirituality sensitive to others. I'm less dogmatic, more open to other people's experience of the divine. As we age, we experience things that aren't easily explained—tragedies, failing health—and we become more reflective. There is so much more to learn about the mystery that is the divine, and I've got this thimbleful of knowledge, and I want more. Earlier, a thimbleful was all I could handle. Not anymore. Our spiritual life has a chance to be richer now, with so many more life experiences to reflect upon.

As told to Lynne Meredith Schreiber. Brent Bill is a Quaker minister in Mooresville, Indiana, and the author of *Sacred Compass: The Way of Spiritual Discernment* (Paraclete Press, 2008).

Because We Are Powerful

30
41 percent of American adults are over 50, the highest percentage in U.S. history.

31
80 percent of Congress is over 50.

32
Half of the Americans who voted in the 2006 elections were 50+.

33
People over 55 own 77 percent of all financial assets in the United States.

34
50+ adults account for 45 percent of U.S. consumer spending, or $2.1 trillion per year.

35
By 2011 the American 50+ population will surpass the 100 million mark.

36 Because we're living longer than ever before

Let's get the distressing stats out of the way first: Citizens in 41 countries have longer average life spans than we Americans

do. In some parts of the United States—portions of the Deep South, the Midwest—life expectancy has actually declined (the big reasons are smoking, obesity, and high blood pressure). The upbeat stats? If you are 50 today, on average you'll live to be 80.5. If you're 65, you'll live to 83.4. In fact, if you go back to our one-celled ancestors, we're doing way better than humans at any point in history.

Average Years of Life for . . .
Americans today: 78
Americans in 1900: 47.3
Europeans in the Middle Ages: 31.3
Ancient Greeks: 28
Cro-Magnons: 25
Amoebas: 2 to 3 days, tops

37 "When you get older, hopefully you've developed the smarts to know that if you wake up in the morning and you're vertical and your kids are healthy, that's 90 percent of being happy. That's it!"

Judge Judy

38 Because you're secure enough to take as much advice as you dish out

If it's true we are judged by the company we keep, the evidence in my favor is compelling: a bevy of strong, self-sufficient, passionate young women, 30—and more—years younger than I am. Being this far past 50 frees me to wallow in their youthful exuberance without competition or regret. I am both their patient sage and their eager student.

Each appeared at different points in my life and from various spots on the globe, and though we are sometimes separated by months, years, even continents, our links are so elastic that we never lose touch. They are dream catchers, all: the brilliant, book-loving hell-raiser, who at 16 was as skilled with her fists as she was with a pen when we met 18 years ago; the enchanting poet/actress; the fierce lawyer; the self-assured entrepreneur.

Early on, each of them evoked an intense whisper in me—"I know her"—and I recognized they were parts of that girl I used to be. We are "like" attracting "like"—as intensely loyal as we are truthful. So, when I confess to feeling fat, the actress dares me to shut up and flaunt it. In the middle of my tiresome ranting, the businesswoman shames me—lovingly—into clearing my space of ancient hurts and weary narratives. If I am weak, the lawyer argues me back to warrior-woman status. When I get stuck, the hell-raiser—now the college student/wife/mother—leads me out.

I admire all the things they are that I will never be, but because I'm older, my instructions to them rarely change: Trust your gut. Get angry. If it scares you, do it. Don't go with the flow unless you started it. Eat dessert first.

My young friends revel in my steady assurances, even as they rescue me from the tedium of old certainties and instruct me in the protocol of cool. Watching them—and listening—is pure joy and wonder.

BERNESTINE SINGLEY (www.BernestineSingley.com) is a writer and lawyer based in Dallas.

39 Because you've seen the world change in inconceivable ways

At 57 years of age, I am nervous about the future—the economy, the environment, to say nothing of those deepening crow's-feet. But the long view sustains me. My grandfather was born in the 1880s to former slaves. I hung on to the stories he told—about a life before cars, plastics, the Wright brothers, the Panama Canal, even before Jim Crow laws.

My father was born in 1915. Despite five strokes, he is still vibrant and funny. He was a technical editor back in the days of computer mainframes, back when FORTRAN and COBOL were the lingua franca of techno-nerds. He regales my son with tales of automobiles that had to be cranked. He recalls lynchings when he was growing up. The integration of the Army. The battle of Anzio. The etymology of the word *smog*.

My father still types letters on an old sticky-keyed Smith Corona. As I craft my own words on a brand-new MacBook Air, I am grateful for the strength that intergenerational engagement brings. I am a black female law professor, something my grandfather could never have imagined. And I am about to e-mail these words through an invisible cushion of whooshing cyberspace, something my father worked to create but still can't entirely grasp.

Across the table my son is writing a school paper about the oil crisis and looks up with a glint of panic. "How," he asks me, "will humanity continue?"

I am not so fearful. Like my son, I worry about the crossroads at which we stand. But I am old enough to appreciate how quickly the course of events can change—for the worse, to be sure, but also for the better, if only the will is there. If my father can remember the very first U.S. smog alert, then my son might live to see the haze subside and the heavens reemerge. The human spirit is amazingly, unexpectedly resilient. Anything can happen.

PATRICIA WILLIAMS is the James L. Dohr Professor of Law at Columbia University and a columnist for *The Nation*.

40 Because you actually enjoy going to high-school reunions

For the first few decades, high-school reunions are like updated versions of an old cartoon show: the hairstyles and voices are a little different, but, really, Archie and Jughead haven't changed that much. Reunions after age 50 are more like *Return to Mayberry,* where Opie's gone bald and Aunt Bee is dead. This is not a bad thing, because while everyone else looks like a jack-o'-lantern left on the porch too long, you haven't changed a bit. You know this is true, because everybody tells you so. (You tell everybody the same thing, but that's just because you're so nice.) And yet these later reunions are somehow more pleasant than those in years past. The smoldering one-up-manship has

pretty much quenched itself; you've filed away a lot of the old jealousies and insecurities that dogged your younger years. At last you're free to enjoy those fleeting connections with your youth. And if you aren't, that old classmate who's now a psychiatrist will gladly give you his card.

BILL NEWCOTT

Because Older Brains Have New Strengths

41 You're a better judge of character

The proof: In tests at North Carolina State University, older folks outperformed younger participants in determining whether people were honest and intelligent.

42 Your brain is more efficient

The proof: Duke University researchers discovered that older individuals use the brain's right and left hemispheres at the same time (typically the brain uses the left for some tasks, and the right for others). "In effect, the mature brain creates a synergy that helps it think outside the box," says Gene Cohen, MD, PhD, author of *The Mature Mind* (Basic Books, 2005).

43 You're less neurotic than you used to be

The proof: Australian scientists found that neuroticism was less prevalent in subjects ages 50 to 79. Brain scans also revealed a more controlled response to fear. The experts' theory: A growing awareness of mortality and a desire for meaning mellows the mind.

MELISSA GOTTHARDT

44 Because you don't tolerate bad service

For years I went to a hairstylist whose end result never quite worked. A nice person, and so proud of owning her own salon—it was fun to spend time with her every couple of months. The friendship was swell—we went through joy, grief, and menopause together—but the hairdo? Not so much. Yet I couldn't leave her; I didn't want her to feel bad. Then I saw the mother-of-the-groom pictures from my son's wedding. Bad hair. Very bad hair. Anyone with a heart would've handed me a baseball cap.

And so, with shaking hands and a sinking stomach, I took my leave. She cried, I cried, and I soon found someone else, who is better than good; sometimes she's great. Yay me. But, wow, how many hundreds of dollars did I spend over the years for bad hair? What is it that holds us to doctors, mechanics, or electricians who don't or won't do what we need? Why do we cling to friendships that take more than they give, or relationships that drag on our hearts like boat anchors? Is it my mother's fault, for tamping down my big teenage mouth with "Be polite; don't make a scene"? Is it my father's, for instructing me to appreciate other people's efforts? "She's doing the best she can," he said about the piano teacher whose breath melted paint. So I dutifully played my scales, never told a waitress that I'd wanted milk, not orange juice, and grew up to gnash my teeth in my sleep.

Finally, the freedom of a fully flowered adulthood dropped the hammer on this Go Along to Get Along baloney. Bad hairstylist? Gone. The plumber who didn't fix the mess under the kitchen sink and charged me anyway? Gone. The old friend who in a three-week period canceled a lunch date four times, then scolded me for arriving ten minutes late? Well, not gone, exactly, but definitely on my pay-no-mind list. The car dealer who tried to muscle me 20 minutes into our first conversation? Summarily exchanged for the nice, slow-moving guy at the dealership down the road. From him, we'll buy two.

No matter how many birthdays we get, the salient lesson remains the same: Life is short. There's never enough time for the people and activities we love, so why allot time (or sleepless nights, or money) to those we don't? Being nice doesn't equal suffering fools; being compassionate does not translate as "take a hosing, write the check, and feel like a sucker." I don't want to waste my time anymore; I don't want to waste yours. Can we make a deal that will make us both happy? Otherwise (and I say this with deep respect for how good you are, how hard you work, and how long we've known each other), you're fired.

LARKIN WARREN

45 Because you realize that trauma can lead to enlightenment

When I used to tell friends, half jokingly, that a potentially fatal disease had actually saved my life, they rarely understood what I meant. I wasn't claiming I was glad to have it. I wasn't pretending to be overjoyed by the prospect of an early departure. I was simply confessing an odd bit of truth. Without the threat of mortal loss, I would never have had the fuel to find my way through terrible dread to something stronger than my fear.

Hardship can render us bitter, selfish, defensive, and miserable. It can also be used as the artery of interconnection, a bridge to other people in pain, as blood in the muscles that push us forward. Crisis takes us to the brink of our limits and forces us to keep moving. When people in extremis call it a blessing, this is the paradox they are describing. It's why men sometimes blossom in wartime and why women are changed by childbirth—they come alive as never before on that knife-blade danger and pain. There's vitality in facing life's extremes, including our own extinction.

Adapted from Mark Matousek's new book, *When You're Falling, Dive: Lessons in the Art of Living* (Bloomsbury USA).

46 Because you grew up in an age before video games

When we were kids, we played outside. Our bodies were hard-breathing little rainbows of energy and earth—red cheeks from running, brown hands from mud, green-grass streaks on our pants. We dreamed of grandiose forts that never got built, had sword fights with sticks while riding our bikes (okay, that was more of a boy thing). But we lived, baby. We lived! Unlike so many kids today, whose every micromanaged, remote-control moment is seemingly spent indoors. Oh, how the play times have changed:

Then	Now
Eating wild berries in the woods	Eating Lunchables on a play date
Climbing trees	Allergy tests
Walking with pals along train tracks	Walking with parents on a leash
Stickball	Xbox
"Be home by dark"	"Answer your cell phone when I call"
Summer camp	Fat camp
Doing cannonballs off the high dive	Wearing floaties in the shallow end
Skinned knees	Carpal tunnel
Jumping on a trampoline	What's a trampoline?

47 Because we can be as fit now as we were at 20 (Just ask Martina)

Tennis legend Martina Navratilova is 52, and she has a message: age is no excuse for being flabby. Too often, she says, 50-plus folks are inactive for so long, they think: Why bother? But Martina isn't buying it. "Age is not part of the equation," she says. "Exercise at your own level. Take a walk. Anything. Once I saw a woman with one leg running on crutches. Another time I saw a man with no legs in a wheelchair playing hockey. So, what is your excuse? A headache? You're too tired? Look in the mirror."

Yeah, yeah—like the eternally buff Martina has any idea what it's like to fight fat. Turns out she does. When she first came to the United States in 1973, she began a love affair with pancakes and eggs, and her rock-hard tennis bod became . . . pudgy. In 1981, despite Martina's having dropped down to a svelte 145 pounds, a friend told her she wasn't in great shape and was wasting her talent.

Thus was born a lifelong commitment to fitness. But you don't have to be as fanatical as Martina. "Start with a ten-minute walk," she says. "Then do more. Go gradually, not too intense. You'll feel better each day. It doesn't have to be painful."

PAT JORDAN

48 "Happiness no longer seems like an unobtainable goal—it can reside in a superb cup of coffee."

MAGGIE FRIEDE, Quincy, Massachusetts

49 "Before I turned 50, I was always pushing to do more. Now I'm able to step back mentally and just look around. Was all this beauty here all along?"

JAN LUFF, Milford, Delaware

50 Because you know who your friends are

It's no mystery at this point. Your old friends are the ones who don't desert you, who share a beer or a tear when life is dark, who make you laugh. (Your new friends do the same; they just haven't been on the job as long.) Harvard professor Daniel Gilbert, PhD, who studies happiness, says we tend to tighten our circle of friends as we age—to focus on those who make us happy now. Yet the squabbling Simon and Garfunkel model of friendship—my "partner in arguments," Simon once called his musical other half—should not be tossed aside like Oscar flinging dirty socks at an exasperated Felix. We need the people who fight with us but will also fight for us. Friendship is like shares in a growing company: the investment isn't easy, but the dividends enrich our lives.

KEN BUDD

Are You Ready for Act II?

Learning professionals nearing retirement age need to start thinking about what they want to do in the next phase of their lives.

PAULA KETTER

The definition of retirement is outdated. The word retirement used to mean "withdrawal from one's occupation or from active working life," but it now has a multitude of meanings, including leaving your current job for entrepreneurship, entering a new phase of life and work, or finding meaning as a volunteer or part-time worker.

Regardless of how you define this term or at what age you begin this new career, you need to ensure that you are ready to leave your current job and start afresh.

"The biggest piece of advice I can give to anyone thinking about retiring is to plan ahead," says Kiki Weingarten, cofounder and coach of Daily Life Consulting. "The time to be laying the groundwork is while you are still working. You need to be in a place psychologically, financially, and emotionally where you can think clearly about the future and your place in it.

"The corporate setting has a tremendous amount of structure, and as much as we complain about it, that structure helps us get up in the morning and plan our day," she adds.

As a workplace learning and performance professional, your skills and competencies can take you far, long after life in your current work is complete. It won't be an end of work for you, just a career transition that could include continuing to work in a reduced role, returning to school for additional training, changing careers, becoming an entrepreneur, volunteering in your community, writing a book, or traveling.

Retirement is a time to be very honest about who you are, what you want to do, and what you do best. If you decide to become a consultant or start a small business for example, you need to ensure that you are ready to work on your own.

"Know clearly what your skills and competencies are and what you don't do well," says Judy Estrin, president of Partners in Enterprise. "Also, you need to answer these questions: Do have what it takes to be by yourself? Do you have the discipline to work by yourself? Are you easily distracted? You need to answer these questions before you decide to be a consultant."

It is critical to know what you do best because as a consultant, you are taking on a substantial risk. You will be doing everything yourself, from faxing and mailing, to doing your own IT support.

Candice Phelan, former director of learning systems at Lockheed Martin, retired recently and relocated to Florida to be near her mother. Her plan was to do some consulting work and stay abreast of what was going on in the field, but she wasn't prepared for the lack of technical support.

"I don't have an IT help desk I can call," she says. "I consider myself computer savvy, but I just didn't have the support of an IT infrastructure."

Ed Betof, former vice president of talent management and chief learning officer at BD, left the corporate world for the academic, as a senior fellow at the University of Pennsylvania. He admits that he wasn't completely prepared for his career change.

"I'm finding that even though I'm engaged in a really rich program at Penn, I'm experiencing the challenge of not having my foot on the gas pedal all the time," he explains. "This career change is also a lifestyle change. Like so many other situations, you need to have a really clear awareness of your personality style, your personal values, and what you want to do because this is a huge change. It's a life-planning situation."

Create a Strategy

Whatever you decide to pursue in this new phase of your life, you need to start planning for it now, before you leave the workplace. Knowing what you want to do is only part of the plan.

"How much time are you going to work? What are your boundaries surrounding work hours and leisure time? You need to have a plan and really stick to it," Weingarten says.

Geoff Bellman, who retired from the corporate world in the late 1970s to become a consultant and then scaled back his "second career" about a decade ago, advises people who are nearing retirement to start preparing for it four years before they leave their current jobs.

"You certainly don't want to go back to work once you've left because you haven't found any place to go or something to do," Bellman says. "If you can use the skills that you liked using in the corporate world, the transition will be a lot easier."

Before you retire, there are several things you need to do to prepare for the challenges ahead.

Decide What You Want to Do

This sounds simple, but many people walk away from their jobs without knowing what they want to do with the next 20 or 30 years of their lives. In search of the answer, ask yourself these questions:

- Do I want to do work that is fun, meaningful, or both?
- How many hours do I want to work?
- Do I want to work a few hours every day for six months and then take six months off, or full time with a few weeks for vacation?
- With what kind of organizational cultures do I want to work?
- Do I want to do volunteer work?

Write a Letter of Introduction for Yourself

Write a letter of introduction as though you are five years into the future, or write a paragraph about what you have been doing for the last five years. "This will give you an idea of where you are today," Weingarten explains. "The best time to do this is while you are still at your old job because you have a certain confidence to sell yourself that will disappear when you leave the workplace."

Start Networking Now

Put the word out to everyone you know that you are starting a new "career." Ask them to pass the information along to people they know. "Networking is so much harder when you are out on your own," says Weingarten. "While you are still working, you can pick up the phone and talk to the people you know. It's easier to get through when you have that corporate identity."

Networking can be one of the most difficult things to do, depending on your personality, your experience doing it, or your future needs. If you don't feel comfortable talking with others or selling yourself, you may want of find a coach to help you prepare for these situations.

Networking can be one of the most difficult things to do, depending on your personality, your experience doing it, or your future needs. If you don't feel comfortable talking with others or selling yourself, you may want to find a coach to help you prepare for these situations. It's critical that you create business cards, practice your pitch, and make eye contact. Don't forget to sign up for profiles on LinkedIn, MySpace, Plaxo, or other social networking forums. These are great ways to meet other people with similar interests.

Fast Facts about the New Retirement Ideal

- There were 34.9 million women aged 55 and above in the United States in 2004. Of those women, 10.7 million were in the workforce (either working or looking for work).
  Source: U.S. Department of labor

- Between 1995 and 2000, the estimated age of retirement for women was 61.4 years.
  Source: U.S. Department of labor

- Nearly four in 10 workers between the ages of 50 and 64 plan to continue to work beyond retirement age. Thirty-one percent of respondents who planned to retire at 65 would reconsider if their employers allowed them to work flexibly.
  Source: Chartered Institute of Personnel and Development survey

- Forty-two percent of men say they definitely want to work beyond 65, compared to 34 percent of women.
  Source: Chartered Institute of Personnel and Development survey

- More than 75 percent of baby boomers have no intention of seeking a traditional retirement.
  Source: The Merrill lynch New Retirement Study

- The ideal retirement for 71 percent of adults surveyed is to work in some capacity. Half of that 71 percent do not plan to ever stop working.
  Source: The Merrill lynch New Retirement Study

To expand your network of contacts, consider joining clubs or professional associations. "Sometimes a great way to get your name out there is to sit on a panel or give a workshop for free or minimal cost," Weingarten says. "Make sure you attend meetings, workshops, and conferences. That is one of the best ways to sell yourself and expand your network."

Estrin agrees, adding that joining clubs and associations can give you a sense of belonging and helps you stay active professionally. "What I discovered about three years into my new life was that I got lonely," she says. "I missed the affiliation of being corporate, but I didn't want to be affiliated, so I found a consortium of other consultants that I met with every four to six weeks just to chit chat.

"I also subscribe to association publications in my field because if I don't, the jargon gets away from me," Estrin adds.

Volunteer Opportunities

A recent Merrill Lynch study finds that boomers want to give back and prefer to pursue "retirement careers" where they can share or pass on knowledge to others through training and teaching. Volunteering ranks high on lists of things boomers want to do in retirement.

You've spent the majority of your life in a rigid corporate structure, so whatever you decide to do, do something you love—whether that's working in a new career or volunteering with a not-for-profit that shares your beliefs and values.

"Volunteering is a great way to keep your skills up if you can afford to do it financially," Estrin says. "There are plenty of places to apply your training skills. Explore the Small Business Economic Development Council in your community, or contact the chamber of commerce in your city."

Weingarten agrees, adding, "Be a mentor, or an advisor, or give talks to kids—there are hundreds of things that you can do every day. Check out message boards and blogs, or visit idealist .org for a list of not-for-profits. There are a lot of things that you can do that don't come naturally to others, so you just have to do a little research."

Planned Phase Out

Part of your work as a workplace learning and performance professional includes creating a succession plan for positions within your company. But, what happens when you decide to retire?

"I worked with the senior vice president of HR to create a current role description for my position," Betof explains. "That description emphasized the mission-critical competencies for the role."

As with any position, keeping your immediate supervisor aware of your plans can make the transition easier for you and the company.

"You can certainly help engineer a replacement using a succession plan," says Phelan. "But another is to ask, 'Is there a better way for this position to be organized?' When I made the decision to leave, I was able to make the case to move my functions to different departments instead of replacing me."

Before you walk out the door, you need to expect that you will be helping with transitioning your successor into your previous role, Betof says. "That will help minimize the risk of that successor."

Once you've told your supervisor of your plans to leave, you need to start thinking about how to transfer the knowledge you have to others in the company. "If there is a bad relationship with the company, tacit knowledge transfer may never happen," Betof explains. "The really important thing is to let the company know what your plans are as soon as possible. If there is a degree of trust between you and your immediate supervisor, it is going to make things a lot easier."

Retiring from corporate life is not as easy as setting a date or deciding on a new "career."

"Be prepared for change," Weingarten says. "In the beginning, there is a big psychological shift. Don't be blindsided."

PAULA KETTER is editor of *T+D;* pketter@astd.org.

Tearing: Breakthrough in Human Emotional Signaling

ROBERT R. PROVINE, KURT A. KROSNOWSKI, AND NICOLE W. BROCATO

Introduction

Tears, a secretion of the lacrimal glands, lubricate the eye, are a response to irritation (e.g., abrasion, onion), improve optical performance by smoothing the otherwise rough corneal surface, and provide the antibiotic lysozyme (Frey, 1985; Sullivan, et al., 2002). Tears are widespread among vertebrates (Frey, 1985), but emotional tears may be unique to humans (Frey, 1985; Walter, 2006). Although there are anecdotal reports of emotional tearing in nonhumans (Masson and McCarthy, 1995), such reports are controversial and it is difficult to establish the cause of tears that may be produced (Frey, 1985). Tearing (lacrimation) by humans is associated with sadness and other emotional states and acts, including crying, grief, despair, frustration, helplessness, powerlessness, pain, happiness, anger, and empathy, as well as yawning, laughing, and sneezing (Frey, 1985; Lutz, 1999; Provine, 2000; Vingerhoets and Cornelius, 2001). The scientific literature about tearing during crying deals with physiology, gender, development, personality, social context, culture, psychopathology, health, and catharsis (Frey, 1985; Vingerhoets and Cornelius, 2001). Remarkably, neither the specialized literature about human crying nor the much broader literature about human emotion and facial expression provides an experimental evaluation of the tacit assumption that tears are a visual signal of sadness or other emotion. This study provides the first test of the role of tears as a visual signal by contrasting the perceived sadness of facial images with tears against copies of those images that had tears digitally removed.

Materials and Methods

Eighty undergraduate students at the University of Maryland, Baltimore County (54 female, 26 male; mean age = 22.0 years (SD = 4.30, range = 18–49) volunteered to participate in a study of sadness perception. UMBC is an ethnically diverse campus (52% white, 22% Asian, 17% African-American, 4% Hispanic, 4% international, 1% Native American) with students from 93 countries.

Fifty color images of faces with obvious tears in their eyes or running down their cheeks, were found by searching for "tears," "crying," and their cognates on online image archives such as *Flickr.* Selected tears (T) images, mostly in frontal and three-quarters perspective, were equally divided between males and females and roughly divided between estimated age (25 preadolescent children, 25 adults) and race (one-third Caucasian, black, and Asian). The 50 "tears" (T) images were edited with Adobe Photoshop to remove the tears, creating 50 matching "tears removed" (TR) images. Fifty tear-free "distracter" (D) facial images with mixed, midrange emotional expressions, were obtained by archive searches ("sports," "careers," etc.), again dividing images into groups based on sex, age and race, and duplicated, yielding 100 D images, and a total of 200 images of all types (T, TR, D). The presentation order of the first 100 images was: D1, T1, D2, TR2, D3, etc. The second 100 images reversed the order of the T and TR (but not D) images in the first 100 stimuli: D1, TR1, D2, T2, D3, etc. Thus, the order of presentation of T and TR image pairs was counterbalanced, with half of T images presented before their TR counterpart, and half of the T images presented after their TR counterpart. The images, cropped and sized to provide similar image scale, were presented in slideshow format, each appearing for 5 s, or until a rating was made, after which the next image would appear. A sample of facial images is not provided because of copyright restrictions and the inability to obtain informed consent of the people portrayed.

Before beginning the study, subjects were given 10 training trials using distracter-type stimuli to confirm that they understood the procedure. Instructions to subjects in both training and experimental trials were presented in on-screen text and read aloud by the experimenter:

> During each 5-second trial you will be shown an image of a person's face on this computer screen. Your task is to estimate the sadness of the person in the image using the 7-point rating scale of sadness from 1 "Not Sad At All" to 7 "Extremely Sad" that appears beneath the person's image. Using the mouse, you will record your response by moving the cursor to the number corresponding to how sad the person in the image appears and click the mouse button.

The study was approved by the Institutional Review Board of the University of Maryland, Baltimore County.

Results

Facial images with tears were rated as significantly sadder in appearance ($M = 5.29$, $SD = .64$) than the same images with tears removed ($M = 4.05$, $SD = .63$), as determined by a repeated-measures ANOVA, $F(1,77) = 27.53$, $p < .01$, $\eta^2 = .26$. The ANOVA used gender as a between-groups factor with age as a covariate. The repeated measures variable had two levels: the average rating of images with tears; and the average rating of the images with tears removed. There were no interaction effects for age or gender with sadness ratings. Also, age was not a significant between-groups factor.

Participants seemed unaware of the experimental design and tear-removal tactic, probably because of the large number ($n = 200$) of D, T and TR images. After the study, a few participants volunteered that some of the images were duplicates, not realizing that half of the images were exact duplicates (D) and the remaining half nearly so (T, TR). No participant commented that some of the "duplicates" had tears and some had tears removed.

Discussion

The finding that tear removal produced a face perceived as less sad was anticipated but provided the first experimental confirmation of folk wisdom that tears are a visual signal of sadness. More surprising was the incidental, anecdotal finding that tear removal often produced faces of ambiguous emotional valence, perhaps awe, concern, contemplation or puzzlement, not simply of less sadness. In other words, faces without tears may not appear very sad. The effect of tear removal can be approximated by using your finger to block-out tears in a photograph.

Emotional tears provide a potent and informative visual signal of sadness that requires facial illumination of the sender and line-of-sight contact by an observer. Tears do not work in darkness or around obstructions. Emotional tears resolve ambiguity and add meaning to the neuromuscular instrument of facial expression, what we term the *tear effect*. Tears are not a benign secretory correlate of sadness or other emotional state. Emotional tears may be exclusively human (Frey, 1985) and, unlike associated vocal crying, do not develop until a few months after birth (Darwin, 1872/1965; Hopkins, 2000). The emergence of emotional tearing during evolution and development is a significant but neglected advance in human social behavior that taps an already established secretory process involving the eye, a primary target of visual attention.

The current study examined a single dimension of tears as a visual signal—their contribution to the perception of sadness. As suggested by the wide-ranging chapters of the text *Adult Crying* (Vingerhoets and Cornelius, 2001), more work must be done to understand the full contribution of tears to the perception of sadness and other emotional states, including their blends; "it is still largely unknown why adults cry and what the function of their crying is" (Vingerhoets, Boelhouwer, Van Tilburg, and Van Heck, 2001, p. 71). Do tears, for example, make a person appear more needy, helpless, frustrated, or powerless, as well as sadder? Do tears amplify a perceived emotional expression, add a unique message, or contribute a subtle nuance interpreted as sincerity or wistfulness? Do tears express a blend of emotions, such as anger and powerlessness? Does a happy face with tears appear more or less joyous, or something in between, perhaps described as "bittersweet?" Are tears more prominent or emotionally potent on dark than light skin? Does the race, sex or age of a tearful face influence ratings of sadness or other emotions? (The current study detected no difference between the sadness ratings of adult men and women, or of adult raters of different age.) Are there interactions between the race, sex and age of sender and recipient of tearful signals, such that, for example, children seem sadder than adults, women seem sadder than men, or same-race individuals seem sadder than individuals of different-race?

A high priority area of future research involves the replication of traditional studies of the perception of facial expressions using tears as a variable. Virtually everything remains to be done. Two approaches would involve variants of the present procedure: examining the effect of tear-removal from facial images, if tears are present; and, adding tears to tear-free facial images, a more technologically difficult procedure. As in the present research on tear removal, the addition of tears to the images of people displaying happy, angry, disgusted, or other faces may yield unanticipated results.

A promising future clinical study involves the examination of emotional experiences of people who are unable to secrete tears because of pathology or agenesis of the lacrimal glands (Sullivan, et al., 2002). This condition of "dry eye" probably has an associated but unappreciated deficit of emotional signaling of the sort experienced by a young female graduate student who shared her story with the senior author. She described the frustration of being forced to explain, at the most difficult of times, and sometimes with quivering voice, her feelings that were once automatically communicated with tears. Her story nicely summarizes the contribution of tearing to the sometimes limited neuromuscular instrument and repertoire of the facial expression of emotion.

References

Darwin, C. (1872/1965). *The expression of emotions in man and animals.* Chicago: Chicago University Press. (Original work published 1872)

Frey, W.H. (1985). *Crying: The mystery of tears.* Minneapolis: Winston Press.

Hopkins. B. (2000). Development of crying in normal infants: Method, theory and some speculations. In R.G. Barr, B. Hopkins, and J.A. Green (Eds.). *Crying as a sign, a symptom, and a signal* (pp. 176–209). London: Mac Keith Press.

Lutz, T. (1999). *Crying: The natural and cultural history of tears.* New York: Norton.

Masson, J.M., and McCarthy, S. (1995). *When elephants weep: The emotional lives of animals.* New York: Delecorte Press.

Provine, R.R. (2000). *Laughter: A scientific investigation.* New York: Viking.

Sullivan, D.A., Stern, M.E., Tsubota, K., Dart, D.A., Sullivan, R.M., and Bloomberg, B.B. (Eds.). (2002). *Lacrimal gland, tear film, and dry eye syndromes 3.* New York: Springer.

Vingerhoets, A.J.J.M., Boelhouwer, A.J.W., Van Tilburg, M.A.L., and Van Heck, G.L. (2001). In Vingerhoets, A. J. J. M., and Cornelius, R.R. (Eds.). *Adult crying: A biopsychosocial approach* (pp. 71–89). Philadelphia: Brunner-Routledge.

Vingerhoets, A.J.J.M., and Cornelius, R.R. (Eds.). (2001). *Adult crying: A biopsychosocial approach.* Philadelphia: Brunner-Routledge.

Walter, C. (2006). *Thumbs, toes, and tears.* New York: Walker and Company.

Robert R. Provine, Department of Psychology, University of Maryland Baltimore County, Baltimore, Maryland 21250, USA. Email: provine@umbc.edu (corresponding author) kurt A. krosnowski, Department of Psychology, University of Maryland Baltimore County, Baltimore, Maryland 21250, USA. Nicole W. Brocato, Department of Psychology, University of Maryland Baltimore County, Baltimore, Maryland 21250, USA.

Acknowledgments—The authors thank Mackenzie D. Whipps and Katie M. Webb for assistance in data collection, Bill Degnan for assistance in programming the display, and Helen R. Weems for editorial suggestions. The manuscript benefited from the suggestions of the editor and two anonymous referees.

Received 22 September 2008; Revision submitted 19 January 2009; Accepted 25 January 2009

Healthy Aging in Later Life

JILL DUBA ONEDERA AND FRED STICKLE

There are many ways in which to describe aging by associating negative factors with growing older (Cuddy, Norton, & Fiske, 2005). In fact, as you are reading this, you probably can mentally note numerous negative factors or disadvantages associated with aging. There are also numerous positive factors associated with the aging process. In this article, several positive factors or ways in which persons can age successfully will be presented.

Positive Factors Associated with Healthy Aging

Certainly, perceptions of aging might contribute to the overall success and satisfaction of growing older (Bowling, 1993). Despite many myths and stereotypes about aging, there are many advantages associated with aging (Knight, 2004). Such advantages include psychological and mental development as well as continued social engagement and intellectual stimulation. In the following section, both of these factors will be briefly discussed.

Psychological and Mental Development with Age

The later years, defined as age 65 or older (Himes, 2001), can be a period of continued psychological growth during which people adapt to new roles and discover creative outlets for their leisure time as well as prepare themselves for the end of life (Lewittes, 1989; Medinger & Varghese, 1981). Upon entering this stage, adults begin to assert the competence and creativity attained during middle adulthood, while also giving additional thought to life's meaning (Knight, 2004). That is, adults may begin to apply the wealth of their life experiences, their perspectives on time, and their adaptations to life crises to personally satisfying answers to the most fundamental of existential questions (Bohlmeijer, Valenkamp, Westerhof, Smit, & Cuijpers, 2005).

Memory, reasoning, information, problem-solving abilities, and mental rigidity or fluidity can influence the capacity of older adults to introspect, assess personal past history, and make plans for the future (Knight, 2004). Through encounters with diverse experiences, decision making, parenting, other forms of tutoring or mentoring of younger generations, and efforts to formulate a personal philosophy, adults can reach new levels of conscious thought (Coleman, Ivani-Chalian, & Robinson, 1999). The accumulation of experiences throughout each older person's life also undoubtedly adds to the framework and self-evaluation of one's life. With such experiences, it may become easier to accept and realize that change, whether linear or cyclic, is a basic element of life at both individual and social levels. As a witness to these changes and varied experiences, older persons exercising positive and hopeful attitudes can aid them in gaining special perspectives on conditions of continuity and change within their culture that can help them shape their own lives (Collings, 2001; Kenel, 2005). In the process of developing a psychohistorical perspective, very old adults can develop a personal understanding of stability and change, effects of history on individual lives, and one's place in the chain of evolution (Haight & Michel, 1998).

Older persons also share a unique place in the process of psychosocial evolution. As parents, grandparents, or great-grandparents, individuals are able to see their lines of descent continue into the fourth generation (Fallon, 1998; Walsh, 1988). Furthermore, older persons are in unique positions that allow them to examine and reflect on how each generation that followed them has added to existing knowledge as well as value bases (Troll, 1996). With these observations and reflections, older persons can choose to embrace the timeless role of keeping family members connected to the past as they knew it by maintaining the value of the oral tradition of history and storytelling. With each story, new connections can be made to the distant past (Knight, 2004). Finally, a greater investment in the future may develop as the very old see in their great-grandchildren the concrete extension of their ancestry three generations into the future.

In summary, the development of one's psyche and cognitions has a circular effect on the psychological and mental health of the individual. That is, while adopting or embracing any of the previously mentioned advantages, it is likely that one's psychological and mental health will be improved or steady.

Successful Aging: The Activity Theory

One of the oldest theories of successful aging was termed the *disengagement theory* (Cummings & Henry, 1961). The disengaged elderly are characterized by infrequent contact with family, friends, and the outside world. It may include a mutual withdrawal by society and the older person. Withdrawal and disengagement are considered to be a natural developmental process. During this process, older persons may experience psychological well-being as well as balance characterized by decreased social interactions and greater psychological distances from those nearby. Although controversial, this theory assumes that successful aging means coping with disengagement successfully (Gamliel, 2001).

The authors of this article advocate for an activity theory that we suggest is a healthy aging theory. According to this model, successful aging occurs as long as persons maintain levels of activity as well as social interactions characteristic of middle age (Bergstrom, Holmes, & Pecchioni, 2000). In other words, older persons need not be expected to disengage or retire from social interactions, physical or mental activities, or other enjoyable experiences. Being both connected and useful to others at an advanced age is both an individual goal and one that supports the well-being of others and society as a whole. Such connections may include finding a substitute partner and/or friends following the death of a loved one. Older individuals also might continue to stimulate themselves in less social ways but more intellectually through books, novels, and educational and technological resources, but even these pursuits can be enhanced by sharing them with others or passing their intellectual curiosities onto younger generations.

Depending on the unique characteristics of the individual, either theory, the disengagement theory or the activity theory, might hold some truth (Chang & Dodder, 1984). Clearly, an older person can disengage and limit social activities while remaining happy, independent, and contented. Ansbacher (1992) has suggested that aging often includes a greater focus on self-interest after people have lived a long time engaged in social interests. At present, it is unclear whether the theories of disengagement and activity can be complementary or are simply contradictory. Both may be limited in explaining an effective recipe for healthy aging. Because some older people may be satisfied with a high degree of social interaction while others are satisfied with a small amount, more information is needed to provide a useful theory of what it means to age with physical, emotional, mental, and relational health.

Criteria for Successful and Healthy Aging

Offenbacher and Poster (1985) offered four normative principles key to aging successfully that are seemingly supportive of the activity theory. These principles, as reported by older individuals themselves, include the following mantras or attitudes: (a) don't feel sorry for yourself: (b) be independent; (c) don't just sit there, do something; and (d) above all, be sociable. Furthermore, the activity theory suggests that when people maintain the attitudes and activities of middle age for as long as possible, while finding substitutes for activities that they must give up, these persons will increase or maintain their overall satisfaction with life (Miller, Soyoung, & Schofield-Tomschin, 1998). These types of active behaviors suggest that living well in later life requires persons to be sociable, active, and independent. Such conducts of living may also benefit others in different age groups; however, this code of conduct specifically offers older individuals sources of self-esteem. Following such a code may tend to promote a sense of vigor and shield against depression or discouragement. Based on the previously mentioned suggestions, the authors present additional reflections on how to carry out such a code.

The Active Lifestyle

The mantras "don't be sorry for yourself" and "don't just sit there" suggest that the very old continue to see their lives as precious resources not to be wasted away in self-pity and passivity (Miller et al., 1998). Doing things, having an impact, and receiving the feedback that action stimulates seem to provide the keys to successful living. In fact, Duay and Bryan (2006) suggest that taking part in volunteer activities, as well as learning and educational experiences, can increase an older person's sense of purpose and personal satisfaction. Furthermore, taking part in such activities has been found to contribute to an older person's psychological well-being as well as more positive views about the aging process (Ritchey, Ritchey, & Dietz, 2001).

Cognitive Orientation

According to Kahana, Kahana, and Zhang (2005), older persons who hold optimistic and hopeful thoughts about the future will achieve meaningfulness in life as well as psychological well-being. More specifically, this dimension of successful aging might be related

to making and planning for short- and long-term goals. Short-term goals may consist of preparing a particular meal for dinner in 2 days or dusting the end table in the bedroom. Long-term goals may include writing a short letter to a friend within the next 3 months or getting through a novel within the upcoming year. Such goals and many others also contribute to any individual's sense of purpose in life as well as reasons to wake up and live each day.

Social Support

For the very old, social support also plays a major role in maintaining well-being and fostering possibilities of transcending any physical limitations that accompany aging (Vance, Wadley, Ball, Roenker, & Rizzo, 2005). Furthermore, social support can play an active role in promoting health and well-being even when a person is not facing a specific stressful situation (Brown & Lowis, 2003). Because social support involves meaningful social relationships, it reduces isolation. People who have intimate companions in later life have higher levels of life satisfaction (Payne, Mowen, & Montoro-Rodriguez, 2006). They feel valued, needed, and a sense of belonging, and in turn, they provide the same value to others. This kind of support may likely to be most appreciated when it comes from friends and neighbors, members of the community who are not bound by familial obligation to care about you but who do care about you anyway. Furthermore, the support system often serves to encourage older persons to maintain their health care practices as well as seek medical attention when it is needed (Cohen, Magai, & Yaffee, 2005).

Very old people are likely to experience declines in physical stamina. They may also have limited financial resources. For the very old to transcend the limitations of their daily living situations, it can be helpful if they are convinced that they are embedded in a network of social relationships in which they are valued (Vance et al., 2005). Their value cannot be based solely on a physical exchange of goods and services. It must be founded on an appreciation of their dignity and a history of reciprocal caring.

Other Criteria for Successful and Healthy Aging
Reciprocity

The value of reciprocity in both emotional and caregiving support is very strong in our culture. Many people want and expect to be able to give about the same as or more than they receive. Nevertheless, many older adults may continue to see themselves as involved in reciprocal, supportive relationships with their friends (Lewittes, 1989). As older adults receive more physical and possibly laborious care from their children when they are ill, they can retain a sense of reciprocal balance by seeing the help they receive now as comparable to the help they gave at earlier stages. In addition, if they experience a feeling of value from their caregivers, it may not be so important to reciprocate in the exchange of tangible resources. Wisdom, affection, joie de vivre, and a positive model of surviving into old age can be intangible resources that are highly valued by members of the support network of older persons (Kenel, 2005). For example, the advice and conversation initiated by older persons may be adequate exchanges for some of the services and assistance being provided by family and friends.

Beginning Early

Being an integral part of a social system does not begin in later life. It can have its origins in infancy with the formation of a mutual relationship with a caregiver. Based on positive social support systems in childhood and early adolescence through identification with a peer group, persons can move into early and middle adulthood with support systems developed through marriage, child rearing, and relationships with coworkers and adult friends (Shaw, Krause, & Chatters, 2004). Payne et al. (2006) also suggest that persons who establish a broad leisure repertoire during earlier life stages will most likely continue this lifestyle into older age.

Staying in Touch with the Present

According to Rikers and Myers (1990), older individuals can enjoy later adulthood by keeping up to date with current events and topics. By attending to current news reports through television and radio stations, forming or joining discussion groups at the local library or senior center on political happenings in the community, or enrolling in related courses at the local community college, older adults glean knowledge that keeps them current as well as in touch with the world around them. Making use of the Internet and e-mail also has been noted to encourage communication between users and their friends and family as well as to serve as a form of entertainment and education (Stark-Wroblewski, Edelbaum, & Ryan, 2007).

Changing Society's Attitudes toward Older Persons

Potentially the most daunting factors related to successful and healthy aging are the perceptions, stereotypes, and myths that society places around older people (Cuddy et al., 2005). Consequently, for older persons to feel confident, while enjoying life as they age, it is imperative that the negative perceptions, ideas, and attitudes in society as a whole, especially as they are reflected in government practices, be challenged with regard to older persons. Such stereotypes can be translated into disrespectful and disempowering behaviors and practices toward older persons by friends and families as well as professional caregivers. It is not uncommon for older persons to then internalize such attitudes. Such internalization can lead to decreased self-worth, self-esteem, and value, thus contributing to the deterioration of one's overall sense of well-being. Our culture needs to embrace the fact that older persons can age successfully and be healthy while doing so.

Case Example: Marcella

To illustrate a case example of an older person who has embraced aging with success and in turn has experienced healthy and enriching consequences, the first author will present a brief picture of her grandmother, Marcella. At the age of 81, Marcella and her husband moved after 25 years from a tight-knit Chicago neighborhood to a nearby suburb. Marcella lived by the mantras "don't feel sorry for yourself" and "don't just sit there." She made efforts to continue her active lifestyle by regularly returning to the city to attend regular Moose meetings and pinochle games. She also sought connections in her new city of residence. In fact, up until the fall of 2006, just months prior to her death, Marcella still was volunteering as her church senior's club secretary. She took notes, kept track of door prizes, and made sure that "get well" letters were sent to members of the club who were ill. It is not surprising that she was completing the minutes on a hospital bed while being diagnosed with cancer at the age of 93. Marcella also incorporated daily and long-term goals. For example, on a daily basis, she was determined to be out of the bath robe by 9 a.m. whether she was feeling good or not. More long-term goals (that incidentally were met) included, but were not limited to, getting through the book *Marley and Me,* picking out a new suit for the community seniors group's Christmas Party, obtaining her passport at the age of 90 to visit a granddaughter in Brazil, and having her

house painted with colors that she picked out at the store (age 92). Marcella not only was engaged with her family, she was an involved friend, making daily calls and writing letters to acquaintances across the country. Finally, Marcella embraced the present. She was a regular reader of the newspaper, attendant of the White Sox games (in her living room), browser of the Internet, and used e-mail to correspond with friends and family. Up until about 3 months prior to her death, on May 2, 2007, Marcella exuberated health by keeping an active lifestyle, staying engaged with family and friends, incorporating mini and large-term goals in her life, and maintaining a positive attitude about herself and others. Finally, her "health" energy also transferred itself onto the people around her, thus affecting the entire system.

Conclusion

In this article, the authors addressed particular aspects of successful aging. Satisfaction, contentment, and health later in life might be due in part to an awareness or reflection of some of the benefits and opportunities that accompany age, such as wisdom and a holistic perspective on life, personally and globally. Other criteria for successful aging may include staying active, maintaining a level of social support, feeling as if one is contributing or reciprocating to others, and developing a foundation for healthy social relationships early in life.

References

Ansbacher, H. L. (1992). Alfred Adler's concepts of community feeling and of social interest and the relevance of community feeling for old age. *Individual Psychology, 48,* 402–412.

Bergstrom, M. J., Holmes, M. E., & Pecchioni, L. (2000). Lay theories of successful aging after the death of a spouse: A network text analysis of bereavement advice. *Health Communication, 12,* 377–406.

Bohlmeijer, E., Valenkamp, M., Westerhof, G., Smit, F., & Cuijpers, P. (2005). Creative reminiscence as an early intervention for depression: Results of a pilot project. *Aging & Mental Health, 9,* 302–304.

Bowling, A. (1993). The concepts of successful and positive ageing. *Family Practice, 10,* 449–453.

Brown, C., & Lowis, M. J. (2003). Psychosocial development in the elderly: An investigation into Erikson's ninth stage. *Journal of Aging Studies, 17,* 415–426.

Chang, R. H., & Dodder, R. A. (1984). Activity and affect among the aged. *Journal of Social Psychology, 125*(1), 127–128.

Cohen, C. I., Magai, C., & Yaffee, R. (2005). Comparison of users and non-users of mental health services among depressed, older, urban African Americans. *American Journal of Geriatric Psychiatry, 13,* 545–553.

Coleman, P. G., Ivani-Chalian, C., & Robinson, M. (1999). Self and identity in advanced old age: Validation of theory through longitudinal case analysis. *Journal of Personality, 67,* 819–849.

Collings, P. (2001). "If you got everything, it's good enough": Perspectives on successful aging in a Canadian Inuit community. *Journal of Cross-Cultural Gerontology, 16,* 127–155.

Cuddy, A. J., Norton, M. I., & Fiske, S. T. (2005). This old stereotype: The pervasiveness and persistence of the elderly stereotype. *Journal of Social Issues, 61,* 267–285.

Cummings, E., & Henry, W. E. (1961). *Growing old, the process of disengagement.* New York: Basic Books.

Duay, D., & Bryan, V. (2006). Senior adults' perceptions of successful aging. *Educational Gerontology, 32,* 423–445.

Fallon, P. E. (1998). An ethnographic study: Personal meaning and successful aging of individuals 85 years and older (doctoral dissertation). *Dissertation Abstracts International, 58,* 4490.

Gamliel, T. (2001). A social version of gerotranscendence: Case study. *Journal of Aging & Identity, 6,* 105–114.

Haight, B. K., & Michel, Y. (1998). Life review: Preventing despair in newly relocated nursing home residents short-and long-term. *International Journal of Aging & Human Development, 47,* 119–142.

Himes, C. L. (2001). Elderly Americans. *Population Bulletin, 56,* 38–40.

Kahana, E., Kahana, B., & Zhang, J. (2005). Motivational antecedents of preventative proactivity in late life: Linking future orientation and exercise. *Motivation & Emotion, 29,* 438–464.

Kenel, M. E. (2005). Personal strengths and the aging process. *Human Development, 26*(1), 5–11.

Knight, B. G. (2004). *Psychotherapy with older adults* (3rd ed.). Thousand Oaks, CA: Sage.

Lewittes, H. (1989). Just being friendly means a lot: Women, friendship, and aging. *Women & Health, 14,* 139–159.

Medinger, F., & Varghese, R. (1981). Psychological growth and the impact of stress in middle age. *International Journal of Aging & Human Development, 13,* 247–263.

Miller, N. J., Soyoung, K., & Schofield-Tomschin, S. (1998). The effects of activity and aging on rural community living and consuming. *Journal of Consumer Affairs, 32,* 343–368.

Offenbacher, D. I., & Poster, C. H. (1985). Aging and the baseline code: An alternative to the "normless elderly." *Gerontologist, 25,* 526–531.

Payne, L. L., Mowen, A. J., & Montoro-Rodriguez, J. (2006). The role of leisure style in maintaining the health of older adults with arthritis. *Journal of Leisure Research, 38*(1), 20–45.

Rikers, H. C., & Myers, J. E. (1990). *Retirement counseling: A practical guide for action.* New York: Hemisphere Publishing Corporation.

Ritchey, L. H., Ritchey, P. N., & Dietz, B. E. (2001). Clarifying the measurement of activity. *Activities, Adaptation & Aging, 26*(1), 1–21.

Shaw, B. A., Krause, N., & Chatters, L. M. (2004). Emotional support from parents' early life, aging, and health. *Psychology & Aging, 19*(1), 4–12.

Stark-Wroblewski, K., Edelbaum, J. K., & Ryan, J. J. (2007). Senior citizens who use e-mail. *Educational Gerontology, 33,* 293–307.

Troll, L. E. (1996). Modified-extended families over time: Discontinuity in parts, continuity in wholes. In V. L. Bengston (Ed.), *Adulthood and aging: Research on continuities and discontinuities* (pp. 246–268). New York: Springer.

Vance, D. E., Wadley, V. G., Ball, K. K., Roenker, D. L., & Rizzo. M. (2005). The effects of physical activity and sedentary behavior on cognitive health in older adults. *Journal of Aging & Physical Activity, 13,* 294–313.

Walsh, F. (1988). The family in later life. In B. Carter & M. McGoldrick (Eds.), *Changing family life cycle: A framework for family therapy* (2nd ed., pp. 311–332). New York: Gardner.

JILL DUBA ONEDERA is an assistant professor in the Department of Counseling and Student Affairs at Western Kentucky University. **FRED STICKLE** is a professor in the Department of Counseling and Student Affairs at Western Kentucky University.

From *The Family Journal,* January 2008, vol. 16, no. 1, pp. 73–77. Copyright © by Sage Publications—JOURNALS. Reprinted by permission via Rightslink.

More Good Years

Want to live longer—and healthier? These secrets from a sleepy Greek island could show you the way.

DAN BUETTNER

In 1970 Yiannis Karimalis got a death sentence. Doctors in Pennsylvania diagnosed the Greek immigrant with abdominal cancer and told him he'd be dead within a year. He was not yet 40 years old.

Devastated, Karimalis left his job as a bridge painter and returned to his native island of Ikaria. At least there he could be buried among his relatives, he thought—and for a lot less money than in the United States. Thirty-nine years later, Karimalis is still alive and telling his amazing story to anyone who will listen. And when he returned to the States on a recent visit, he discovered he had outlived all the doctors who had predicted his death.

On Ikaria, a mountainous, 99-square-mile island, residents tell this story to illustrate something they've known all their lives: on average, Ikarians outlive just about everyone else in the world.

Ikaria's heart disease rate is about half the American rate, and its diabetes rate is one-ninth of ours.

For three weeks in April, I led a scientific expedition to Ikaria to investigate the reasons for the islanders' remarkable longevity. It was part of my research into the earth's few Blue Zones: places where an extraordinarily high proportion of natives live past 90. Our team of demographic and medical researchers—funded by AARP and *National Geographic*—found that an amazing one in three Ikarians reaches 90. (According to the U.S. Census Bureau, only one in nine baby boomers will.) What's more, Ikarians suffer 20 percent fewer cases of cancer than do Americans and have about half our rate of heart disease and one-ninth our rate of diabetes. Most astonishing of all: among the islanders over 90 whom the team studied—about one-third of Ikaria's population who are 90 and older—there was virtually no Alzheimer's disease or other dementia. In the United States more than 40 percent of people over 90 suffer some form of this devastating ailment.

How do we explain these numbers? History tells part of the story.

In antiquity Ikaria was known as a health destination, largely for its radioactive hot springs, which were believed to relieve pain and to cure joint problems and skin ailments. But for much of the ensuing two millennia, civilization passed over this wind-beaten, harborless island. To elude marauding pirates, Ikarians moved their villages inland, high up on the rocky slopes. Their isolation led to a unique lifestyle.

Over centuries with no outside influences, island natives developed a distinctive outlook on life, including relentless optimism and a propensity for partying, both of which reduce stress. Ikarians go to bed well after midnight, sleep late, and take daily naps. Based on our interviews, we have reason to believe that most Ikarians over 90 are sexually active.

But what about the Ikarians' culture best explains their long lives? To find out, we let visitors to AARP.org/bluezones direct our team's quest. Our online collaborators voted on what we should research next. One day, for example, we interviewed hundred-year-old Ikarians to discover what they'd eaten for most of their lives. The next day we investigated the chemical composition of herbal teas.

In all, we found 13 likely contributors to Ikarian longevity. The formula below may be the closest you'll get to the fountain of youth:

Graze on greens. More than 150 varieties of wild greens grow on Ikaria. Some have more than ten times the level of antioxidants in red wine.

Sip herbal teas. Steeping wild mint, chamomile, or other herbs in hot water is a lifelong, daily ritual. Many teas lower blood pressure, which decreases the risk of heart disease and dementia.

Throw out your watch. Ikarians don't worry about time. Work gets done when it gets done. This attitude lowers stress, which reduces the risk of everything from arthritis to wrinkles.

Nap daily. Ikarian villages are ghost towns during the afternoon siesta, and science shows that a regular 30-minute nap decreases the risk of heart attack.

Walk where you're going. Mountainous terrain and a practice of walking for transport mean that every trip out of the house is a mini workout.

Phone a friend. With the island's rugged terrain, family and village support have been key to survival. Strong social connections are proven to lower depression, mortality, and even weight.

Drink goat's milk. Most Ikarians over 90 have drunk goat's milk their whole lives. It is rich in a blood-pressure-lowering hormone called tryptophan as well as antibacterial compounds.

Maintain a mediterranean diet. Around the world, people who most faithfully stick to this region's diet—a regimen high in whole grains, fruits, vegetables, olive oil, and fish—outlive people who don't by about six years. The Ikarian version features more potatoes than grains (because they grew better in the mountains) and more meat than fish (because the sea was a day's journey away).

Enjoy some Greek honey. The local honey contains antibacterial, anticancer and anti-inflammatory properties. (Unfortunately, the health benefits of Ikarian honey do not extend to American honey, as far as we know.)

Open the olive oil. Ikaria's consumption of olive oil is among the world's highest. Residents drizzle antioxidant-rich extra-virgin oil over food after cooking, which preserves healthful properties in the oil that heat destroys.

Grow your own garden (or find farmers' markets). Fruits and vegetables eaten soon after picking are higher in compounds that decrease the risk of cancer and heart disease.

Get religion. Ikarians observe Greek Orthodox rituals, and regular attendance at religious services (of any kind) has been linked to longer life spans.

Bake bread. The island's sourdough bread is high in complex carbohydrates and may improve glucose metabolism and stave off diabetes.

Do Ikarians possess the true secret to longevity? Well, some combination of their habits is helping them live significantly longer than Americans, who live on average to age 78. We can't guarantee that Ikarian wisdom will help you live to 100. But if Yiannis Karimalis's example is any indicator, it may help you outlive your doctor.

DAN BUETTNER is the author of *The Blue Zones: Lessons for Living Longer From the People Who've Lived the Longest* (National Geographic, 2008).

Lost and Found

Promising therapy for Alzheimer's draws out the person inside the patient.

BARBARA BASLER

The woman wore a plain housedress and a big apron, its pockets stuffed with plastic checkers. Head down, eyes blank, she shuffled aimlessly around the activity room. Cameron Camp, a research psychologist who was visiting this assisted living home in Kentucky, watched the 70-year-old woman for a moment. Then, he recalls, "I went up to her and gave her one of our books—the one on Gene Kelly, the dancer—and asked her to please read a page."

He pauses, remembering the woman and the skeptical staff— and the very next moment.

"She took the book and read aloud—clear as a bell," Camp says with a smile. "A shocked staffer turned to me and said, 'I didn't even know she could speak. That's a miracle.'"

Camp heads the Myers Research Institute in Beachwood, Ohio, and his cutting-edge work with patients in all stages of Alzheimer's has left him improbably upbeat—because he sees miracles like this day after day.

His research is part of a sea of change in the care of Alzheimer's patients who are in the later stages of the disease: "Ten to 15 years ago these people were institutionalized, and their care involved physical or chemical restraints," says Kathleen O'Brien, vice president of program and community services for the Chicago-based Alzheimer's Association, which, with the National Institutes of Health, has helped fund Camp's work.

Psychologist Cameron Camp says patients live in the moment. "Our job is to give them as many good moments as we can."

"Today," she says, "more than 70 percent of those with Alzheimer's are cared for in the family home, and we talk about controlling the disease and enhancing daily life for those who have it."

Alzheimer's, the most common form of dementia in people over the age of 65, affects 4.5 million Americans. An irreversible brain disorder, the disease robs people of their memory and eventually impairs most of their mental and physical functions.

While research typically focuses on preventing Alzheimer's or delaying its progress in the early stages, some medical specialists and long-term care professionals are investigating activities that will help patients in the later stages.

"We can't stop cell death from Alzheimer's," Camp explains. "But at any stage of dementia there is a range of capability. If you give people a reason to get out of bed, activities that engage them and allow them to feel successful, they will be at the top of their game, whatever it is."

Camp, 53, began his research 10 years ago when he looked at the activities developed for young children by the educator Maria Montessori, whose "method" is followed today in Montessori schools around the world. There, children learn by manipulating everyday objects like balls, seashells and measuring spoons in highly structured activities that engage children but rarely allow them to fail.

Camp adapted these kinds of exercises for older people with dementia, tailoring them to the individual's background and interests, and found he could draw out the person inside the patient.

"Suddenly, they just wake up, come alive for the moment," he says.

That happened to Mary Anne Duffy's husband when they took part in Camp's research. James Duffy, 77, has Parkinson's disease and dementia and is confined to a wheelchair in a nursing home in Mentor, Ohio.

"James loved woodworking," Duffy says, "and he liked fixing things, so the researcher brought him a small box to paint, nuts and bolts to put together, puzzles." Before her husband began the activities, she says, he "just sat there, nodding off."

But when he was working a puzzle or painting a box, "James actually smiled—something I hadn't seen for a long time," Duffy says. "And he would talk. That was amazing."

People with Alzheimer's "live in the moment, and our job is to give them as many good moments as we can," Camp says. "We need to be thinking about these people in a new way. Instead of focusing on their problems and deficits, we need to ask what strengths and abilities remain."

People had assumed, for instance, that the woman with the checkers in her apron pockets was too impaired to read. But studies have found that reading is one of the very last skills to fade away. "It's automatic, almost a reflex," Camp says.

"If the print is right," he says as he flips through one of his specially designed books with big, bold letters, many Alzheimer's patients can read.

One goal of Camp's work has been to turn his research into practical how-to guides for professional and family caregivers. Published by the Myers Research Institute, the guides have been translated into Chinese, Japanese and Spanish.

While long-term care residences may have some activities for dementia patients—like coloring in a picture or listening to a story—often they don't have activities "that are meaningful, that call on an adult's past," Camp says. "And even people with Alzheimer's are bored if an activity isn't challenging or interesting."

Much of Camp's research is with residents at Menorah Park Center for Senior Living in Beachwood, which is affiliated with Myers Research. After Alzheimer's patients were given the large-print books that he and his colleagues developed, many could read aloud and discuss the books.

A brief biography of Leonardo da Vinci, for instance, talks about some of his wildly imaginative inventions, like a machine that would let soldiers breathe underwater so they could march underneath enemy ships, drill holes in their hulls and sink them.

"It's a wonderful, wacky idea," Camp says. "Dementia patients react to it just as we do. They love it. They laugh, they shake their heads. They talk about it."

Education Director Lisa P. Gwyther of the Bryan Alzheimer's Disease Research Center at Duke University Medical Center recalls visiting a facility where she saw Alzheimer's patients themselves teaching some of the simple activities they had learned to preschool children. "I was so impressed with the dignity and the purpose and the fun that was observable between the older person and younger child," she says. Camp's work has been rigorously studied in a number of small pilot projects, she adds, "which means this is a reliable, valid method."

At Menorah Park, Camp and his team look at what basic skills remain in those with dementia: Can the person read, sort, categorize, manipulate objects? Then they customize activities for those skills.

"We had one man who loved baseball," Camp says. "We had him sort pictures of baseball players into American and National leagues. Another man who loved opera sorted titles into operas by Puccini and operas by Verdi."

The activities help patients maintain the motor skills needed to feed themselves or button buttons. They also trigger memories, then conversations that connect the patient and the caregiver.

People with dementia won't consciously remember the activity from one session to the next. But, Camp says, "some part of them does remember, and eventually they will get bored. So you can't have them match the same pictures each time."

It doesn't matter if patients make mistakes, Camp adds. "What's important is that they enjoy the process."

Mike Skrajner, a project manager for Myers Research who monitored an Alzheimer's reading group at Menorah Park, recalls one morning when the group was reading a biography of Gene Kelly and came to the part where Kelly tells his father he is quitting law school—to take ballet lessons. "They stopped right there and had a great conversation about how they would react to that news," he says. "It was a wonderful session, and at the end they all wound up singing 'Singin' in the Rain.'"

Manipulating everyday objects helps patients maintain skills for feeding themselves or brushing their teeth.

Camp's research shows that people who engage in such activities tend to exhibit fewer signs of agitation, depression and anxiety.

George Niederehe, acting chief of the geriatrics research branch of the National Institute of Mental Health, which is funding some of Camp's work, says a large study of patients in long-term care facilities is needed for definitive proof of the effectiveness of Camp's approach. But his method could be as helpful to caregivers as it is to people with Alzheimer's, he says, because it would improve "staff morale, knowing they can do something useful for these patients." And that, he adds, would enhance the overall environment for staff and residents alike.

One vital part of Camp's theory—like Montessori's—is that residents need activities that give them a social role, whether it's contributing at a book club or stirring lemonade for a party.

The Menorah Park staff worked with one patient, a former mailman, who loved folding pieces of paper stamped with "Have a Nice Day!" He stuffed the notes into envelopes and delivered them to other residents.

"What we try to do," Camp says, "is let the person you remember shine through the disease, even if it's only a few moments a day."

To Learn More

- To download samples of Cameron Camp's activities for dementia patients, go to www.aarp/bulletin/longterm.
- The caregiver's manual "A Different Visit" costs $39.95 plus shipping, and the special large-print books for Alzheimer's patients cost $5.95 each (or six copies for the price of five) plus shipping. To order, go to www.myersresearch.org, or write Myers Research Institute, 27100 Cedar Road, Beachwood, OH 44122.
- For general information, go to the Alzheimer's Association website at www.alz.org.

For nine simple habits you can adopt that may delay dementia, see the September-October issue of *AARP The Magazine*.

Life after Death

If life is a journey, what is the destination? We asked people 50 and over to share their most deeply held beliefs. The result is an illuminating glimpse into America's spiritual core.

BILL NEWCOTT

For all the nudging and pushing and jockeying for position among the sweaty tourists who surround me on the floor of the Sistine Chapel this summer morning, it's nothing compared with the cyclone of activity going on up there on the front wall.

In Michelangelo's painting *The Last Judgment* there's little doubt about who's going where. On the left, a swirl of saints and martyrs ascend Heavenward, their faces a mix of rapture and shock. They soar triumphantly, flanking the figure of a Risen Christ. On the right, it's a decidedly downward trend, a slightly more populated mix of eternal unfortunates being dragged, pushed, and hurled into the abyss. I step around behind the altar—a vantage virtually no one else seems interested in—and marvel at the nearly hidden figures of three apelike creatures, seemingly the gatekeepers of a fiery furnace that is glimpsed just beyond.

In appearance and execution *The Last Judgment* is archetypical Mannerist art. But the fact is, the nuts and bolts of Michelangelo's vision are shared by the vast majority of 50-plus Americans.

In an exclusive survey of 1,011 people 50 and over, AARP THE MAGAZINE sought to learn just what Americans in the second half of life think about life after death. Over the years we've seen countless surveys examining Americans' attitudes and beliefs about the afterlife, but we wanted to hear specifically from the AARP generation—those who are more than halfway to the point of finding out, once and for all, precisely how right or wrong they were about life after death.

To begin, we found that people 50 and over tend to be downright conventional in their basic beliefs: nearly three quarters (73 percent) agree with the statement "I believe in life after death." Women are a lot more likely to believe in an afterlife (80 percent) than men (64 percent).

A copyeditor I once knew insisted that you should always capitalize the word *Heaven*. "Heaven," he explained, "is a place. Like Poughkeepsie."

Two thirds of those who believe also told us that their confidence in a life after death has increased as they've gotten older. Among them is 90-year-old Leona Mabrand. Born in North Dakota, she moved to Oregon in her 20s, married—and watched, one by one, as every member of her family passed on before her. "I'm the only one left of my family tree," she says, her voice a mix of pride and sadness.

Turning down her radio to chat one recent afternoon—Paul Harvey is one of her favorite companions these days—she tells me that the longer she lives, the more miracles she sees, and the more that convinces her that what her Christian faith tells her about the hereafter is true.

77% are not frightened by thoughts of what happens after death.

"The Lord has shown me a lot of good miracles happen," she says. "I'm looking forward to seeing my husband and my family and all those who have gone to their rest before me."

Of course, Christians like Leona aren't the only ones with their eye on an afterlife.

"It reflects our multicultural environment," says Barnard College professor of religion Alan F. Segal, author of *Life After Death: A History of the Afterlife in Western Religion* (Doubleday, 2004). "Most Americans believe they will be saved no matter what they are. In the '60s and '70s there was this thought that the boomers were not particularly religious; they were busy finding jobs and setting up house. But as they entered their fourth decade, they returned. I'm not sure it was a religious revival—it may have been they were just returning."

It may also reflect a repudiation of the long-held notion that science is the source of all of life's answers, adds Huston Smith, Syracuse University professor emeritus of religion and author of the 2.5 million-copy-selling *The World's Religions: Our Great Wisdom Traditions* (HarperSanFrancisco, 1991).

"Belief in an afterlife has risen in the last 50 years," he says. "Serious thinkers are beginning to see through the mistake modernity made in thinking that science is the oracle of truth."

Believers show general agreement over the choice of destinations in the afterlife, as well: 86 percent say there's a Heaven, while somewhat fewer (70 percent) believe in Hell.

After that, the groups break down into subsets. While most people 50 and over believe there's life beyond the grave, there's a spectrum of visions regarding just what's ahead.

Location, Location, Location

A copyeditor I once knew insisted that you should always capitalize the word *Heaven*. "Heaven," he explained, "is a place. Like Poughkeepsie." He'd be in the minority among those 50 and over who believe in Heaven. Just 40 percent believe Heaven is "a place," while 47 percent say it's a "state of being." As for the alternate destination, of those who think Hell exists, 43 percent say it's a "state of being"; 42 percent say it's "a place" (although not, presumably, like Poughkeepsie). "Heaven's a place, all right," says Ed Parlin, 56, of Salem, New Hampshire, about Heaven. And he's got some ideas of what to expect. "It's a better place than this is—that's for sure," he says. "And I guess everybody gets along. It's always a beautifully clear day, and sunny, with great landscaping."

86% believe in Heaven.

"Americans see life after death as a very dynamic thing," says Barnard College's Segal. "You don't really hear about angels and wings, sitting on clouds playing melodies. A lot believe there will be sex in the afterlife, that it'll be more pleasurable, less dangerous, and it won't be physical, but spiritual. They talk about humor in the afterlife, continuing education, unifying families—like a retirement with no financial needs."

There's a line in Matthew's Gospel that states: "It is easier for a camel to go through the eye of a needle than for a rich man to enter the kingdom of God." And perhaps not so coincidentally, our survey shows the richer people are, the less likely they are to believe there's a Heaven. Among those with a household income of $75,000 or more per year, 78 percent believe in Heaven—compared with 90 percent of those earning $25,000 or less. Similarly, 77 percent of college-educated people think there's a Heaven, compared with 89 percent of those who have a high school diploma or less.

The Price of Admission

While the overwhelming majority of Americans 50 and over believe in Heaven, there's a lot of splintering when it comes to just what it takes to arrive there. The largest group, 29 percent of those who believe in Heaven, responded that the prerequisite is to "believe in Jesus Christ." Twenty-five percent said people who "are good" get in. Another 10 percent said that people who "believe in one God" are welcomed into Heaven. Likewise, 10 percent took a come-one, come-all philosophy, saying everyone gets into Heaven.

94% believe in God.

And while 88 percent of people believe they'll be in Heaven after they die, they're not so sure about the rest of us. Those responding said 64 percent of all people get to Heaven. And many think the percentage will be a lot smaller than that.

"Fifteen percent," says Ira Merce of Lakeland, Florida. He admitted it's just a guess on his part, but he's still not happy about it. "I'd like to see the percentages turned exactly around, but I can't see it happening. If you read Scripture, it says, 'Broad is the way that leads to destruction, and narrow is the way that leads to eternal life.' "

Among those who told us they believe in Hell, their attitudes about who goes there generally mirrored the poll's results about Heaven. Forty percent of those who believe in Hell said "people who are bad" or "people who have sinned" go there; 17 percent said, "People who do not believe in Jesus Christ" are condemned to spend their afterlife in Hell. And in what has to be the understatement of all eternity, Ed suggests, "It's probably a place where you're gonna do things that you don't like to do."

70% believe in Hell.

Second Time Around?

Twenty-three percent of those responding said they believe in reincarnation—meaning there are a fair number who have an overlapping belief in Heaven and a return trip to Earth. The percentage was highest in the Northeast (31 percent), and boomers were most likely to believe in reincarnation.

"It's controversial here [in the United States], but reincarnation is a mainstay of the Eastern religions—Hinduism, Jainism, and Sikhism," says Ishani Chowdhury, executive director of the Hindu American Foundation. "You see more and more people of the younger generation weighing it at the same level as Western religions and not dismissing it."

Adds Jeffrey Burton Russell, professor emeritus of history at the University of California, Santa Barbara, and author of *A History of Heaven* (Princeton University Press, 1998): "If you took this study 50 years ago, the belief in reincarnation would be down at about one percent. Generally, the traditionally clear Christian vision of Heaven has declined, while the vaguer visions of the continuation of life have taken its place."

One true believer is Linda Abbott of St. Louis. "We have to come back," she tells me. "We come back over and over until we get it right!"

More than half of those responding reported a belief in spirits or ghosts—with more women (60 percent) than men (44 percent) agreeing. Boomers are a lot more likely to believe in ghosts (64 percent) compared with those in their 60s (51 percent) or 70s or older (38 percent). Their belief is not entirely based on hearsay evidence, either. Thirty-eight percent of all those responding to our poll say they have felt a presence, or seen something, that they thought might have been a spirit or a ghost.

"We've had some strange experiences," says Ed, who once lived in a house he suspected might be haunted. "Doors closing that shouldn't close, things falling down when you know they're stable. Kind of like someone on the other side was trying to get our attention."

Still, despite all those great stories about old haunted houses in the Northeast and Deep South, it was respondents from the West (50 percent) who were especially likely to say they'd felt the presence of a spirit or a ghost.

What's with That White Light?

Can you die and live to tell the tale? Some people come awfully close, and a few return with a remarkable story: of euphoria, a bright light (sometimes at the end of a tunnel), encounters with dead relatives, or an out-of-body experience, in which they feel as if they're hovering over their physical body. Scientists call these near-death experiences, or NDEs; polls show 4 to 5 percent of Americans say they've had one.

Some experts dismiss NDEs as nothing more than an altered state of consciousness. "It's very likely that REM [rapid eye movement] sleep and the arousal system of the brain are contributing to NDEs," says Kevin Nelson, M.D., a University of Kentucky neurophysiologist. His research suggests that people with NDEs have a "different brain switch" that blends sleep with wakefulness—which reduces the ordeal of dying to a dreamlike state.

But lots of people believe NDEs are glimpses of the afterlife—and there's some data to indicate there's something happening beyond the realm of physiology.

Some of the most intriguing findings come from Pim van Lommel, a retired cardiologist from the Rijnstate Hospital in Arnhem, Netherlands, who followed 344 survivors of cardiac arrest; 18 percent reported having had NDEs while their brains showed no wave activity. This perplexes van Lommel because, he says, "according to our current medical concepts it's impossible to experience consciousness during a period of clinical death."

"The out-of-body component of the NDE is actually verifiable," says Sam Parnia, MD, PhD, a critical-care physician at New York City's Weill Cornell Medical Center. He says patients who report watching their own resuscitation from above may have had visions—or they may be recollecting false memories. He plans to place markers, visible only from the ceiling, in emergency rooms across the United Kingdom, then quiz patients who report having had NDEs.

"If they correctly identify these targets," says Parnia, "that suggests the experience was real."

—Anne Casselman

No Place to Go

Nearly one quarter of those responding agreed with the statement "I believe that when I die, that's the end." It's not the sort of statement that invites a lot of questions for clarification, but Tom, a friendly, outspoken fellow I chatted with from the Lake Champlain region of upstate New York, took a shot at it.

To the question "Is there life after death?" Tom responds, "Nope. I've always felt that way. Life's short enough without having to worry about something you can't do anything about anyway. It's just reality, you know? I mean, I'm a Catholic."

Tom waits while I lift my jaw from the table. A *Catholic?*

"Sure. They preach life after death, you know? I just say, hey, people preach a lot of stuff. You just gotta make up your own mind about things. I go to Mass. I live my life like there's life after death, but I don't believe there is. If it's true, well, hey, it's a plus. But if it ain't, I didn't lose nothing."

He laughs, and I laugh with him. (He does ask that I not divulge his last name, and I wonder if that's to cover his tracks just in case God picks up this issue of AARP THE MAGAZINE.) Nonetheless, it's interesting that Tom tries to live as if there were an afterlife, even though he doesn't believe in one. It seems to echo what others tell me about how their beliefs in the hereafter—or lack thereof—impact the way they live their lives. Surprisingly, few confess their beliefs have any effect at all. And everyone I talk to agrees we should be living our lives according to a moral code—which many would define as God's code—whether there's a God at all, or a reward awaits.

As 90-year-old Leona puts it, "I just want to be faithful to Jesus every day and do what's right."

The sentiment, I discovered, is echoed across a wide spectrum of belief—and disbelief. "Atheists celebrate life, but we know death is a reality," says Margaret Downey, president of Atheist Alliance International. "We believe the only afterlife that a person can hope to have is the legacy they leave behind—the memory of the people who have been touched by their lives."

No matter what your belief, adds Omid Safi, former cochair for the study of Islam at the American Academy of Religion, "even though we use words like *afterlife,* or the *next life,* the *life beyond,* it is actually a great mirror about how people like to see themselves now, and the way they see God, and the way they see themselves interacting with other people."

For my money, there have been two great books written about the afterlife: Dante's *The Divine Comedy* and C.S. Lewis's *The Great Divorce.* Of course, Lewis's book is funny, and shorter, so it's better: a guy gets on a commuter bus and finds himself on a tour of Heaven and Hell. Still, both writers seem to reach similar conclusions: whether we choose to take any side in the afterlife conversation, the reality is heading relentlessly toward us. We can straddle the line between belief and unbelief all we want, but in a world where we love to split the difference when it comes to spiritual matters, where inclusiveness often means reaching consensus on conceptual matters, the answer to the ultimate question of life after death leaves no room for quibbling. The position you took during your earthly life is either spot on or dead wrong.

The figures on Michelangelo's monumental fresco seem ready to tumble over me, and I figure it's time to make room for some new tourists. At the back of the Sistine Chapel, I notice two doors: a large one to the left and a smaller one to the right. I ask an English-speaking tour guide which way I should go.

"That way"—he points to the right—"is a lovely long staircase. And if you keep going, there's a shortcut to St. Peter's Basilica. That way"—he jerks his head to the left—"you snake through a dozen more galleries and stand on a two-hour line to get into the basilica."

He pauses, then adds, "It's Hell."

Additional reporting by Emily Chau.

Navigating Practical Dilemmas in Terminal Care

HELEN SORENSON, MA, RRT, FAARC

Introduction

It has been stated that one-fourth of a person's life is spent growing up and three-fourths growing old. The aging process is universal, progressive, irreversible and eventually decremental.[1] Cellular death is one marker of aging. When cells are not replaced or replicated at a rate constant enough to maintain tissue or organ function, the eventual result is death of the organism.

Although not an unexpected endpoint for any human being, death unfortunately is often fraught with turmoil and dilemmas. Patients, family, friends, caregivers and health care professionals often get caught up in conflicting opinions regarding how terminal care should be approached. For the patient, the result often is suboptimal symptom management, an increased likelihood of being subjected to painful and often futile therapy and the unnecessary prolonging of death. For the family and friends of the patient, the psychosocial consequences can be devastating. Conflict at the bedside of a dying loved one can result in long-lasting and sometimes permanent rifts in family relationships.

There are some complicated issues surrounding terminal care, such as fear, lack of trust, lack of understanding, lack of communication, and stubbornness on the part of both the physicians and family members. There are moral, ethical, economic, cultural and religious issues that must be considered. Some of the dilemmas in terminal care come up more frequently than others. This paper will discuss some of the more commonly encountered ones. And possible interventions and/or alternate ways of coming to concordance regarding end-of-life care will be presented for consideration by the reader.

Fear/Death Anxiety

A degree of fear is the natural response of most individuals to the unknown. Despite many attempts at conceptualization and rationalization, preparing for death involves coming to terms with a condition unknown in past or present experience. Fear of death has been referred to in the literature as death anxiety. Research indicates that younger people have a higher level of death anxiety than older people.[2] The reasons are not difficult to understand. Younger adults in our society are often shielded from death. Many young adults may not have had close contact with individuals dying from a terminal or chronic disease. When younger people confront death, it is most likely that of a grandparent, a parent, a sibling or a friend. Death is commonly from an acute cause. Grief is intense, with many unanswered questions and psychological ramifications.

Older adults have had more experience with death, from having lost a spouse, colleagues, a friend or relatives over the years. They undoubtedly will have experienced grief and worked through loss at some time in their life. Older adults may be more apt to express the fear of dying alone.

When facing a terminal diagnosis and impending death older adults are more likely to be concerned with "mending fences" and seeking forgiveness for perceived wrongdoing. There is a need on the part of many adults to put their affairs in order and resolve any outstanding financial matters. Some interesting research on death anxiety and religiosity conducted by Thorson & Powell[3] revealed that persons higher in religiosity were lower in death anxiety.

How can the potential dilemma caused by fear be circumscribed? Possibly allowing patients to discuss the issue may ease death anxiety, but patients may be advised not to talk about funeral arrangements, since "they're not going to die." While well intended, the statement may not be helpful. Instead of preventing the patient from discussing "depressing thoughts," encouraging frank discussions about end-of-life issues may ease death anxiety. Asking the patient to verbalize his or her fears may lead to understanding the fears and alleviate the anxiety they cause.

It is important to guard against treating dying patients as though they are no longer human. For example, asking if a person would like to talk to a minister, priest or rabbi does not impinge the religious belief of the patient—it simply allows another avenue to reduce death anxiety.

Issues of Trust

Patients who have been under the care of a personal physician for an extended period of time generally exhibit a high level of trust in the diagnosis, even when the diagnosis is that of a terminal disease. Good end-of-life care requires a measure of continuity among caregivers. The patient who has had the same physician from the onset of a serious illness to the terminal stages of the disease has a substantial advantage.[4]

Planning, family support and social services, coordinated to meet the patient's needs, can be more easily arranged if there is an atmosphere of trust and confidence.

Health care today however, has become increasingly fragmented. A physician unknown to the family and/or patient may be assigned to a case. It is difficult for very sick patients to develop new relationships and establish trust with an on-going stream of care providers.[5] When circumstances are of an immediate and critical nature, issues of trust become paramount. Lack of trust in the physician and/or the health care system can erode into a lack of confidence in a diagnosis, which often results in a conflict between the patient, the family and the health care system.

Navigating this dilemma can be challenging. Recommending that the services of a hospitalist or a palliative care team be requested may be beneficial. Patients and families who are versed in the standard of care for the specific terminal disease may be in a better position to ask questions and make suggestions. Trust is associated with honesty. Conversely, trust can be eroded by what is perceived as the incompetence of or duplicity by health care providers.

An increased, concerted effort to communicate effectively all pertinent information to a patient and family and members of the health care team caring for the patient may not instantly instill confidence, but it may forestall any further erosion of trust. It is a good feeling to think that everyone on the team is pulling in the same direction.

Issues of Communication

Communication, or lack of adequate communication, is problematic. A recent article published in *Critical Care Medicine* stated, "In intensive care settings, suboptimal communication can erode family trust and fuel so called 'futility disputes'."[6] Lack of communication does not imply wrongdoing on the part of the caregivers, nor does it imply lack of comprehension or skills in patients and families. The message is delivered, but not always in language that is readily understandable. While the message may be received, at times it is not comprehended due to the nature of the message or the emotional state of the recipient.

A few years ago, during a conversation about end-of-life care, a nurse shared with the author a situation she had encountered. The patient, an elderly female, had undergone a biopsy of a tumor. The physician, upon receiving the biopsy report, asked the nurse to accompany him to the patient's room to deliver the results. The patient was told "the results of the biopsy indicate that the tumor was not benign, so I am going to refer you to Dr. ***, an oncologist, for further treatment." The physician asked for questions from the patient and, receiving none, left the room. The patient then got on the phone, called her family and stated: "Good news, I don't have cancer." The nurse left the room and called the physician, who expressed surprise that the patient had misunderstood the message. Reluctantly, he returned to the patient's room and in simple terms told her that she did indeed have cancer and that Dr. *** was a cancer specialist who would discuss treatment options with her and her family. Did the physician, on the first visit, tell the patient she had cancer—of course. Did the patient receive the message—unfortunately, no.

Although anecdotal, the case demonstrates a situation in which there was poor communication. Had the nurse not intervened, how long would it have been before the patient was adequately apprised of her condition?

Because quality communication with patients and families is imperative, the dilemma deserves attention. Many articles have been written, discussing optimal times, situations and environments best suited for end-of-life care discussions. Unfortunately, end-of-life does not always arrive on schedule or as planned.

Because of the severity of some illnesses, intensive care units may be the environment where the futility of further care becomes apparent. Intensive care units are busy places, sometimes crowded, and replete with a variety of alarms and mechanical noises on a continual basis. About 50 percent of patients who die in a hospital are cared for in an intensive care unit within three days of their death. Over thirty percent spend at least ten days of final hospitalization in an intensive care unit.[7] This is a particularly sobering reality for patients with chronic lung disease. Many COPD patients have had serious exacerbations, have been admitted to intensive care units, and many have been on mechanical ventilation. Fortunately, the medications, therapeutic interventions, and disease management skills of physicians and therapists often can turn the exacerbation around. Unfortunately, the airway pathology may not be reversible.

How and when and with whom should communication about the gravity of a situation be handled? Ideally, it should occur prior to any crisis; realistically, when it becomes obvious that a patient is unlikely to survive. Regardless of the answer, effective communication is vitally important.

Because few intensive care unit (ICU) patients (less than 5%) are able to communicate with the health care providers caring for them at the time that withholding/withdrawing life support decisions are made,[8] there is a real need to share information with and seek input from the family.

A recent article published as a supplement to *Critical Care Medicine* reviewed the importance of talking with families about end-of-life care. Although few studies provide hard evidence on how best to initiate end-of-life discussions in an ICU environment, Curtis, et al.[9] provides a framework that could serve as a model for clinicians and families alike. The proposed components of the conference would include: preparation prior to the conference, holding the conference, and finishing the conference.[9]

Preparing in Advance of the ICU-Family Conference

It is important for the participating clinician to be informed about the disease process of the patient, including: diagnosis, prognosis, treatment options, and probably outcomes of various treatments. It is important also for the clinician to identify areas of uncertainty or inconsistencies concerning the diagnosis, prognosis, or potential treatments. Any disagreements between sub-specialists involved in the care of the patient should be resolved before the family conference. Additionally, in preparing for the family conference, it is advantageous for the clinician to have some familiarity with the attitudes of the family and the patient toward illness, life-extending therapy, and death. When possible, the determination of who will attend the conference should be done advance of the conference. The location of the conference should also be pre-determined: a quiet private setting with adequate comfortable seating is ideal. Asking all participants to turn off cell phones and pagers is appropriate and will prevent unwanted distraction. (If the patient is able to participate in the conference but is too ill to leave the ICU, then the conference should take place in the patient's room in the ICU.)

Holding the ICU Family-Conference about End-of-Life Care

Assuring that all participants are introduced and understand the reason for the conference will facilitate the process. It is also helpful to discuss conference goals and determine what the patient and his or her family understand about the prognosis. If the patient is unable to participate in the conference, it may be opportune to pose the question: "What would the patient want?" Explaining during the conference that withholding life-sustaining treatment is not withholding care is an important distinction. Another recommended approach to achieve concord in the conference is to tolerate silence. Giving the family time to absorb any information they have just received, and allowing them to formulate questions, will result in better and more goal-oriented discussions.

When families are able to communicate the fears and emotions they may have, they are better able to cope with difficult decisions.

Finishing the Conference

After the patient and/or family have been provided with the facts and have achieved an understanding of the disease and the treatment issues, the clinician should make recommendations regarding treatment options. It is a disservice, for example, to give family members the impression that they are single-handedly making the decision to "pull the plug" on a loved on. Soliciting any follow-up questions, allowing adequate time, and making sure the family knows how to reach you, should end the conference on a positive note.

Understanding Choices

Another commonly encountered dilemma in terminal care is the number of choices involved, as well as the medical terminology that sometimes mystifies the choices. Advanced directives, living wills, health care proxies, durable powers of attorney for health care; what they are, what they mean, how much weight they carry, are they honored, and does everyone who needs them have them? Not long ago during a conversation with a chaplain at a hospital, the advice shared with me—to pass on to others—was to give family members the gift of knowledge. The final gift you give them may be the most important gift of all. Let them know your wishes.

When advanced directives became available in the late 1980s, it was presumed that the document would solve all the problems and that terminal care would adhere to the patient's wishes. The Study to Understand Prognoses and Preferences for Outcomes and Risks of Treatment (SUPPORT), initiated in 1988, however, showed severe shortcomings in end-of-life care.[10]

Advanced directives, as a legal document, have not necessarily lived up to expectations. A viable option is a Durable Power of Attorney for Health Care, in which a trusted individual is designated to make health care decisions when the patient cannot.

Another option is to have advanced planning sessions with family members. If the patient and his or her family can come to consensus about terminal care in advance, and the doctor is in agreement with any decisions, unnecessary suffering probably can be avoided. (When death becomes imminent and the patient's wishes are not followed, waste no time in seeking a meeting with the hospital ethics committee.)

Adaptive Techniques

There is no "recipe" that, if followed precisely, will allow for the successful navigation of all potential dilemmas. There is no way to prepare for each eventuality that accompanies terminal illness and death. Knowledge remains the safest shield against well-meaning advice-givers. Asking questions of caregivers is the best defense against misunderstanding and mismanagement of the patient.

The University of Iowa Research Center is working on an evidence-based protocol for advanced directives, which outlines in a step-by-step fashion assessment criteria that factor in the patient's age, primary language, and mental capacity for making health care treatment decisions. The protocol also provides a check-list format for health care providers, the documentation thereof is easily accessible and in a prominent position in the patient's chart.[11]

Another alternative health care benefit being proposed is called MediCaring, which emphasizes more home-based and supportive health care and discourages hospitalization and use of aggressive treatment.[12] While not specifically aimed at solving end-of-life care issues, there may be parts of MediCaring that mesh well with terminal care of the oldest old.

Whether in a home setting, a community hospital or an intensive care unit, terminal care can result in moral, ethical, economic, religious, cultural and/or personal/family conflict. Even when death is universally accepted as a normal part of the life cycle, there will be emotional dilemmas to navigate around. Additional education and research initiatives, however, may result in increased awareness that this currently is an unsolved problem, for the patient, the family, and the health care providers. Notwithstanding, however, the medical community should continue to persevere in trying to understand patients' and families' fears and needs, the need for quality communication with questions and answers in lay vocabulary. The clinician's task is to balance communication and understanding with medical delivery.

References

1. Thorson JA. *Aging in a Changing Society,* 2000. 2nd Ed. Taylor & Francis, Philadelphia, PA.
2. Thorson JA & Powell FC. Meaning of death and intrinsic religiosity. *Journal of Clinical Psychology.* 1990;46: 379–391.
3. Thorson JA & Powell FC. Elements of death anxiety and meanings of death. *Journal of Clinical Psychology.* 1998;44: 691–701.
4. Lynn J. Serving patients who may die soon and their families. *JAMA.* 2001;285(7): 925–932.
5. Pantilat SZ, Alpers A, Wachter RM. A new doctor in the house: ethical issues in hospitalist systems. *JAMA.* 1999;282: 171–174.
6. Fins JJ & Soloman MZ. Communication in the intensive care setting: The challenge of futility disputes. *Critical Care Medicine.* 2001;29(2) Supplement.
7. Quill TE & Brody H. Physician recommendations and patient autonomy: Finding a balance between physician power and patient choice. *Ann Internal Med.* 1996;25: 763–769.
8. Prendergast TJ & Luce JM. Increasing incidence of withholding and withdrawal of life support from the critically ill. *Am J Respir Crit Care Med.* 1997;155: 15–20.
9. Curtis JR et al. The family conference as a focus to improve communication about end-of-life care in the intensive care unit: Opportunities for improvement. *Critical Care Medicine.* 2001;29(2) Supplement. PN26–N33.
10. Pioneer Programs in Palliative Care: Nine Case Studies (2000). The Robert Wood Johnson Foundation in cooperation with the Milbank Memorial Fund, New York, NY.
11. Evidence-based protocol: Advanced Directives. Iowa City, IA: University of Iowa Gerontological Nursing Interventions Research Center. 1999. Available; [http://www.guideline.gov/index.asp].
12. Lynn. J. et al. MediCaring: development and test marketing of a supportive care benefit for older people. *Journal of the American Geriatric Society.* 1999;47(9) 1058–1064.

HELEN SORENSON, MA, RRT, FAARC Assistant Professor, Department of Respiratory Care, University of Texas Health Science Center at San Antonio in San Antonio, Texas. Ms. Sorenson is also Managing Editor of "Emphysema/COPD: The Journal of Patient Centered Care."

Test-Your-Knowledge Form

We encourage you to photocopy and use this page as a tool to assess how the articles in *Annual Editions* expand on the information in your textbook. By reflecting on the articles you will gain enhanced text information. You can also access this useful form on a product's book support website at *http://www.mhhe.com/cls*.

NAME:

DATE:

TITLE AND NUMBER OF ARTICLE:

BRIEFLY STATE THE MAIN IDEA OF THIS ARTICLE:

LIST THREE IMPORTANT FACTS THAT THE AUTHOR USES TO SUPPORT THE MAIN IDEA:

WHAT INFORMATION OR IDEAS DISCUSSED IN THIS ARTICLE ARE ALSO DISCUSSED IN YOUR TEXTBOOK OR OTHER READINGS THAT YOU HAVE DONE? LIST THE TEXTBOOK CHAPTERS AND PAGE NUMBERS:

LIST ANY EXAMPLES OF BIAS OR FAULTY REASONING THAT YOU FOUND IN THE ARTICLE:

LIST ANY NEW TERMS/CONCEPTS THAT WERE DISCUSSED IN THE ARTICLE, AND WRITE A SHORT DEFINITION:

We Want Your Advice

ANNUAL EDITIONS revisions depend on two major opinion sources: one is our Advisory Board, listed in the front of this volume, which works with us in scanning the thousands of articles published in the public press each year; the other is you—the person actually using the book. Please help us and the users of the next edition by completing the prepaid article rating form on this page and returning it to us. Thank you for your help!

ANNUAL EDITIONS: Human Development 10/11

ARTICLE RATING FORM

Here is an opportunity for you to have direct input into the next revision of this volume.
We would like you to rate each of the articles listed below, using the following scale:

1. **Excellent: should definitely be retained**
2. **Above average: should probably be retained**
3. **Below average: should probably be deleted**
4. **Poor: should definitely be deleted**

Your ratings will play a vital part in the next revision.
Please mail this prepaid form to us as soon as possible.
Thanks for your help!

RATING	ARTICLE	RATING	ARTICLE
	1. The Identity Dance		20. A "Perfect" Case Study: Perfectionism in Academically Talented Fourth Graders
	2. Seeking Genetic Fate		21. The Angry Smile
	3. Fat, Carbs, and the Science of Conception		22. Where Personality Goes Awry
	4. The Mystery of Fetal Life: Secrets of the Womb		23. The Blank Slate
	5. Truth and Consequences at Pregnancy High		24. Girls Gone Bad?
	6. HHS Toned Down Breast-Feeding Ads: Formula Industry Urged Softer Campaign		25. Disrespecting Childhood
	7. Reading Your Baby's Mind		26. Don't Blame the Caveman
	8. Vaccination Nation		27. The End of White America?
	9. Long-Term Studies of Preschool: Lasting Benefits Far Outweigh Costs		28. A Peaceful Adolescence
	10. How to Help Your Toddler Begin Developing Empathy		29. Young, Gay, and Murdered
	11. Easing the Separation Process for Infants, Toddlers, and Families		30. Interview with Dr. Craig Anderson: Video Game Violence
	12. Accountability Comes to Preschool: Can We Make It Work for Young Children?		31. Jail Time Is Learning Time
	13. "Early Sprouts": Establishing Healthy Food Choices for Young Children		32. Finding a Job in the 21st Century
	14. Get Smart		33. Hold Me Tight
	15. An Educator's Journey toward Multiple Intelligences		34. Emotions and the Brain: Laughter
	16. In Defense of Distraction		35. 50 Reasons to Love Being 50+
	17. Informing the ADHD Debate		36. Are You Ready for Act II?
	18. Ten Big Effects of the No Child Left behind Act on Public Schools		37. Tearing: Breakthrough in Human Emotional Signaling
	19. Single-Sex Classrooms Are Succeeding		38. Healthy Aging in Later Life
			39. More Good Years
			40. Lost and Found
			41. Life after Death
			42. Navigating Practical Dilemmas in Terminal Care

BUSINESS REPLY MAIL
FIRST CLASS MAIL PERMIT NO. 551 DUBUQUE IA

POSTAGE WILL BE PAID BY ADDRESSEE

McGraw-Hill Contemporary Learning Series
501 BELL STREET
DUBUQUE, IA 52001

NO POSTAGE
NECESSARY
IF MAILED
IN THE
UNITED STATES

ABOUT YOU

Name   Date

_____

Are you a teacher? ❏ A student? ❏
Your school's name

_____

Department

_____

Address   City   State   Zip

_____

School telephone #

_____

YOUR COMMENTS ARE IMPORTANT TO US!

Please fill in the following information:
For which course did you use this book?

_____

Did you use a text with this ANNUAL EDITION? ❏ yes ❏ no
What was the title of the text?

_____

What are your general reactions to the Annual Editions concept?

_____

Have you read any pertinent articles recently that you think should be included in the next edition? Explain.

_____

Are there any articles that you feel should be replaced in the next edition? Why?

_____

Are there any World Wide Websites that you feel should be included in the next edition? Please annotate.

_____

May we contact you for editorial input? ❏ yes ❏ no
May we quote your comments? ❏ yes ❏ no

NOTES

NOTES

NOTES

NOTES

NOTES

NOTES

NOTES

NOTES